Contents

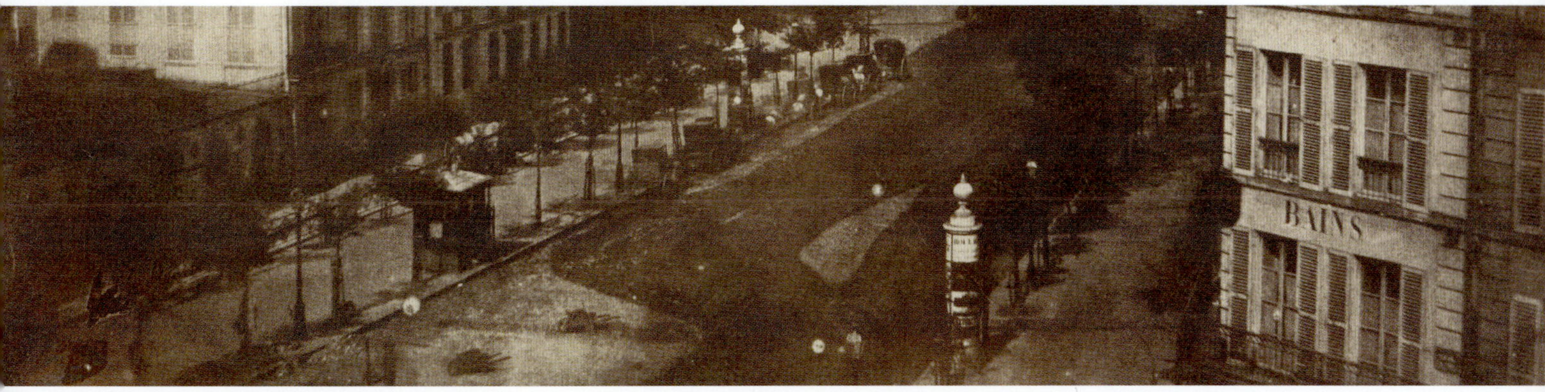

Introduction to Photography

Chapter 1

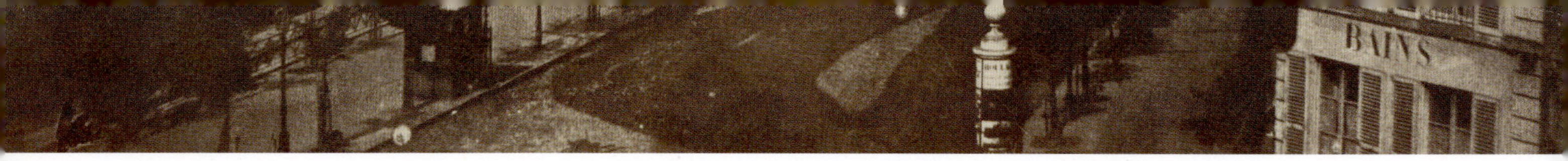

Hello and welcome to The School of Photography. I'm Marc Newton and in this book, we are going to learn about the Art and Science of Photography.

Before we begin, I'll just tell you briefly how this book works. The Complete Guide to Photography book is divided into chapters with accompanying tasks for you to complete.

You're going to need a notebook, so make sure you keep one to hand as we go through the book. As you learn photography, or anything in fact, you make mistakes along the way. We all learn from our failures and your notebook is there to note down every time you do something wrong. What's really important is to know how to correct those wrongs. That is how we learn, and here's where I come in.

I will teach you the art and craft of photography, so that when you make a mistake, you'll know how to correct it - and after a bit of practice - you'll never make those same mistakes again. So remember, it's okay to make mistakes; it doesn't mean you've failed or it's too complicated for you.

That mistake has just given you a new opportunity to learn.

Ok, I'm going to start off by asking you this one question:

What is Photography?

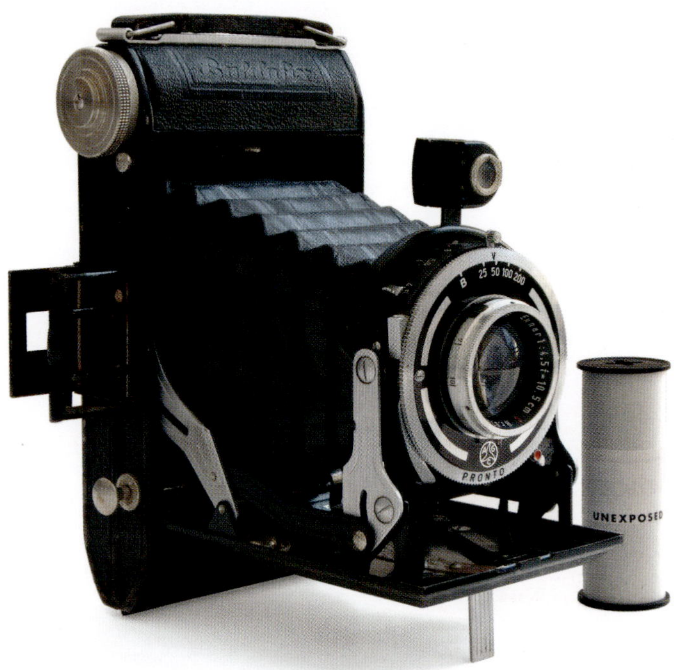

Grab your notebook and write down some answers.

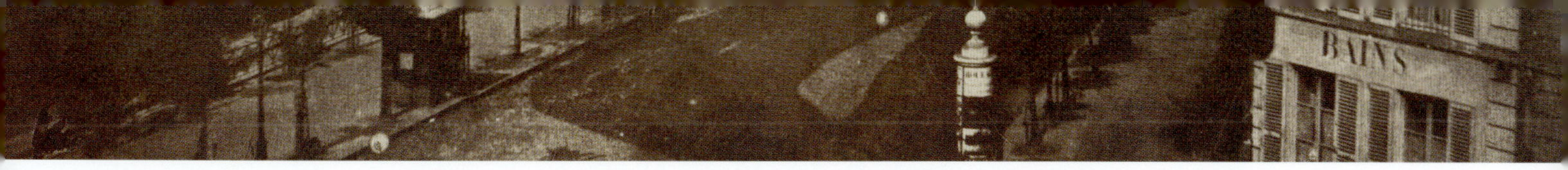

I hope you have lots of things written down - it's an open-ended question with lots of different answers.

Common answers are:
- It's an art form
- It captures memories
- It records history
- It's a way of capturing a scene

  ...and so on.

Of course, it's all of these things, but essentially photography is the capturing of light.

Photography is a science; it was invented by scientists, not artists. You need to learn the science, or craft, of photography first, then you can get creative with that knowledge.

You might get that lucky shot, but you won't be able to be consistently good or consistently creative without that full control over the science of photography.

The craft of photography has been the same since its invention in the 1830s and it will continue to be the same forever.

This is because it's a science - it's the laws of physics at work.

It's essentially about capturing light beams.

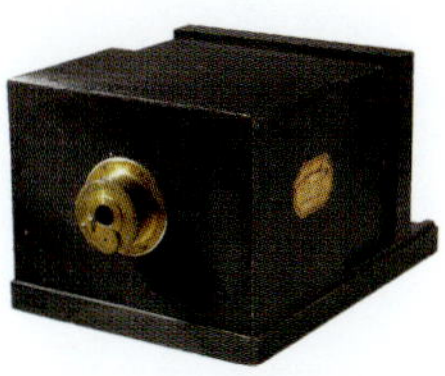
1830

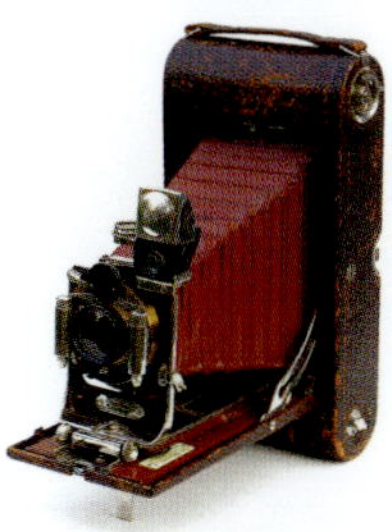
1890

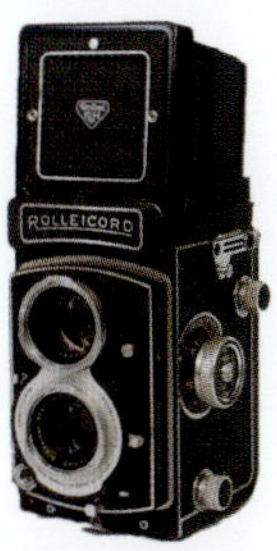
1930

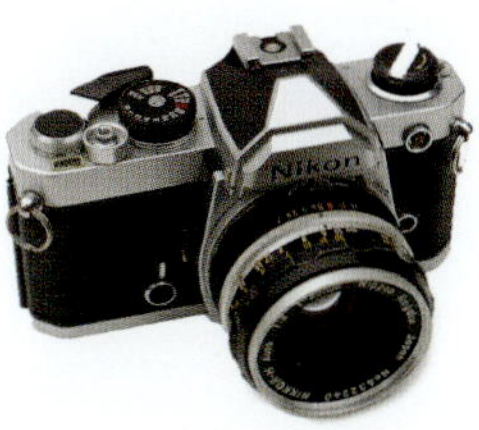

1975

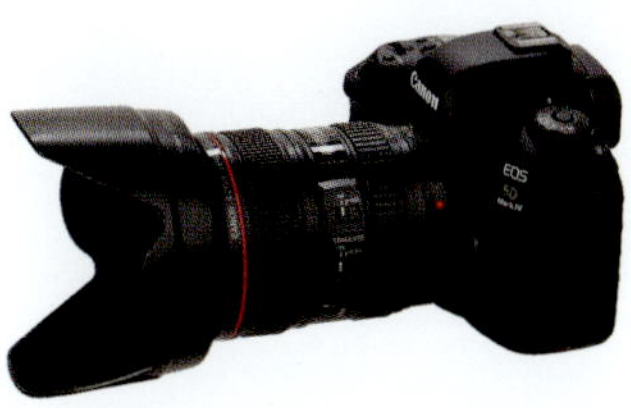
2020

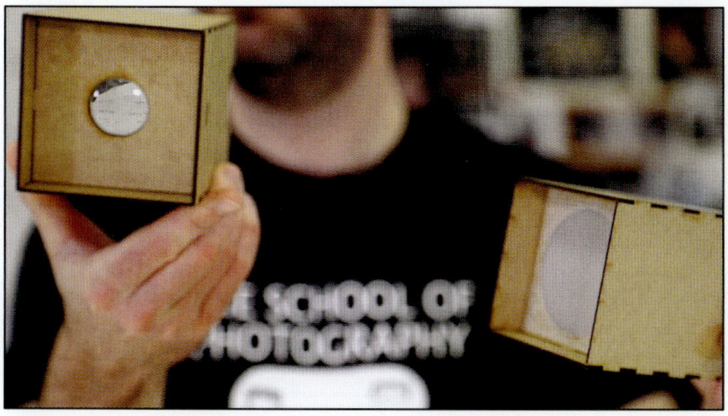
You focus the image by moving the smaller box in and out of the larger box.

This is a camera obscura, the most basic form of a camera. Light travels through the lens at the front and hits an imaging plane, in this case, a piece of tracing paper. This creates an image.

This essentially, is photography.

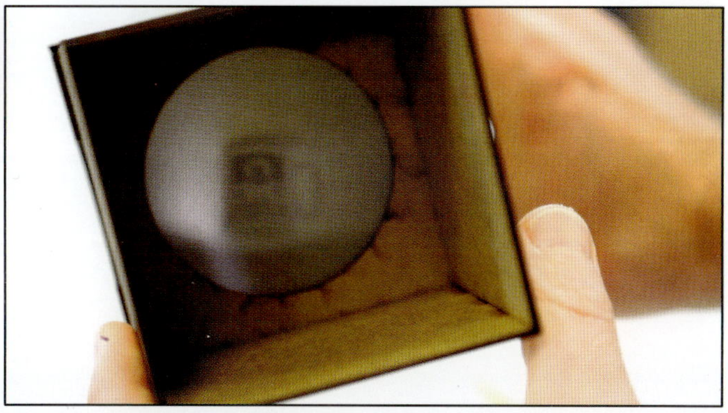

Camera obscuras have been around for hundreds of years but no one could capture the image they saw. It wasn't until the 19th Century when this was able to happen.

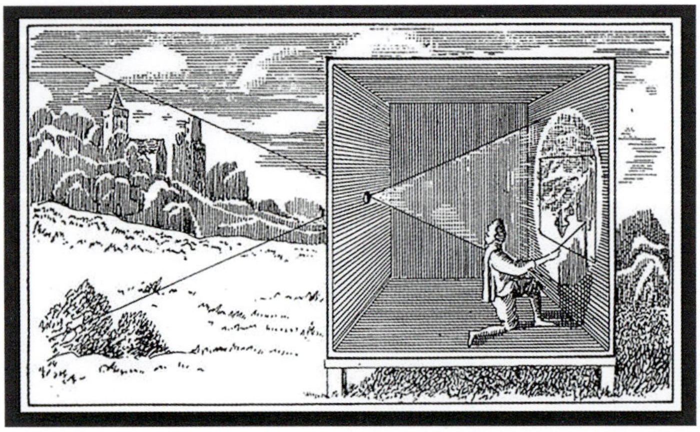

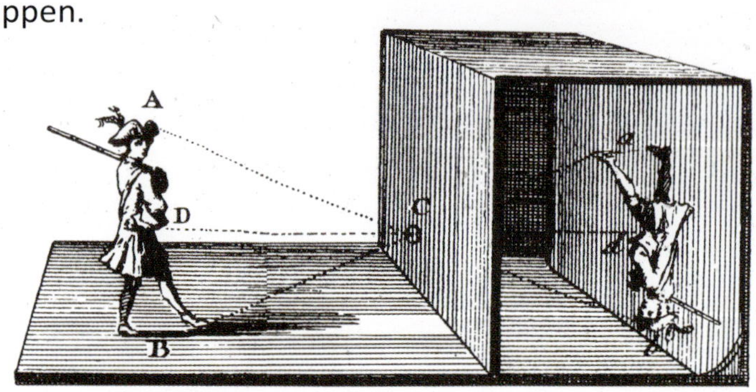

An illustration showing a camera obscura flipping an image upside down and back to front. (above)

An illustration of a camera obscura at work. (left)

Now we'll look at some old photographs to show how photography has essentially stayed the same for many years.

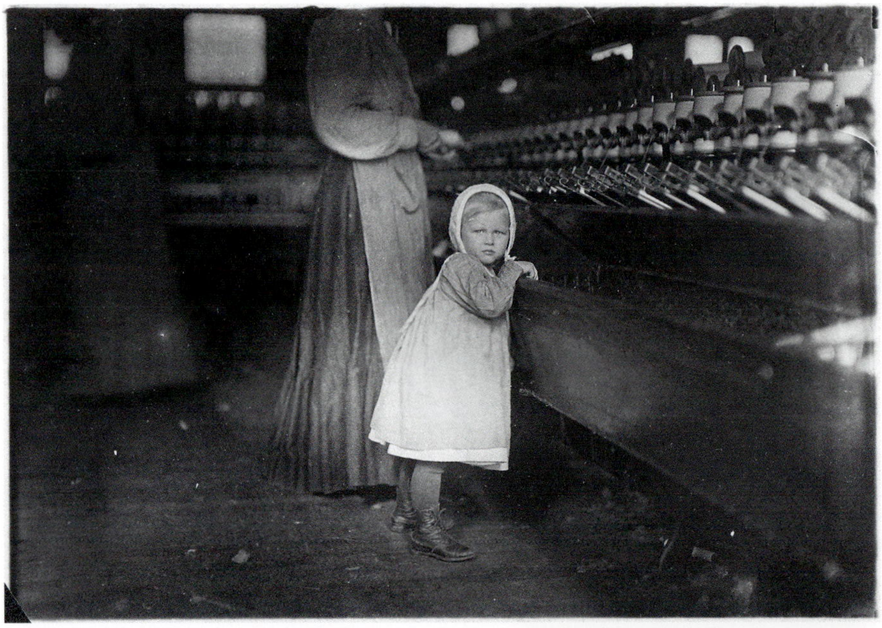

This photo from 1908 shows a young girl in a factory.

The photo is blurred in the background which is an effect called Shallow Depth of Field. To get this effect you need to use a wide aperture.

This photo was taken after the San Francisco earthquake in 1906.

The foreground and background are sharp and this is an effect called Long Depth of Field. To get this effect you need to use a small aperture.

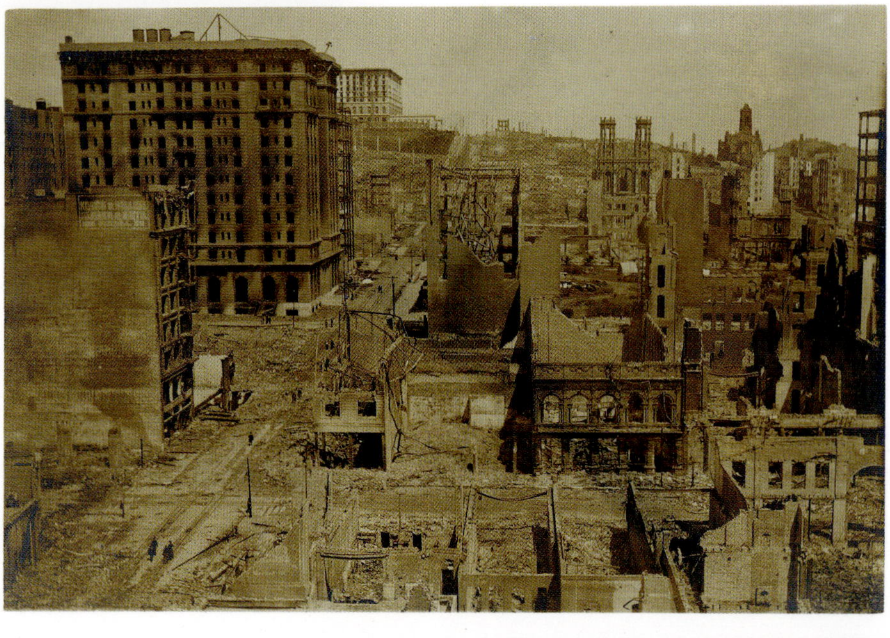

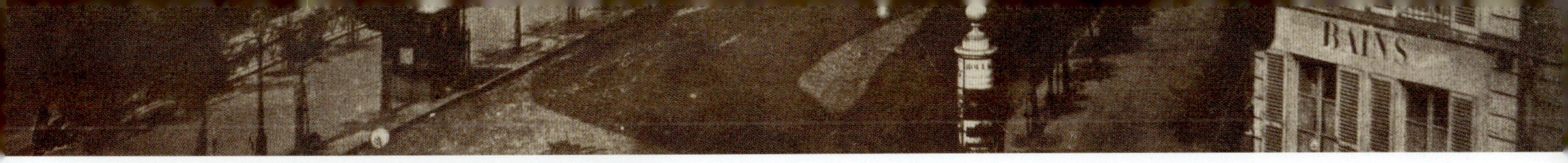

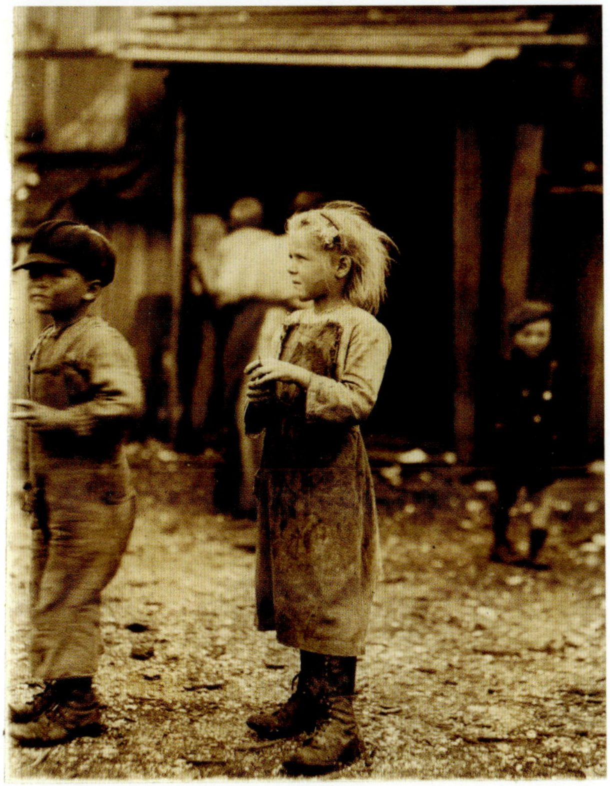

This photo from 1912 shows a shallow depth of field again, yet the boy on the left is blurred. This is because he was moving whilst the picture was taken but the girl wasn't.

This is caused by using a slow shutter speed.

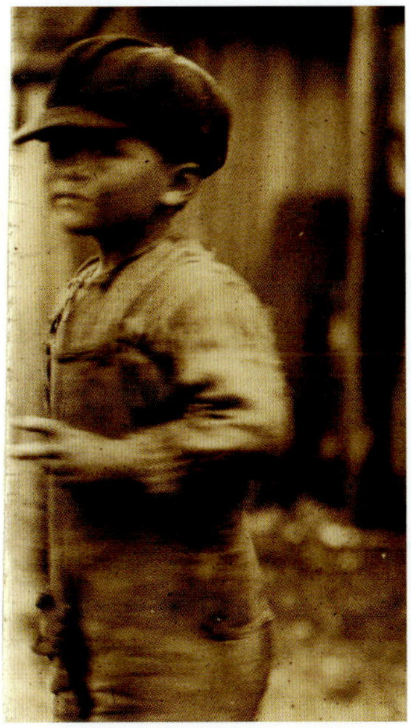

These old photos show that the capture of light was the same all those years ago. Depth of field is controlled by the aperture, and movement is controlled by the shutter speed. The principle has always stayed the same; light travels through a lens and is captured on an image plane.

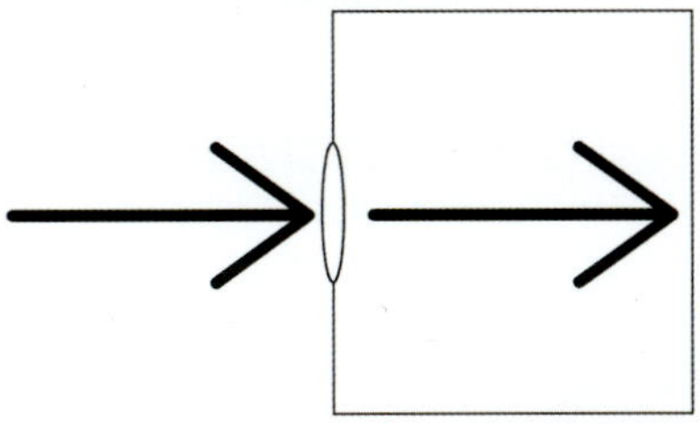

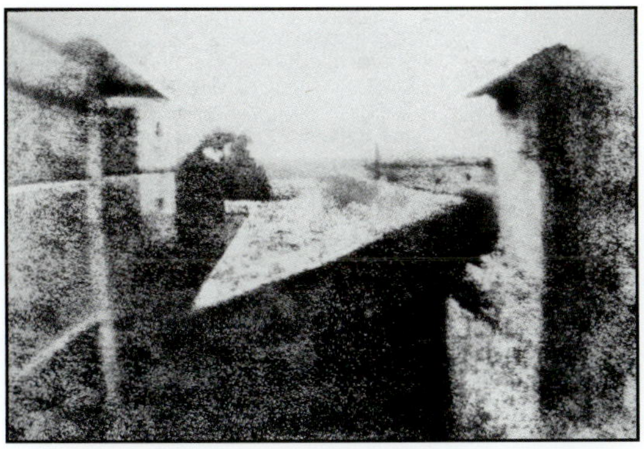

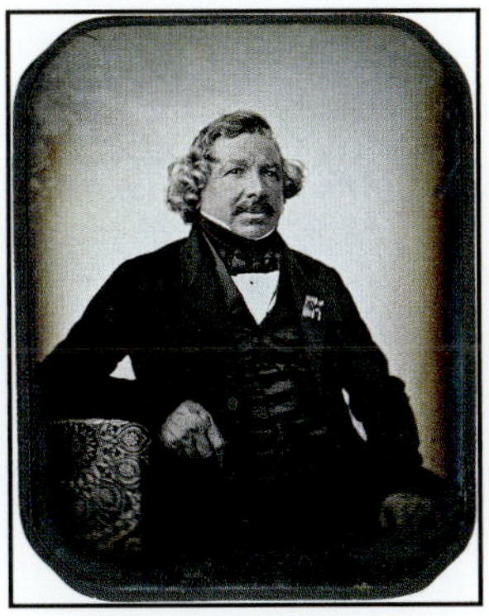

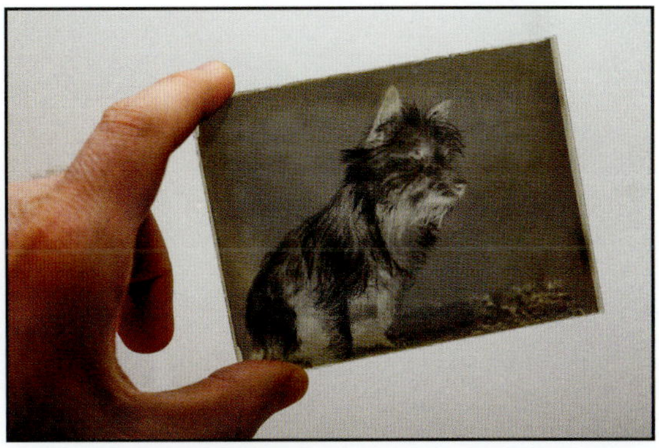

The oldest surviving photo ever taken
"View from the window at Le Gras"

1a

1b

When photography was first invented, light was captured onto metal [1a] and paper, then it was glass [1b], then came plastic film [1c] and now it is a digital chip [1d], but the process of light beams travelling through a lens and being captured has been the same and will continue to be the same.

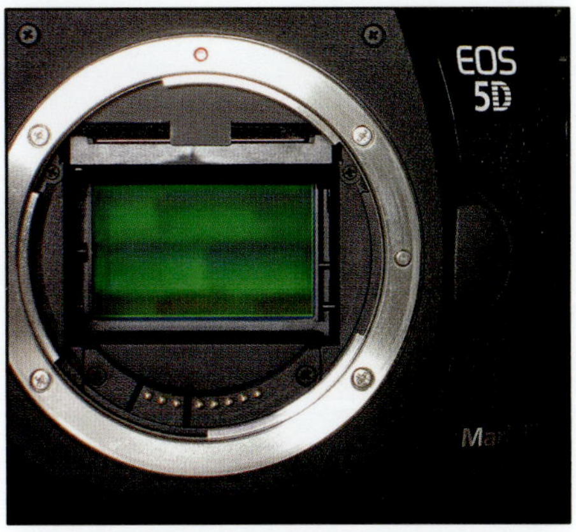

1d

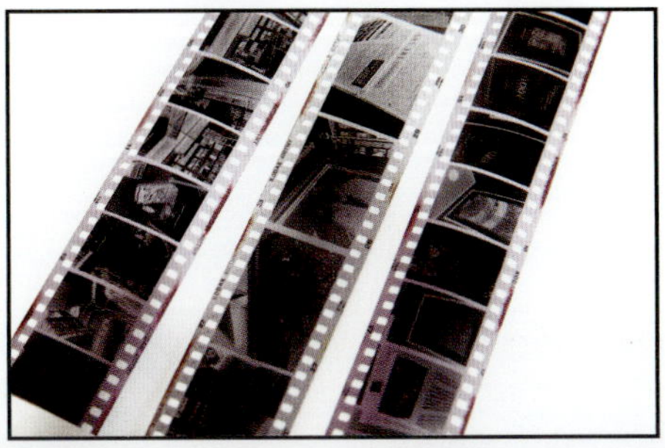

1c

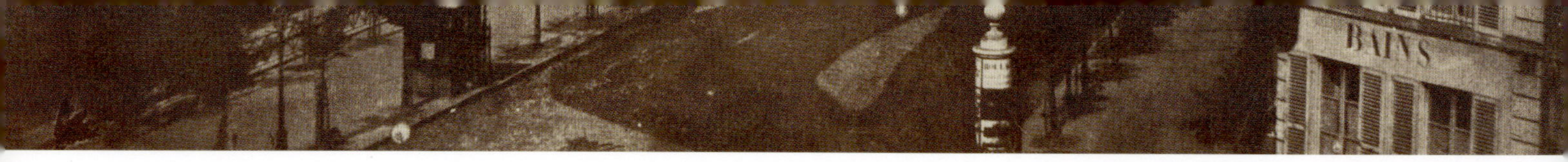

It’s because of those reasons that we only use the manual settings in this book. This is so we learn to control the aperture, the shutter speed, the ISO and so on.

Most modern settings on cameras are just gimmicks, they are selling points from the manufacturer; they actually make things more confusing.

So we’ll use just the manual settings. Not only does this allows us to take control, but it also allows us to understand what mistakes have been made. And like I said before, once you understand those mistakes, you can correct them very easily.

That is learning!

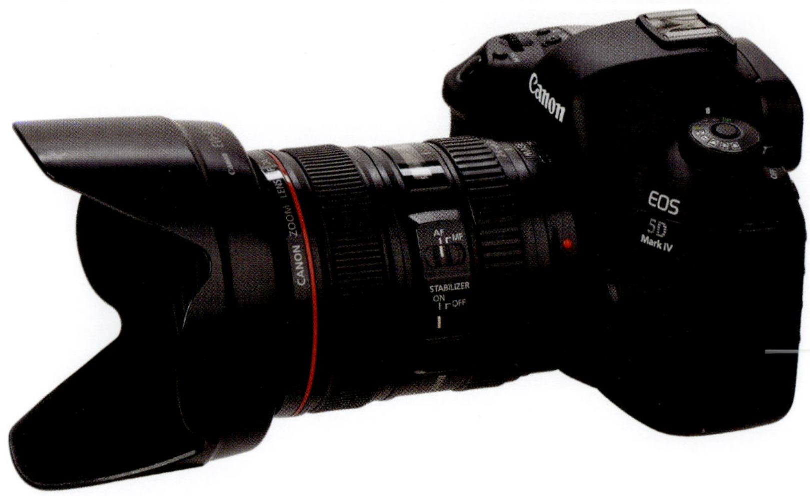

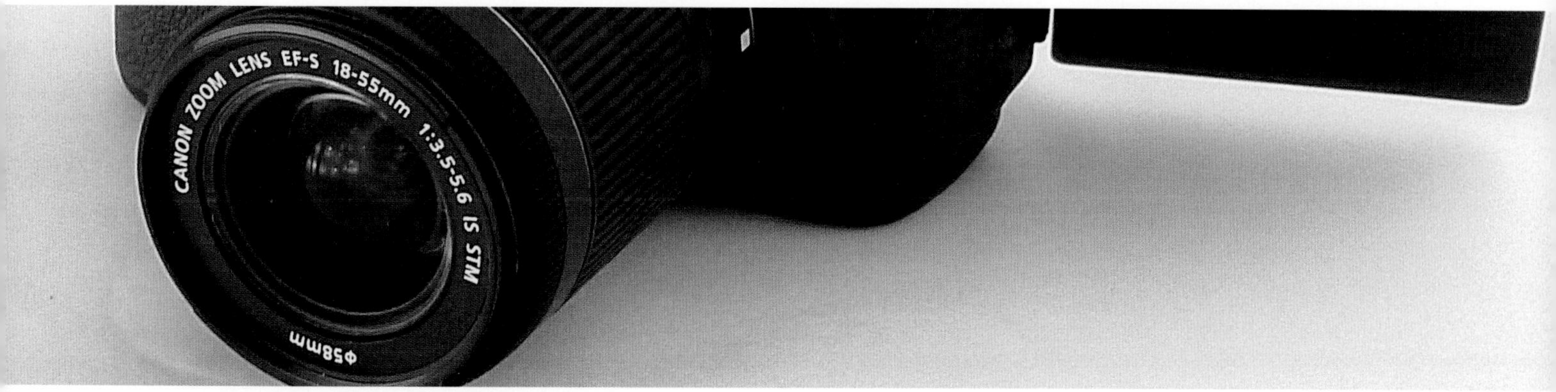

Camera Kits and Recommended Equipment

Chapter 2

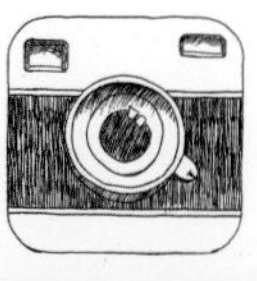

There are four main types of cameras that you can buy for general use.

Compact

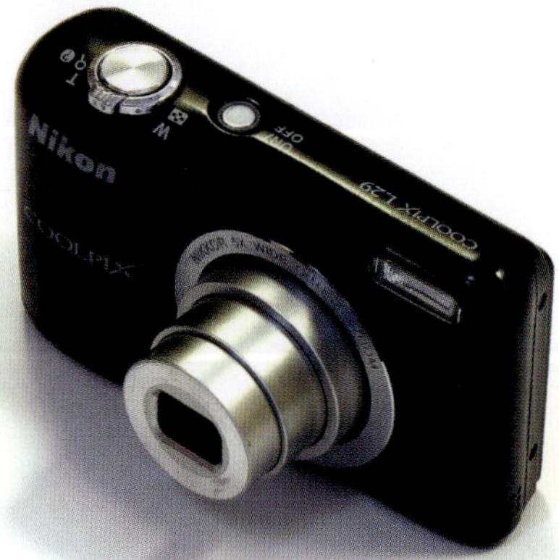

Bridge

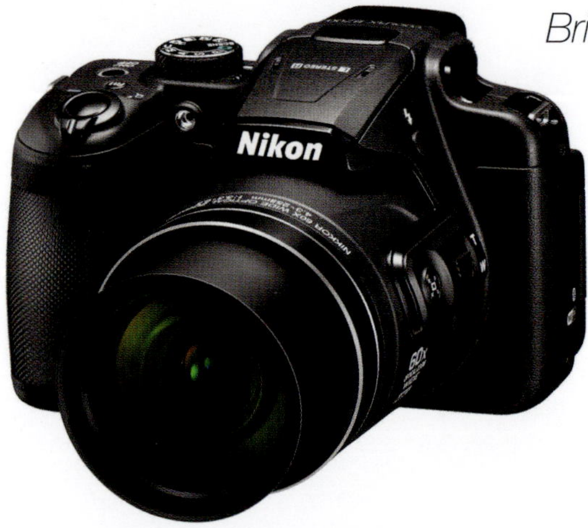

Mirrorless (Compact system)

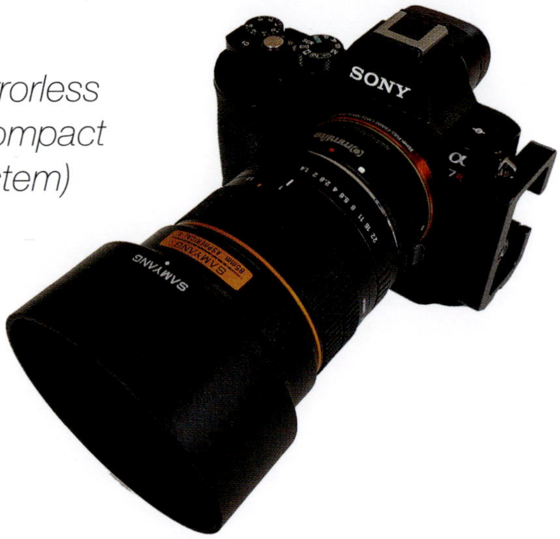

DSLR

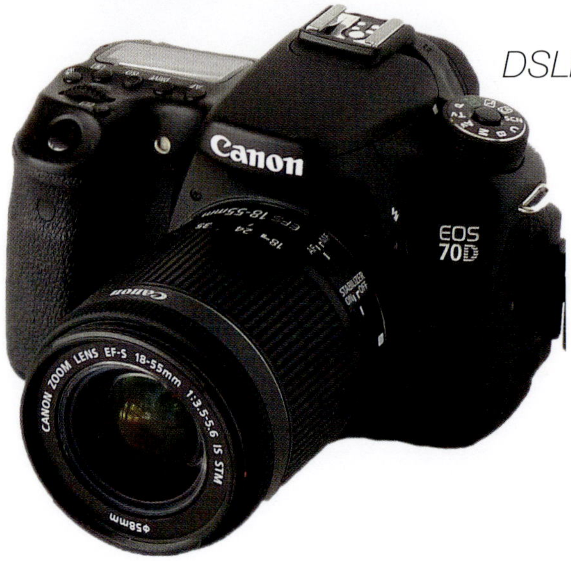

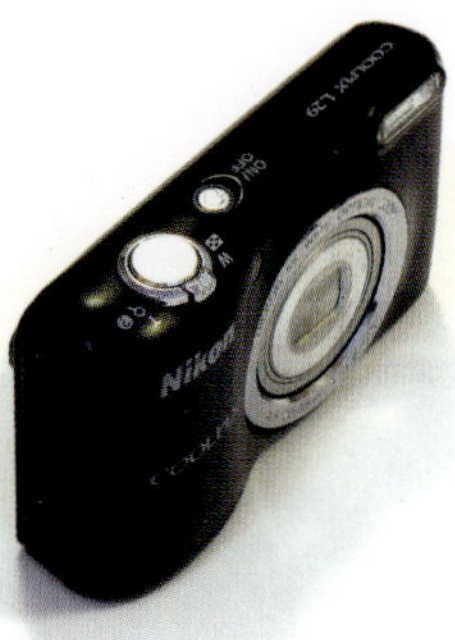

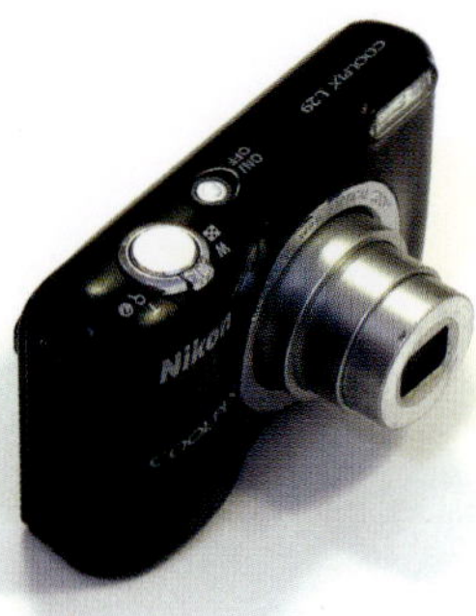

Compact camera

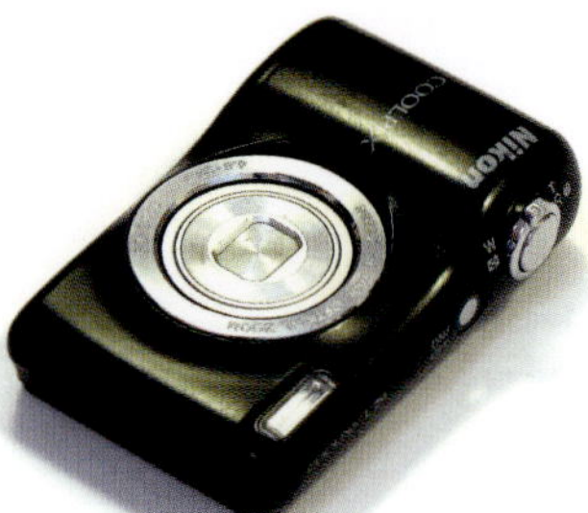

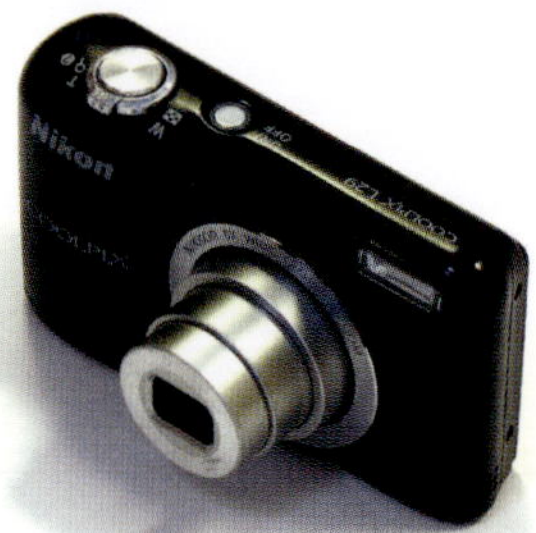

Once extremely popular, these cameras are becoming increasingly obsolete as mobile phone cameras can do the job just as well - and sometimes better.

However, these cameras still do have some use, as some models are waterproof, for example.

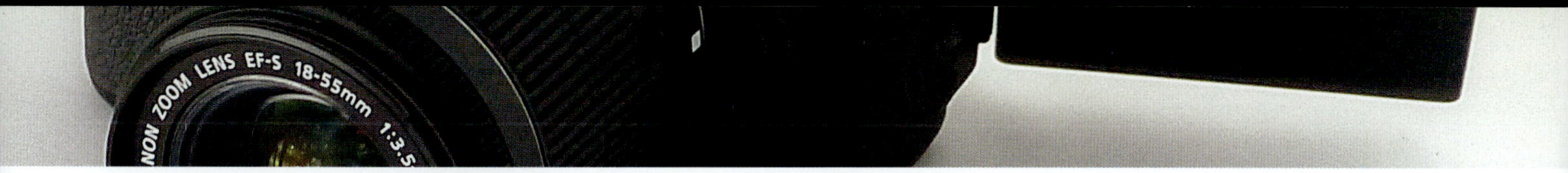

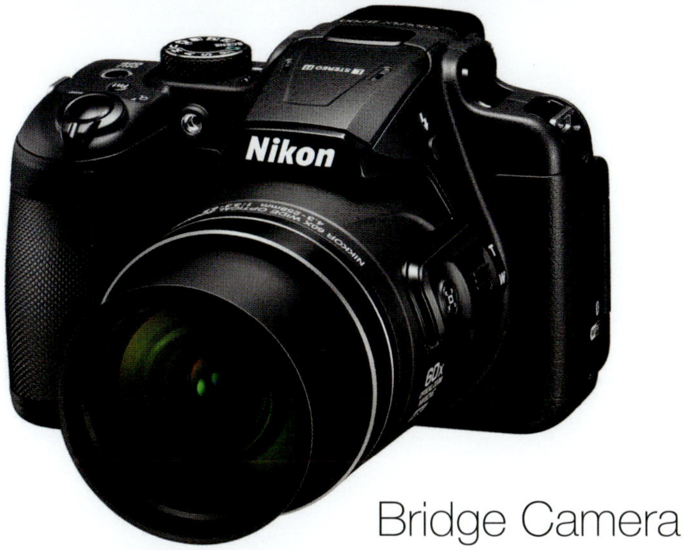

Bridge Camera

Bridge cameras are a combination of a compact and an SLR. Smaller than an SLR and with a bit more control over image taking than a compact. These cameras can also be cheaper than SLR cameras.

However, the lens cannot be changed on a bridge camera, and although there is a slight element of control, the manual settings are usually very hard to get to.

These cameras are aimed at the 'point-and-click' market, therefore, I wouldn't recommend buying one for learning photography, as you need to get to those manual settings quickly, to start taking control of your photography.

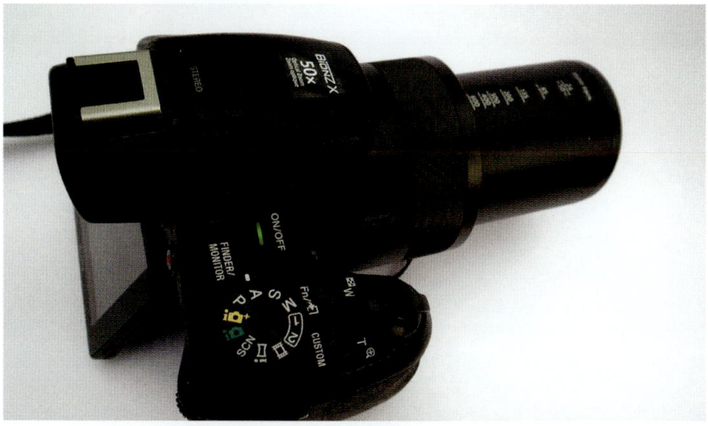

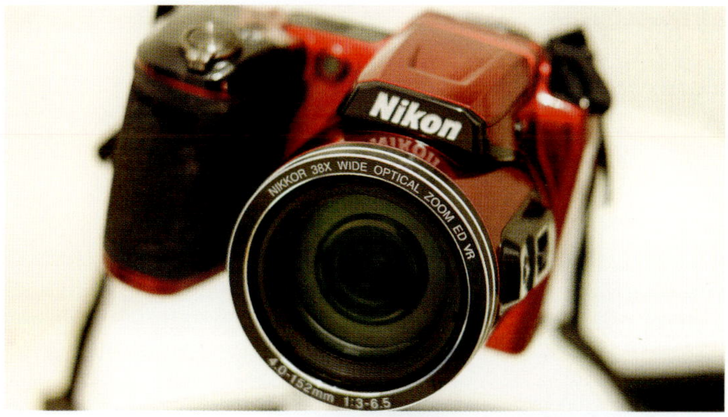

Mirrorless or Compact System camera

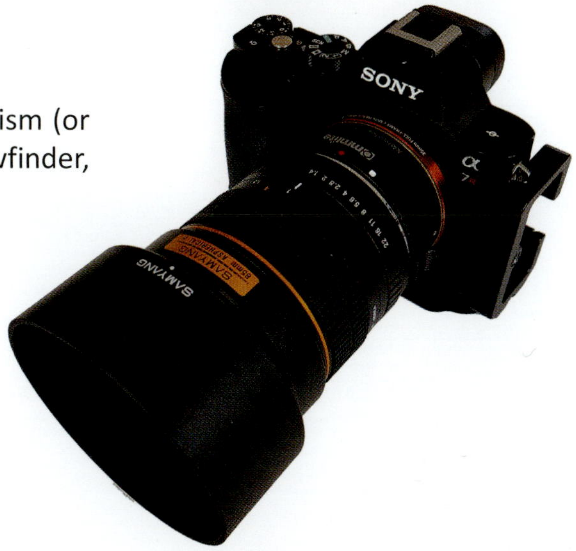

Mirrorless cameras are called such because they lack the prism (or mirrors) used in most cameras. Instead of a traditional viewfinder, they have a digital screen.

These can be very good as they generally give you access to the manual settings more easily, and they are much better quality than bridge or compact cameras. You also have the option of using different lenses.

The really good ones are very expensive and aimed at professionals, whereas the cheap ones are aimed at 'point-and-click' photographers.

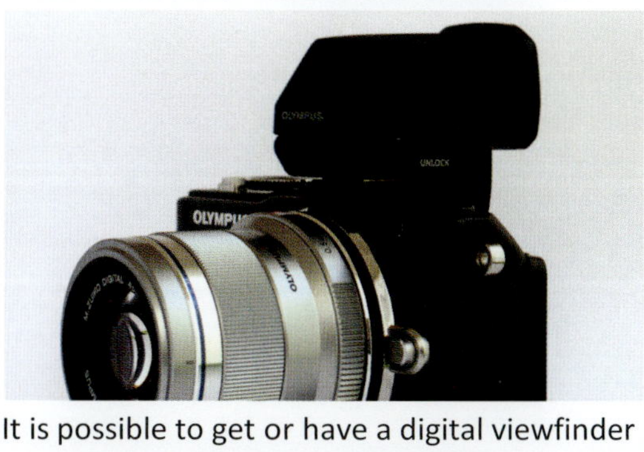

It is possible to get or have a digital viewfinder on mirrorless cameras.

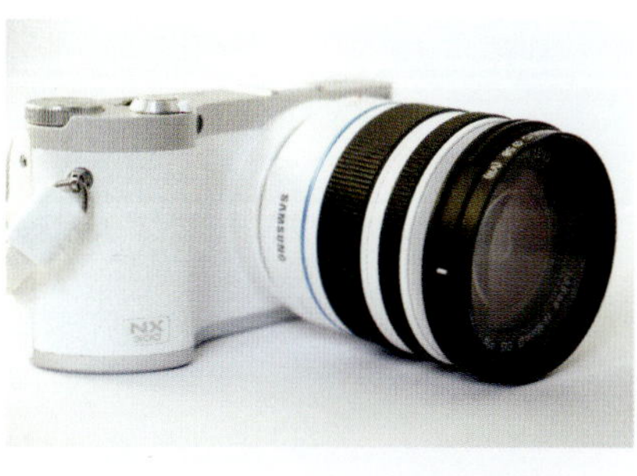

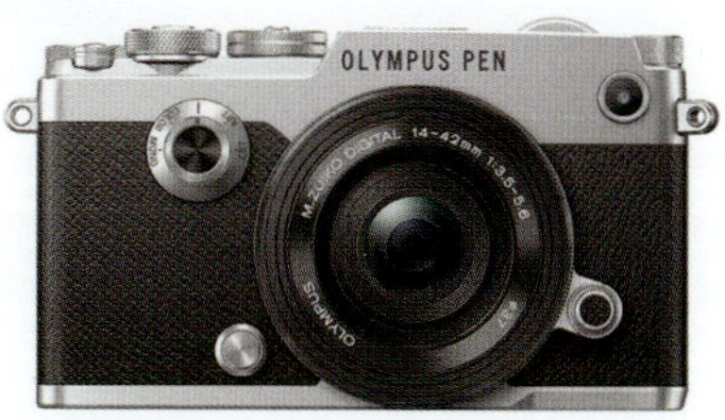

Digital Single Lens Reflex camera (DLSR)

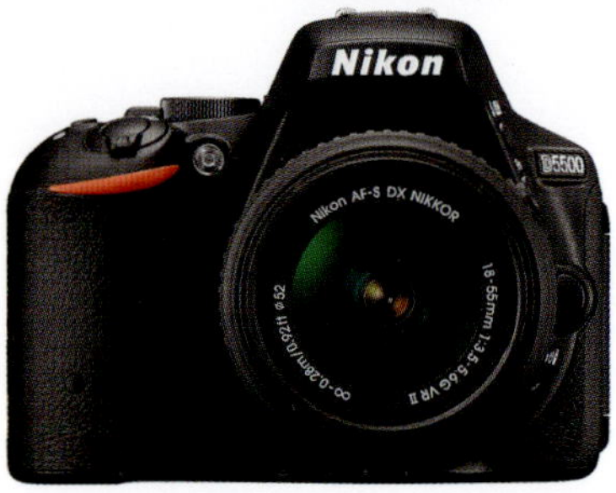

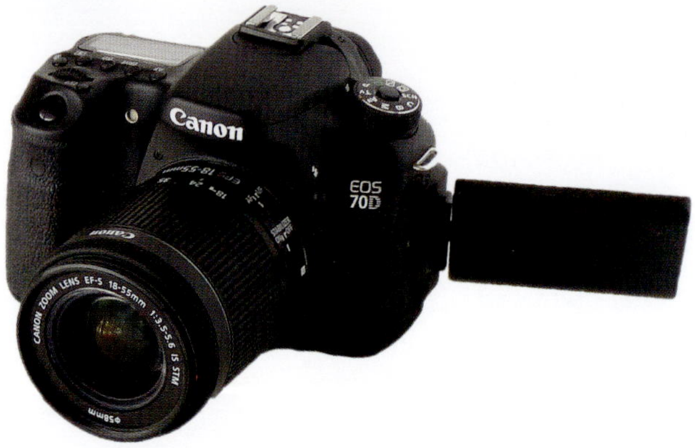

DSLR cameras are arguably the best type of camera for learning photography. The lenses are interchangeable, all the manual settings are easy to get to, they generally produce good quality images, and they have a better built-in flash.

What's more, they are good value and upgradable. As you learn photography, you might want to get better lenses and a camera body. DSLRs give you that flexibility by offering more advanced equipment for a range of budgets.

If you really want to learn photography and have a limited budget, the DSLR camera is perfect.

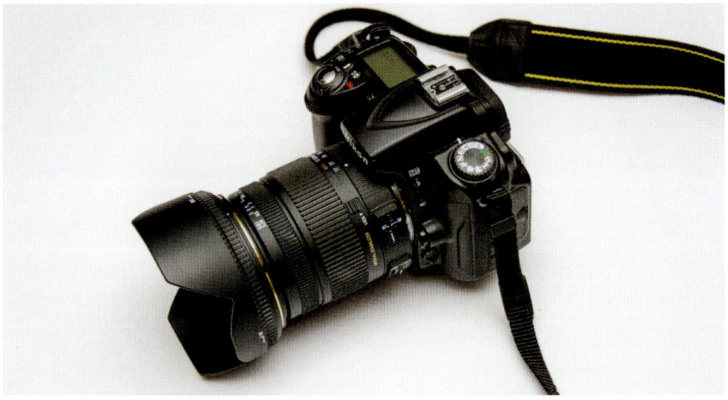

Essential equipment

Your first piece of essential equipment is a tripod. The tripod must be sturdy and stable. You need a tripod that will fully support the weight of your camera. Avoid the cheap, thin, flimsy ones!

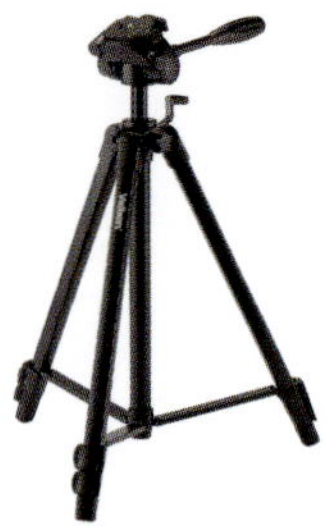

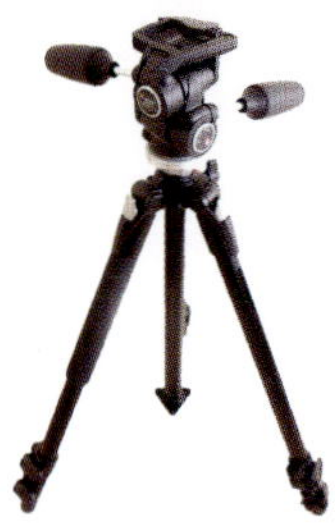

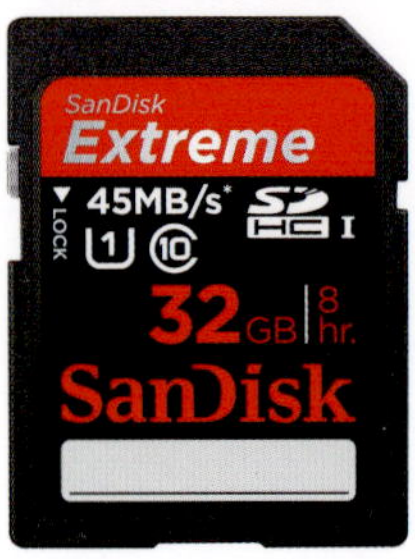

Carry a spare SD card with you, as they can become full on a long shoot.

Also have a spare battery for your camera if you can.

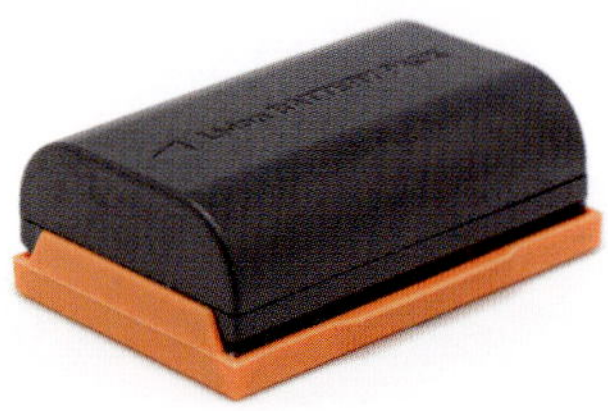

In addition to this, a lens cleaning kit is also a good piece of equipment to have. Most people don't notice the huge effect that a dirty lens can have on the quality of their photos. Carry a camera cleaning kit and keep your lens clean at all times.

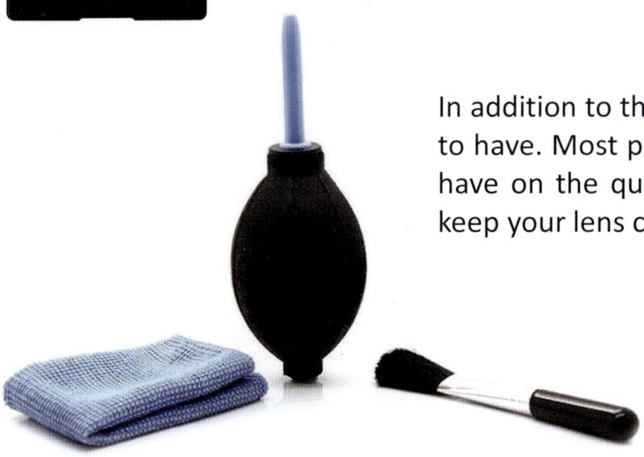

Essential equipment

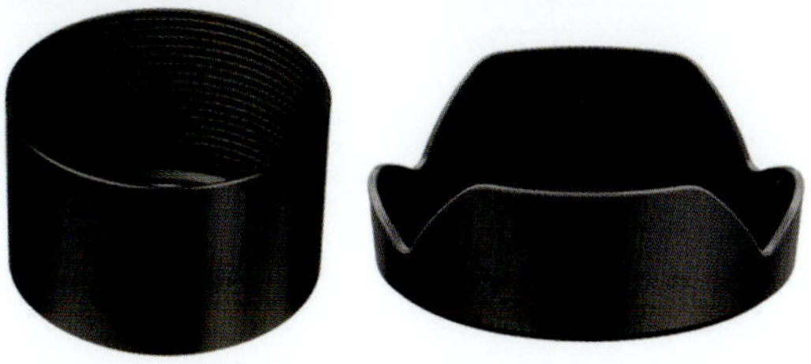

A lens hood will help reduce lens flare and give more contrast to your shots.

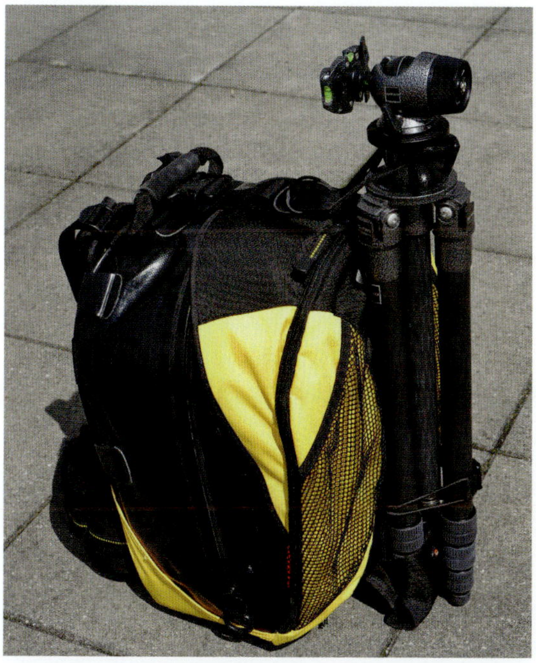

Lastly, a camera bag is another essential piece of kit as it protects all of your equipment.

I personally prefer the rucksack type of bag as it is very handy for keeping on your back all day with minimal effort.

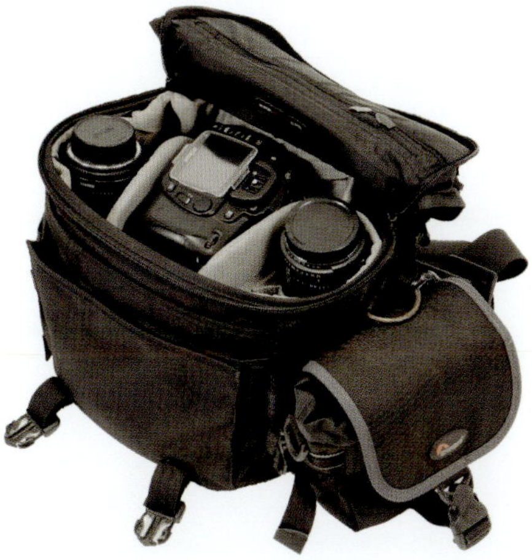

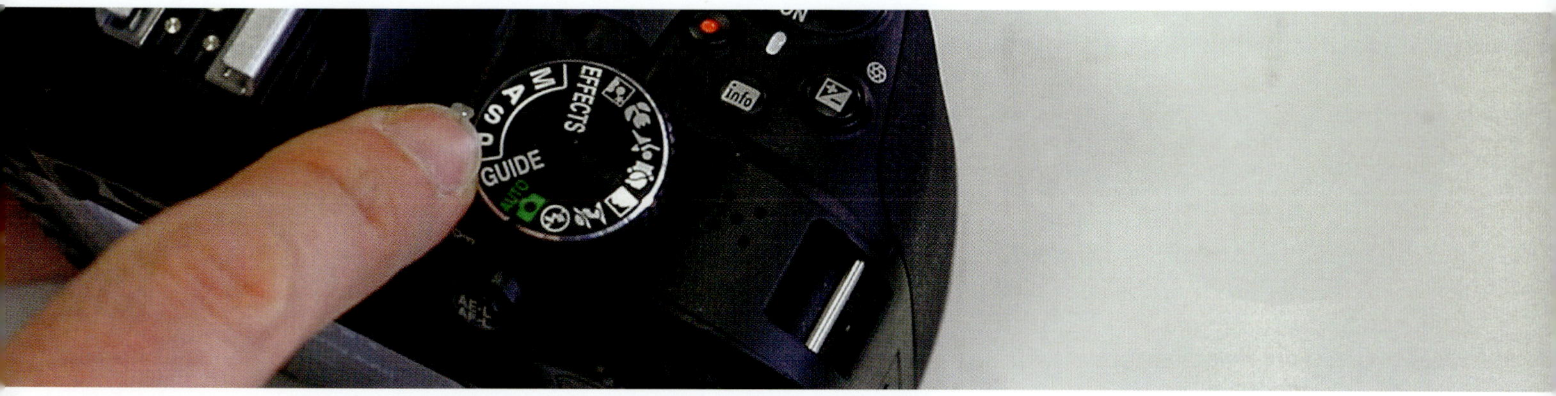

Introduction to Camera Settings

Chapter 3

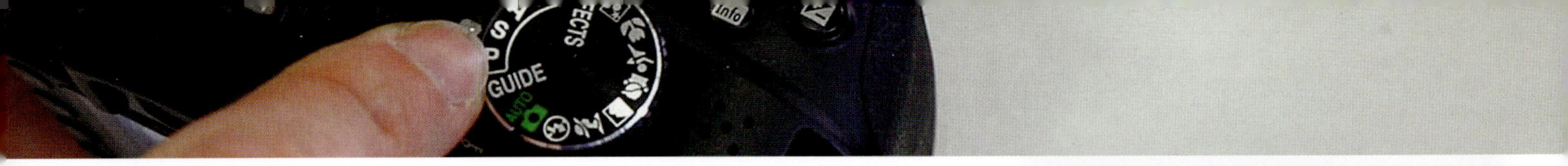

You can use most DSLRs and mirrorless cameras in Auto or Manual modes.

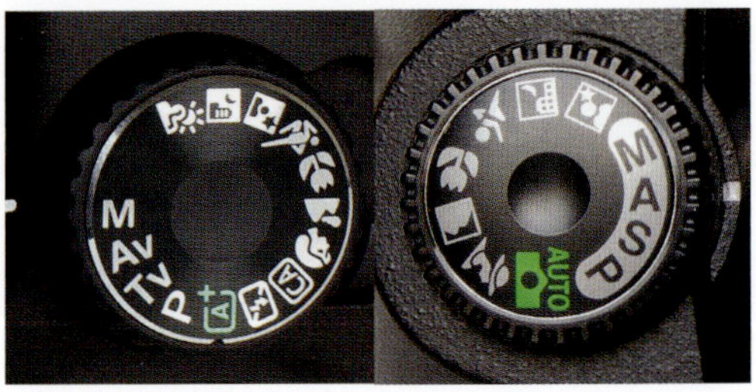

On the top of the camera, there will be a wheel with letters and pictures on e.g. Av, Tv, S, A, a picture of a mountain etc. These symbols are your camera modes.

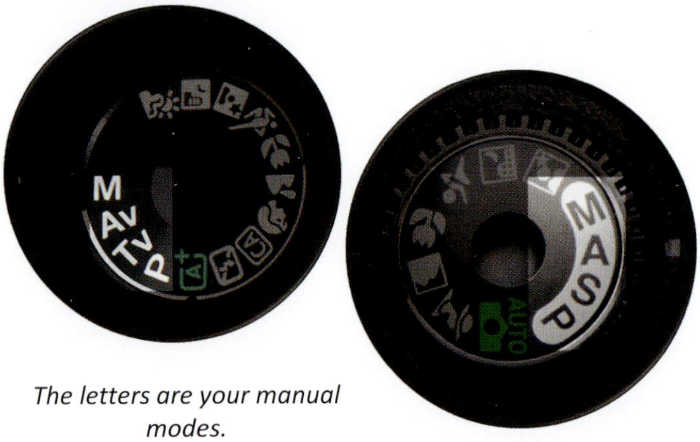

The letters are your manual modes.

Auto modes like Portrait (the head symbol) will automatically give you the largest aperture possible. The Landscape mode (the mountain symbol) will give you the smallest aperture possible.

To be creative, 'you' need to take control of elements like the aperture. Therefore, from now on, **automatic modes are BANNED!**

Below is a brief description of the manual modes on your camera. Don't worry about not knowing what the photographic terms mean for now, we will go through these in much more detail as the book progresses.

P: Program. The most automatic of the manual modes. Gives you an exposure that can be changed quickly to give different visual effects.

Tv or S: Shutter speed priority. Here you set the shutter speed and the camera will set the rest to give the correct exposure. A kind of 'semi-automatic' mode.

Av or A: Aperture priority. Here you set the aperture and the camera will set the rest to give the correct exposure. Another 'semi-automatic' mode.

M: Manual. Here you are in full control of the camera.

Program mode

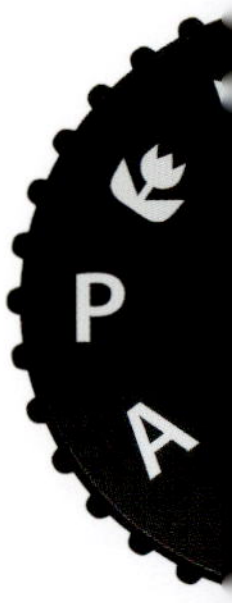

This is the most 'auto' setting in the manual modes. It sets the largest aperture to start with like Portrait mode. However, you can change the exposure very quickly for different visual effects i.e. to get the background blurred or sharp.

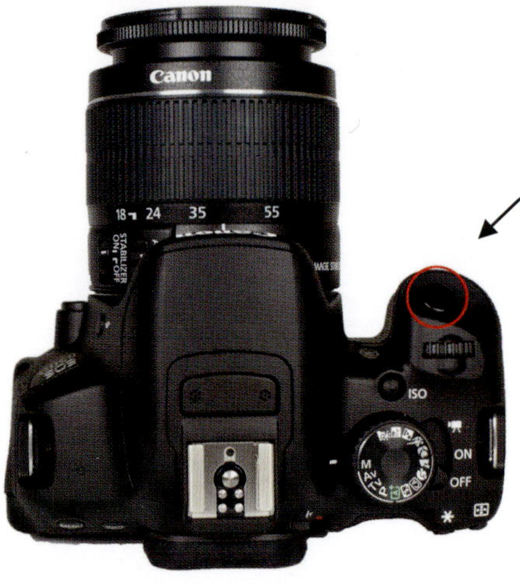

In Program, you get an exposure by pressing the shutter release button half way down. This will bring up lots of numbers on your screen or along the bottom as you look through the viewfinder. Then to change the exposure settings, twist the dial (*below*).

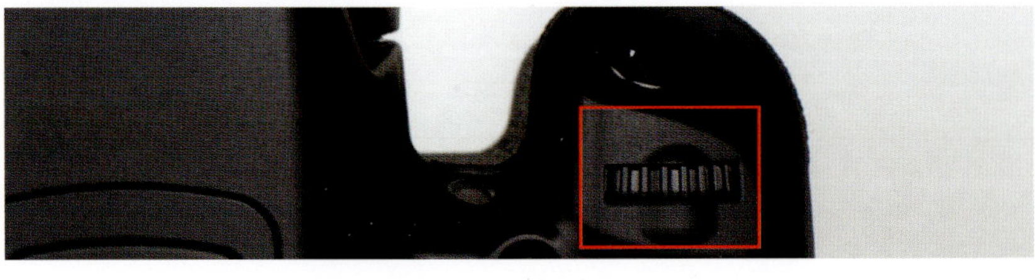

This will be on the back of some cameras

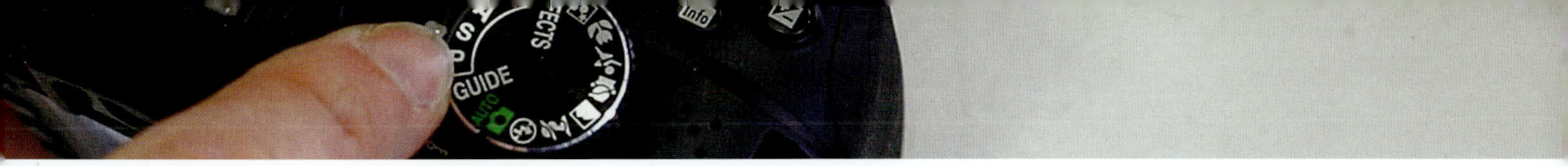

I don't expect you to know what any of the numbers on the back of the camera mean yet, just know that they change and that will in turn change the visual effect of the image. As the book progresses we will learn in much more detail what those numbers mean.

It's important to know that learning is layered, that doesn't just apply to photography, it's any learning. Learning something new is like building bricks in a wall, you need to start from the bottom and work up, you can't just put the top bricks in as there's nothing underneath to support them. For instance, in photography, there's no point jumping into learning about apertures and depth of field when you know nothing about the focal lengths of lenses, you'll just confuse yourself further. It'll be like jumping into a racing car when you don't know how to drive. So in this book we are going to learn one stage at a time so that the past knowledge will support the future knowledge, like bricks building up a wall!

Task

I'm going to set you your first task now, think of it as a warm up.

Take shots with your camera on all the manual settings and turn your dial to change the exposure (those numbers) between shots. E.g. set your camera to the Tv or S mode, take a shot > turn the dial several times > Take another shot. Then do the same in the other modes. Make a note of what goes wrong.

Here is a brief description of each of the 4 manual modes again:

P: Program. The most automatic of the manual modes. Gives you an exposure that can be changed quickly to give different visual effects.

Tv or S: Shutter speed priority. Here you set the shutter speed and the camera will set the rest to give the correct exposure. A kind of 'semi-automatic' mode.

Av or A: Aperture priority. Here you set the aperture and the camera will set the rest to give the correct exposure. Another 'semi-automatic' mode.

M: Manual. Here you are in full control of the camera.

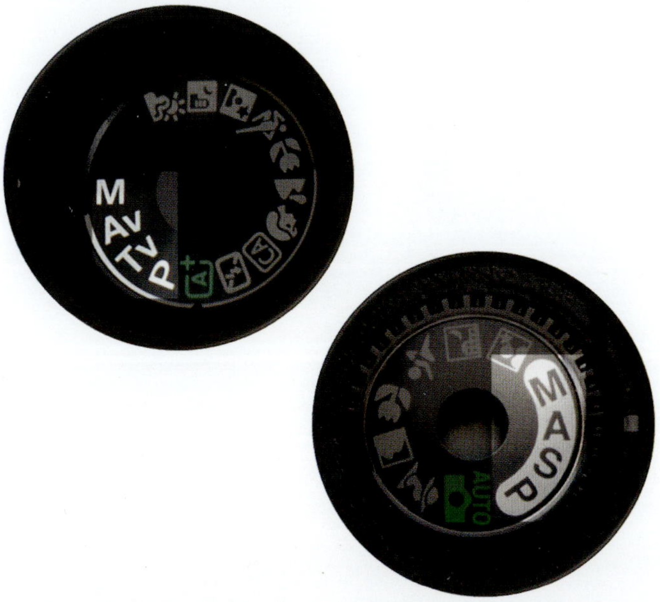

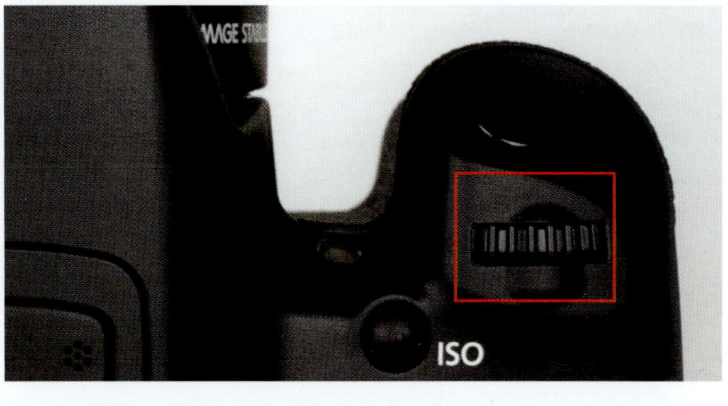

This will be on the back of some cameras

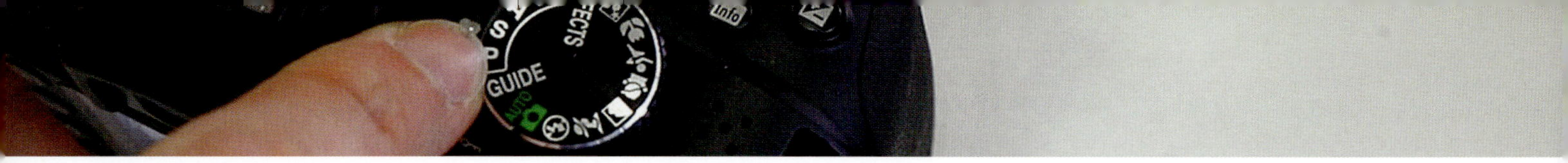

I hope you've had a good play around there, I just wanted you to get moving around your camera and note down what went wrong. Only 3 things can go wrong with your exposure and that's it! Your pictures can be too dark, too light or they might blur. Basically, it break downs to this:

If your picture is too dark, not enough light has entered the camera; the image has been underexposed to light.

If your picture is too light, too much light has entered the camera; the image has been overexposed to light.

If you have a blurred picture, light has entered the camera slowly whilst the camera or subject was moving, commonly referred to as camera shake.

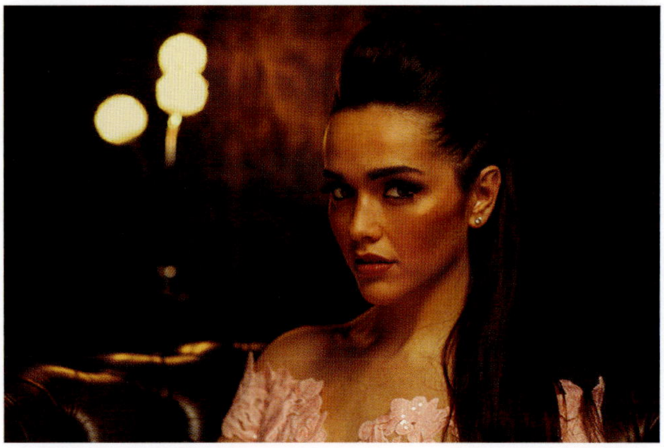

Correct Exposure

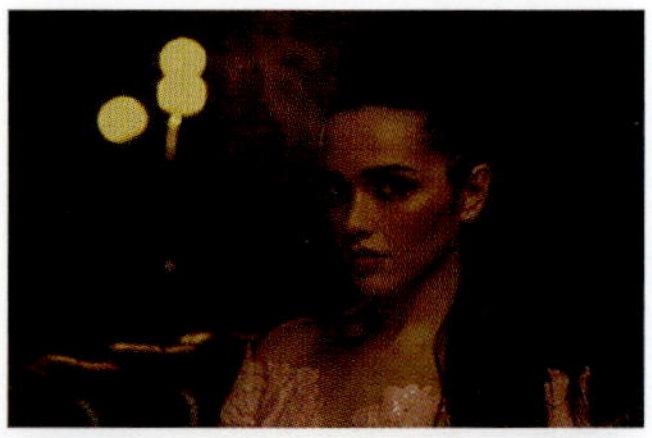

Underexposed

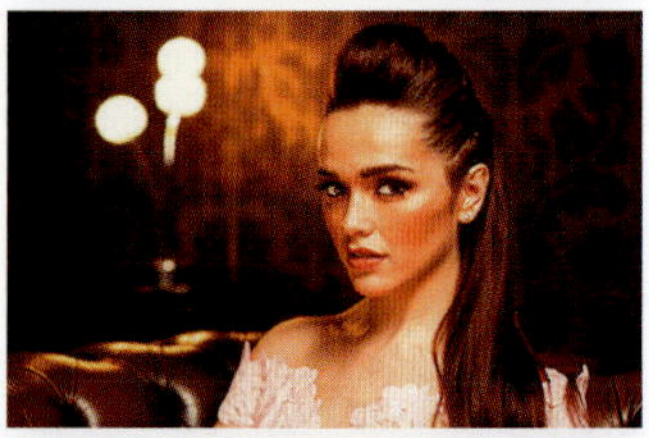

Overexposed

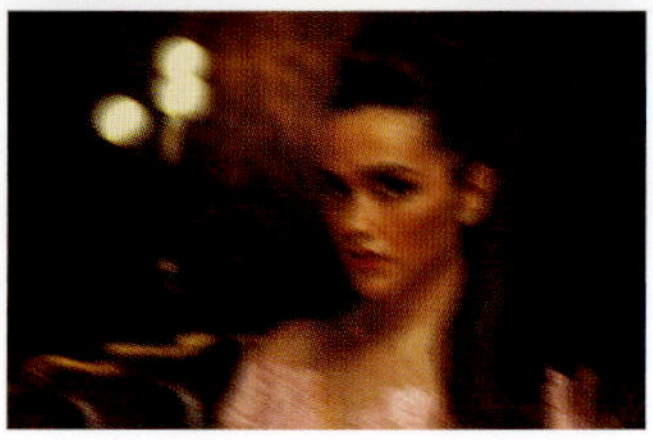

Light entered the camera slowly (Camera shake)

That's pretty much it. Your job, as a learning photographer, is to know how to correct those wrongs or even better, not do them in the first place!

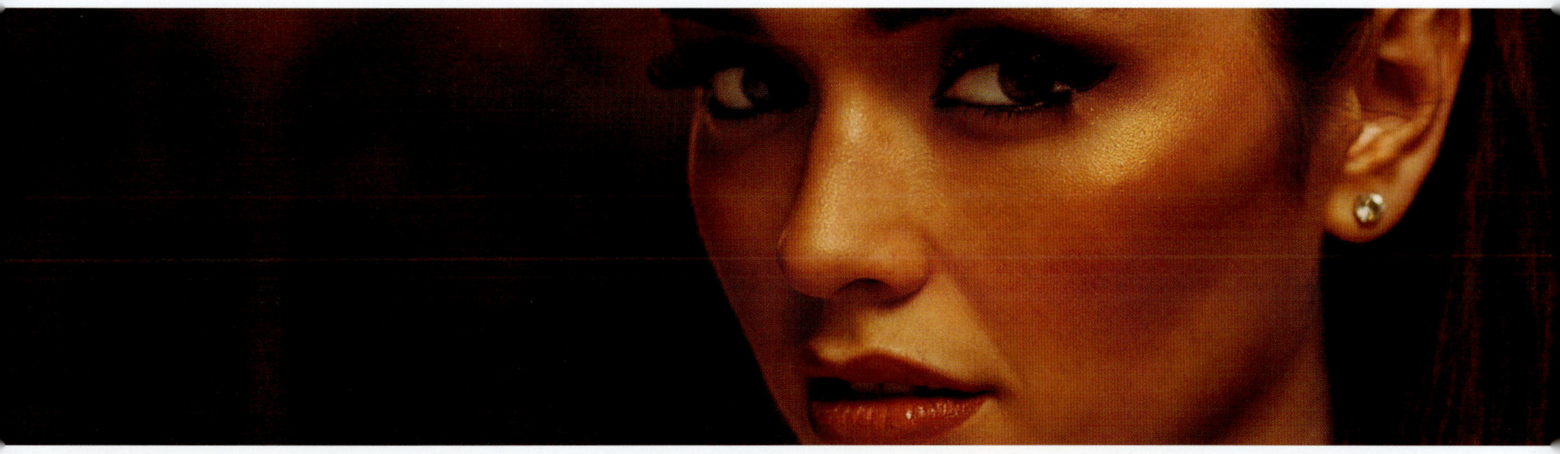

Focusing – Best Practices and Settings

Chapter 4

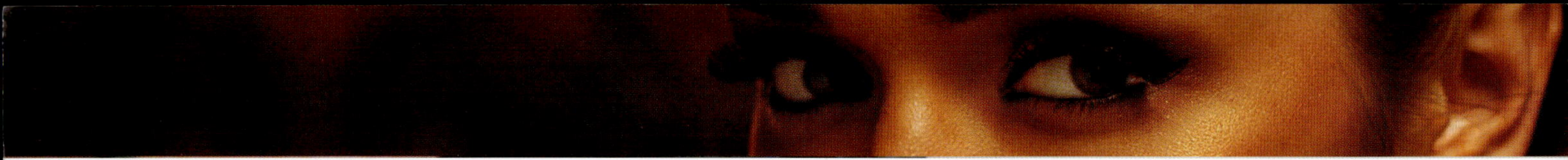

One of the first things to take control of in photography is your focus point. It can be taken for granted that you just hold the camera up and it focuses. But cameras will tend to focus on the most contrast-y thing in the frame due to their automatic settings and you might not want that to be the focus point. You need to take control and focus on what 'you' want.

The focus point of the image is where a viewer's eye will go first and is normally the most important part of the image. Take for example, this photo of a model.

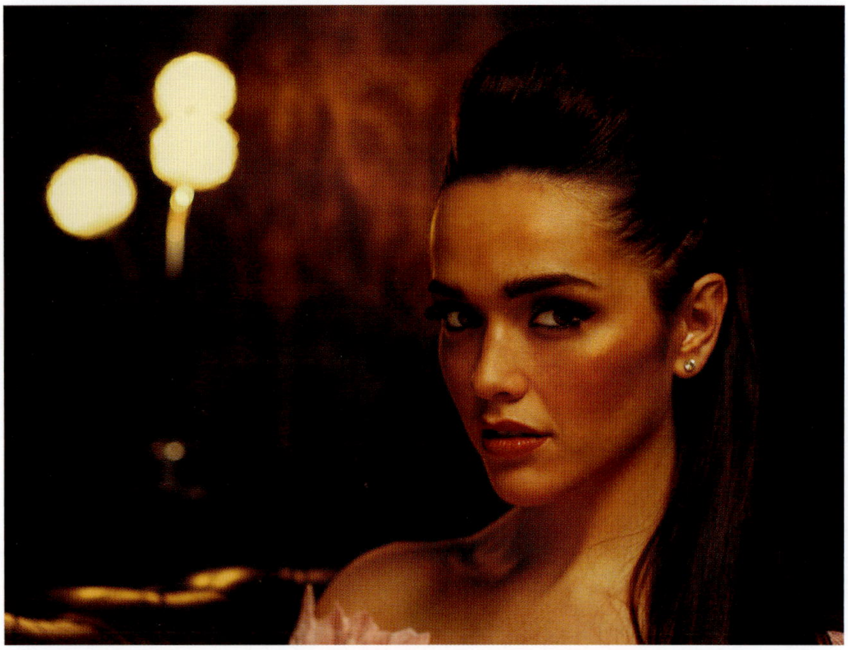

Your eye is immediately drawn to the eye of the model. And one of the reasons for this is because it's the focus point of the picture.

If we crop in, we can see that the right eye of the model is sharp, and the left eye is soft. This precise control of your focus point is what you're aiming for.

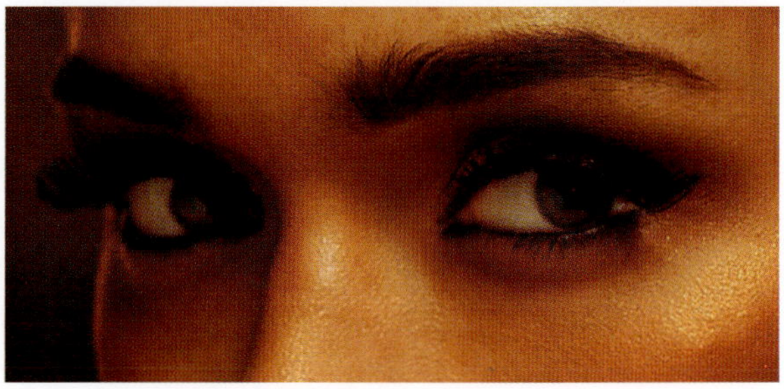

Controlling where your focus point is, is very important to get right from the start.

Things to note before we start:

1. Auto focusing, on all cameras, needs some detail to focus onto. For instance, it will not focus on a plain white wall but will focus on a picture hung on that wall. The camera needs to see some contrast to focus onto.

2. Your shutter release button has two settings. You press half way down to focus and fully down to take the shot.

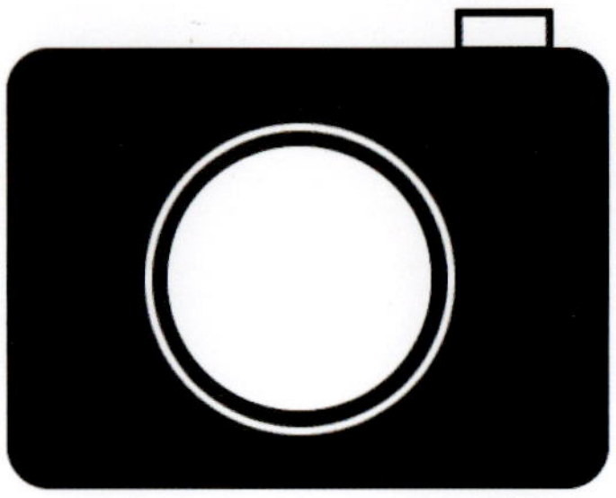

Normal

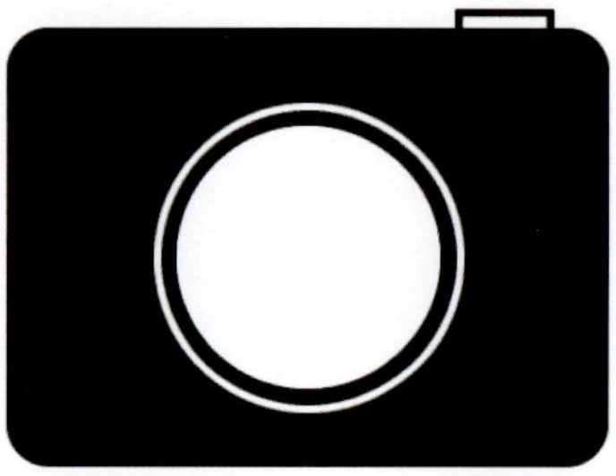

Press half-way down to focus

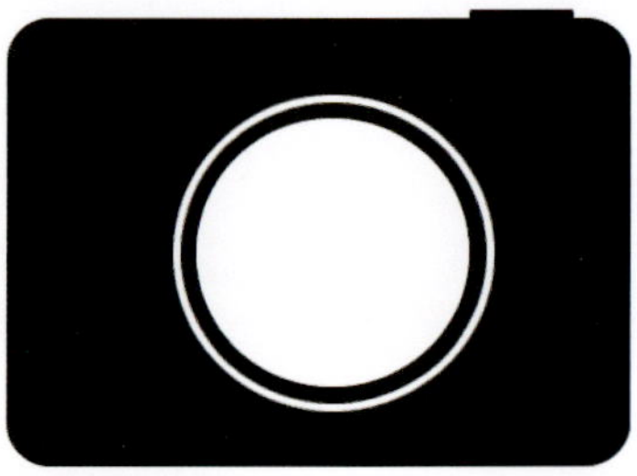

Press fully to take the picture

3. Lenses have limits on how close you can get to an object. If you're too close, your camera won't focus onto it.

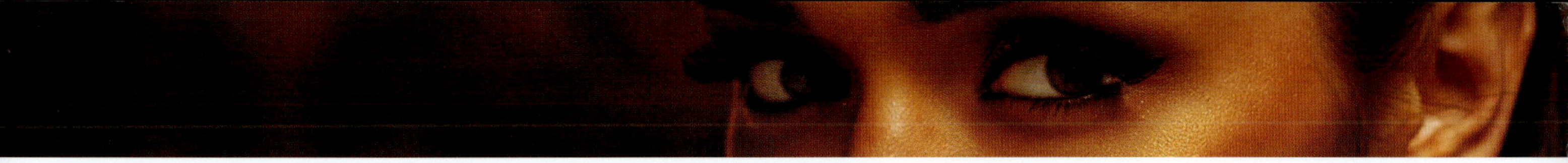

Focus Settings

There are various focus settings on various cameras but here are the most common:

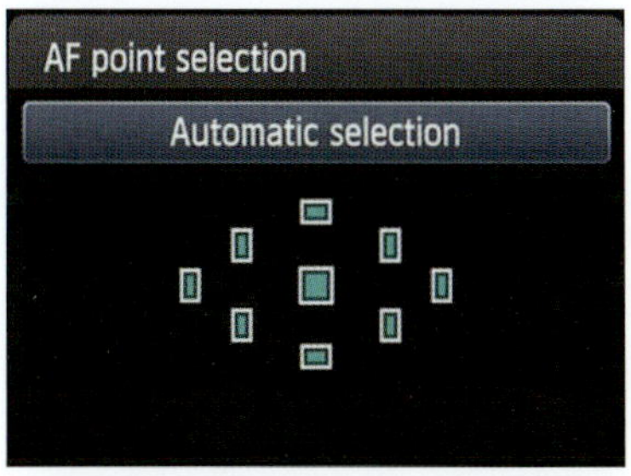

Automatic selection – The camera will focus on the most prominent part of the image. Generally, this will be what is big and near to the camera.

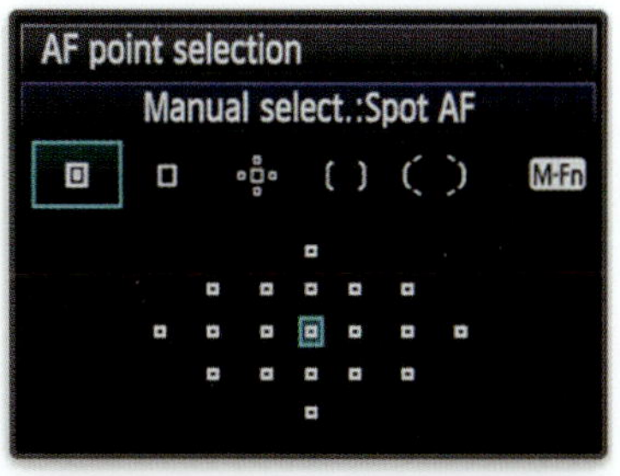

Spot auto focus – This is where you can tell the camera to focus on a particular part of the frame, for instance the centre of the frame.

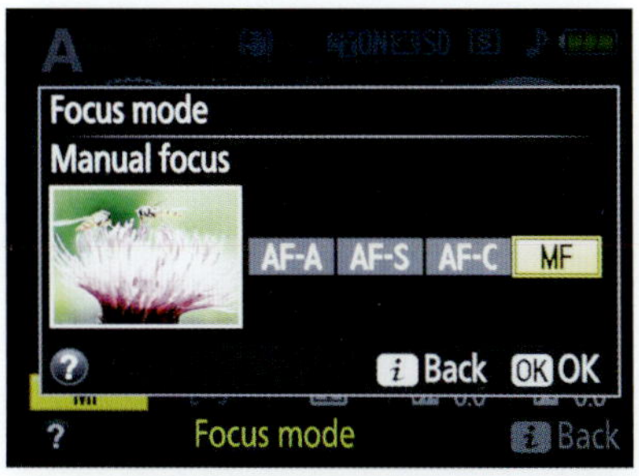

Manual focus – You control this manually from the lens. Good for low contrast or low light situations. You can switch to manual focus on most lenses by flicking a switch on the side of the lens from AF to M.

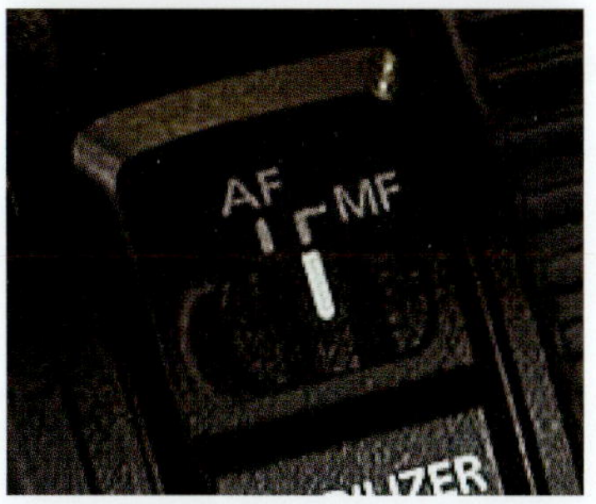

Spot Auto Focus

To start, we are going to use the spot auto focus setting and set the focus point to centre frame. Below is a guide on how to do this on most popular cameras, other camera models and brands may vary slightly. Simply look up Spot Auto Focus in your camera's manual if this is the case.

Canon

Press the button with this symbol:

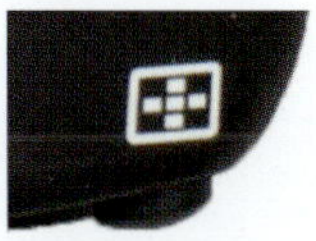

This should bring you to the focus mode screen which looks something like this (*right*). Use the navigating arrows on the back of your camera to get the dot in the centre of the frame.

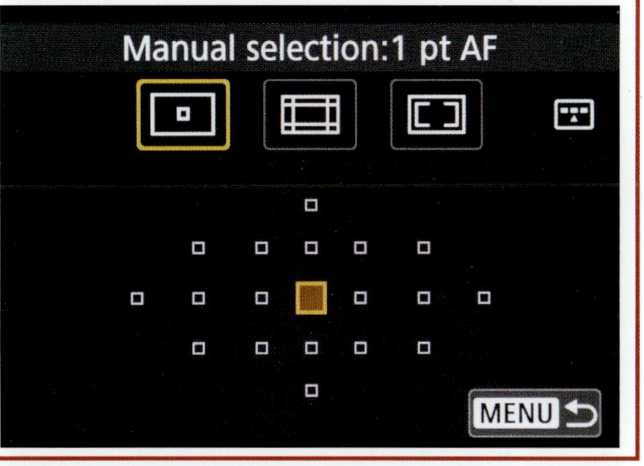

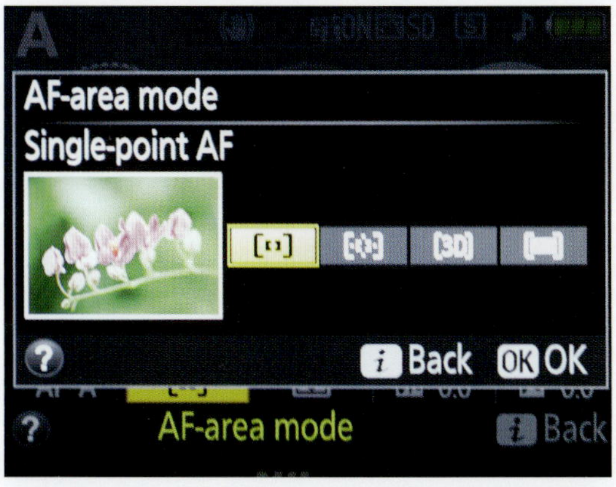

Nikon

Press the *i* button on the back of the camera to open the setting strip at the bottom or side of most screens.

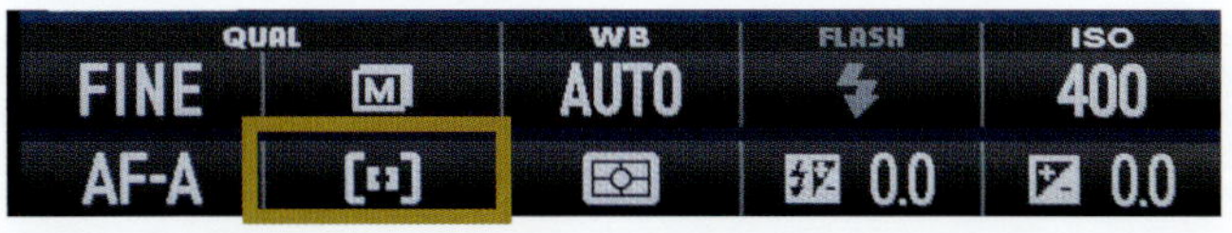

Then use the navigating arrows to select 'AF-area mode'. Then select Single-point AF mode (*pictured left*).

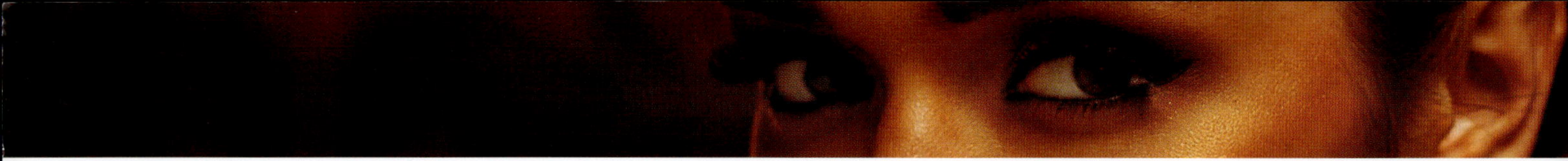

Focusing Modes:

Then you have your focusing modes.

The first being Single-Shot mode which is called One-shot focusing on Canon and AF-S on Nikon and others. This mode is generally used for shooting things that aren't moving, for example when shooting portraiture or landscape shots.

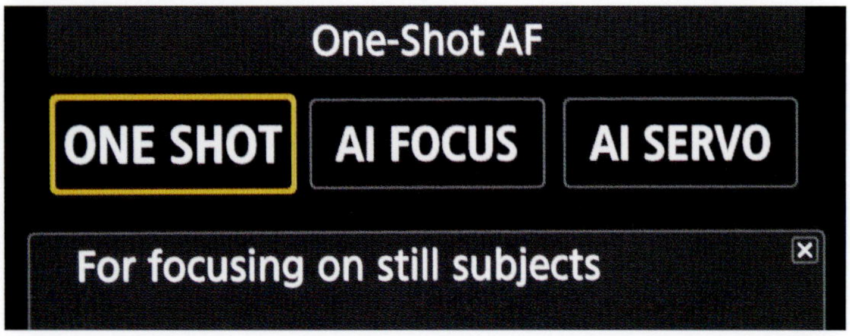

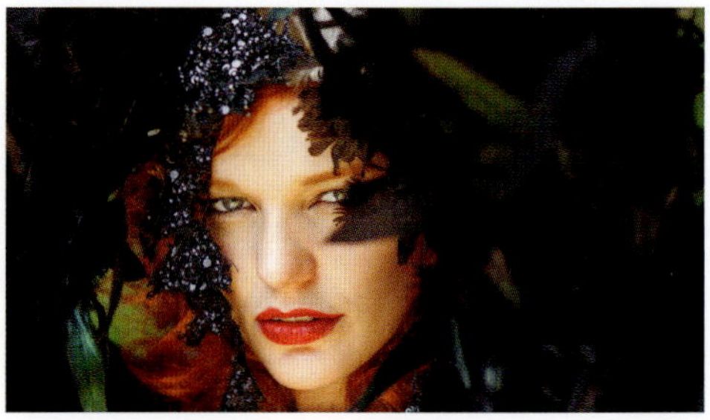

You then have continuous shooting which is called AI Servo on Canon and AF-C on Nikon and others. This mode is usually used for moving objects like a fast-moving bike or car. The camera will change the focus automatically to track the moving object.

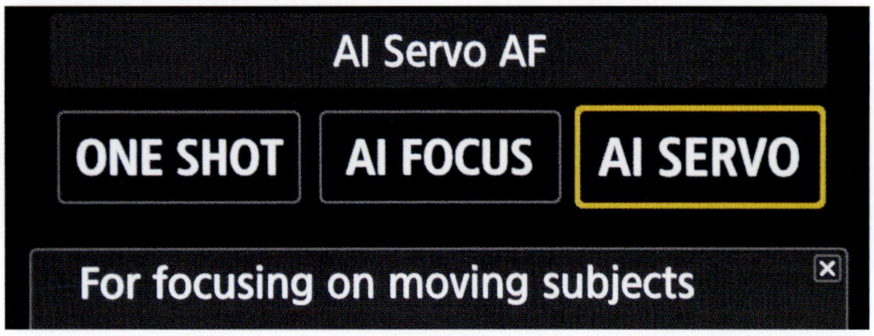

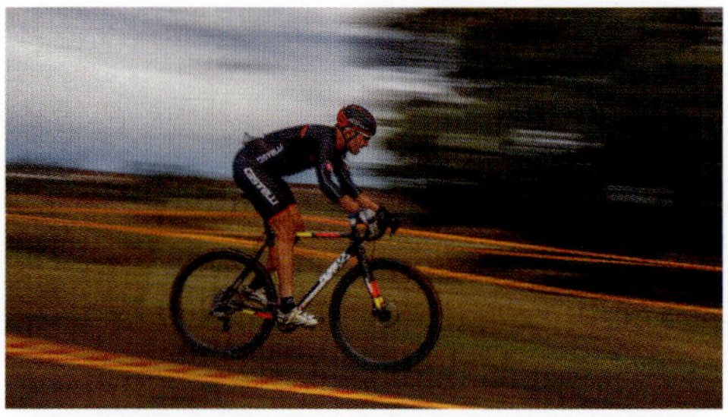

On some cameras, you also have an Auto detect setting, called AI Focus on Canon and AF-A on Nikon. In this mode, the camera decides if something is moving in the shot. You generally want to leave this off as you want to take full control of the focusing on your camera.

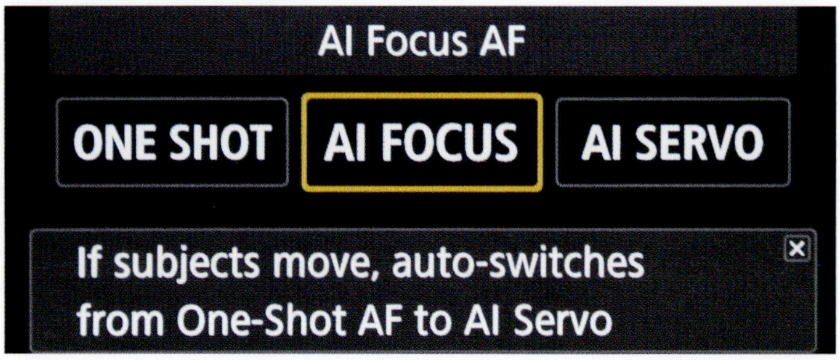

For now, we're just going to use Single Shot or One Shot as that's the mode you'll be using most of the time, and it's best for learning photography.

On the following page is a guide on how to do this on most popular cameras, other camera models and brands will vary. Simply look up Focusing Modes in your camera's manual if this is the case.

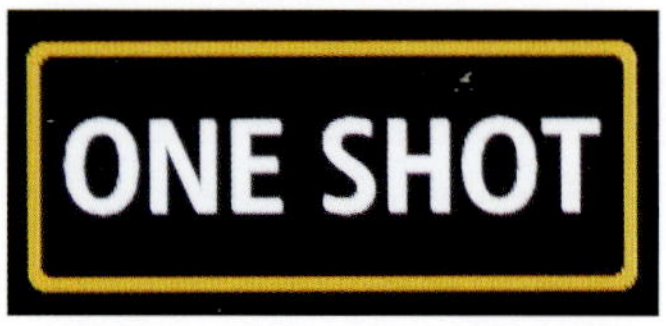

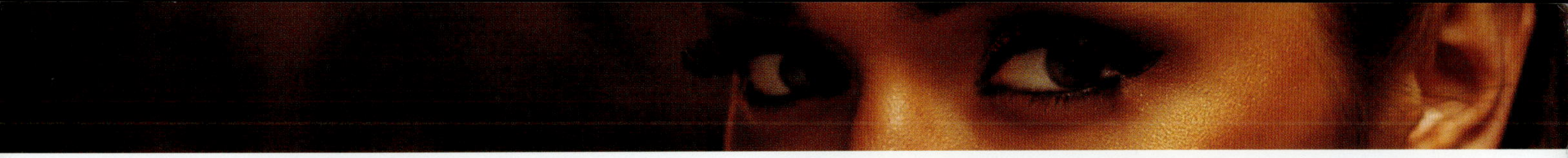

Canon

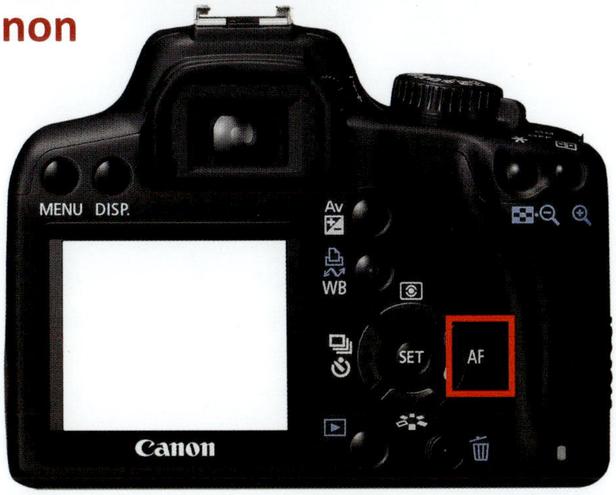

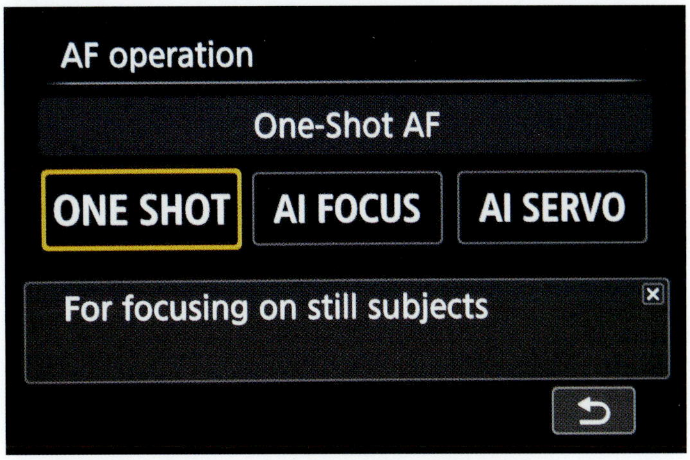

Press the AF button, then the AF operation screen should come up. Select 'One Shot'.

Nikon

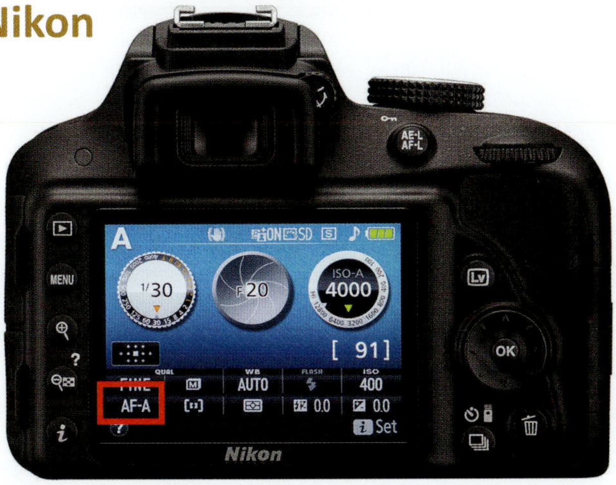

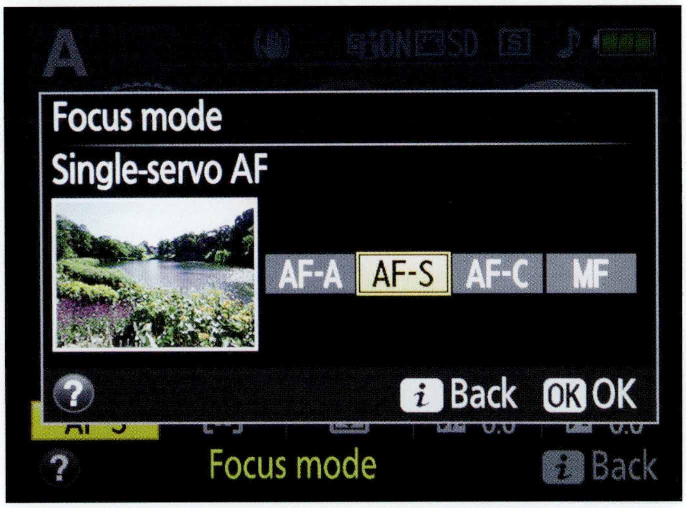

Press the i button and then using the navigator arrows, go to the Focus Mode and select Single-servo AF

Task

Ok, we're going to do a little task to get you practicing taking control of your focus point. But firstly, here's how to hold your camera correctly:

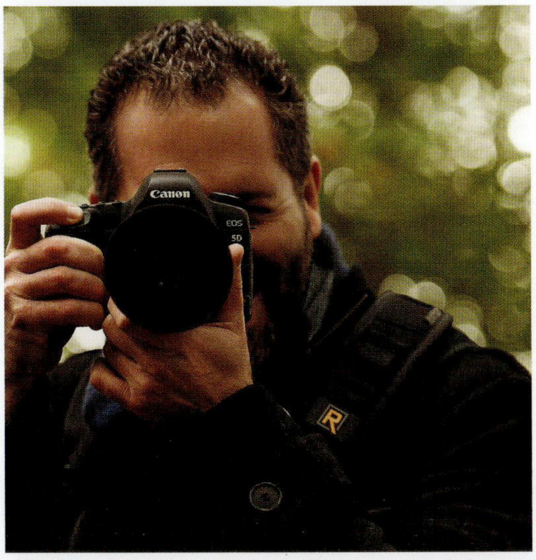

1. Put your right hand around the grip.
2. Put your left hand underneath the camera, resting the lens on your hand.

This is a stable position which allows you to go from shooting landscape to portrait very quickly.

It will also help reduce what's called camera shake and generally make you feel more comfortable with your camera.

Give it a go now and just practice holding the camera correctly whilst snapping a couple of shots.

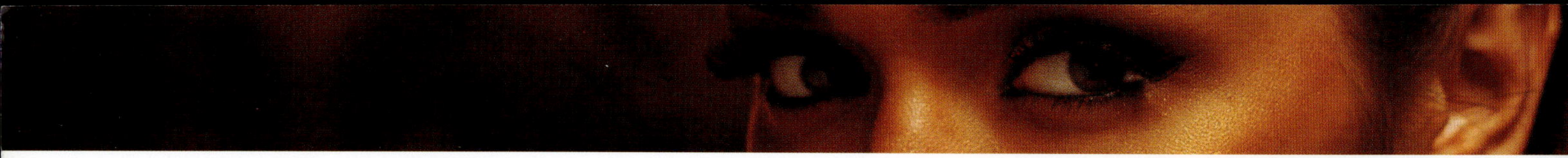

Task

Taking control of your focus point

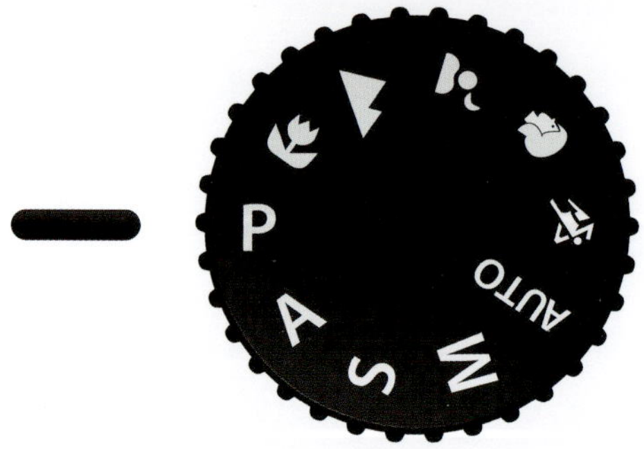

- Set your camera to P (program setting).
- Set your camera to 'Spot AF' or 'Single Point AF'.
- Set the AF (Auto Focus) point to the centre of the frame.
- Set your camera to One Shot AF or AF-S (single shoot mode).

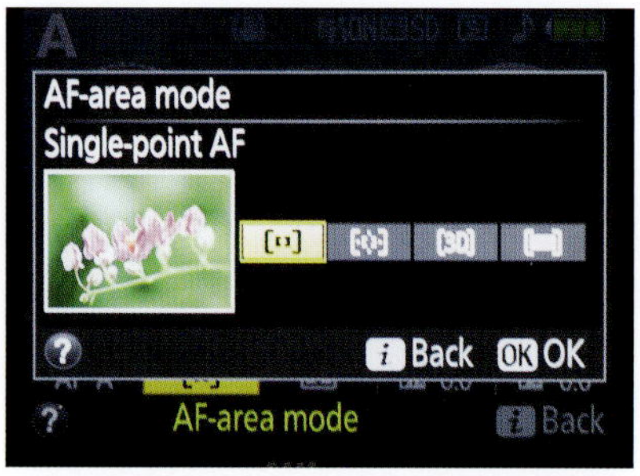

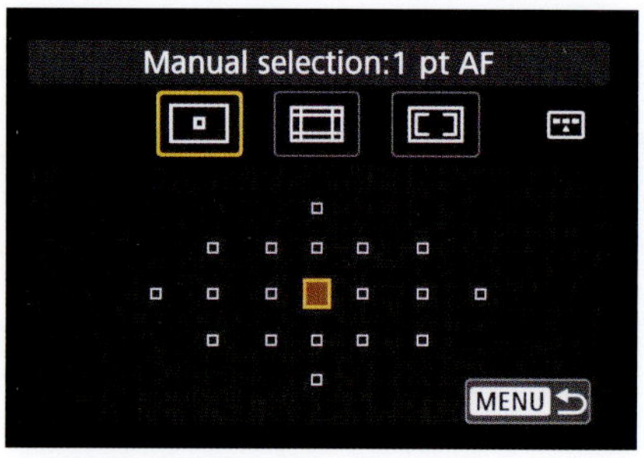

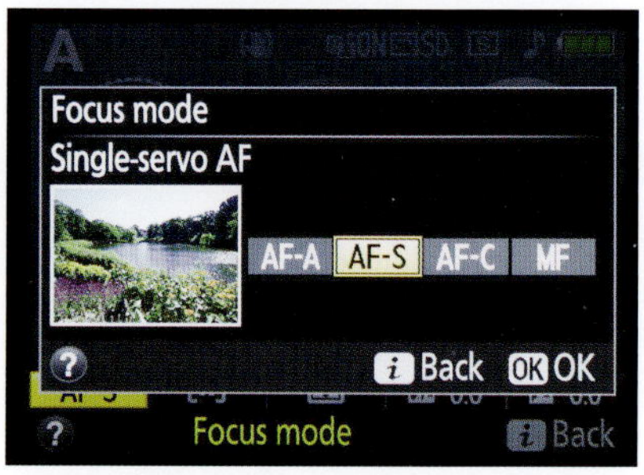

- Set your ISO to Auto (Look up how to do this in your camera's manual) and make sure you have lots of light in the room. We will learn about ISO in much more detail later in the book.
- Zoom your lens in to about 35-50mm (below right). Again, we will learn a lot more about lenses later in the book. Remember, learning is layered, we will be learning one step at a time.

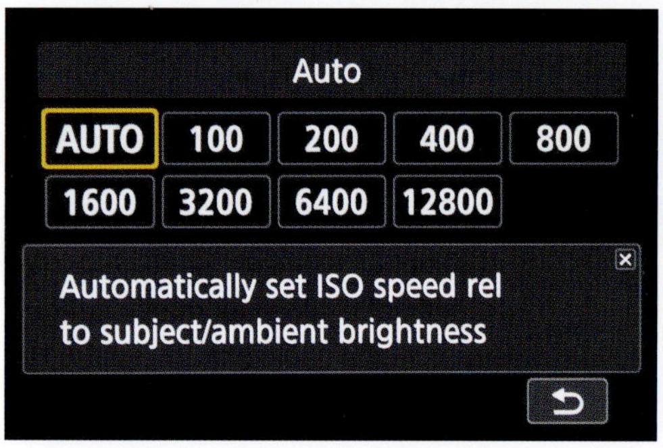

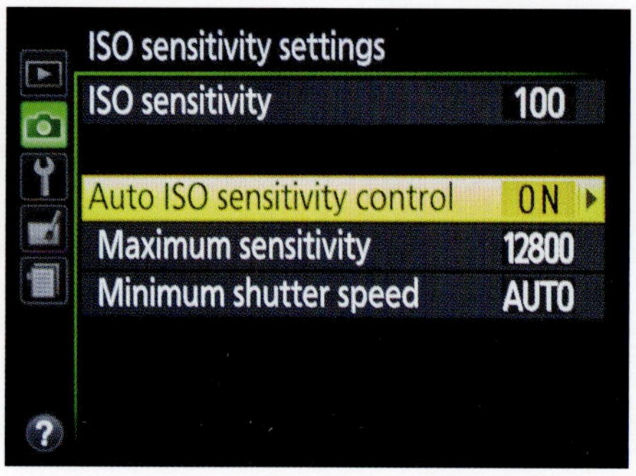

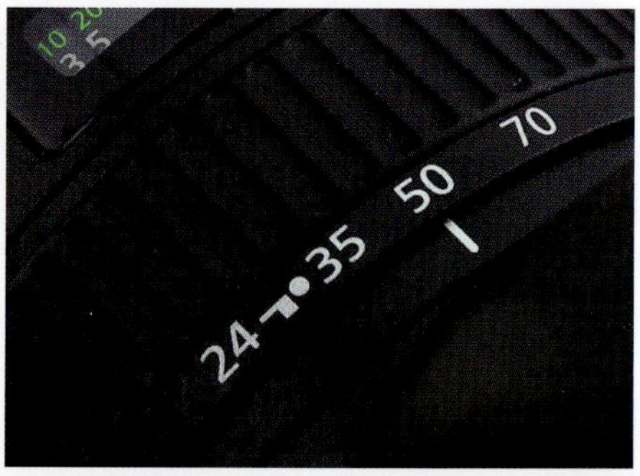

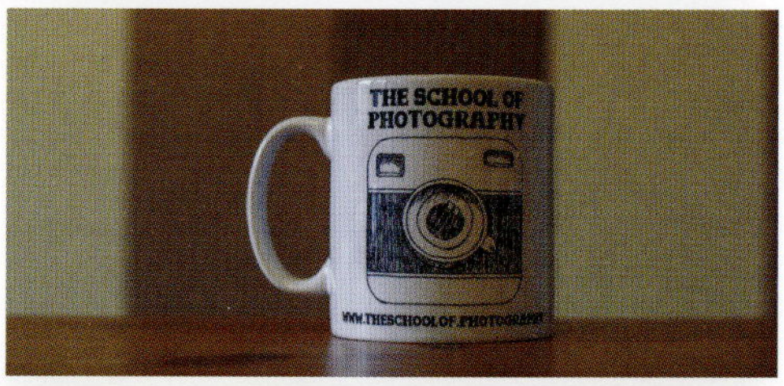

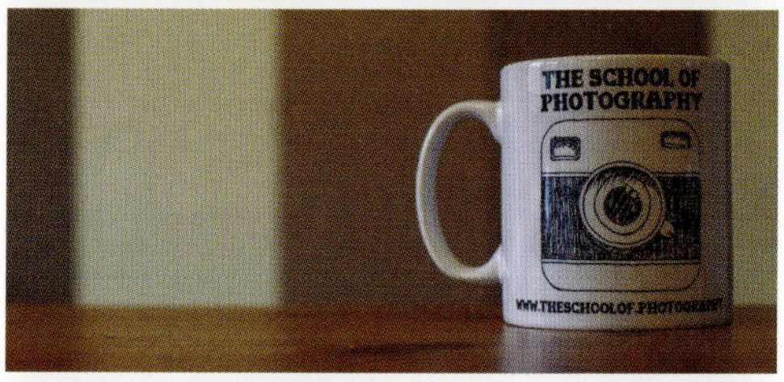

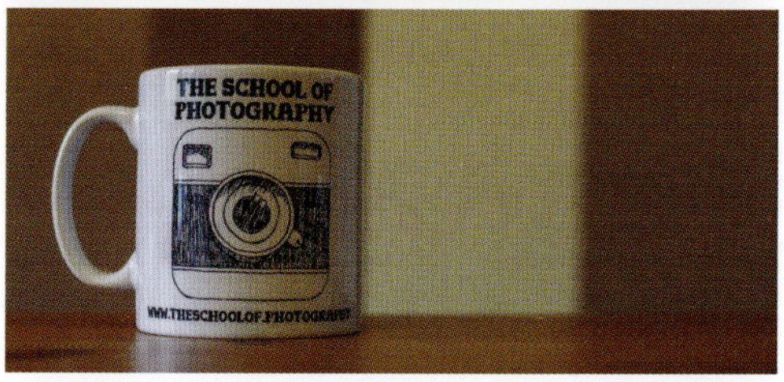

- Choose an object to photograph and make sure you have a distance of at least 5 meters between your object and the background.
- Make sure your object is around 1 meter away from your camera.
- Focus on your object by pressing the shutter half-way – Take the shot by pressing all the way down.
- Now focus on the subject again but this time keep your finger pressed half way on the shutter release button and move your camera to place the object in the right side of the frame. **Do not release your finger in the process.** Take the shot by pressing all the way down.
- Repeat the process so the focus point is now on the left of your frame.
- You are aiming to get images similar to those right.
- Remember the process: **1 – Focus, 2 – Reframe, 3 – Shoot.**

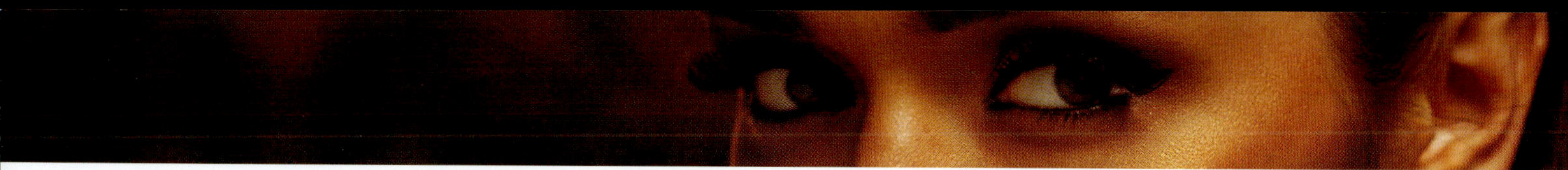

Ok, you've just taken your first steps to controlling your photography; the focus point will now go exactly where *you* want it to go. Let's recap:

- Auto focusing needs some detail to focus on – it won't focus on a plain wall or in the dark because it can't see anything.
- Your shutter release has two settings: half-way to focus, fully down to take the shot.
- If you're too close to something, the camera won't focus so move back a bit and zoom in if you have to.
- While you're practicing, it's best to have the camera set to One-Shot Focusing or AF-S, and the camera set to the Spot Auto Focus setting, placing your focus point to the middle of your frame. Then you can quickly focus on the point that you want and move that focus point to anywhere in the frame.

And that's focusing done! Practice it some more if you need to, and then move on to the next chapter.

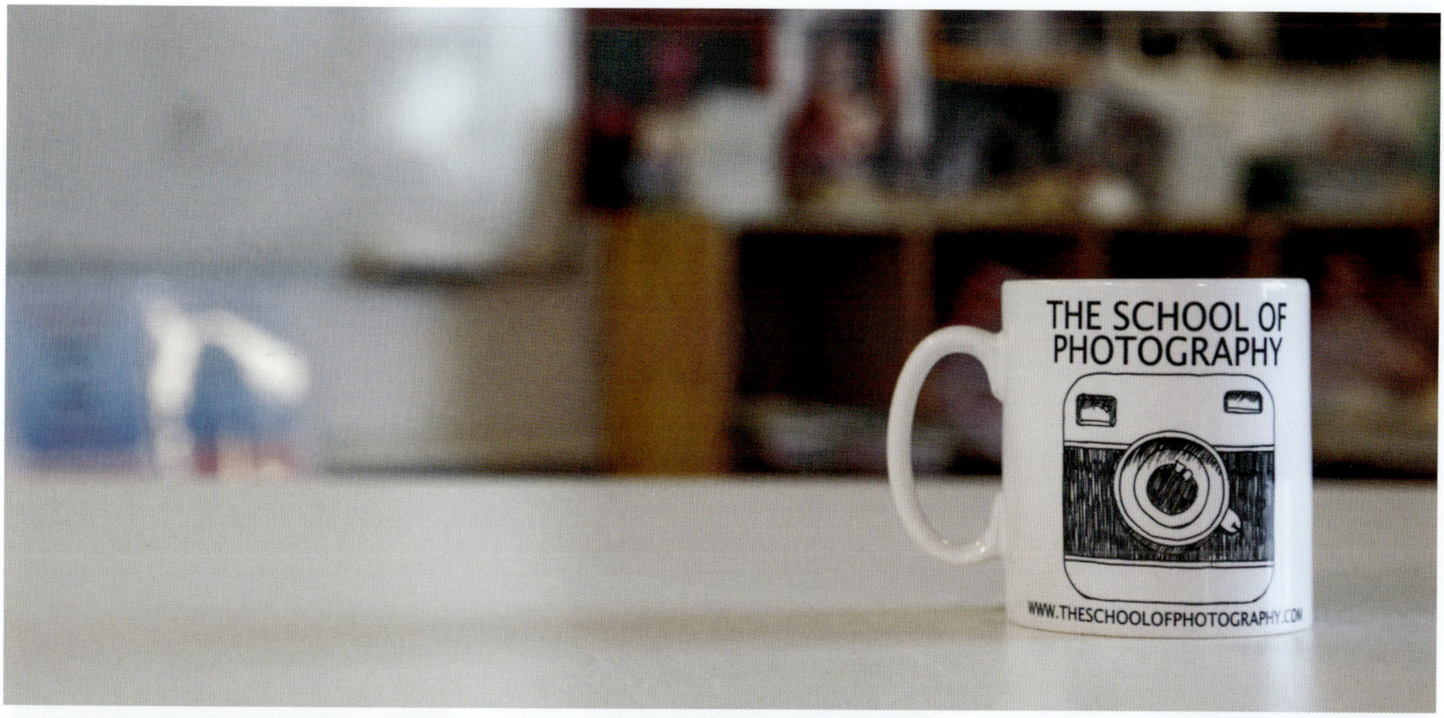

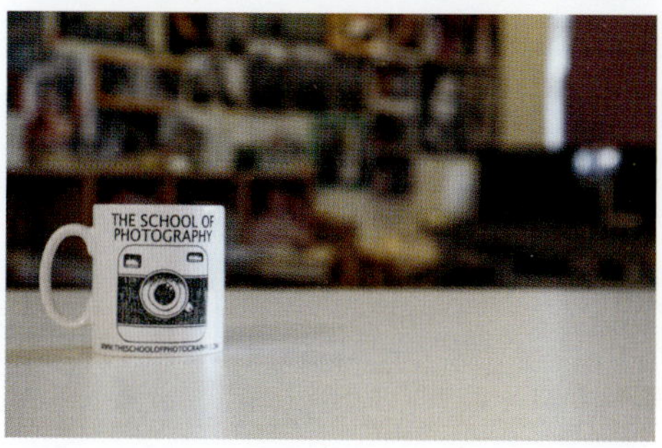

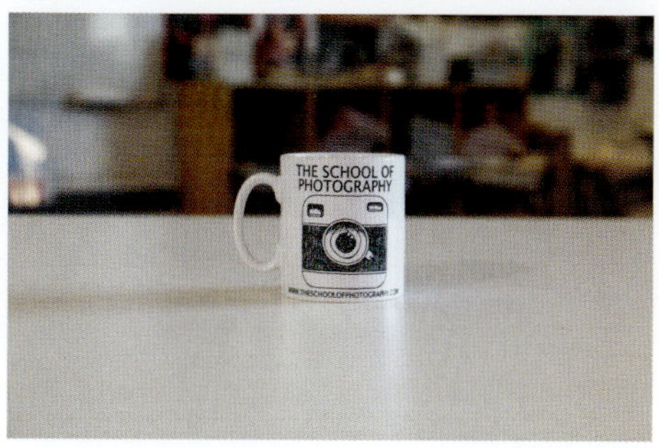

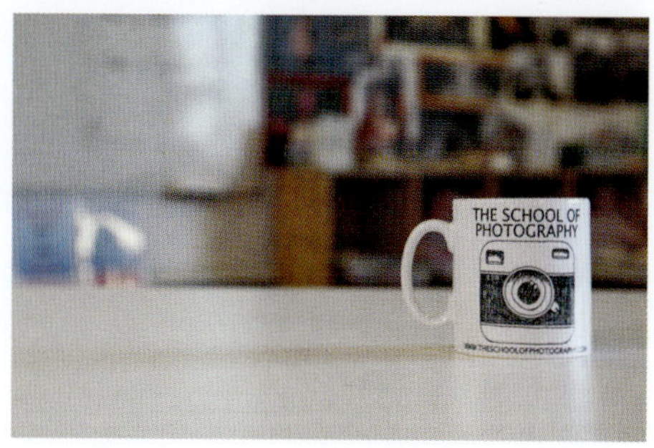

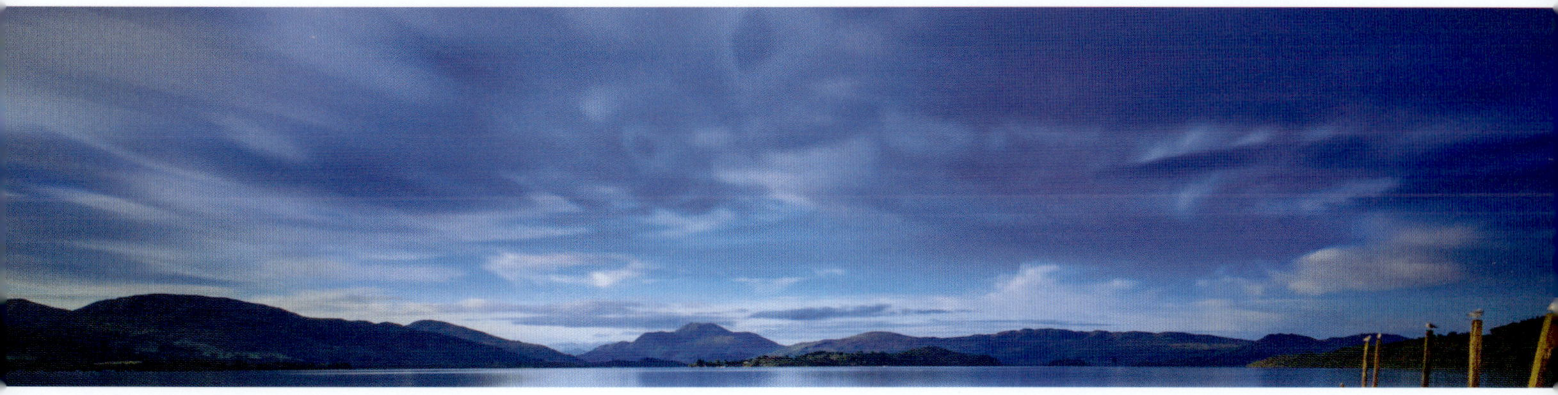

Composition

Chapter 5

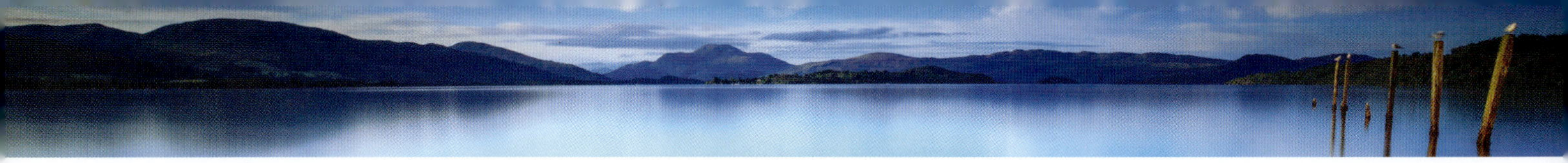

In this chapter we are going to talk about composition.

Now Composition, in my opinion, is one of the most important parts of photography. If I had to put one thing on top of everything else to get right, it would be composition. This is because you can make your shots look 10 times better without any technical knowledge, just with the knowledge of how composition works.

In the dictionary, the word composition means combining or putting together different parts to form a whole. Composition can apply to many subjects including music and writing – when you compose a song, you could start with the drums and then bring in the guitar after 10 seconds and then the vocals after another 10 seconds and in doing that, you are composing that song in that way.

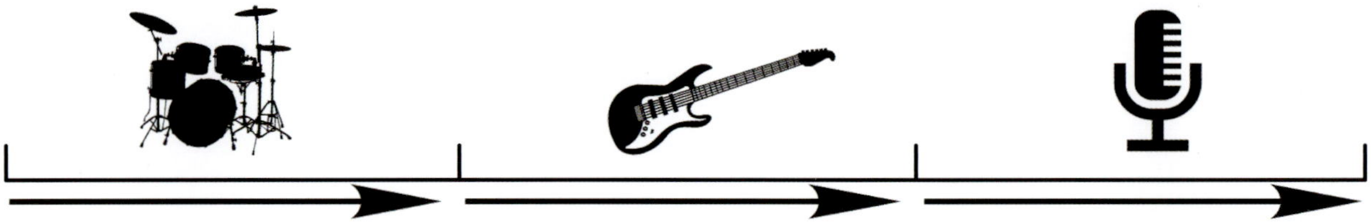

But if you move the vocals to the start and put the drums at the end, you are changing the composition of that song – Composition applies to any creation that is put together using different parts.

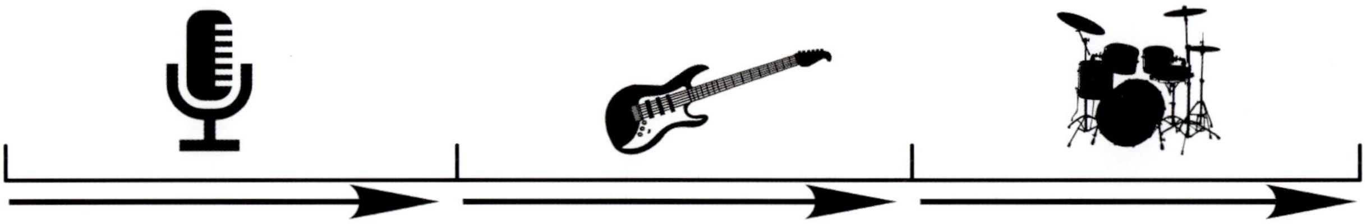

In photography, composition is how you arrange the elements of your scene, within your frame. This could mean what's in the foreground, the background, your subject, props etc. In short, everything within your frame is an element of that picture and if you change one of those elements, let's say you move your subject from the left of the frame to the right of the frame, you have just changed the composition of that shot. Let's look at some examples.

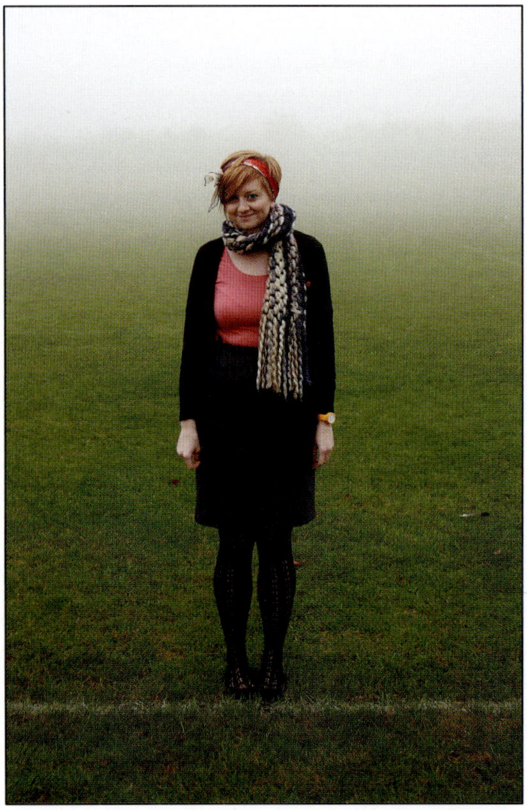

Here is a nice normal shot; she is centre of the frame, looking at the camera and smiling.

But now let's change the 'composition' of the shot - the positioning of the model within the frame.

All I've done in this shot is move closer to the model, position her to the left of the frame and asked her to not smile as much. It's completely changed the mood of the image.

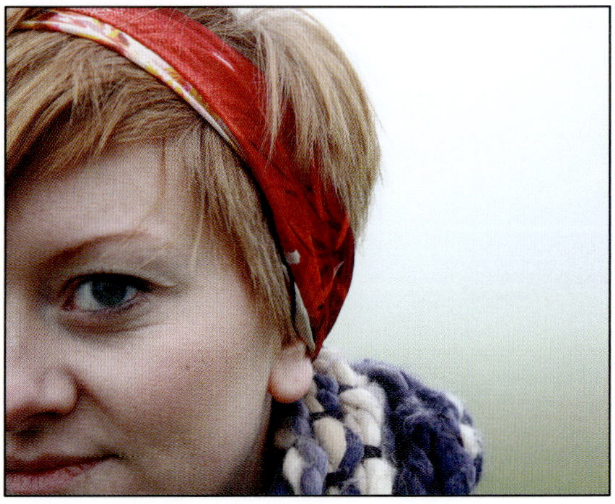

You have the same person in the same place, but you have two different compositions, which are giving two separate feelings.

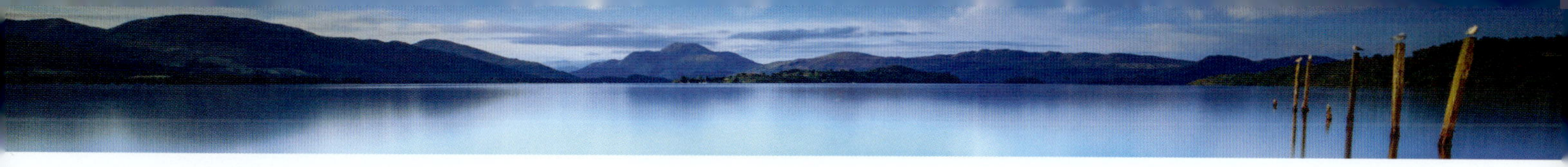

It's really important to know that it's you, the photographer, that controls the composition of your shots. Let's take this one step further.

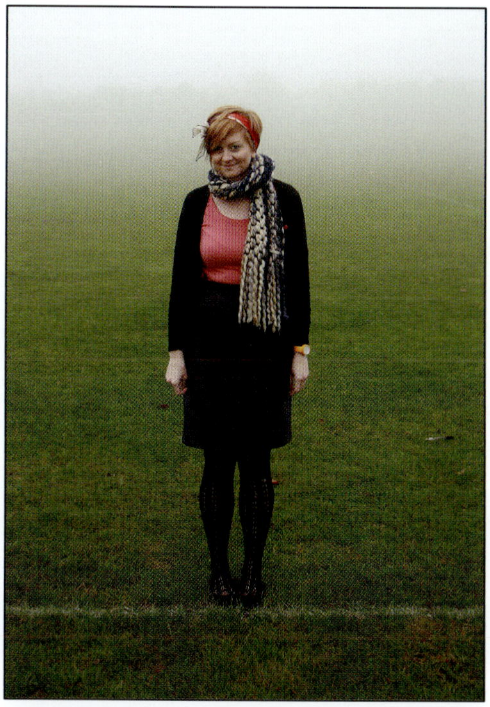

Here is the first image again. Nice, normal, model is in the centre of the frame.

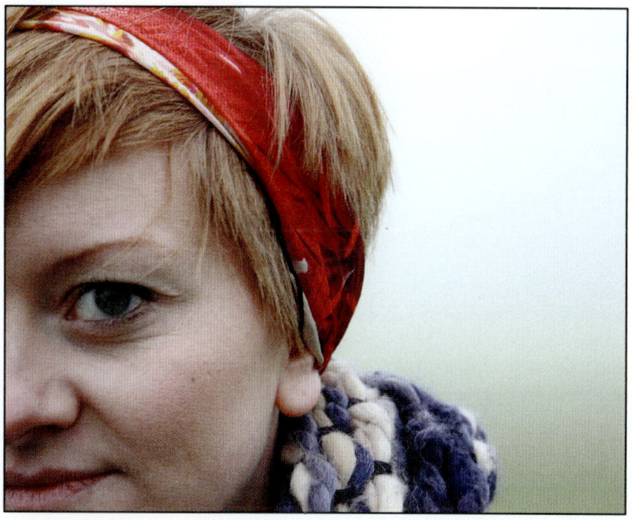

Here's the close-up image, more focused on the face, model looking straight into the lens, giving a more intimate feeling.

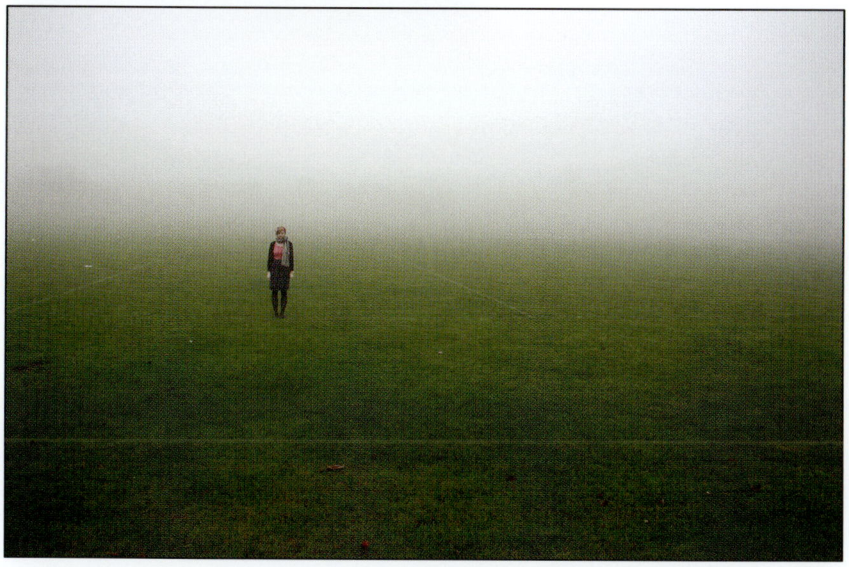

In this image I have moved back to make the model small within the scene; I wanted to create a sad, desolate feeling so I changed the composition of the shot to try and get that feeling.

Again, it's me that has moved, not the model. I have controlled the composition of this shot to give a different mood.

Now I can tell you that she is a very happy person. She's certainly not sad like that image suggests, and that's because photography lies, and it's you that makes it lie.

You can do this just through a clever use of composition. You can make someone look happy when they are sad and vice versa. You are in control of the composition.

So again, we have the same person in the same place, but 3 different compositions giving 3 different moods.

Let's just look at one more where the viewpoint has totally changed.

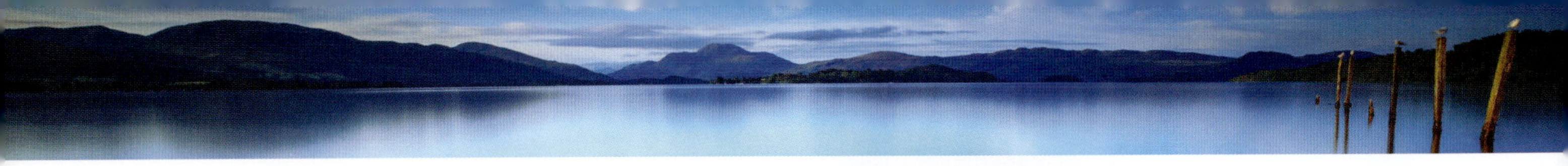

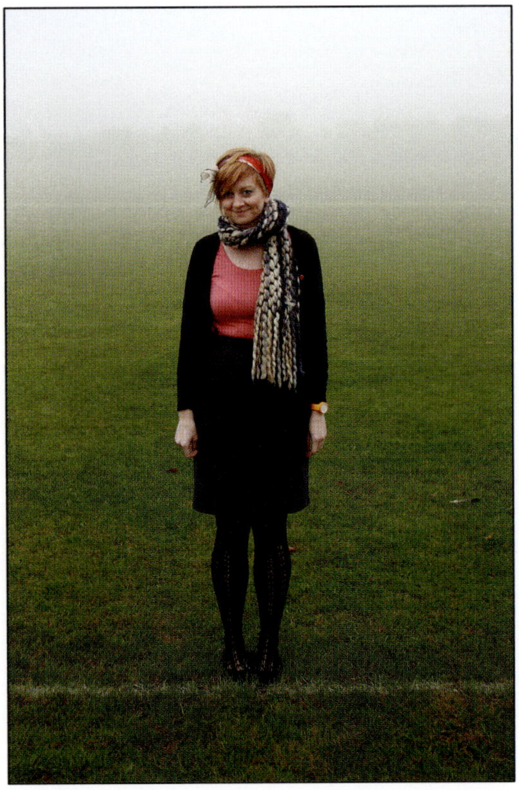

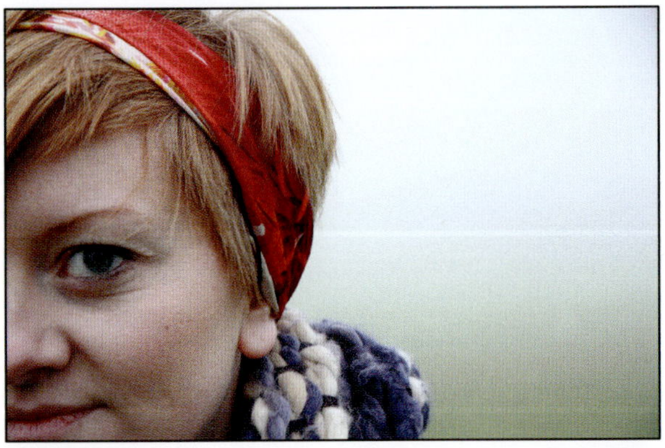

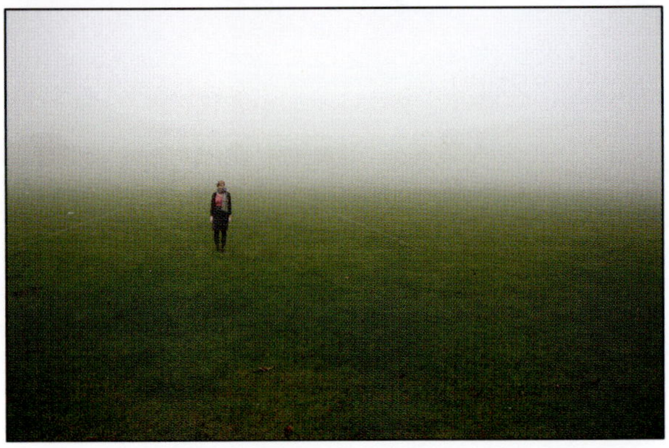

With the other 3 shots, they were pretty much taken at a normal eye height - that's me standing normally, holding the camera to my face and taking the picture. The viewpoint of your picture is where you place the camera to take the shot.

A shot up high will have a high viewpoint, a shot on the ground will have a low view point. Here you can see I've used a low viewpoint, the camera has been rested on the ground looking up.

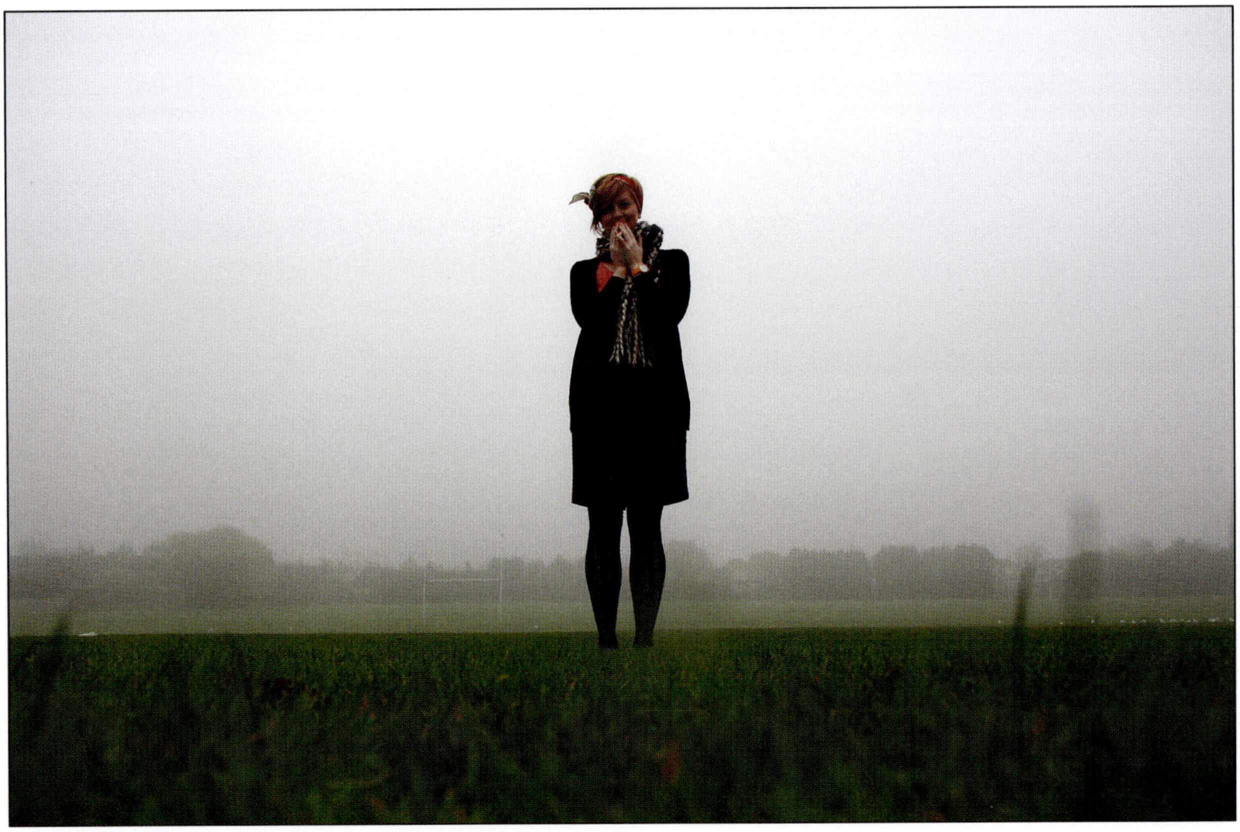

This has totally changed the composition of the image.

Most people just continue to take pictures at eye level, but moving your viewpoint is a really easy way to change your composition and give more interest to the image.

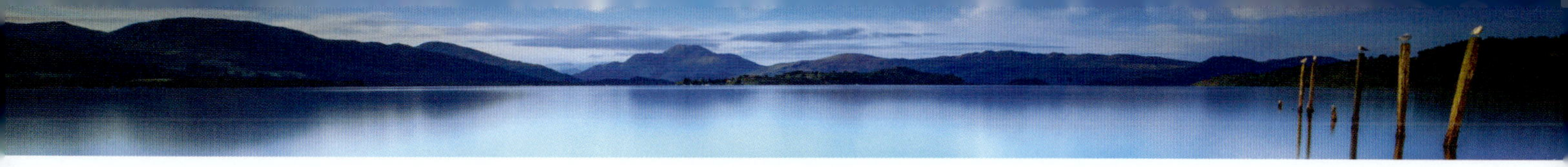

Task

I want you to start to analyse and think about the effect composition has on imagery. Firstly, write down as many words as you can to describe each of the images below (such as happy, sad, desolate and so on). Then write down what it is that's giving each image its own characteristics or feelings.

Let's go back to the beginning where I said that composition is how you arrange the elements in your scene. How has the changing of the elements within each of these pictures i.e. the foreground, position of model etc. changed the feeling of the image?

You could say "the close up picture gives a much more intimate look as you can see clearly into the models eyes". And lastly, just say which ones are your best and worst, and why that is.

That's your first task, I want you to analyse how different compositions affect the mood of the shot.

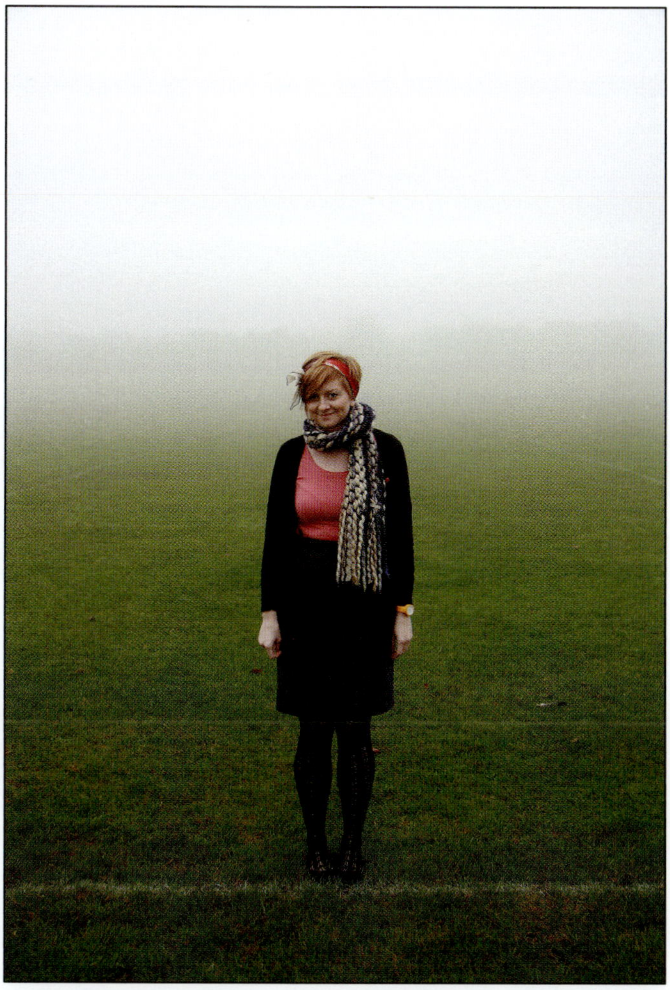

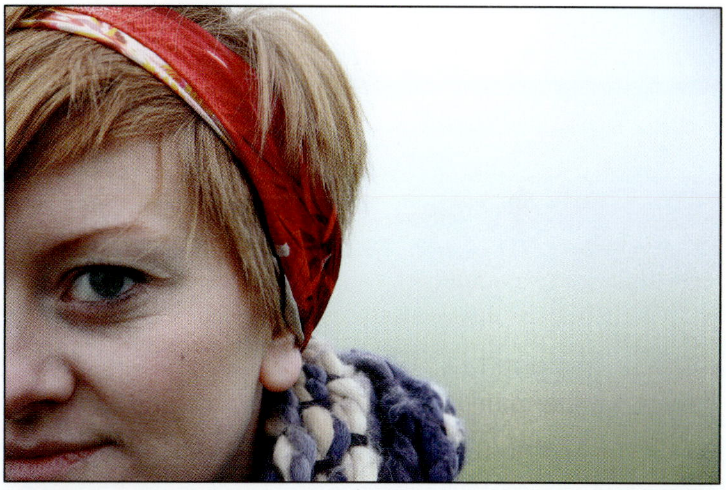

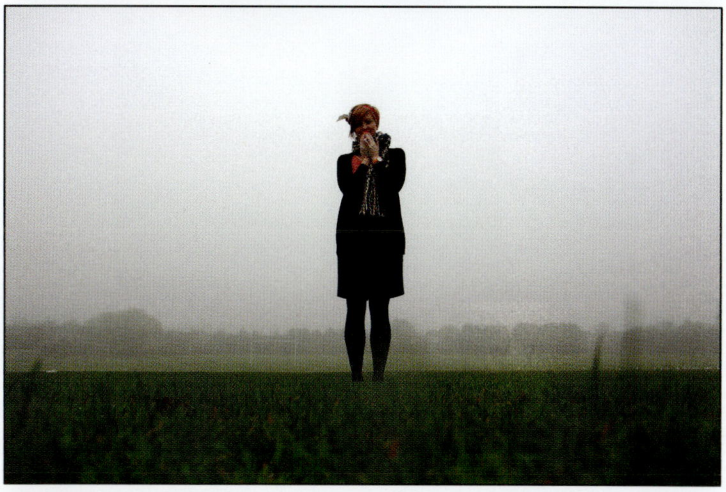

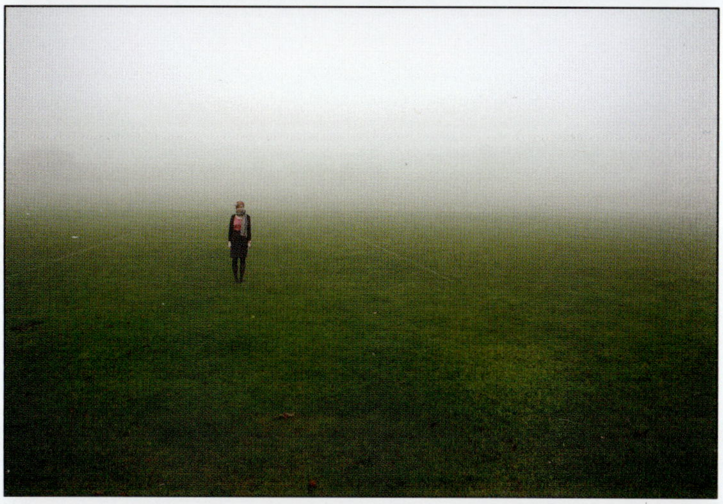

Analyse the 'composition' of these shots

1. Write down as many words as you can to describe each image.
2. What elements have given each image its different look or feeling?
3. Which one is your favourite and why?
4. Which one is your worst and why?

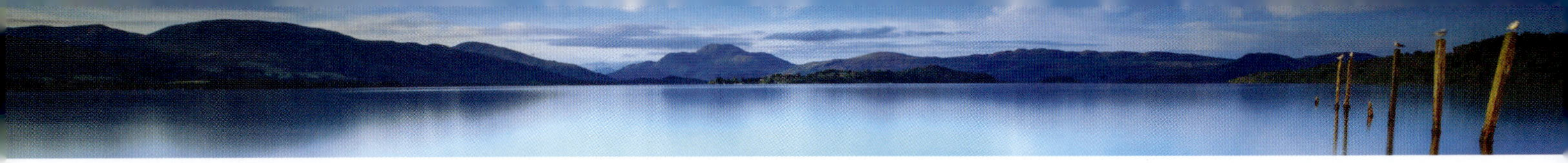

There's no wrong or right answers to those questions, it's your opinion that counts. It's just as important to analyse photography as it is to make it. This is, after all, how you come up with your own style.

Remember this – anything that is in your shot is part of your composition, and it is there because you wanted it to be there. So if you have a lamp post coming out of someone's head, or a wheelie bin in the background with a stray cat coming out of it, from now on it's there because you want it to be there.

You control the composition of your shots, and it's one of the easiest things to master, that will start giving you great results.

Rules of Composition

Now when it comes to composition there are certain rules you can follow that will make your pictures seem more pleasing to the eye, or enhance a certain feeling you're going for.

These rules of composition are not just things that photographers have invented, it's actually down to human nature. The way humans view and interpret things is an evolutionary thing, and you can use these rules to your advantage to get a better-looking images.

I'm going to show these rules, then set you some tasks so you can put them into practice yourself.

Rule of Thirds

The first rule to talk about, and probably the most popular, is The Rule of Thirds. The Rule of Thirds means to place the main part of your image within one third of the frame.

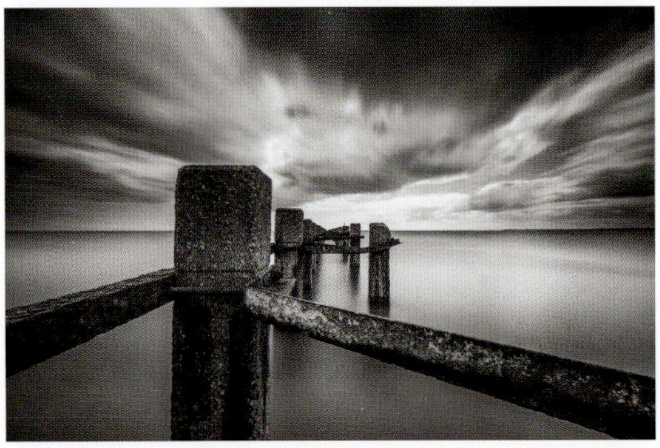

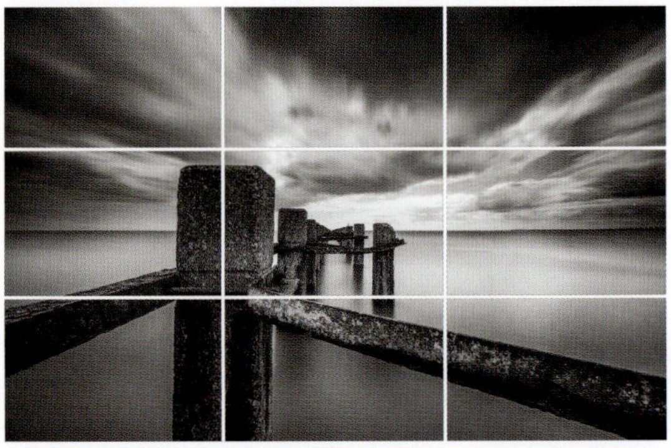

Another easy way to do this is to just place the main part of the image, in this case, the face, just off centre.

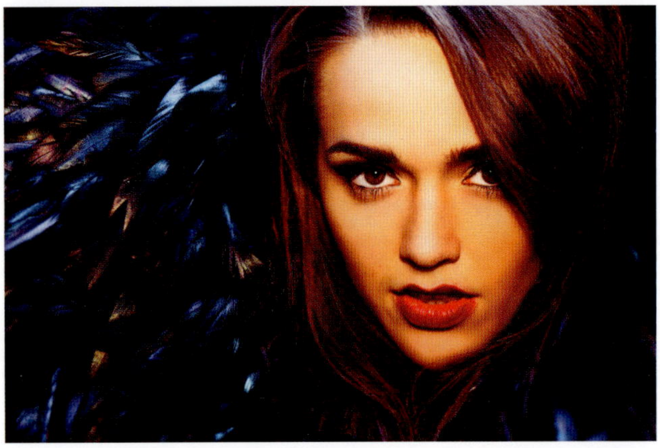

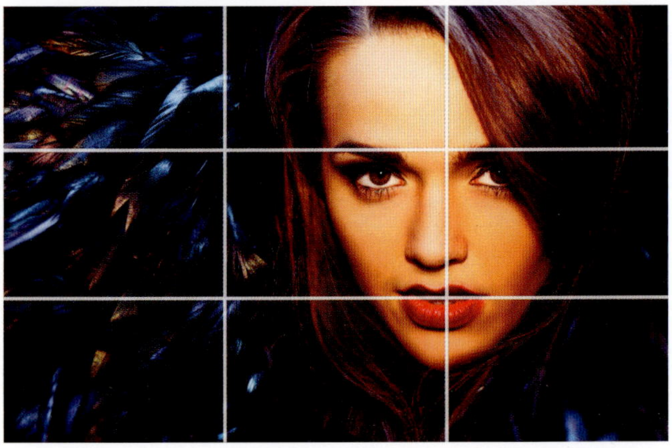

When you position the main part of your image within one third of the frame it tends to sit more naturally within your brain. This is because, in nature, things tend to be quite random, nothing's placed in an order.

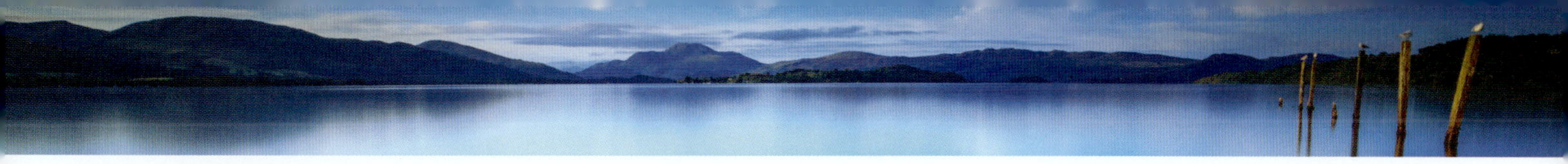

Think of trees in a forest; you don't see them growing dead straight, or in perfectly formed lines without human intervention. Nature will grow and form its own random patterns. Your brain subconsciously knows this so when something is dead centre in a picture, it doesn't sit naturally in people's minds. Putting things just off centre, in one third of the frame, makes the shot look more natural and tends to sit easier in the viewer's eye. Here's some examples.

Compare the pictures below. The first question is, *which one has a more natural feel*? Then the second question is, *which one follows the rule of thirds*? Write down your answers in your notebook.

1

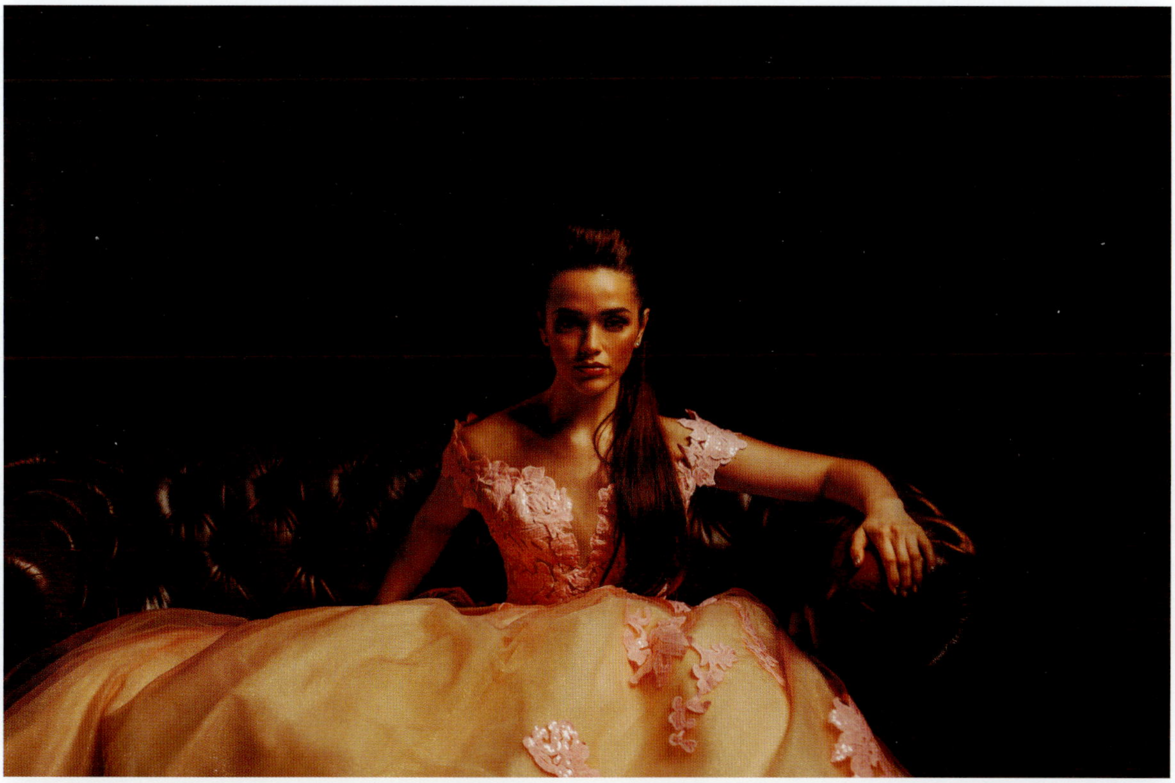

2

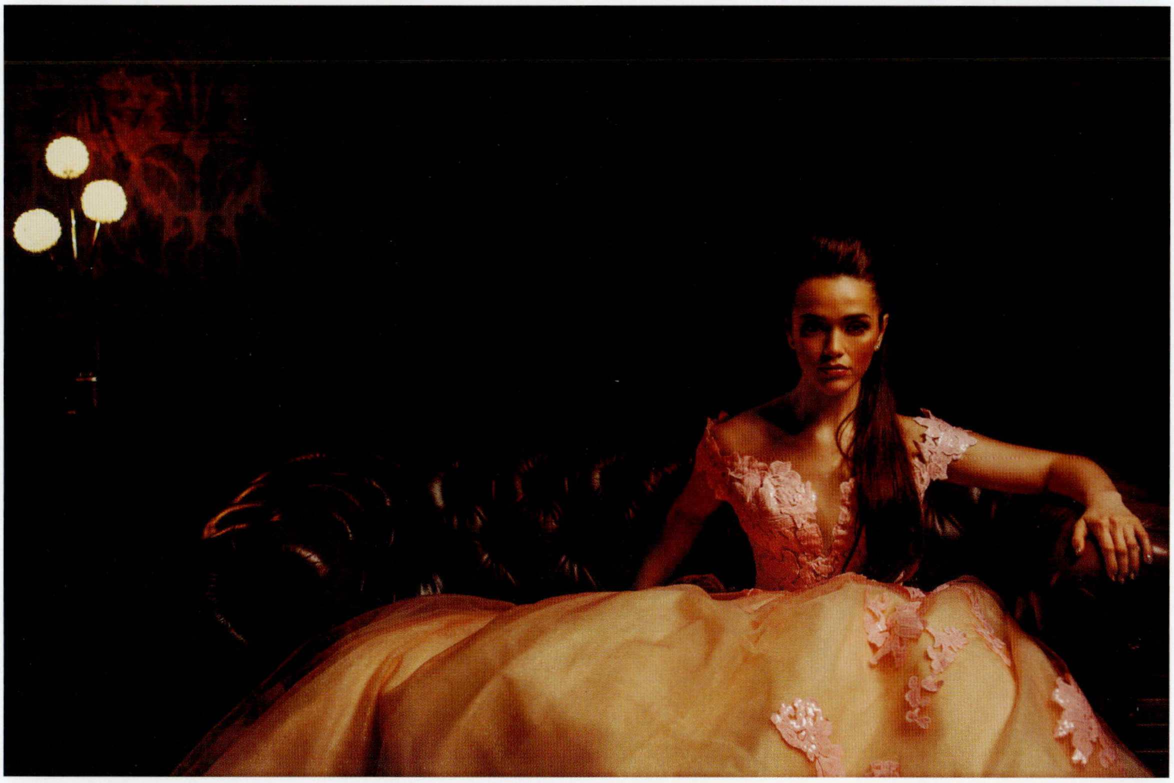

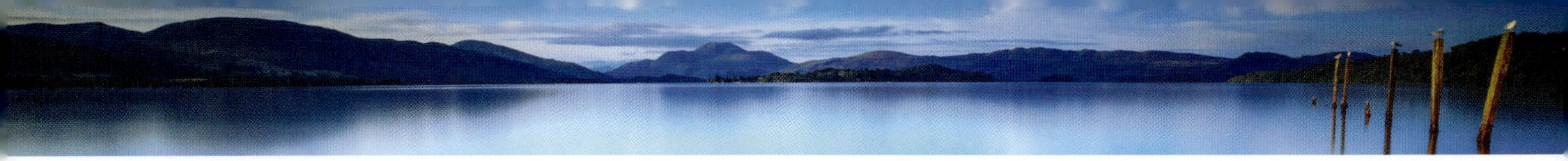

On occasions you might get people say number 1, and I'll come to why that is a bit later, but in general people will say number 2. This is because number two follows the rule of thirds, it sits more naturally in the frame, and more naturally in the viewer's eye.

1

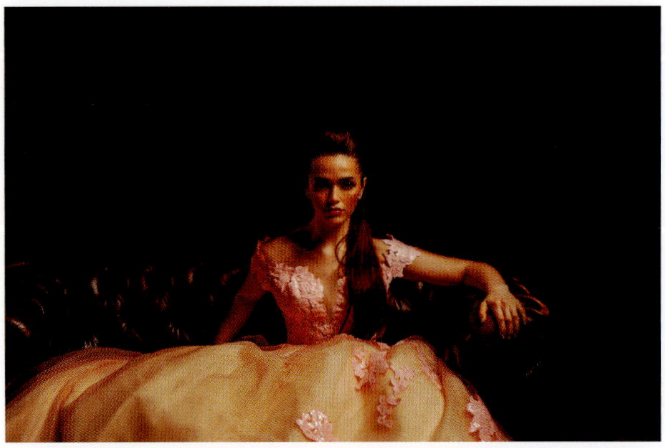

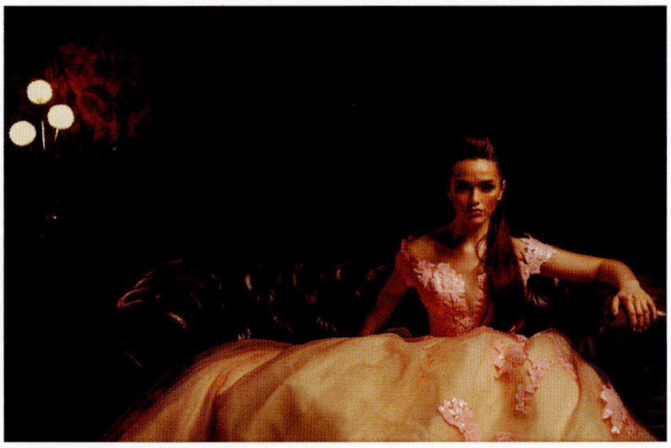

2

The rule of thirds can also apply to the horizon line.

You'll find that landscape photography often uses the rule of thirds by placing the horizon line on one of the thirds - this is to get either more of the land, or more of the sky, in the shot; whichever has more interest.

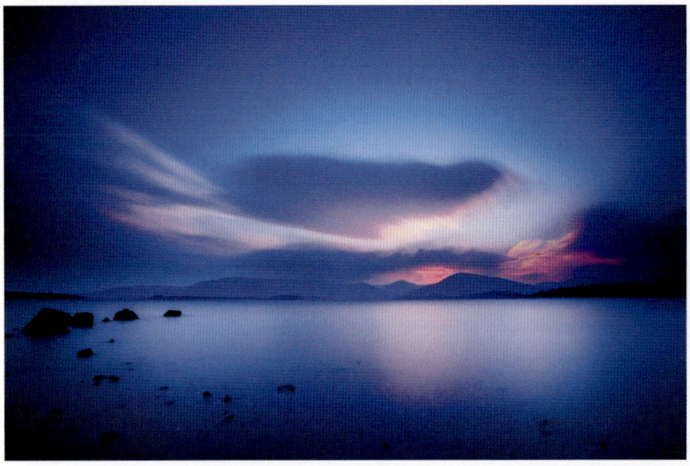

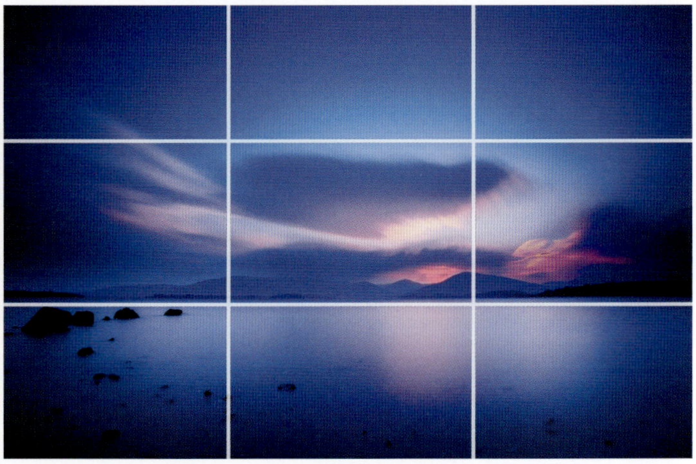

Let's look a few more rules of photography before I set you your task and get you working!

Rule of Odds and Evens

If you use an even number of things in your shot, you can really enhance that feeling of tension, or unease. This again goes back to nature being random and a carefully arranged even number of objects, or in this case people, will sit uneasy in the viewer's eye; you don't know where to look first.

This is a really good way to get people to stare for longer at an image. People tend to do this because it's not something they're used to seeing. A perfectly arranged, even number of people staring into the lens for instance.

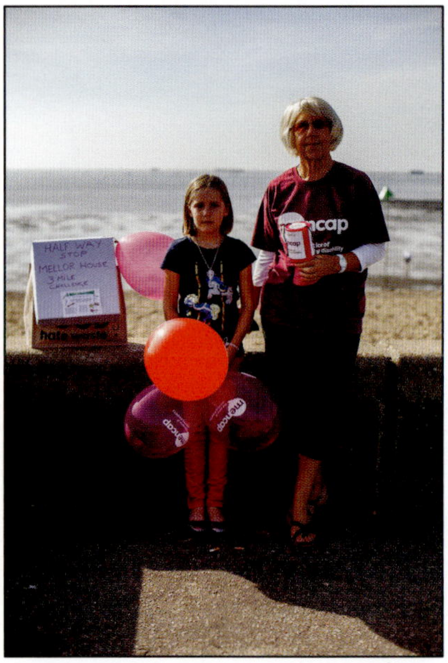

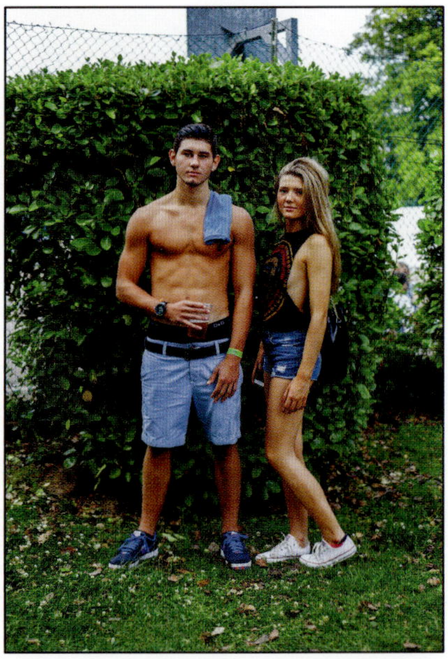

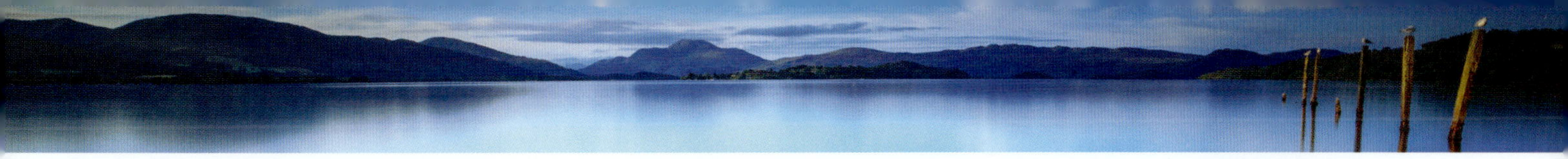

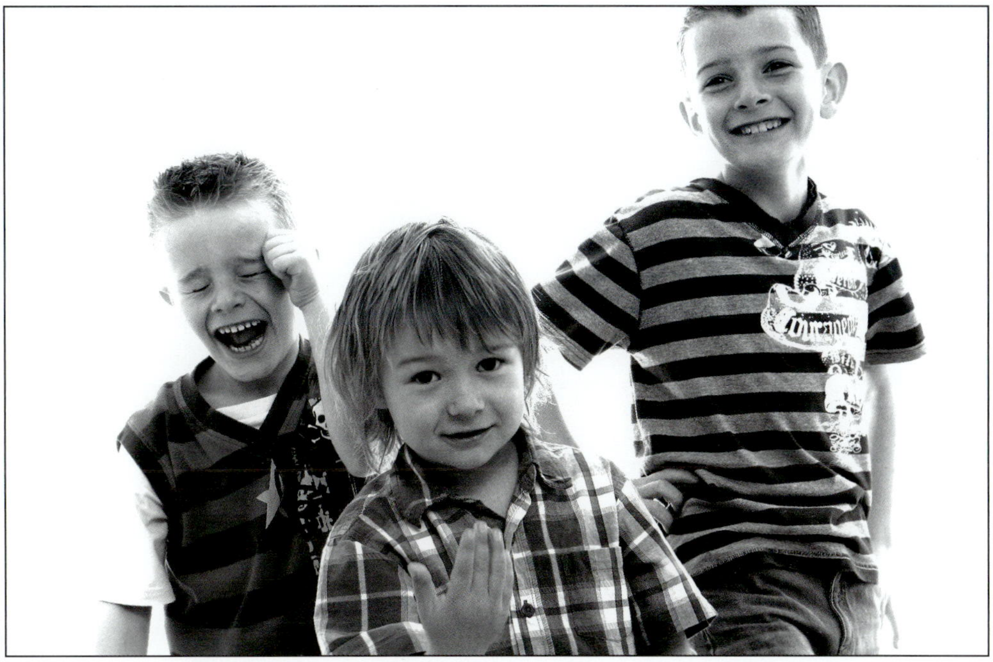

Whereas if you use an odd number of things you can enhance a natural feel. One that will make you smile, or feel at ease. You can also use an odd number of things to draw the viewer's eyes to the middle object. Just think about who you looked at first in this image.

You can bet 9 times out of 10, that the viewer will look directly at the middle person first. And you can control that by a simple use of composition.

Remember - composition is there to enhance the look of your shot, not make it. So if you've got two people in your shot and they're laughing and having a good time, that feeling of tension won't be there. Use composition to enhance the feeling of your shot.

Let's look at some more.

Rule of Triangles

Look at this image. This is an old Victorian family picture. Can you spot any triangles in this image?

Take your time and write some ideas down in your notebook if you want.

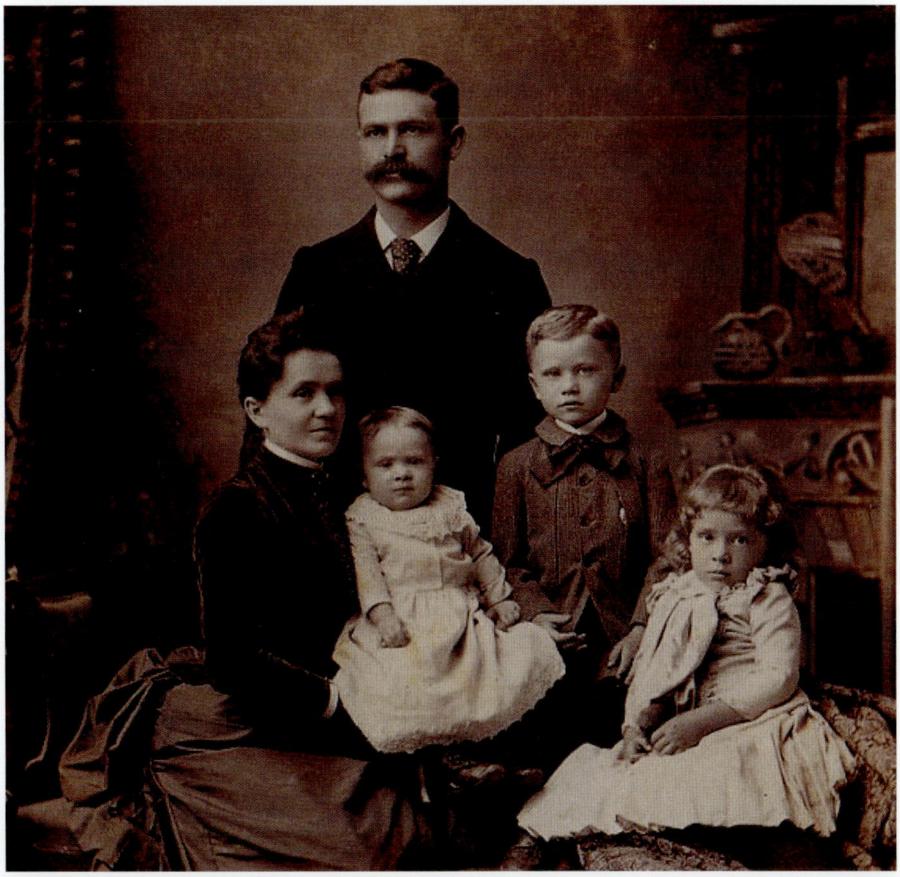

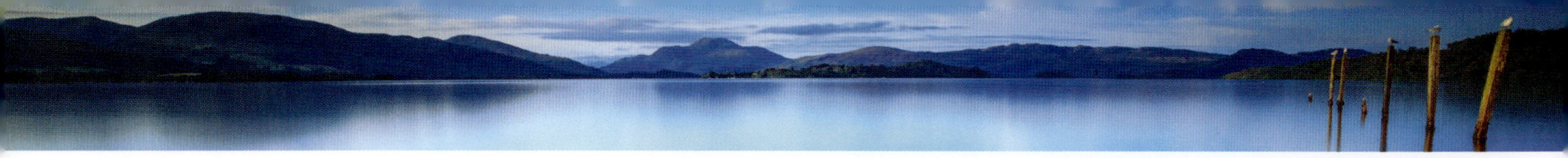

Hopefully you have seen that all the people together form a big triangle, which was common for a Victorian family photograph - the man's head being the top of that triangle. So the next question is this:

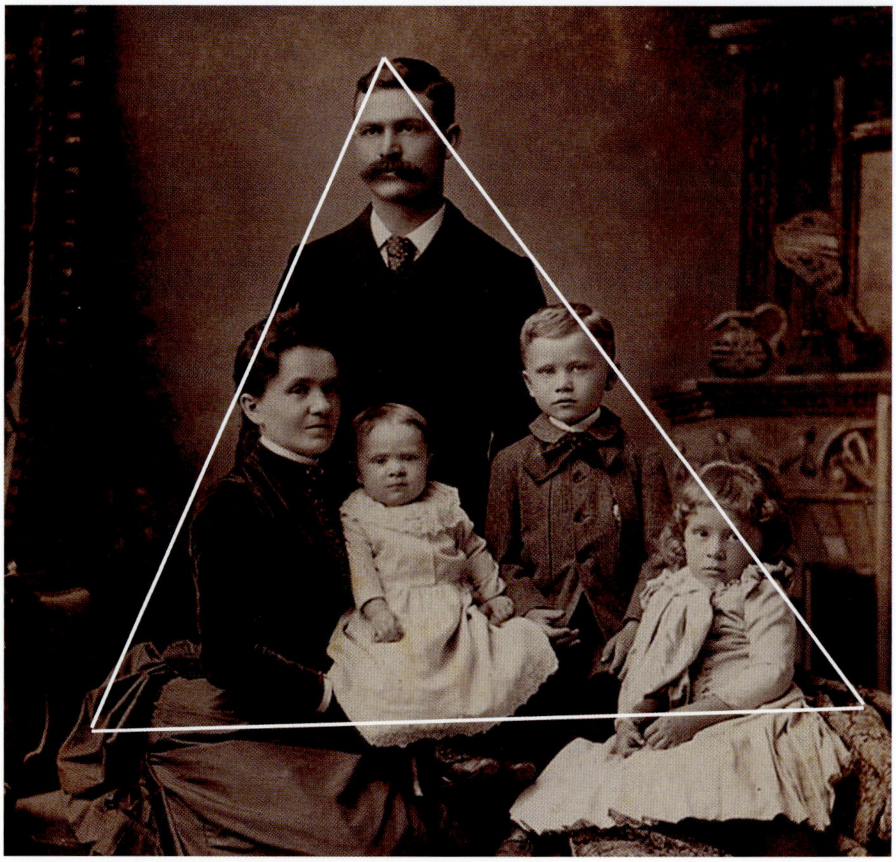

Why were triangular compositions often used in these Victorian family portraits?

Take some time to write down some answers in your notebook if you want.

Triangles tend to form stable, solid looking compositions. Triangles are the strongest shapes in nature and in construction because any added force is evenly spread through all three sides. Think of roofs of houses or the Pyramids.

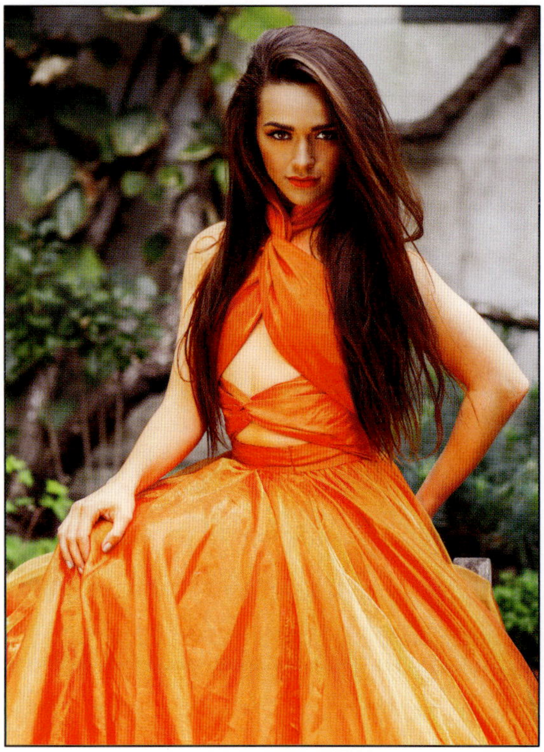

Subconsciously, our brains know this and that is why if you use a triangular composition, you enhance a feeling of strength or hierarchy. In this case it's been used to show the hierarchy throughout the family. The man sitting proudly at the top with his family below him. He is in charge of that family.

If you want someone to look powerful, get them to sit up straight, look down onto the camera and hold their arms and shoulders wide. Create a triangular composition to enhance a feeling of strength.

Rule of Space

Now let's look at the rule of space. Take a look at these two images (*right*).

Which one looks better and why? Write down some notes.

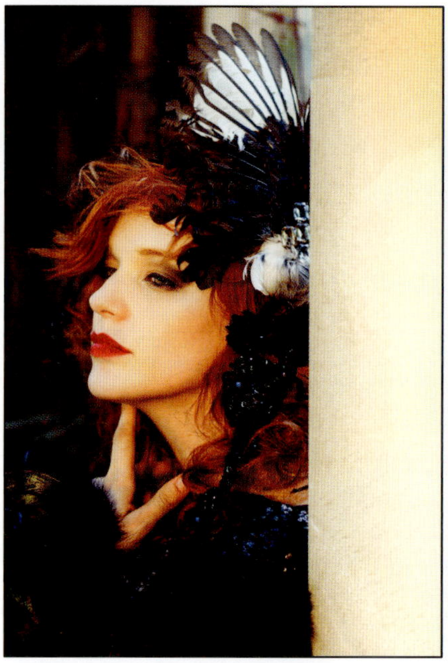

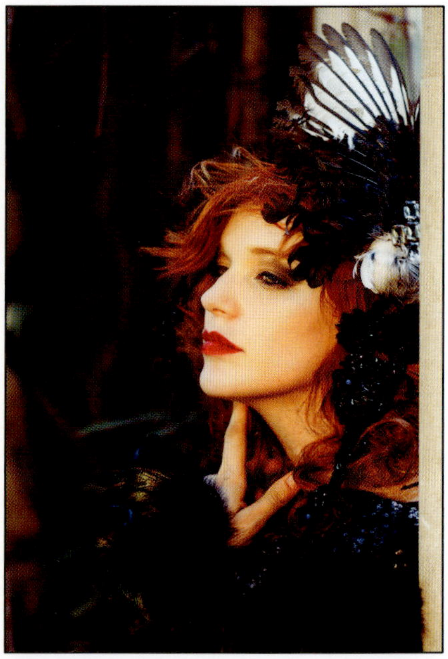

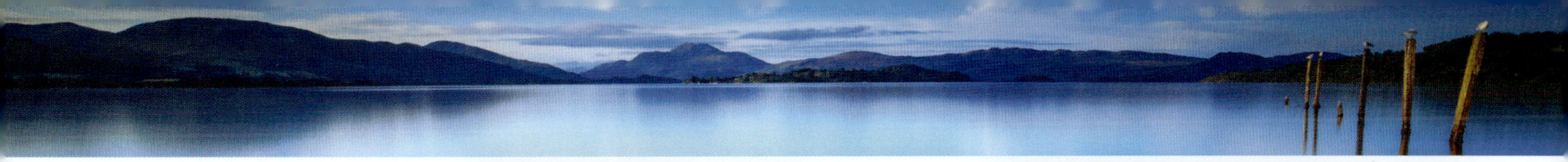

On the right, the model sits much more naturally within the scene. This is because she is looking into the space.

Having space in an image can be a good thing as long as it's placed correctly.

On the left, she looks like she has been squeezed into the frame. It just looks cramped and squashed in.

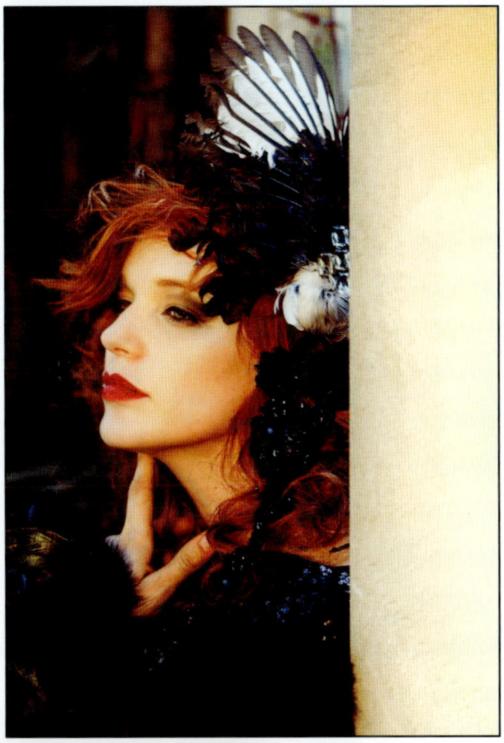

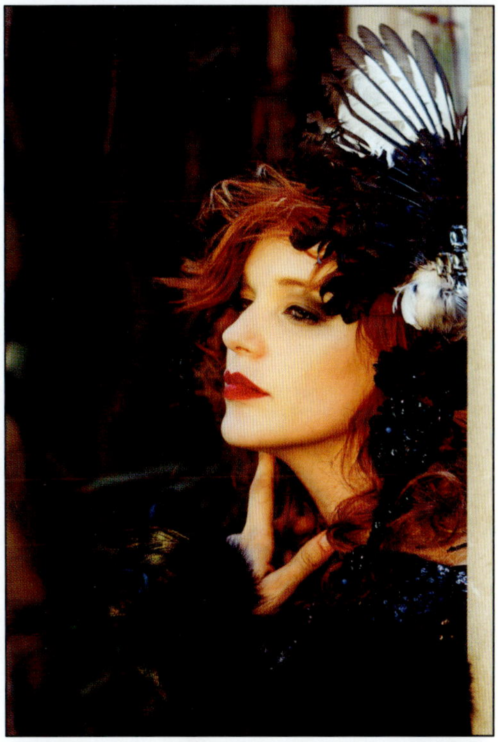

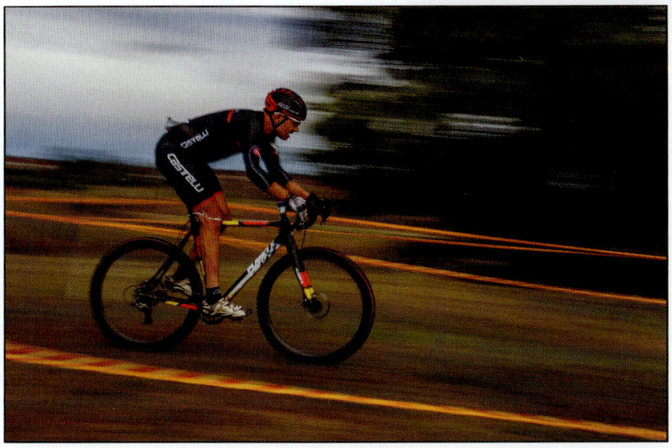

The same rule also applies to things moving, always have the space in the direction the object is moving. In this case a mountain bike.

Frame Within a Frame

Now let's look at a technique called frame within a frame. Frame within a frame means exactly that, you find something to frame your main subject and include that in your picture, therefore creating a frame within a frame.

This image here is a nice simple example of that. Someone looking through the hole of a bin.

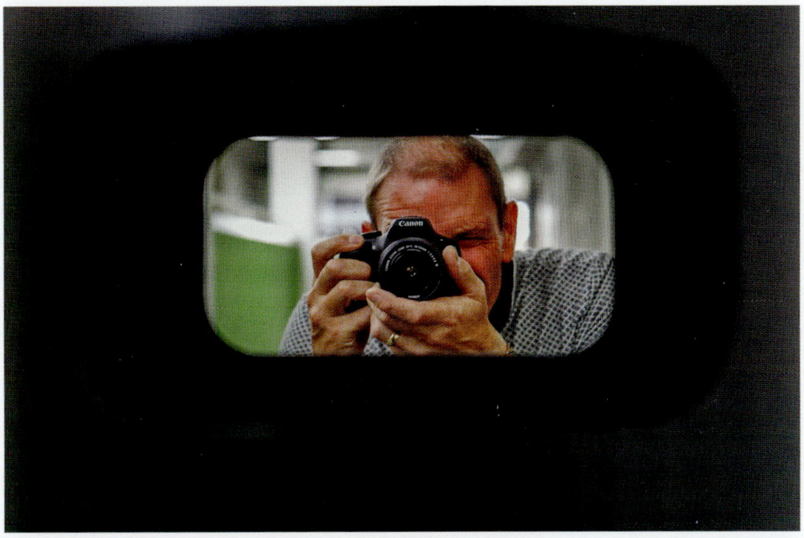

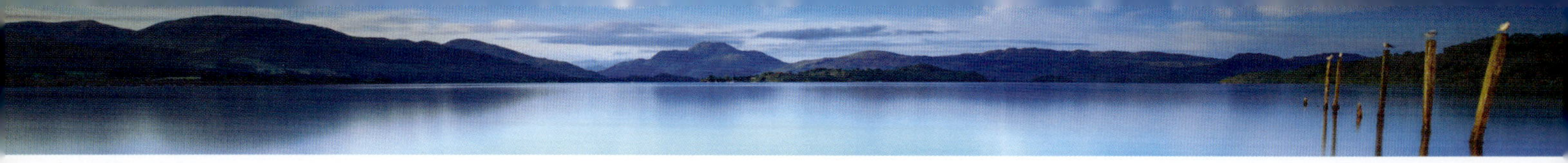

Another simple example is having someone looking through an opening, or in front of a window and including the frame in the shot. It's a great way to lead your viewers' eye into the main part of the image.

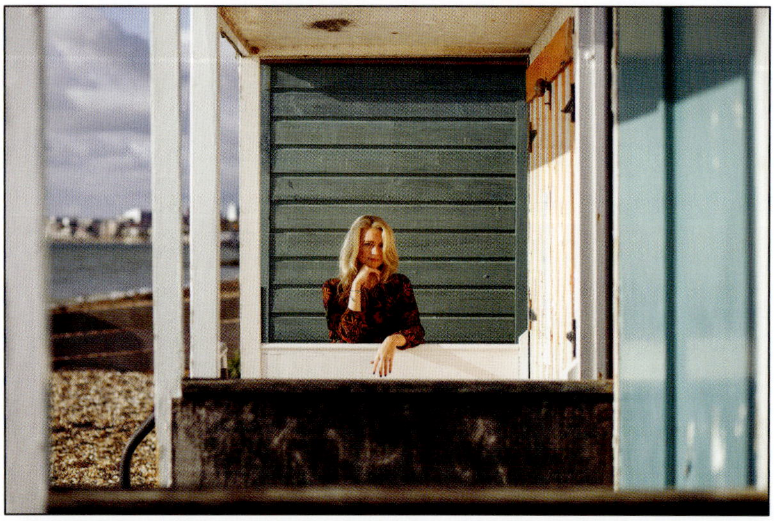

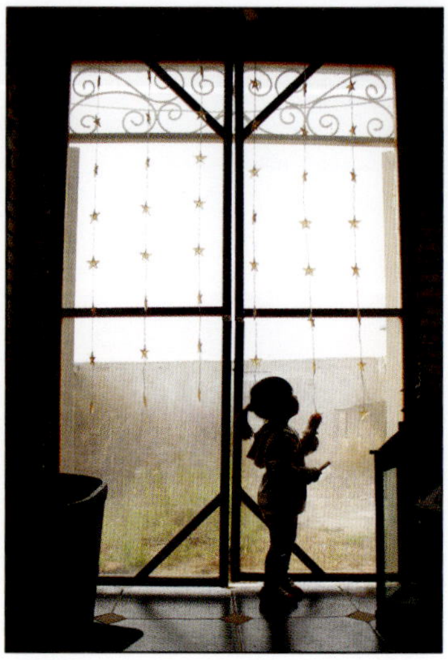

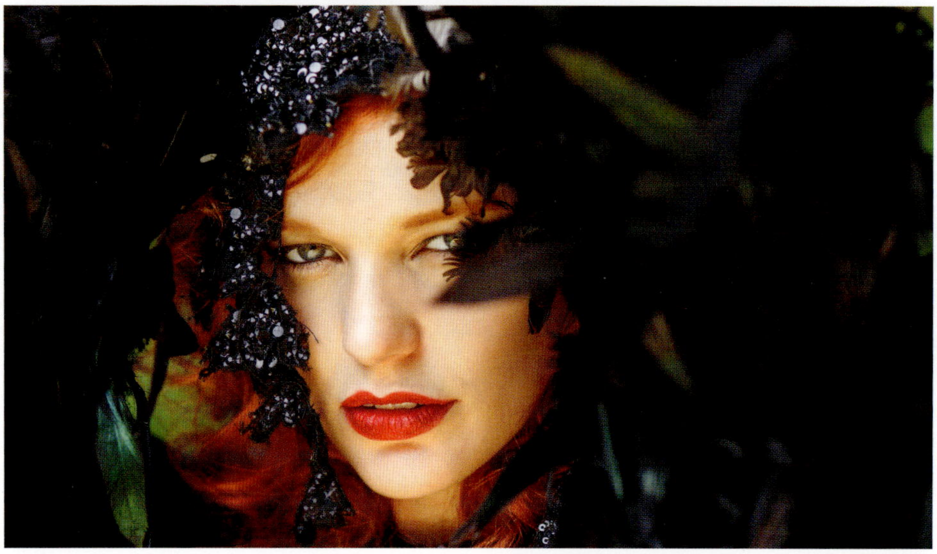

But you can be a bit more creative with this technique.

In this image the model had a dress on which had feathers going down the arms, so I asked her to hold her arms above her head to create this frame of feathers which I could shoot through.

A good tip is to shoot through the arms of the model, or through a furry coat or even a scarf.

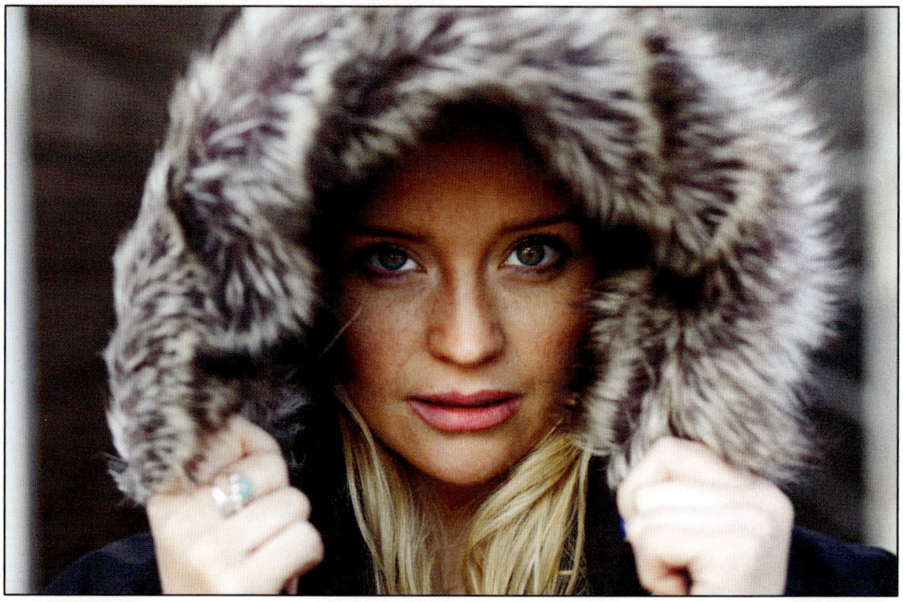

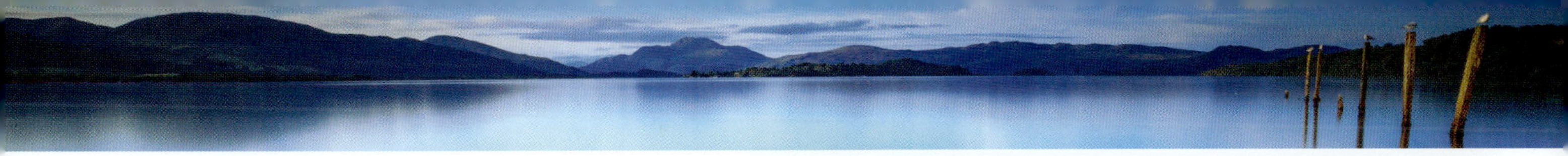

Symmetry

The next composition technique to look at is using symmetry.

Using symmetry blows the whole idea of the rule of thirds out of the window. How can symmetry look good if the rule of thirds looks good?

Remember that these composition techniques are there to enhance the feeling of the shot. So, where the rule of thirds will give you a more natural composition, using symmetry will give you an unnatural look. It can create a clinical, clean and ordered look.

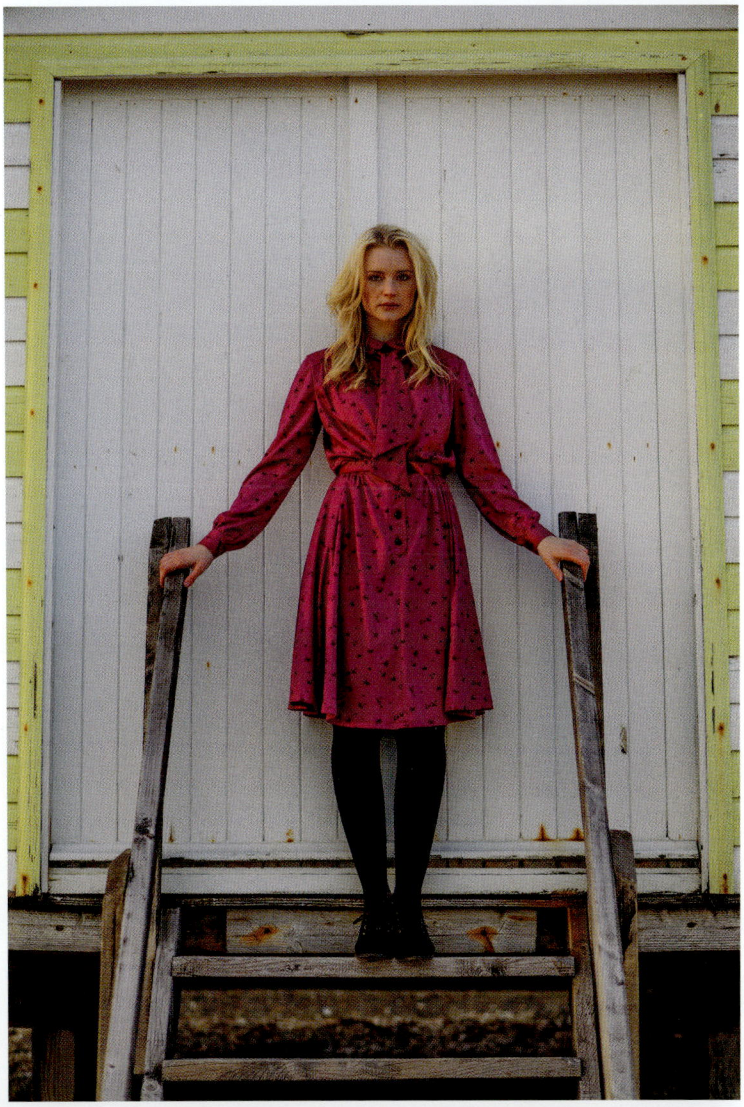

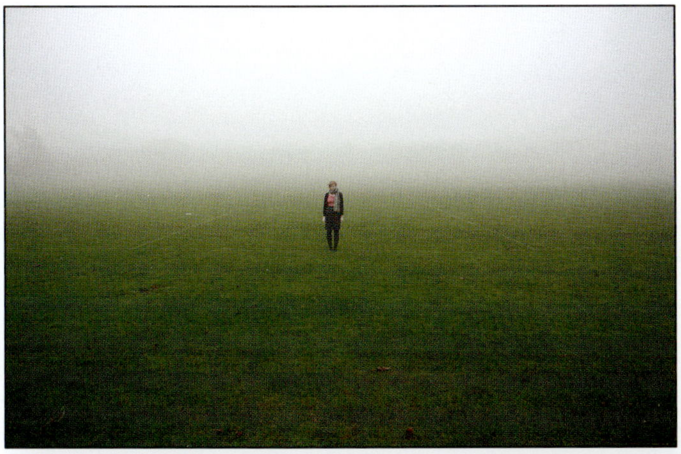

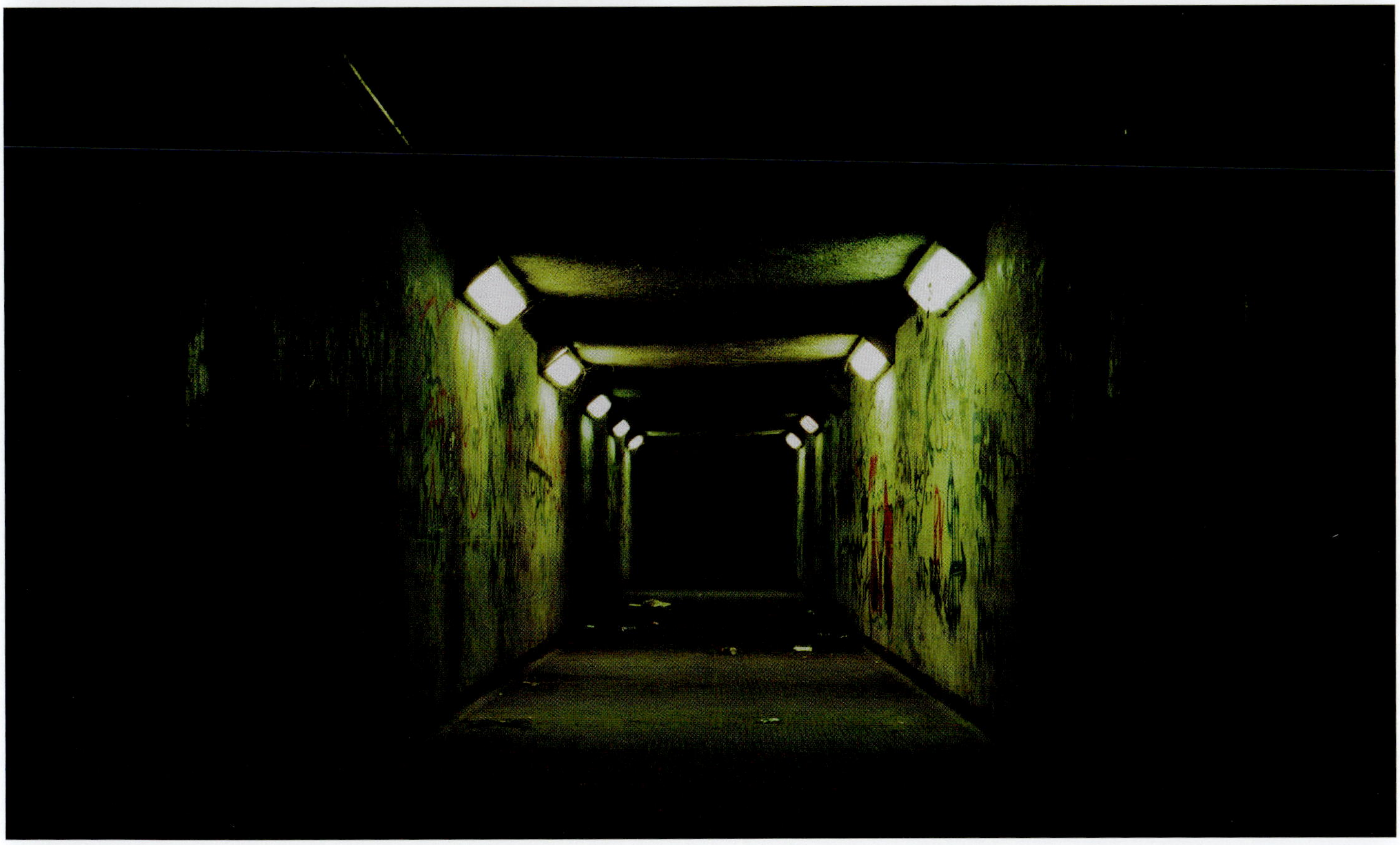

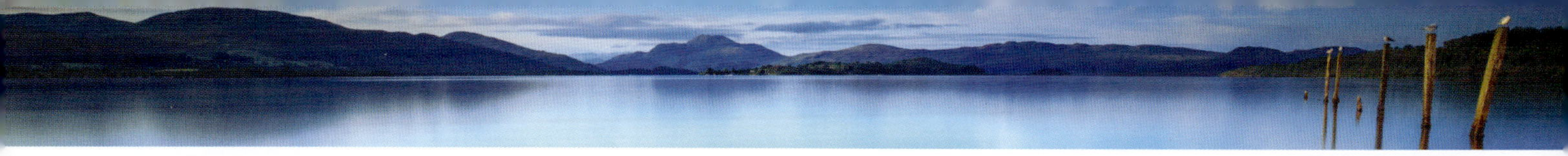

Leading Lines

The Leading Lines technique is where you use objects within your scene to lead the viewer's eye from the foreground of the image, to the background. In this shot I've used a fallen tree in the foreground to lead you into the wooden posts, which then lead you into the distance.

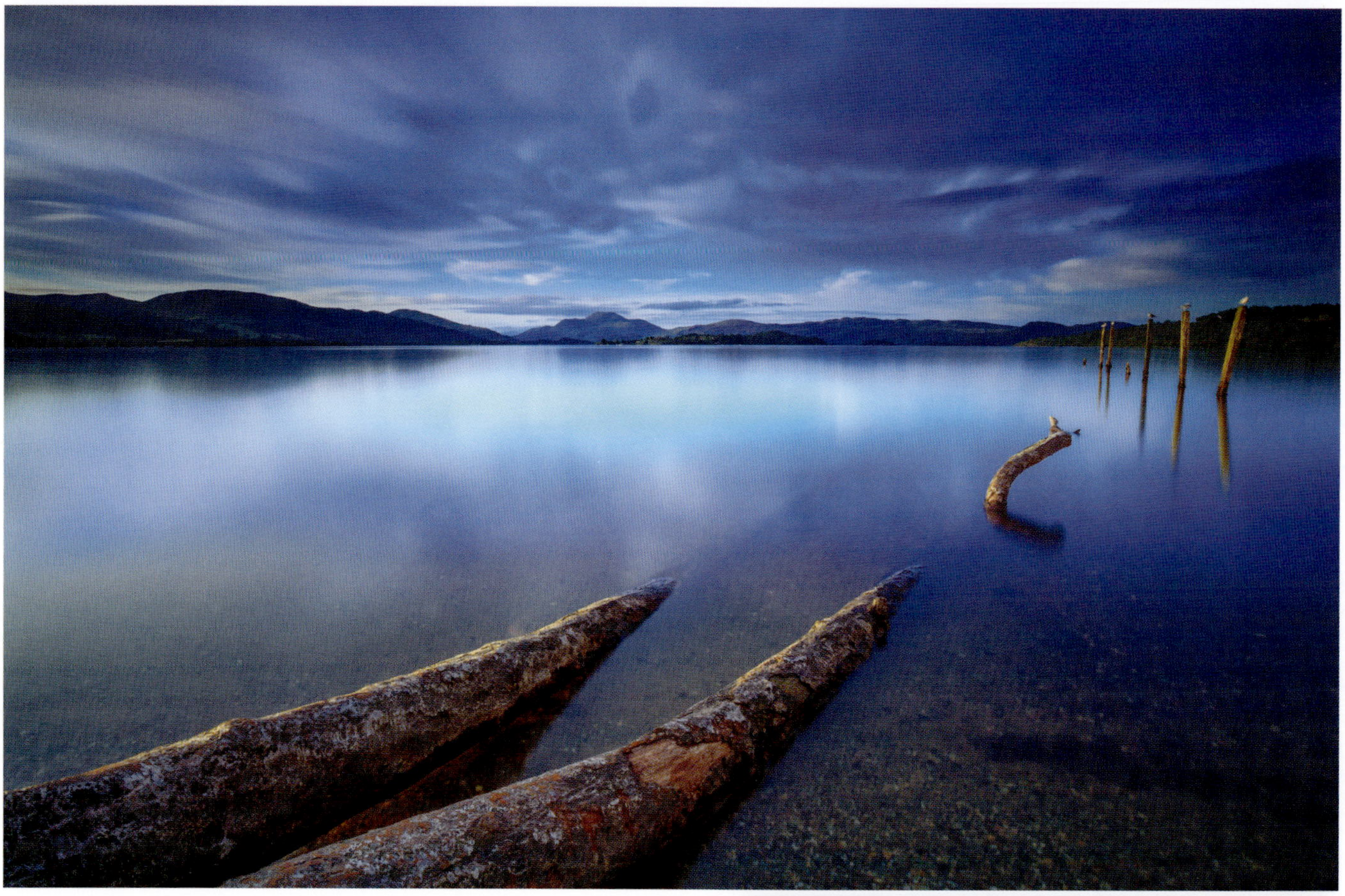

In this shot (*right*) I used this path to lead your eye into the scene. Leading lines are a great way to add interest into the foreground of landscape shots.

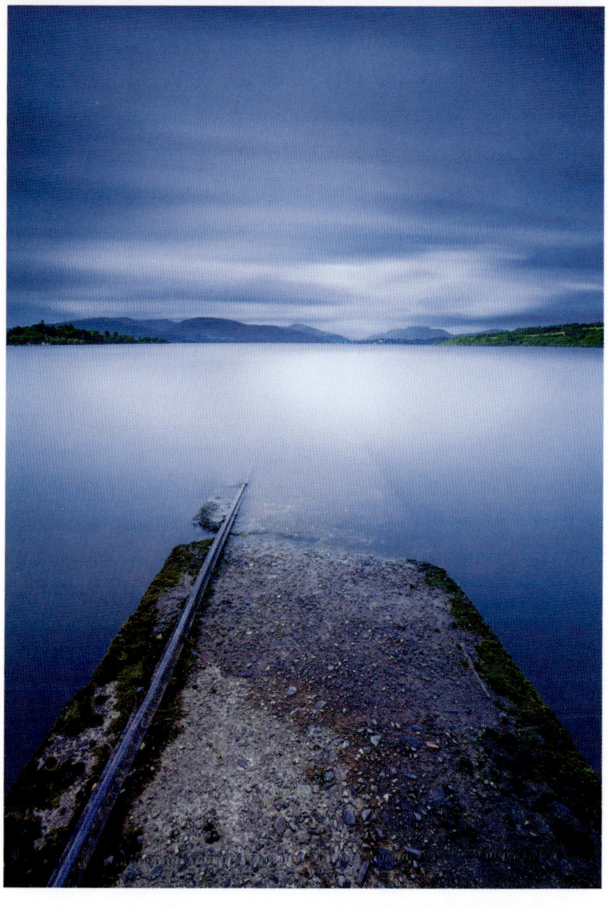

There are a lot more rules of composition but the ones I have discussed here are the most common.

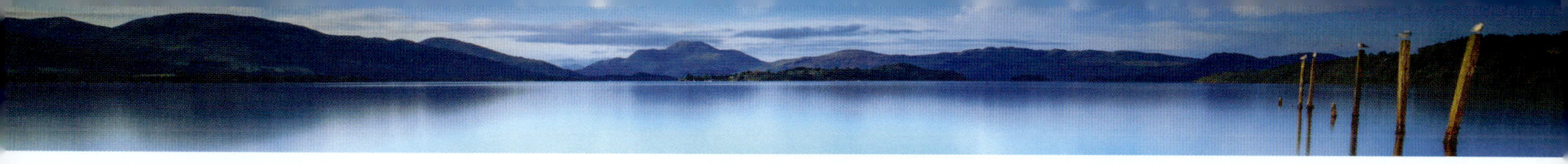

Task

Control the 'Composition' of your shots

1. Take shots which show the use of good composition. Set your camera to the 'P' setting and put your ISO on Auto.

Chose all or a few of the following to practice with.

You can use people, buildings, landscapes etc. What matters is how you are using composition to enhance the look of your shot.

Rule of Thirds – Rule of Odds & Evens – Rule of Triangles – Using Space – Frame within a frame – Symmetry – Leading Lines

Remember everything that is in your frame is there because you want it to be.

2. Note down which composition has worked best and why?

3. And note down which one hasn't worked and why?

Remember, making mistakes is important; it's important for learning. Make notes so you don't make those mistakes again.

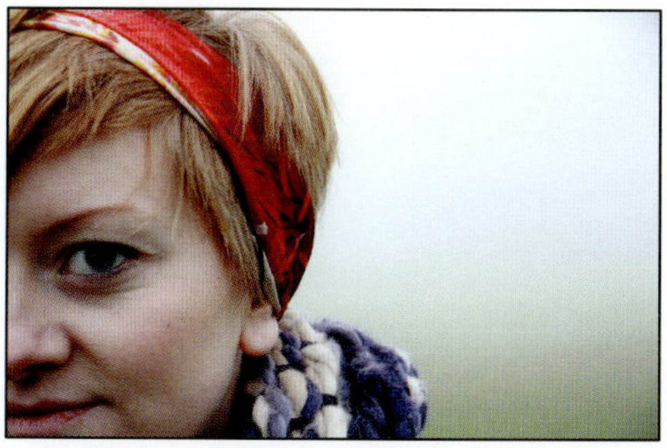

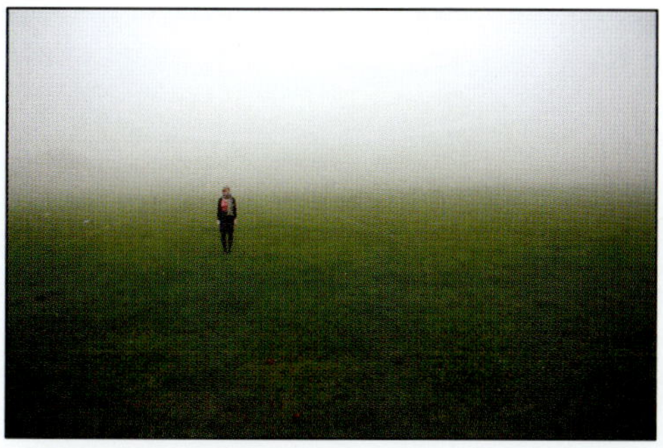

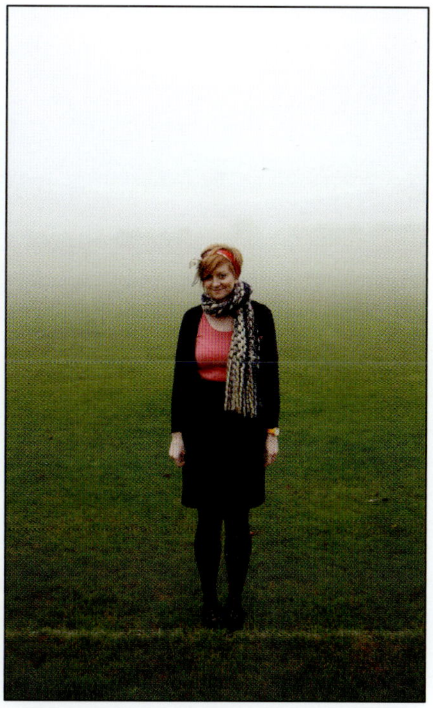

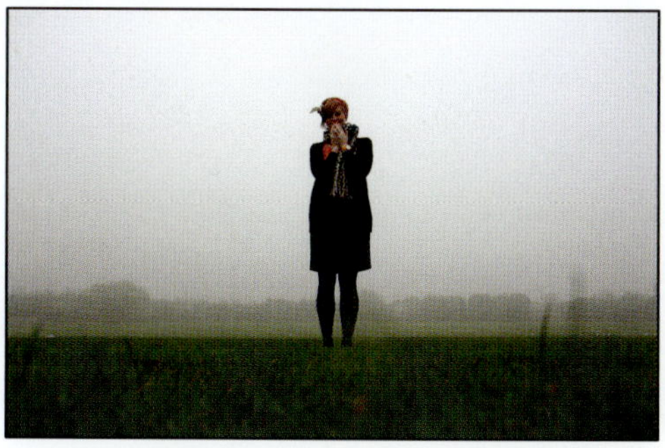

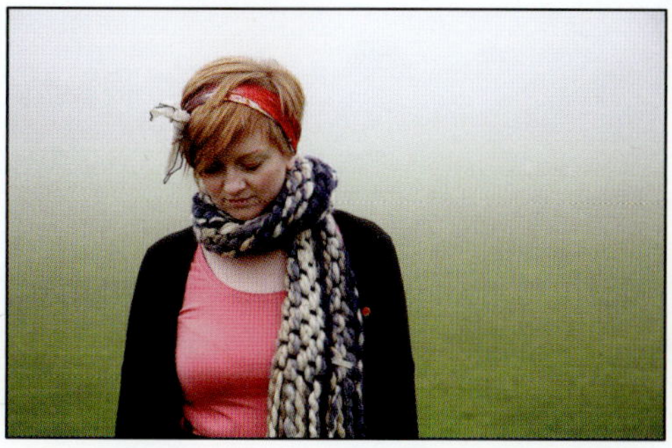

We always like to see students' work here at The School of Photography. So, if you want to show us, tag your pictures on social media with #theschoolofphotography so we can see them.

To view video tutorials on using composition in photography go to www.theschoolofphotography.com and type composition in the search bar.

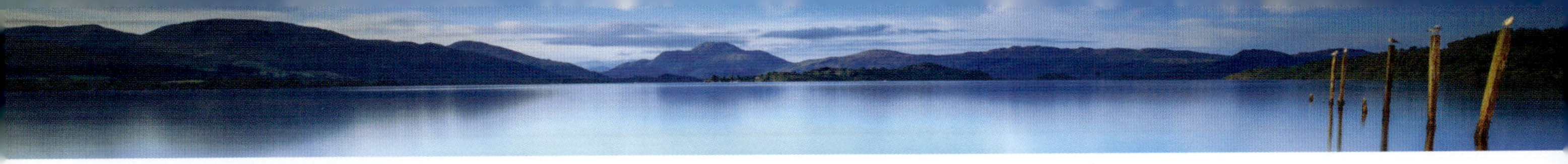

Let's recap on what we've looked at.

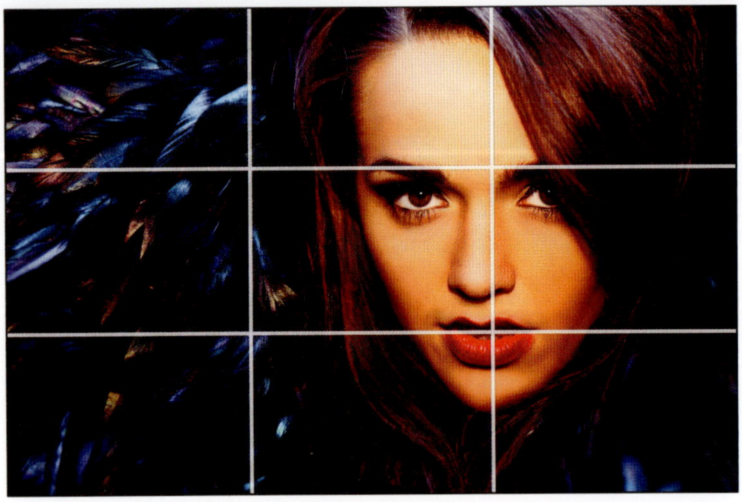

Rule of Thirds – Place your main subject within one third of the frame. When you position the main part of your image within one third of the frame it tends to sit more natural within the viewers eye.

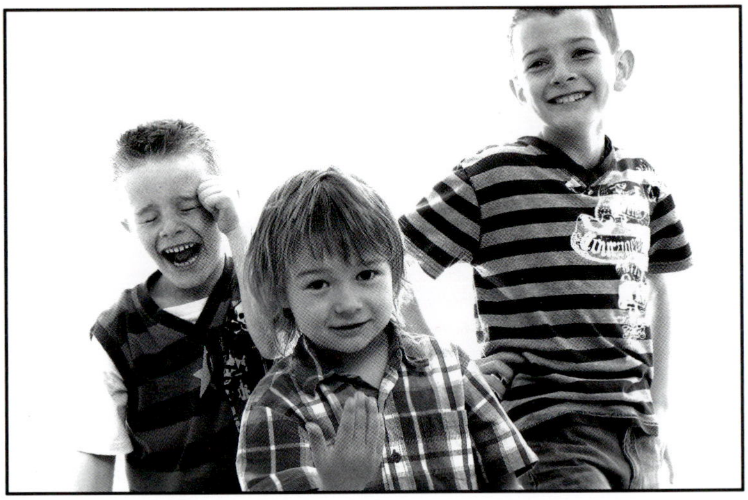

Rule of Odds - An odd number of subjects in an image often has a more natural feel. You can also use an odd number to draw the viewers eye to the middle object.

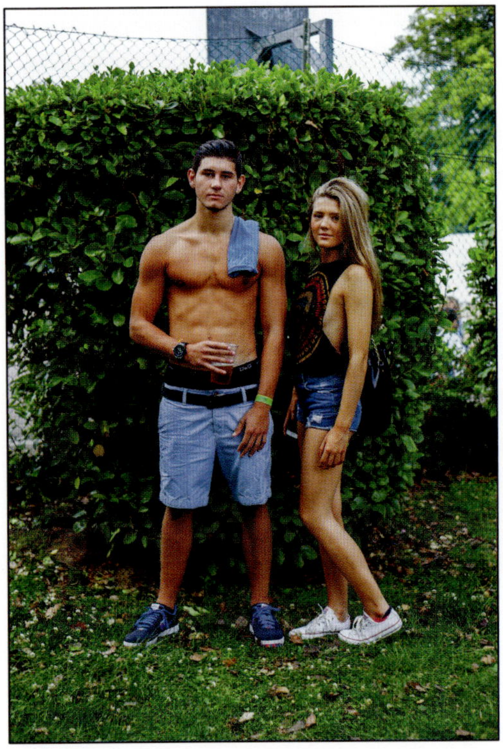

Rule of Evens –
An even number of objects can enhance a feeling of tension or an unnatural look.

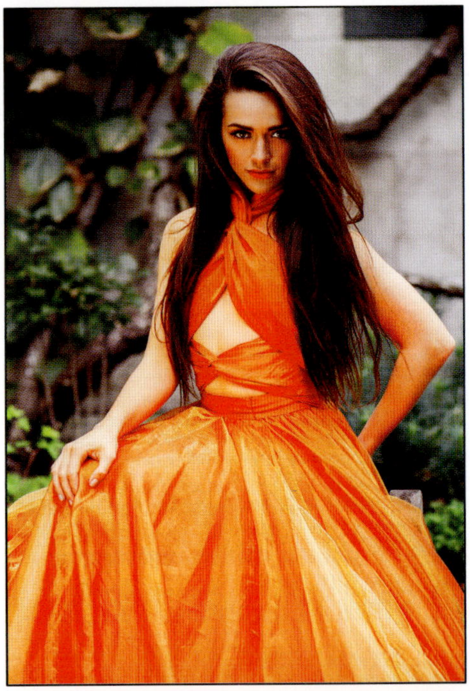

Rule of Triangles – Triangular compositions can be used to enhance a feeling of strength.

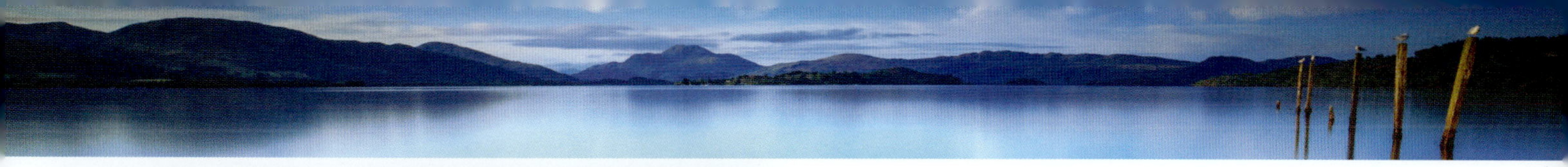

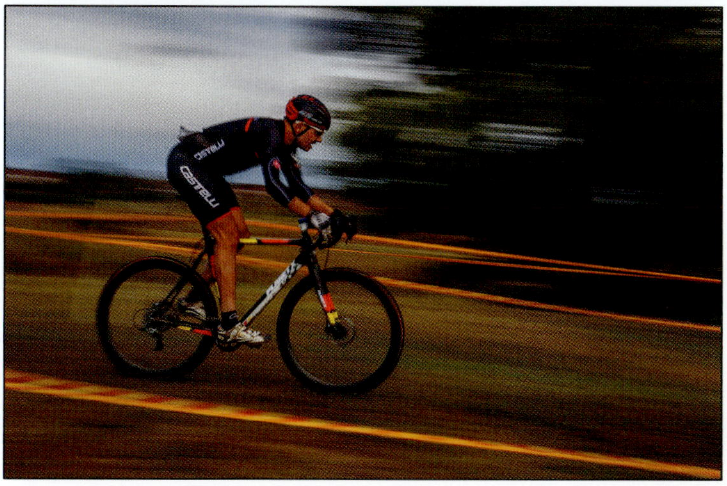

Using Space – Place empty space in the direction the person is looking or the object is going. This will allow for the person, or moving object to move into the space.

Frame within a frame – Find something to frame your main subject and include that in your picture, therefore creating a frame within a frame. Gives more interest to the picture and focuses the eye to the main part of your image.

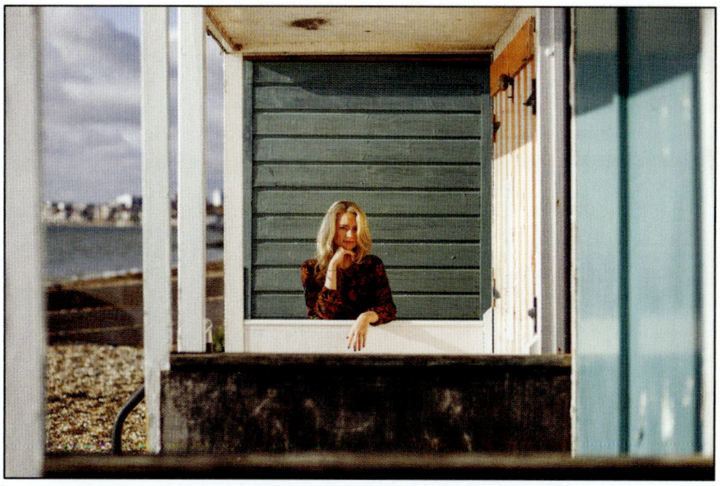

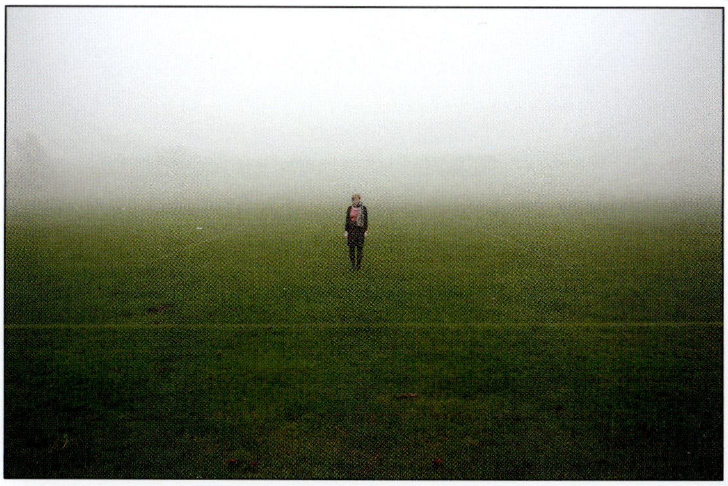

Symmetry – Using symmetry will give you an unnatural look. It can create a clinical, ordered feeling.

Leading Lines - Use objects within your scene to lead the viewers eye from the foreground of the image, to the background.

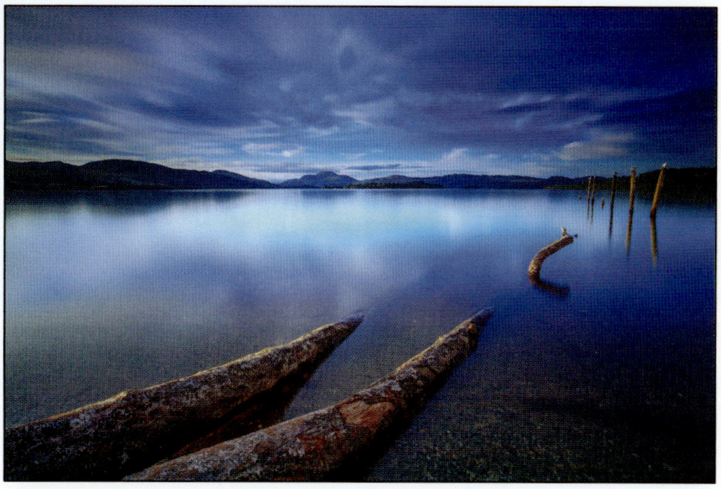

That's the end of this chapter on Composition, now go outside, give it a go, then move onto the next chapter when you are ready.

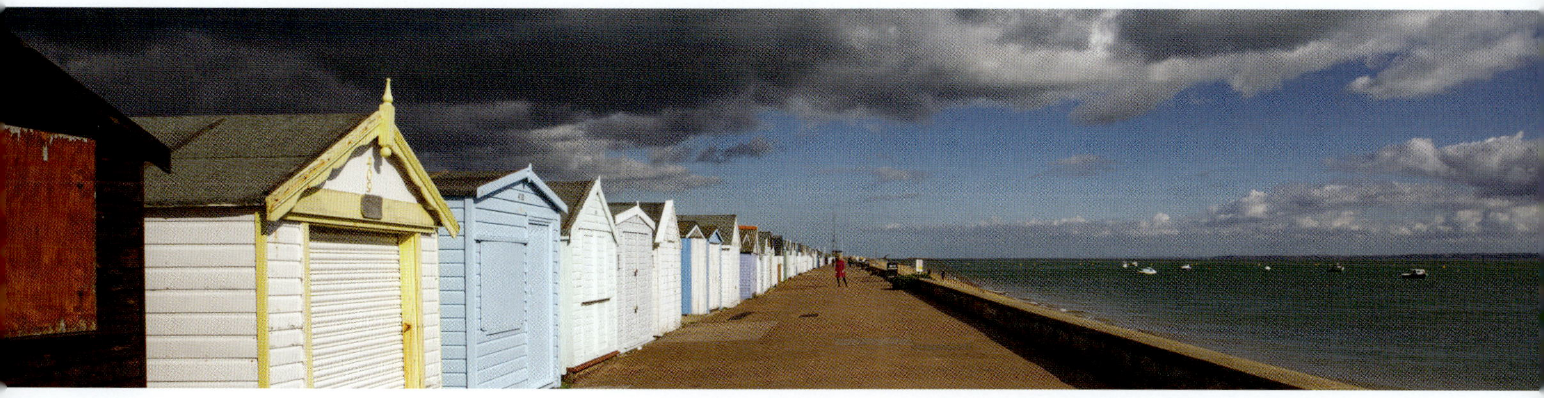

Lenses and Focal Lengths

Chapter 6

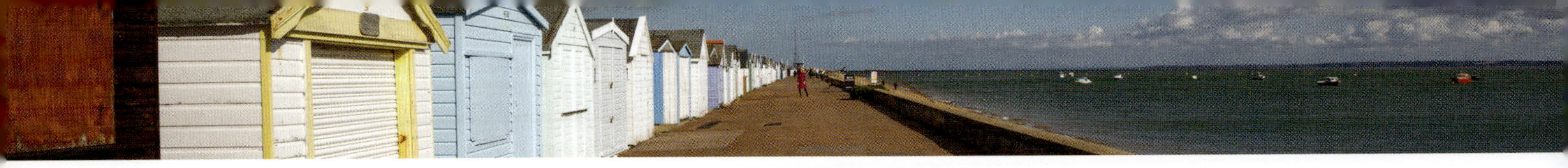

Lenses

This chapter is about camera lenses and their focal range. Firstly, let's look at the types of lenses you can get. One is called a Fixed Focal Range Lens, sometimes it's referred to as a Prime Lens, and the other is a Zoom Lens.

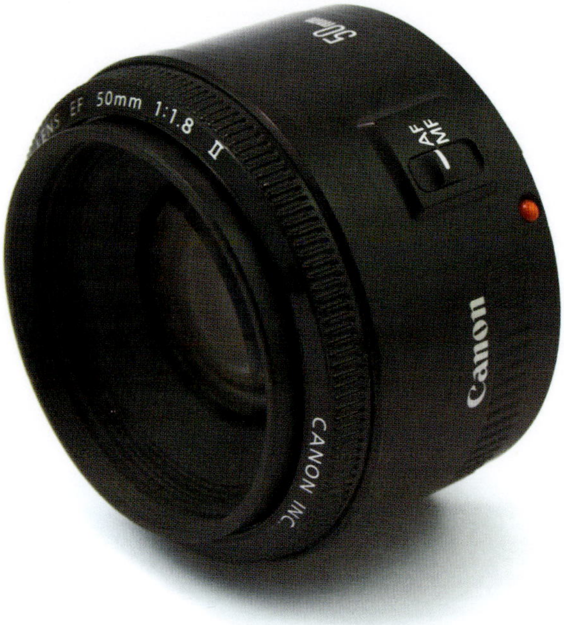

A Prime Lens has a Fixed Focal Range. That means you can't zoom in or zoom out - you have to physically move forwards and move backwards to enable you to get more or less in your shot.

The pros to these types of lenses is that they have much better optics and you can get wider apertures built into them for less cost. We are going to cover what apertures are and the benefit of wider apertures in another chapter.

The con to this lens is that it has a fixed focal range. But, in my opinion, I find that having a fixed focal range is not such a bad thing, it makes you think about framing and the composition more, as you physically have to move around to use it. So personally, there's not much wrong with a Prime Lens and I recommend you get one if you can.

Better Optics
Wider Apertures
Less cost

Fixed focal range

Then you have a Zoom Lens. A Zoom Lens zooms forwards and backwards to get more or less in a shot.

The pros to these are one lens fits all, you can zoom in and out of objects quickly.

The cons to these types of lenses are that they generally have a reduced image quality and smaller apertures. If you want better quality and wider apertures in a zoom lens, they will generally cost a lot of money.

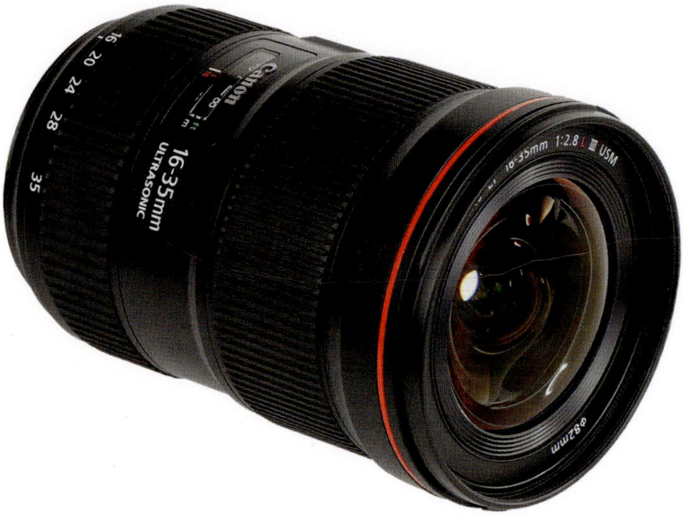

Zoom in and out very quickly

Generally lower quality
Smaller Apertures
Good ones are usually expensive

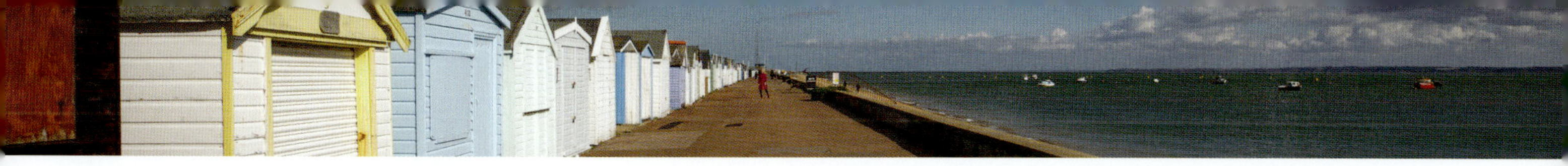

Focal Lengths

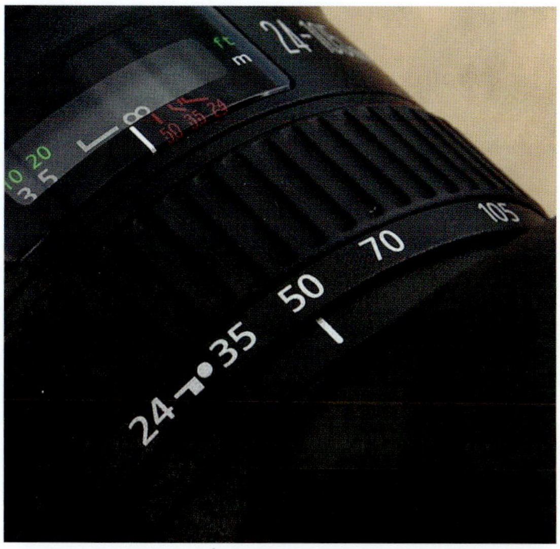

Before we look at what focal lengths are, I want to explain to you where to find them on your camera.

If you look at the top of your lens, you will see a little red or white dot or line, depending on your camera. As you twist your lens in or out you'll see that it corresponds with a number. That is your focal length. So, when the white line matches up with the number 50, your current focal length is 50mm. Whatever that dot/line corresponds with, that is current focal length you will be shooting at.

To put it in an nutshell, the smaller the number, the wider the angle of view - the smaller the number the more you're going to get into your shot. The more zoomed in you are, the higher the number, and the less you're going to get into your shot.

Let's look at the effect this has on an image. Here, I am zooming through the focal lengths to show the effect it has.

16mm

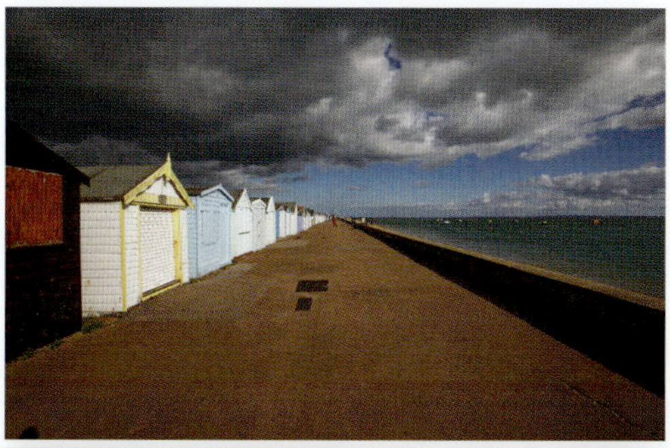

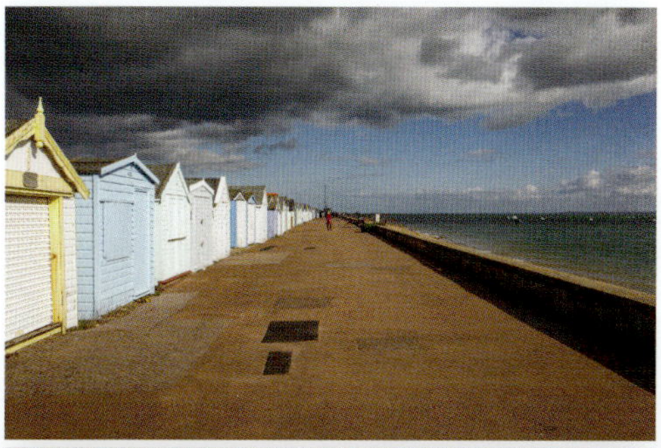

28mm

35mm

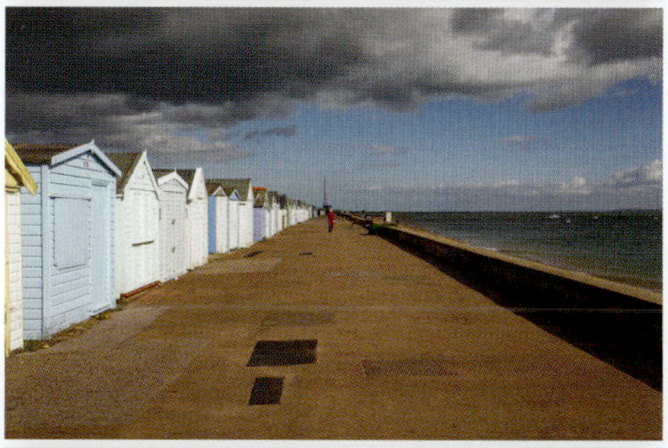

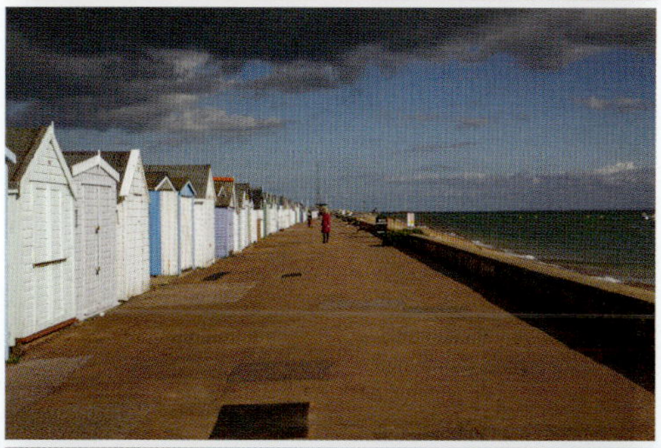

50mm

80mm

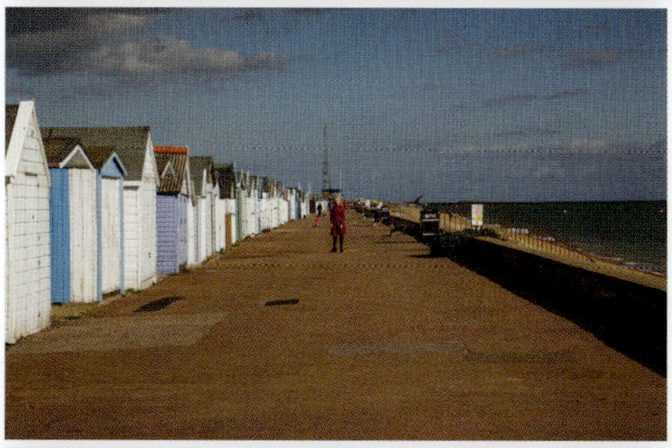

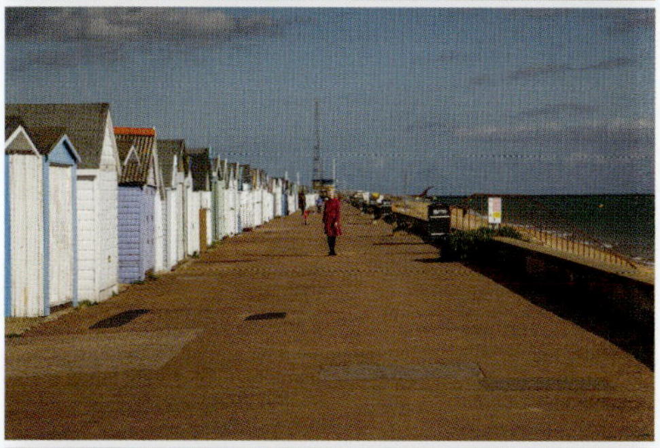

100mm

200mm

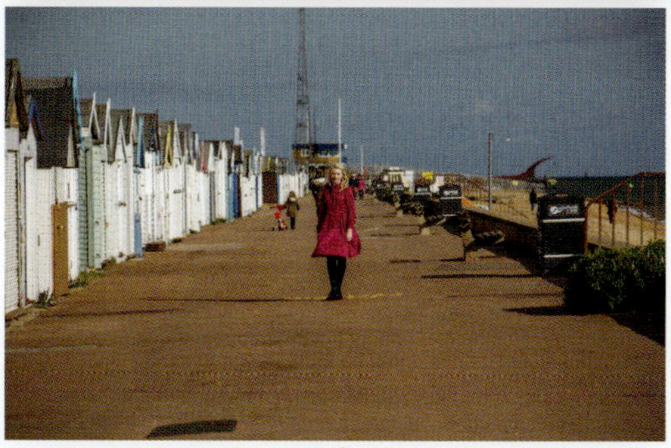

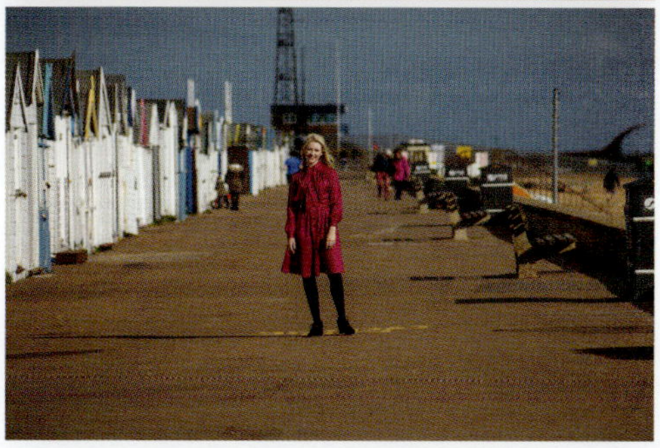

300mm

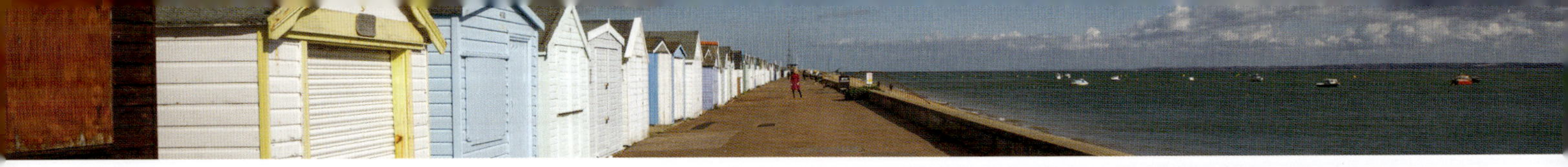

A lot of people think that a zoom lens is just to get closer, or zoom out if you're too close to something. In general, the learning photographer will use their zoom lens because they can't be bothered to move forward or back. That's not a good thing to do!
You need to use the focal range of the lens to get the desired effect that you want, not because you can't be bothered to move forwards and backwards. That's really important and here's why...

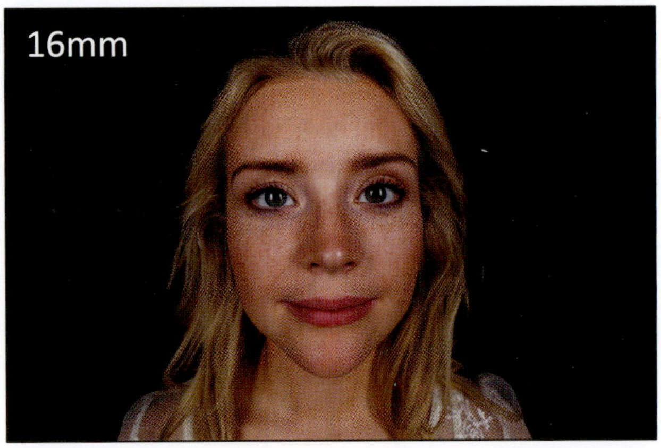

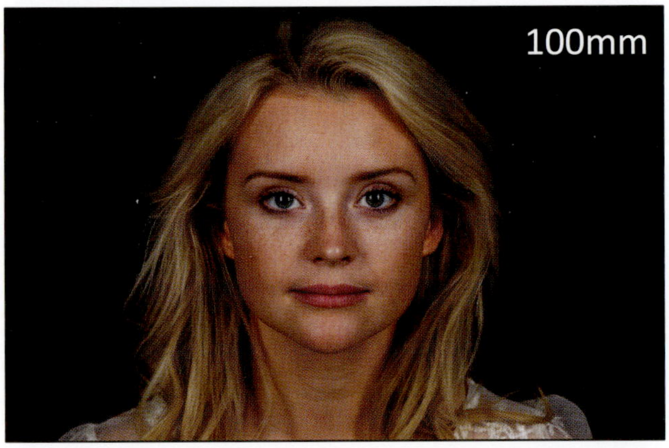

Here's a picture of someone taken at an ultra-wide angle. This picture was taken at a focal length of 16mm using a full frame camera. I'll come to full frame cameras in more detail soon.

The picture here is the same person but this picture was taken at a focal length of 100mm.
Look at the difference in the 2 pictures. That is solely down to the focal length used - you could be forgiven to think that it's not even the same person.

Let's look at the same picture again through a variety of focal lengths.

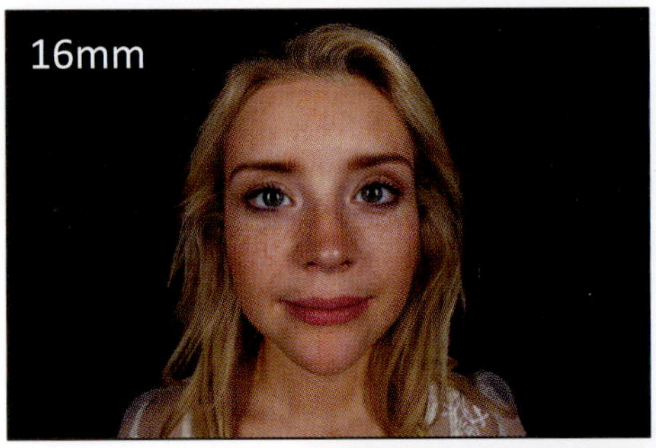

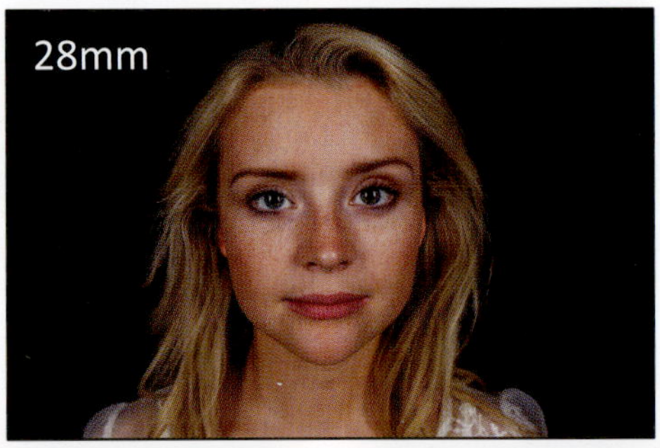

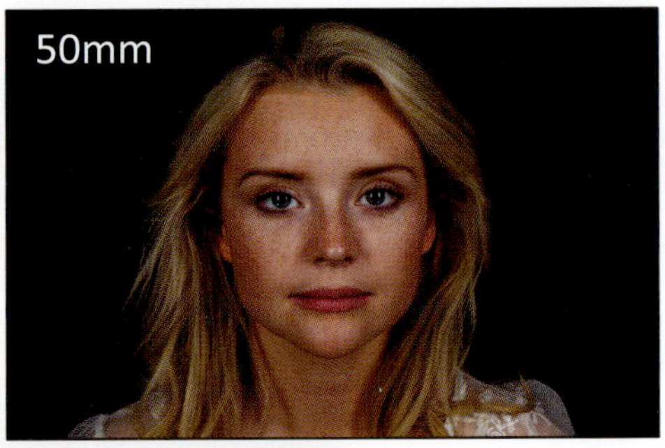

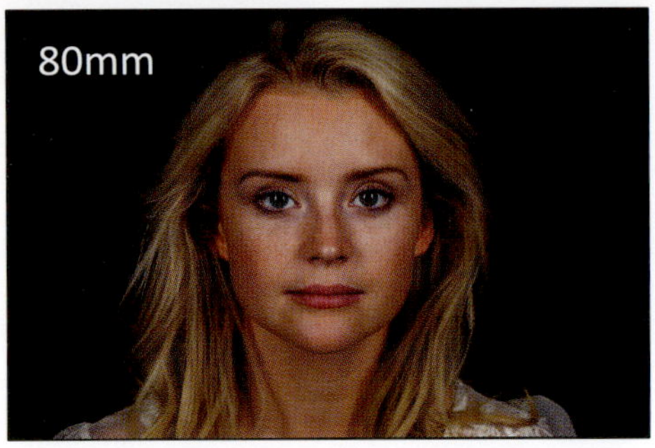

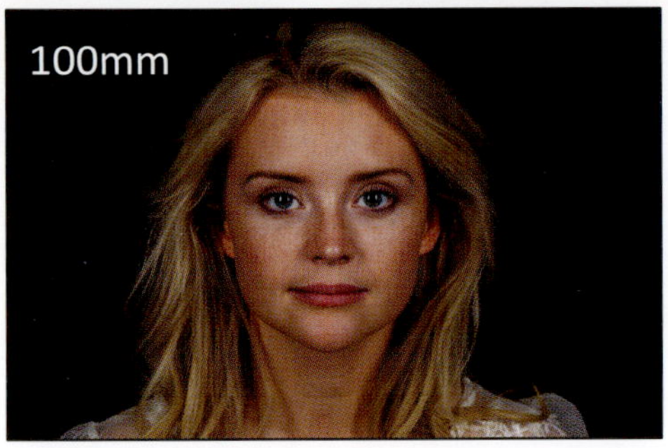

50mm - This picture is really important because it's actually how your eye sees. Using 50mm focal length on a full frame camera will give little distortion or obscurity to the picture. This means you can take a picture at this focal length, put that picture next to the person and it should look exactly the same, without any distortion at all – this is known as a standard lens.

80-85mm - This is a very good focal length for portraiture, as it compresses the face a little bit giving a more flattering portrait.

Notice through these pictures how the head is framed the same in each shot. For instance, the nose is dead in the centre of each image and the head size is taking up roughly the same amount of space in each frame - This is because you're going to be doing this yourselves in your task.

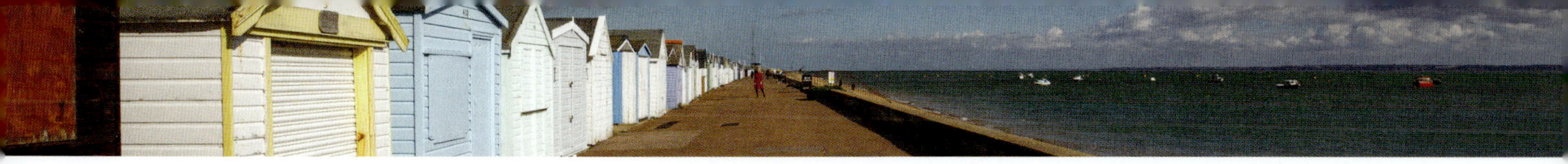

Task

For your task, it's best to use something cubical or a face close up to see the distortion fully. Here I have demonstrated this with a bus shelter.

I want you to physically see, with your own equipment, the effect that the lens's focal length has on objects.

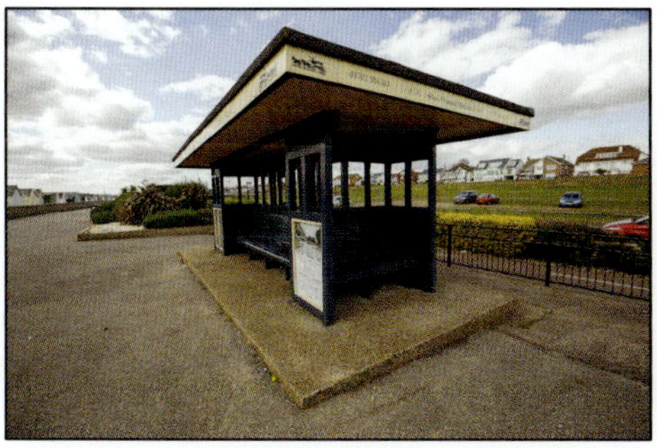

16mm

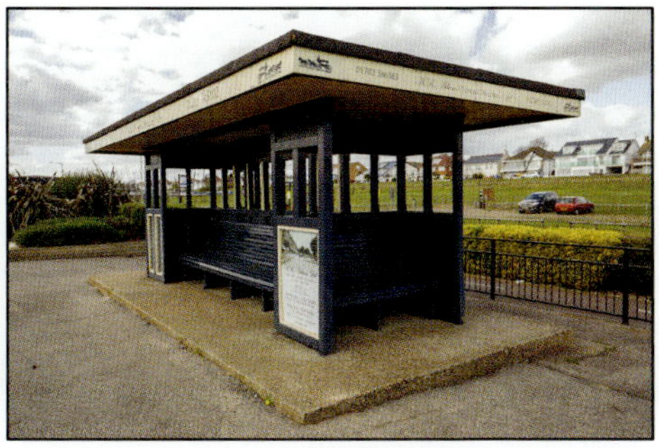

28mm

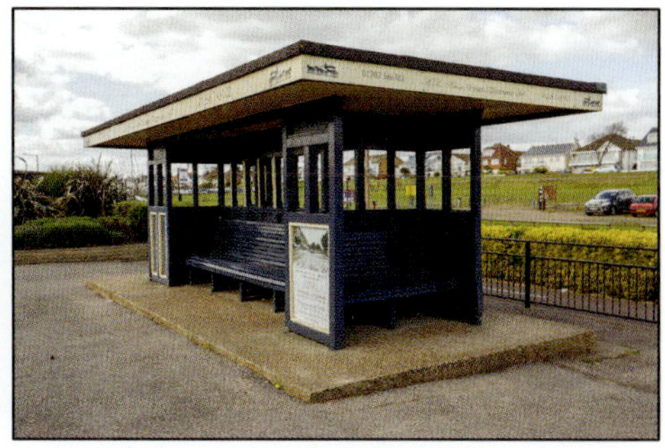

35mm

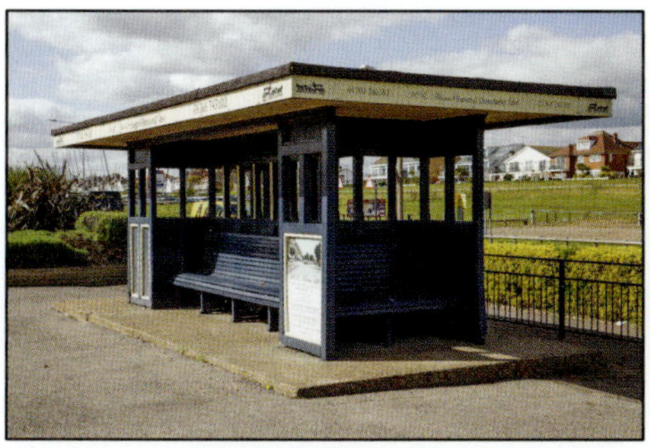

50mm

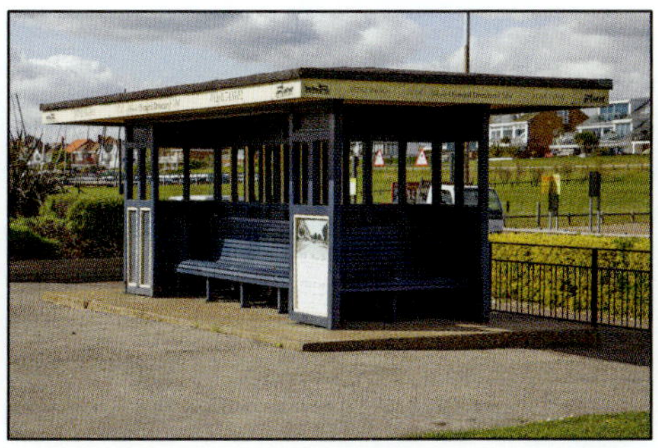

80mm

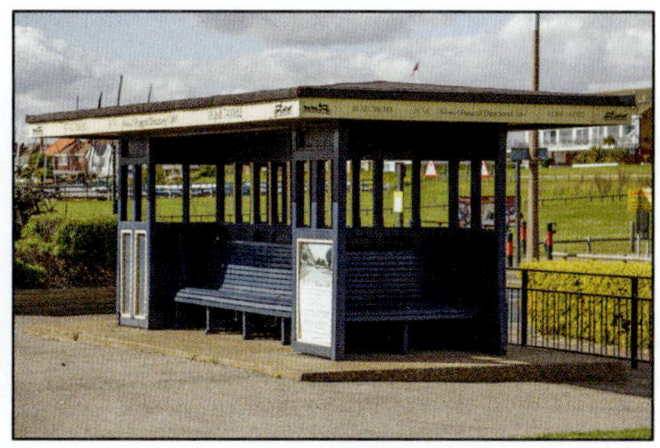

105mm

- Take pictures of the same object with different focal lengths and notice how focal lengths can distort an object. Don't worry if you don't have the same numbers shown above, simply start at your lowest number and work up in stages.

- Set your camera to P (program mode) – Put your ISO on Auto – Have your focus point set to centre frame.

- Frame the object the same in each picture e.g. Fill the frame with the object equally in each shot - Make sure your wide angle shot is as close to the object as possible - Have your focus point the same in picture.

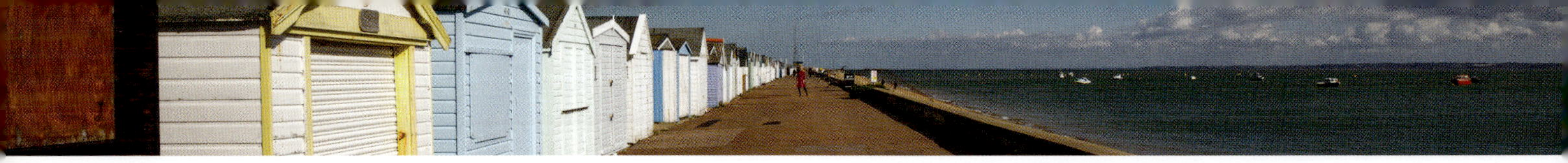

Sensor Sizes

So I hope you've had fun doing that task. Now, I want to talk to you about sensor sizes as that also has an effect on the focal length that you use. A 50mm focal length will look different on what's called a full frame sensor camera, a crop sensor camera and a micro 4/3 camera. Your sensor is what captures the light and is held in the camera body.

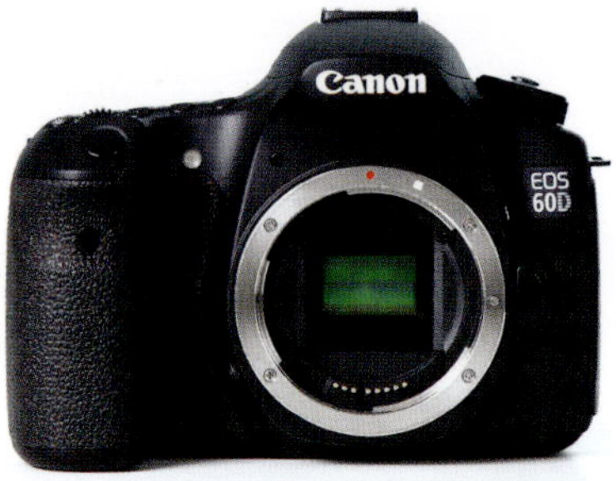

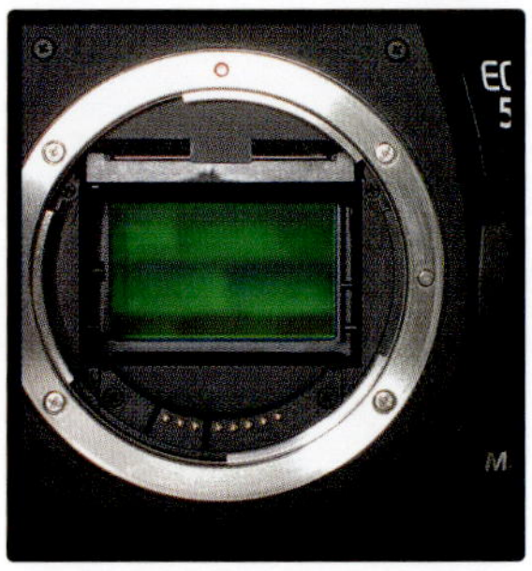

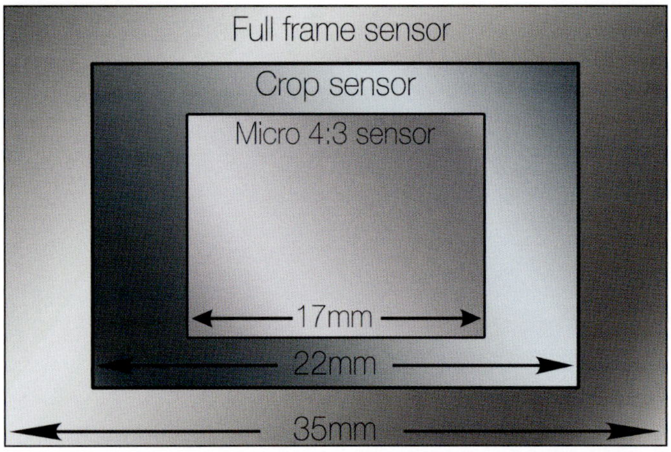

The main difference between a full frame and a crop sensor is its size. The full frame sensor is based on the old 35mm negatives which means it's 35mm along its longest side whereas a crop sensor is smaller - it's around 22mm on its longest side and a micro 4/3 sensor is 17mm along its longest side.

The main reason manufacturers do this is costing. A full frame camera will cost you a lot more money; it's generally what professionals use.

The quality of the image is going to be better on the full frame but it will be minimal and only visible on high end pro shots or big prints so don't worry too much about this as you're learning. What it does effect though, is the amount you can fit into your frame. Let's look at the effect of this in an actual picture.

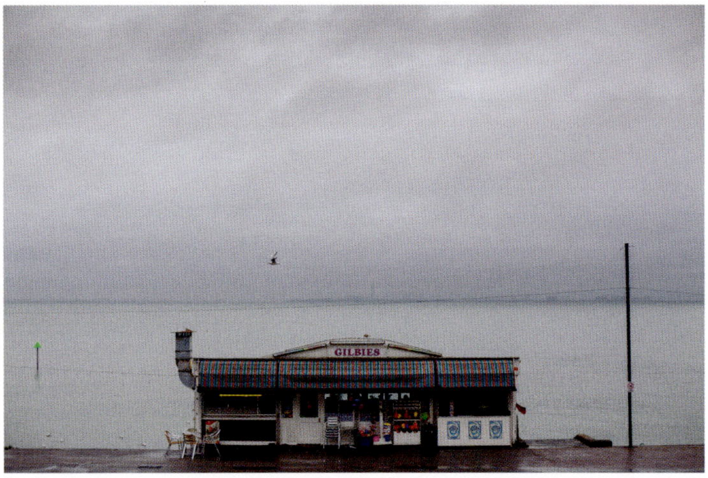

Here we have a picture that's been taken on a full frame camera and the focal length used was 50mm.

If I took the same shot with a crop sensor camera, and set the lens to 50mm, I would have got this which is a cropped in version of that image.

To get the equivalent look on a crop sensor, I would simply have to zoom out. On the crop sensor camera you would have to zoom out to 31mm to get the equivalent of 50mm on a full frame camera.

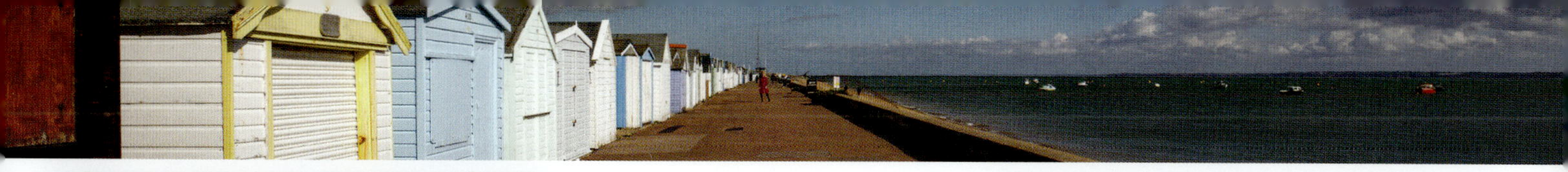

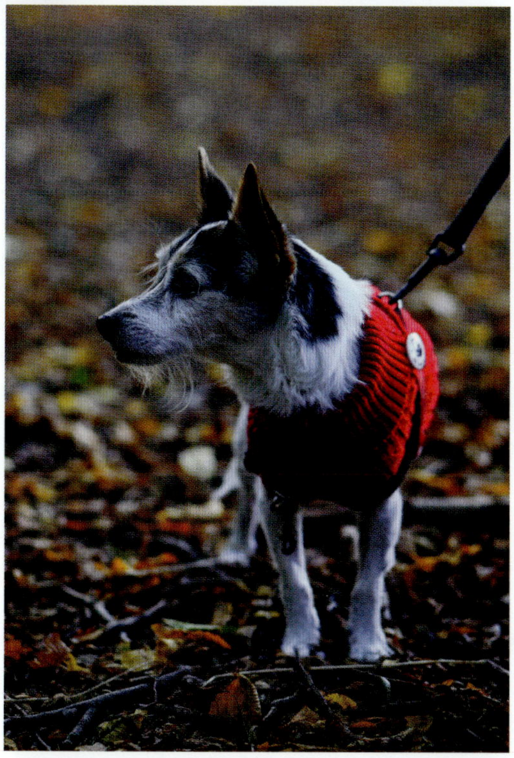

Let's look at another example. Here we have my little dog Jake taken on a full frame camera with a focal length of 80mm (*left*).

If that was a focal length of 80mm on a crop sensor camera it would look like this on the right.

So, to get the equivalent look on a crop sensor camera you would zoom out to 50mm.

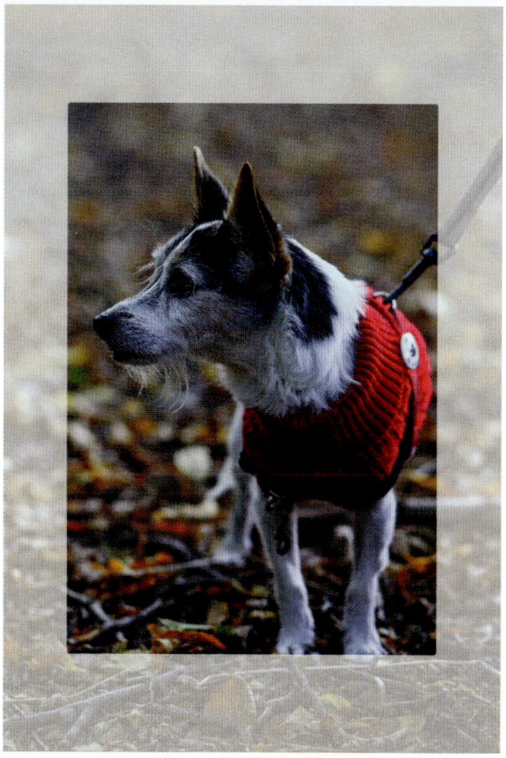

50mm focal length on a crop sensor camera is equivalent to 80mm on a full frame camera and 40mm on a micro 4/3 camera (see table below).

I know this all sounds confusing and to be honest it's not something you have to worry about too much unless you're going to change cameras. But you do need to know what types of focal lengths suit what types of subjects.

Of course, you can use any focal length for any picture and it is good to experiment, but there are general focal lengths that will suit certain subjects.

Full Frame Cameras, 35mm sensor	Crop sensor or APS-C 'common cameras' 22mm sensor (approx)	Micro 4:3 Cameras 17mm sensor	Type of lens and typical use
16mm focal length	11mm	8mm	Ultra Wide Angle
28mm	17mm	14mm	Wide Angle - good for landscapes
50mm	31mm	25mm	Standard Lens – as your eye sees
80mm	50mm	40mm	Good for portraiture
100mm	62mm	50mm	Good for Macro (Close up photography)
200mm and above	125mm	100mm	Zoom lens – good for wildlife and sports

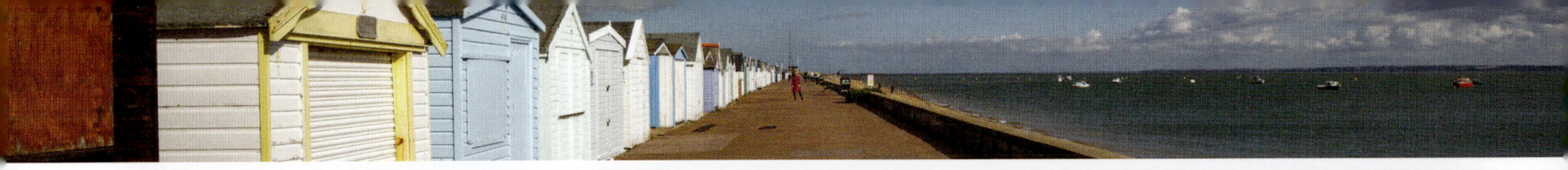

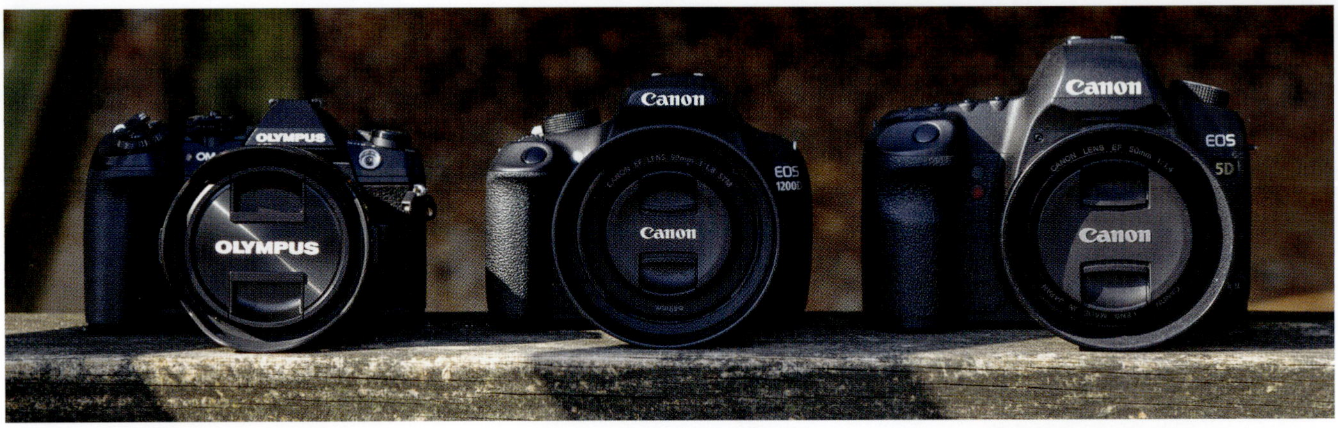

Olympus OMD
Micro 4:3 Camera

Canon EOS 1200d
Crop Sensor Camera
(APS-C)

Canon EOS 5d
Full Frame Camera

Below is an example of a shot taken on a full frame camera at a focal length of 16mm. To get this look on a crop sensor camera you would have to use a focal length of 11mm and on a Micro 4:3 camera a focal length of 8mm. These focal lengths would be called ultra-wide angle and they're really good for taking those obscure landscape shots where you capture a lot of the scene in the picture.

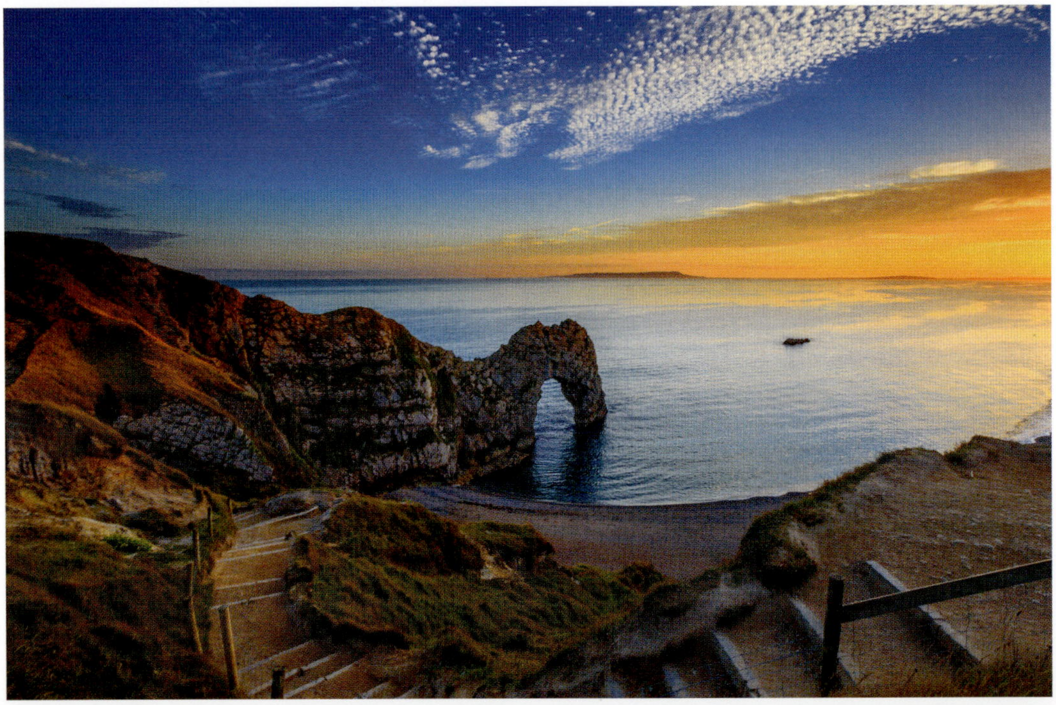

Full Frame Cameras, 35mm sensor	Crop sensor or APS-C 'common cameras' 22mm sensor (approx.)	Micro 4:3 Cameras	Type of lens and typical use
16mm focal length	11mm	8mm	Ultra Wide Angle

A standard DSLR camera with a standard kit lens will probably have a widest angle of approximately 17mm. The equivalent of that will be 28mm on a full frame camera and 14mm on a Micro 4:3 camera. They're good for general wide angle shots and landscapes.

28mm	17mm	14mm	Wide Angle - good for landscapes

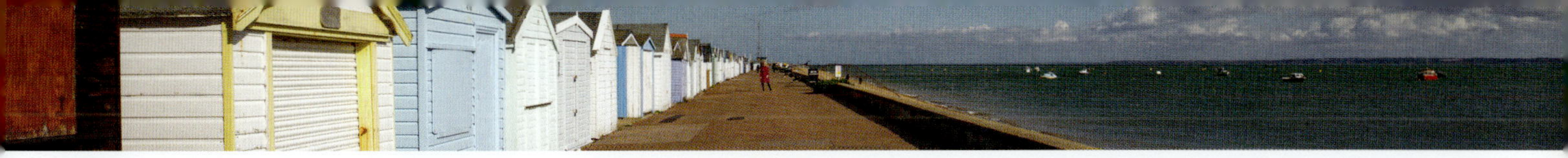

Full Frame Cameras, 35mm sensor	Crop sensor or APS-C 'common cameras' 22mm sensor (approx.)	Micro 4:3 Cameras	Type of lens and typical use
50mm	31mm	25mm	Standard Lens – as your eye sees

50mm on a full frame, 31mm on a crop sensor and 25mm on a micro 4:3 camera is a standard lens as this is how your eye sees. If you want something to look natural then this is a good focal length to use.

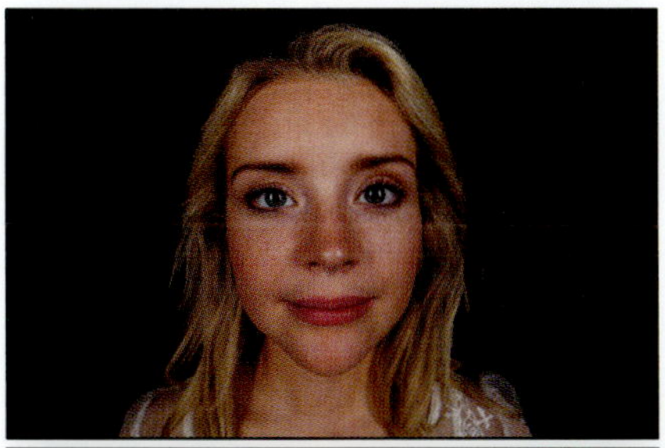

16mm – The face is distorted.

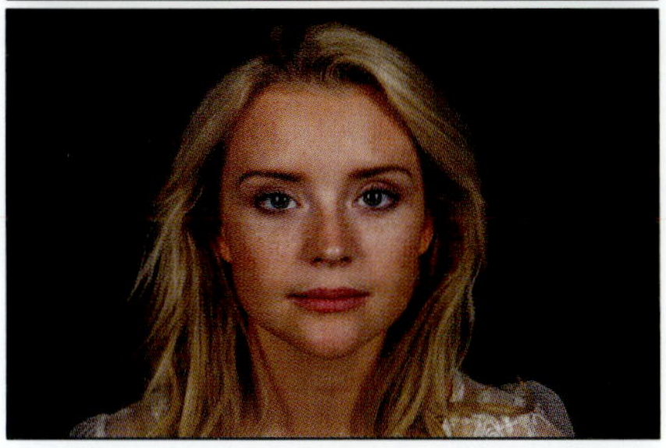

50mm – As your eye sees.

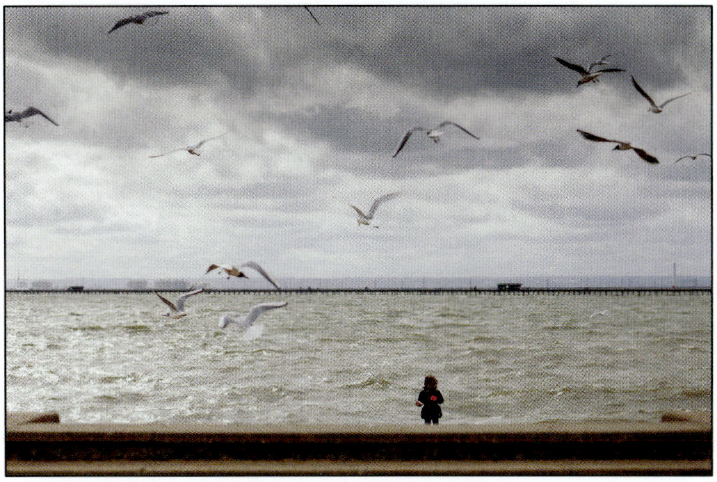

Commonly used in documentary and product photography.

Full Frame Cameras, 35mm sensor	Crop sensor or APS-C 'common cameras' 22mm sensor (approx.)	Micro 4:3 Cameras	Type of lens and typical use
80mm	50mm	40mm	Good for portraiture

80mm on a full frame, 50mm on crop sensor and 40mm on a Micro 4:3 camera is really good for portraiture. It throws the background out of focus and compresses the face in a little (*right*).

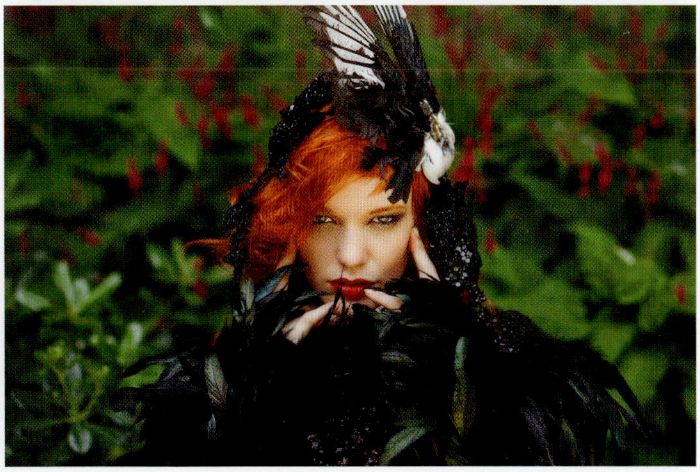

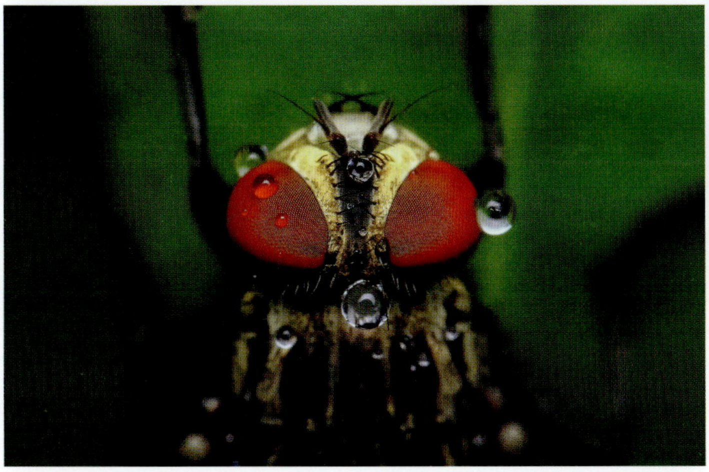

As you zoom in further to 100mm on a full frame you'll get good Macro shots (*left*).

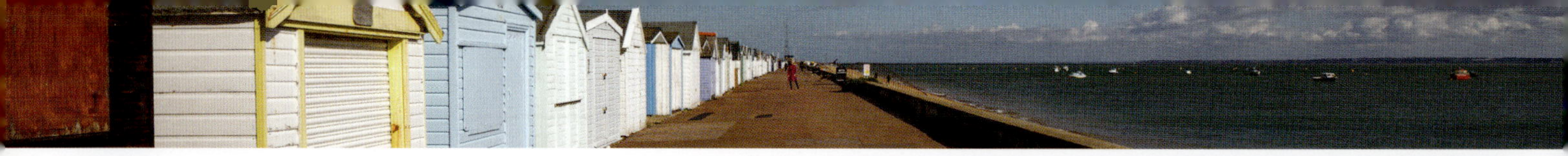

Full Frame Cameras, 35mm sensor	Crop sensor or APS-C 'common cameras' 22mm sensor (approx)	Micro 4:3 Cameras 17mm sensor	Type of lens and typical use
200mm and above	125mm	100mm	Zoom lens – good for wildlife and sports

Zooming in further, you get the lenses generally used for Sports or wildlife Photography where you need to photograph things that are far away.

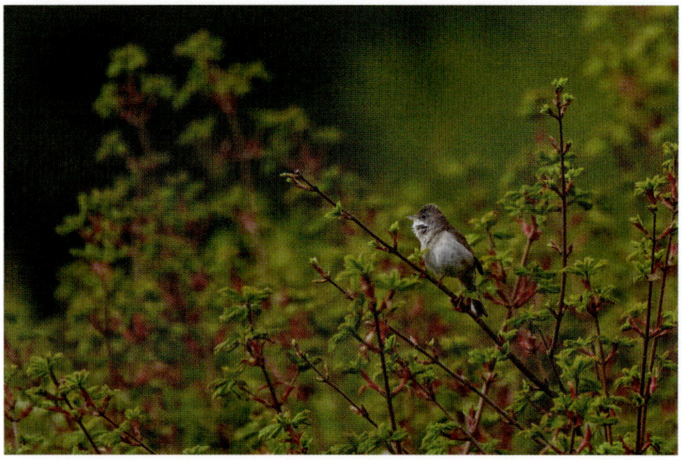

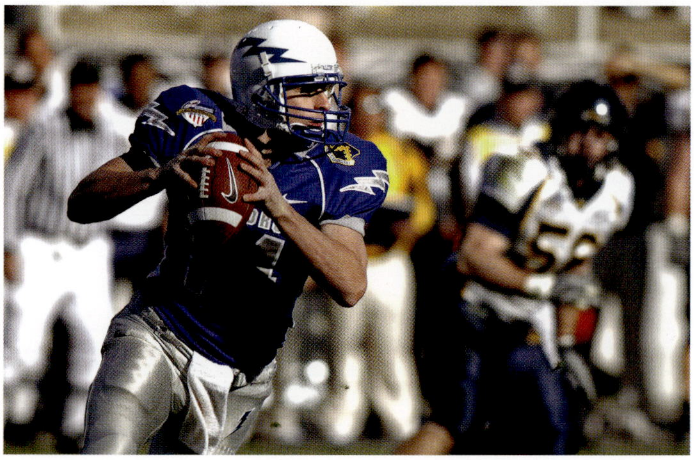

So have a practice with your task and make sure you're comfortable with how different focal lengths can affect the look of your shots then move onto the next chapter.

To view a video tutorial on camera sensor sizes go to www.theschoolofphotography.com and type sensor size comparison in the search bar.

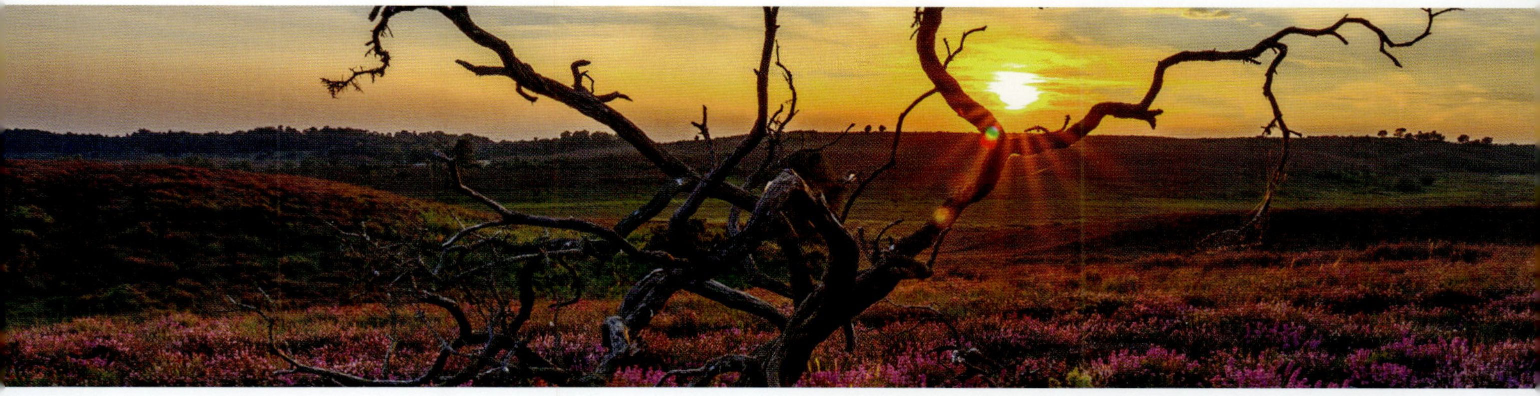

Metering

Chapter 7

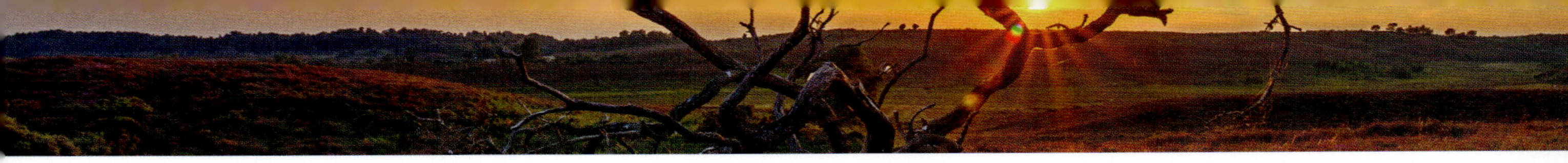

Every modern DSLR has something that's called a Metering Mode.

Knowing how metering works and what each of the metering modes do is very important in photography as it helps control exposure with minimum effort and it helps you take pictures in unusual lighting situations, for instance, situations where you have a lot of contrast between lights and darks - for example a shot where you have a person standing in front of a bright window.

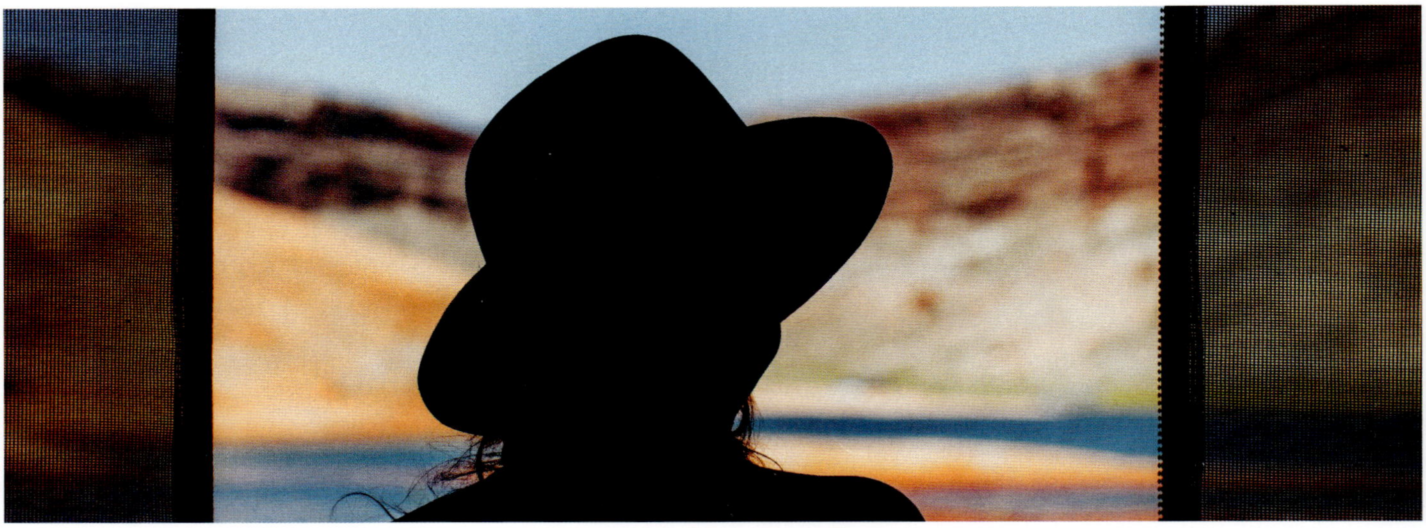

Exposure in photography is something we are going to cover in much more detail later on in this book but to briefly give you an understanding of it, an exposure is how much light you let into the camera. Too much light and the photo becomes too bright - overexposed. Not enough light and the photo becomes too dark - underexposed. Metering in your camera is what determines the correct amount of light needed for any particular shot.

Firstly, lets show you where your metering settings are on your camera. Below is a guide for common cameras. Other cameras will be very similar to this so just refer to your user manual under Metering if you get stuck.

Canon

- Press the info button to bring up this screen.
- Using the touch-screen, or the navigator wheel, select the symbol highlighted below and press set or tap it on the touch-screen.

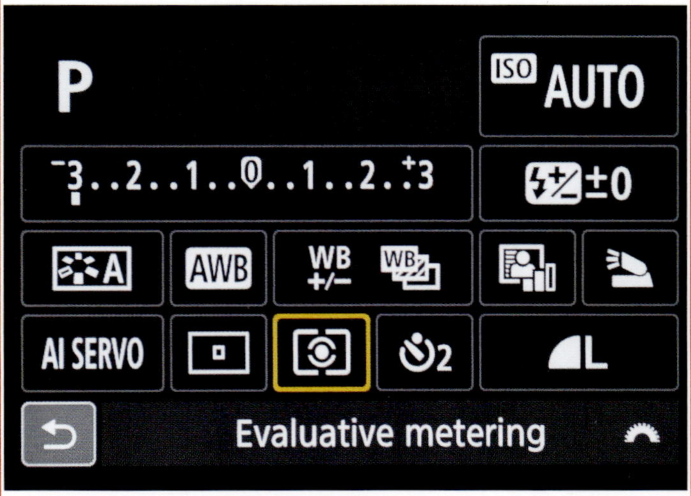

Nikon

- Press the i button and the bottom setting strip should come up.
- Using the navigator wheel or buttons, select the symbol highlighted below.

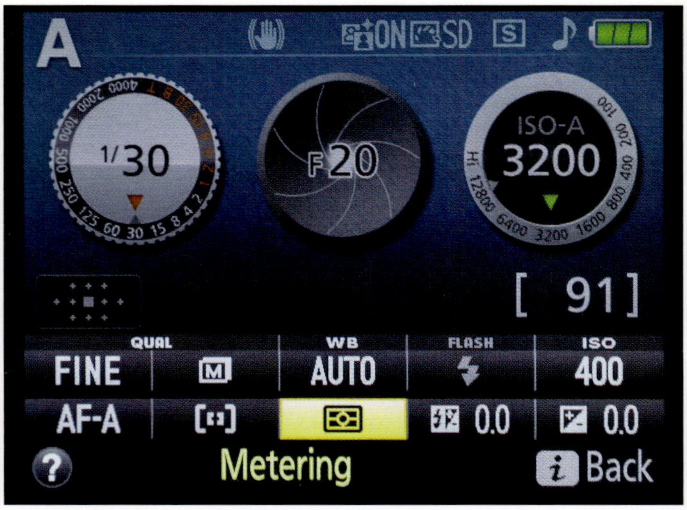

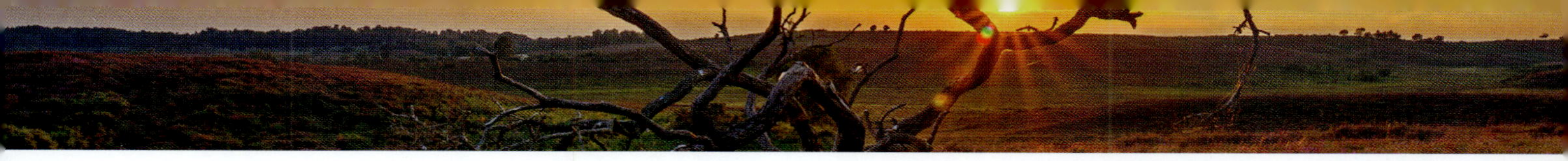

There are several different metering modes on your camera.

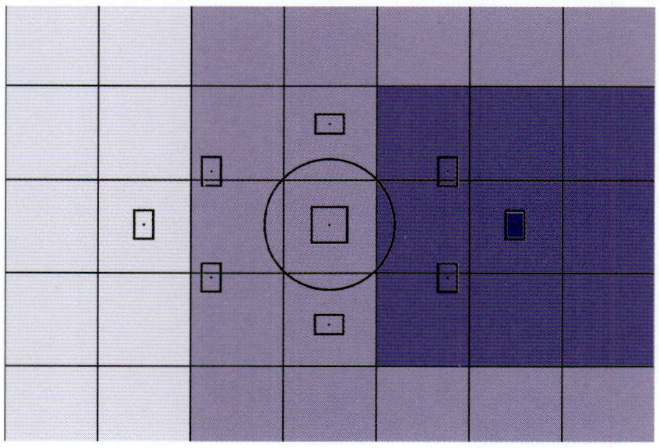

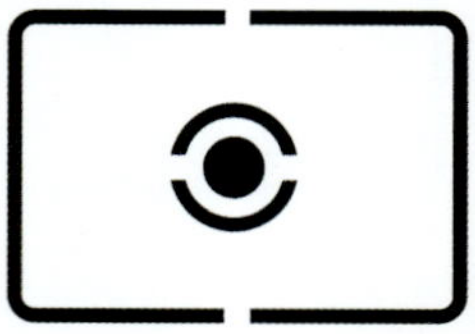

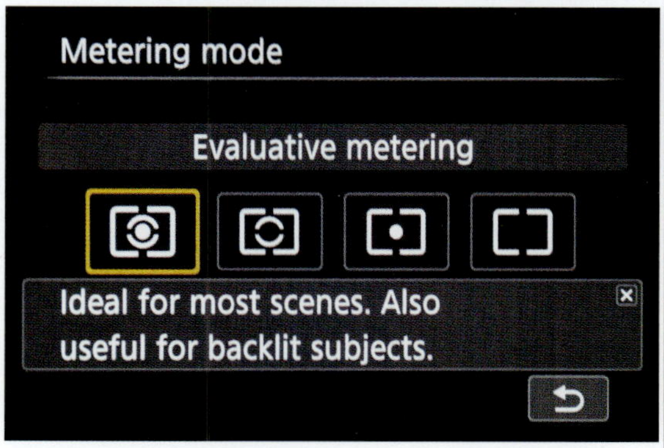

The first one is called evaluative or matrix metering, depending on what camera you have. That's the default metering mode and works really well. It measures the light from across the frame but puts a bias where the focus point is.

On this picture (*above left*) the dark blue dot is where the focus point is and where most of the information is recorded from; directly surrounding that is where it takes further information from and sounding that is the rest. It mixes all 3 areas together and gives you a balanced exposure.

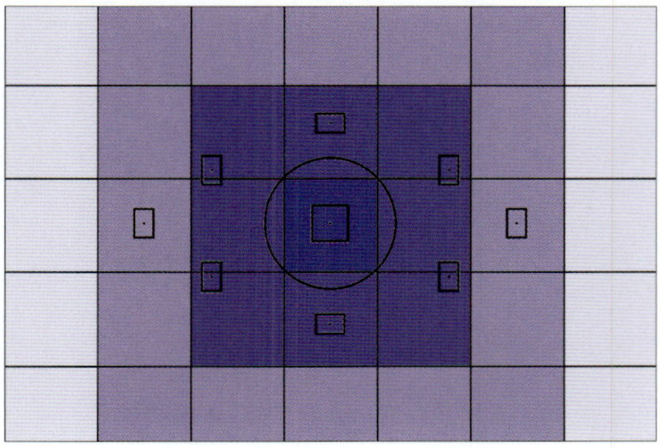

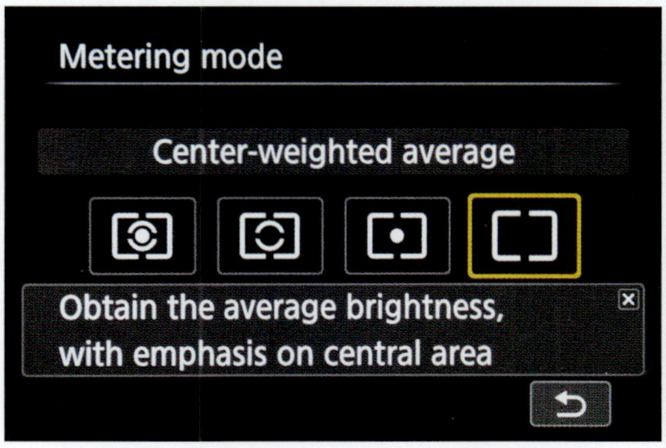

The next one is called Centre weighted or Average Metering. This measures light from across the whole frame but its bias is around the centre. It ignores the focus point. This can be good for landscape situations when you might be focusing something in the foreground but you want the camera to balance the exposure for the whole shot.

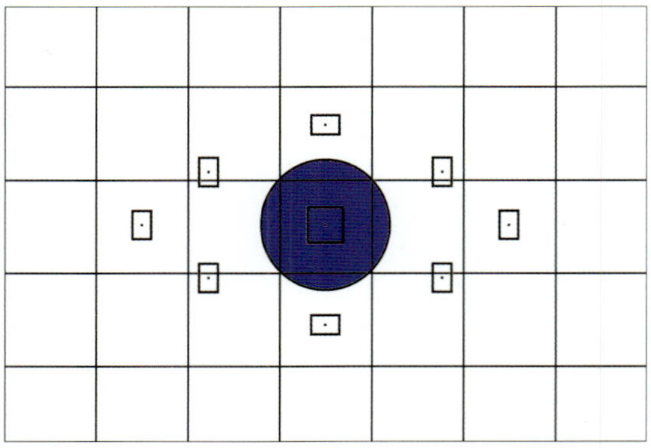

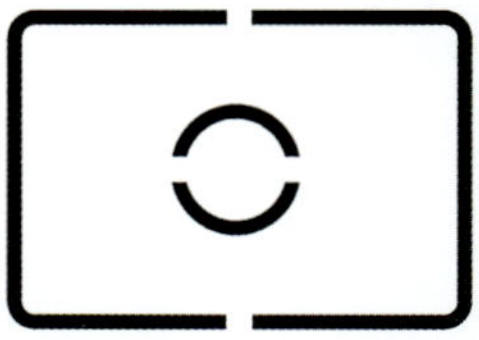

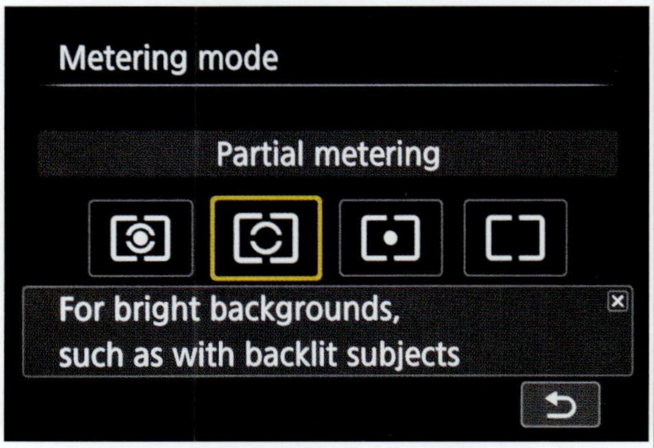

On some cameras you have Partial Metering. What this does is measure light from a small part of the picture around your focus point, approx. 10% of the frame around the focus point.

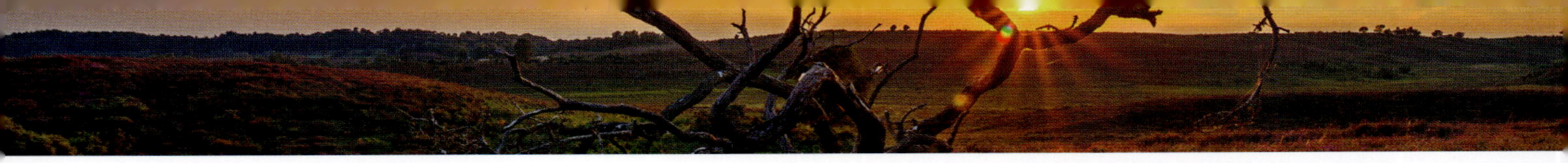

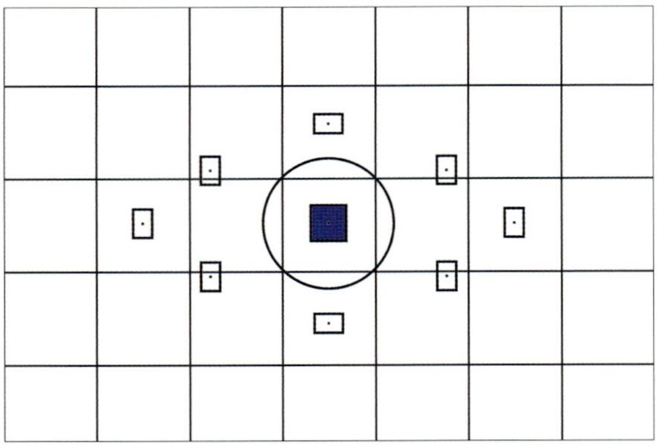

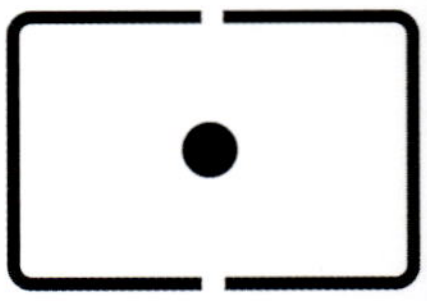

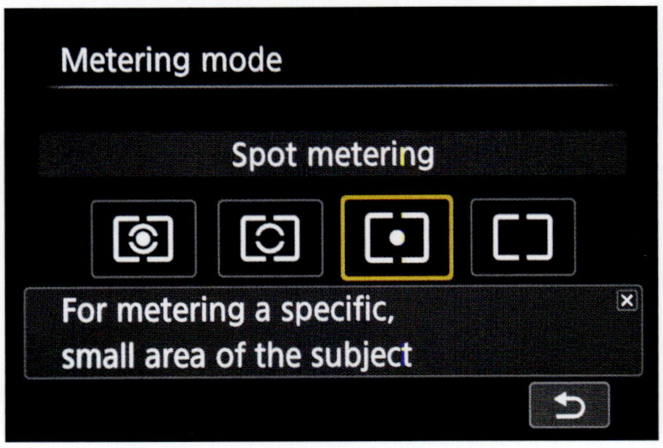

Then there is spot metering and spot metering does exactly that. It meters from an exact spot – your focus point, approx. 2-4% of the image area. Partial and spot metering are good settings for challenging lighting situations especially when you have a moving subject.

Task

I want you to find a challenging situation. A really easy way to do that is put an object in front of a window so you have something very dark against something very bright. Take shots on different metering modes and note down the difference.

Have a practice with that and then move on when you're ready.

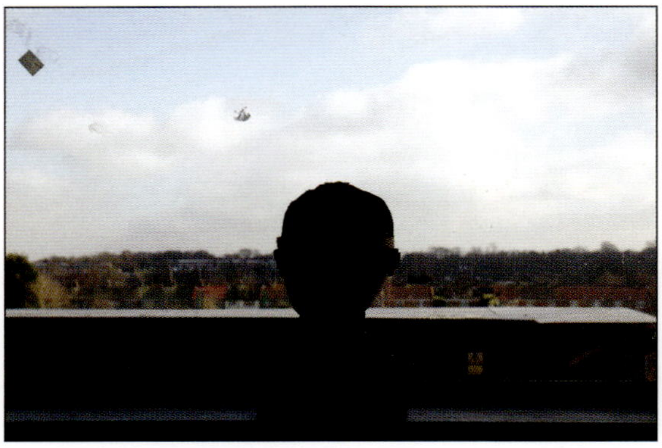

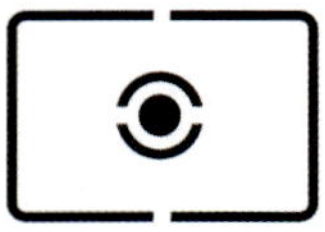

Evaluative or Matrix

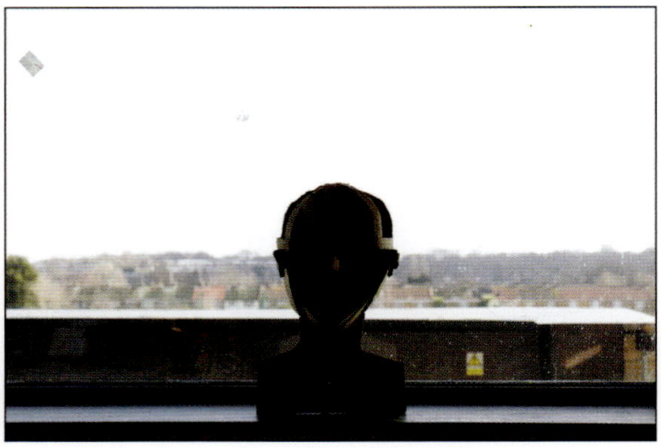

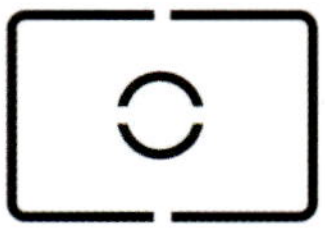

Partial

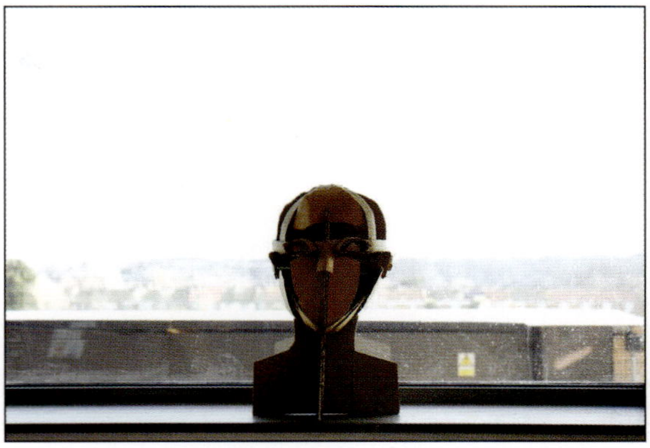

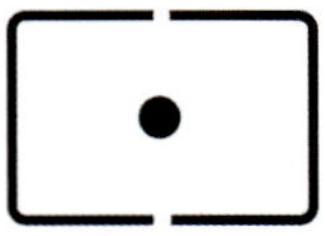

Spot

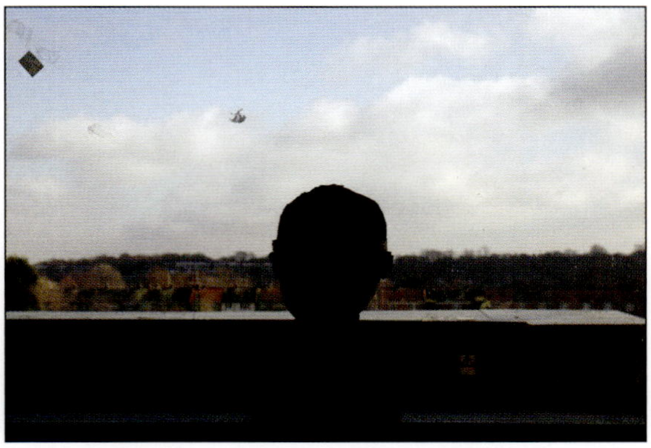

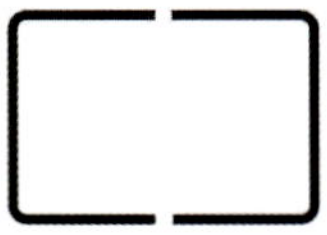

Centre Weighted

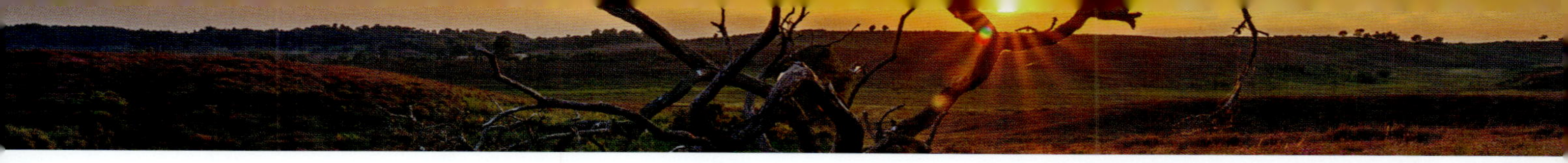

As well as metering, there is another way to control exposure. It's called Exposure Compensation and it's really simple to use. You simply use exposure compensation to make your pictures brighter or darker.

For example, imagine you're taking a picture of a sunset and it has come out too bright. By using exposure compensation, you can tell the camera to let in less light, to under-expose the picture, and in that process the picture is going to come out darker, meaning the sunset is going to come out darker, therefore giving you a much deeper, better-looking sunset.

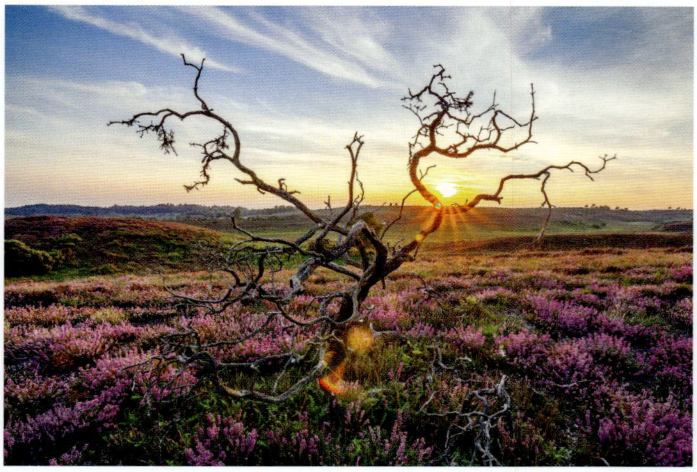

Original exposure

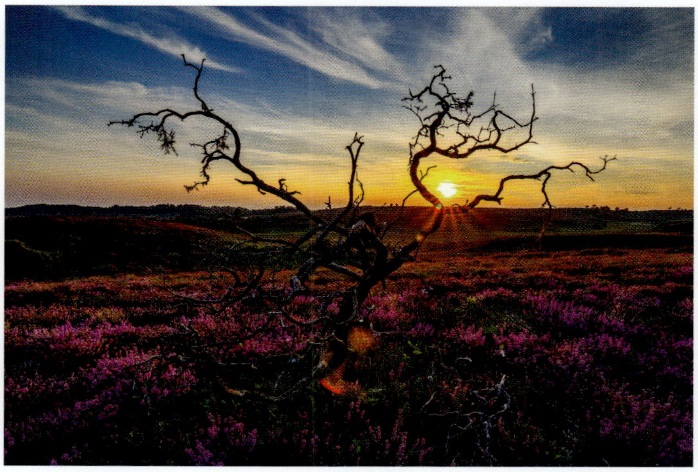

With exposure compensation

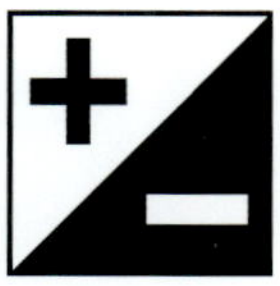

This is the Exposure Compensation symbol found on most cameras

Here's how to do that technique on your cameras. Again, this is a guide for common cameras; other brands will be very similar. Refer to your camera's manual under Exposure Compensation if you get stuck.

Canon

On a Canon, press the button that looks like this:

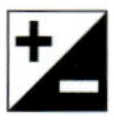

and whilst holding that down, move the dial on the back or top of your camera to move the dot left or right of the '0' (highlighted below). The '0' is correct exposure, the '– numbers' being under-exposed, and '+ numbers' being over-exposed.

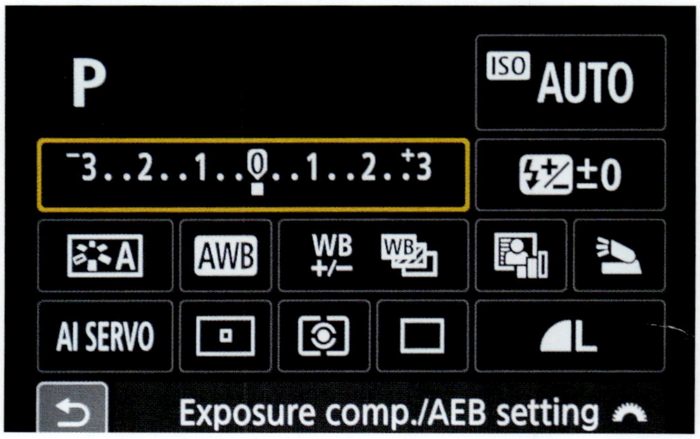

Nikon

On a Nikon, find the exposure compensation button:

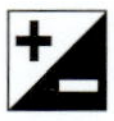

Then, holding this button down, use the dial at the back or front of the camera to move the exposure to the '+ number' or '– number'. The '– numbers' being under-exposed, and '+ numbers' being over-exposed (highlighted below).

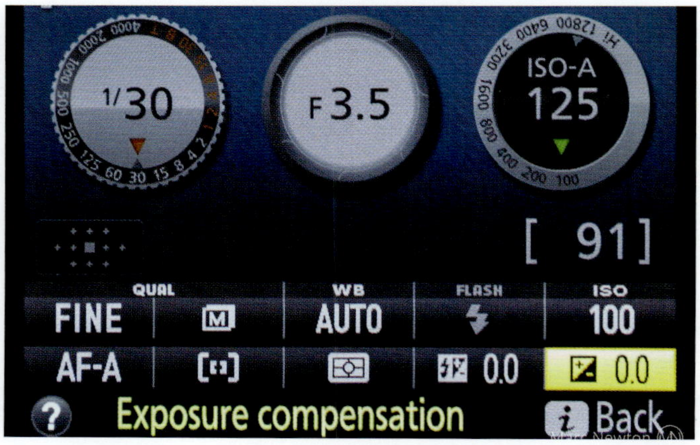

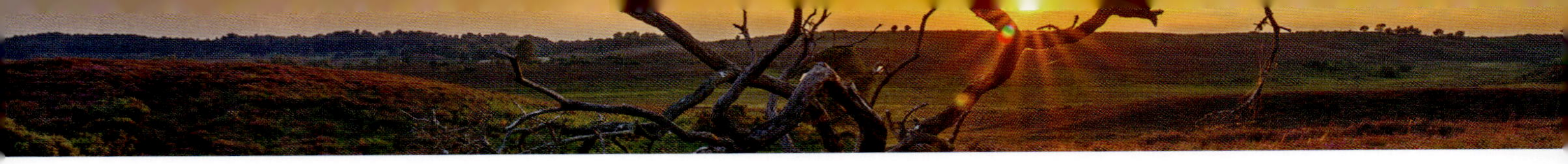

Task

Practice using exposure compensation.

Set your camera up in one position and take some pictures at different exposures e.g. -1, -2, +1, +2 etc. If your camera goes to 3 or 4, try that as well.

0

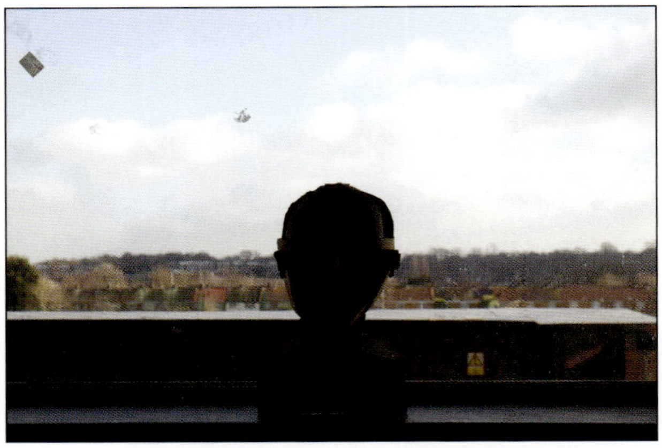

- 1

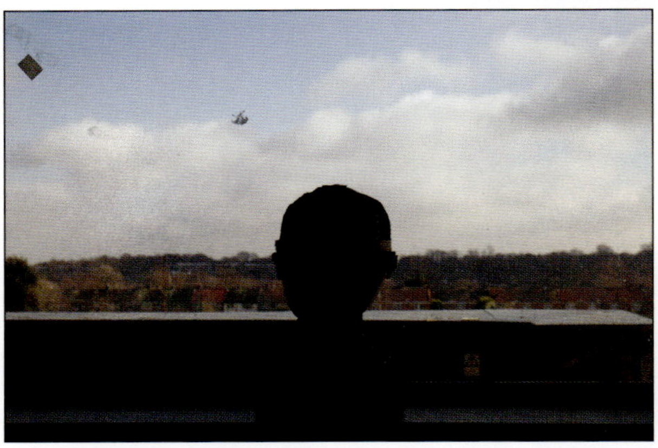

+1

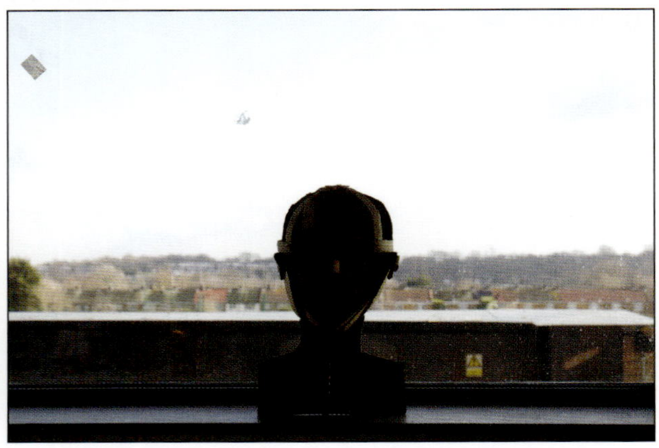

- 2

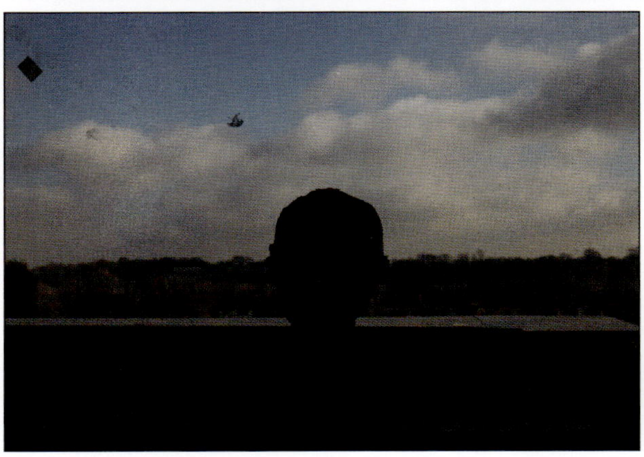

+ 2

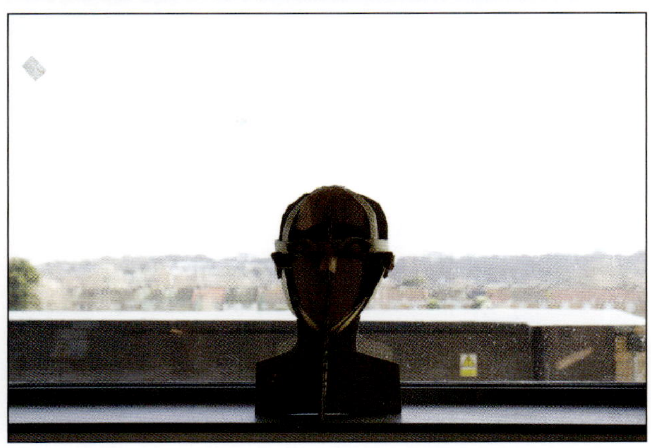

- Set your camera to ‘P’ and the ISO to Auto.
- Take one shot at the camera’s normal exposure.
- Using Exposure Compensation change the exposure to –1 and take another picture.
- Now change the exposure to -2 and take another picture.
- Repeat the process throughout your cameras range e.g. +1, +2 etc.

- Compare each shot and notice the difference in its brightness.

By doing this you have just controlled the exposure of your shots!

Important – Make sure you put your camera back to ‘0’ when you finish this task.

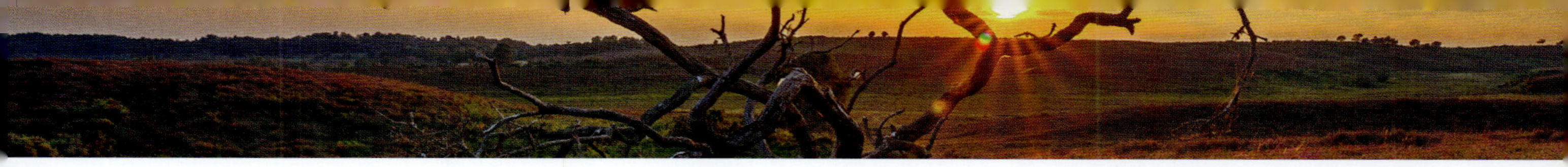

Let’s recap on this chapter.

- You have different types of metering modes on your cameras that can be used to your own advantage. The 2 main ones being Evaluative (or Matrix Metering) and Spot Metering.
- Spot Metering will help you out in difficult situations when you just need to meter for one particular object.
- Then you have exposure compensation. Exposure compensation is a really quick and easy way to just brighten up or darken your pictures. Really good for sunsets, someone standing in front of a window or to create silhouettes.
- Generally if you leave it on the cameras default setting which is Evaluative or Matrix Metering, the camera does a really good job. You would only use these settings if the exposure is not coming out correct i.e. if your picture is coming out too dark or too light.

There are more advanced ways to control the exposure of your shots and we’ll cover that later. For now this is a good way to understand exposure and just get a bit more control over the look of your shots.

Have a good practice with that and when ready, move onto the next chapter.

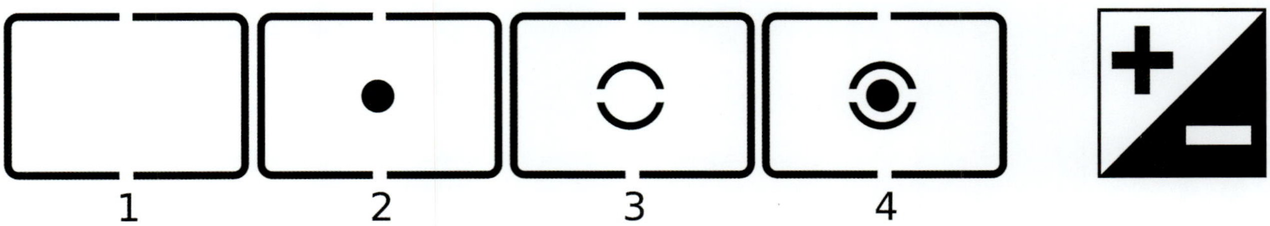

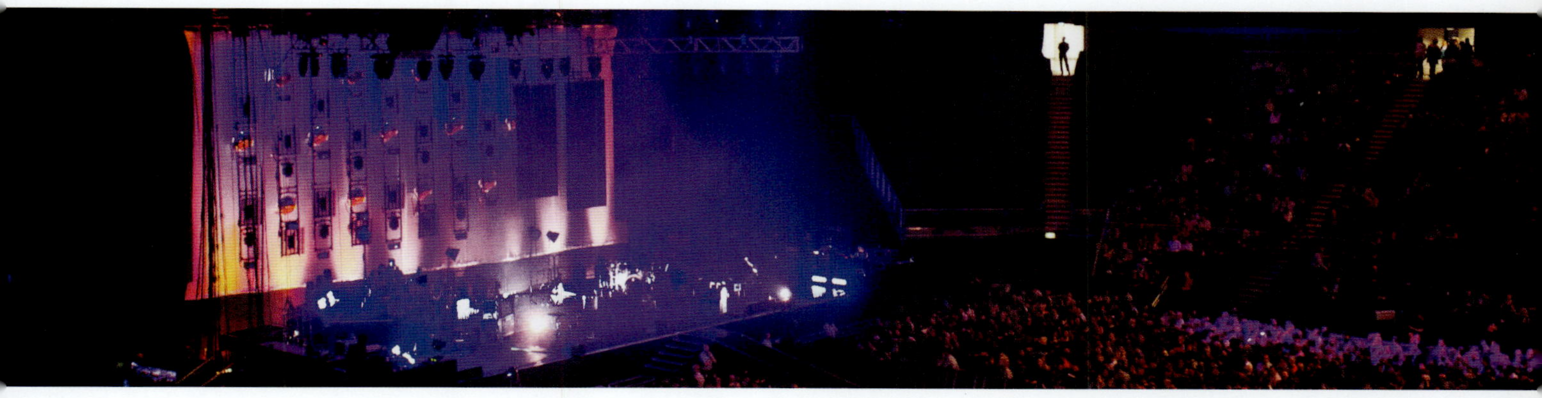

ISO

Chapter 8

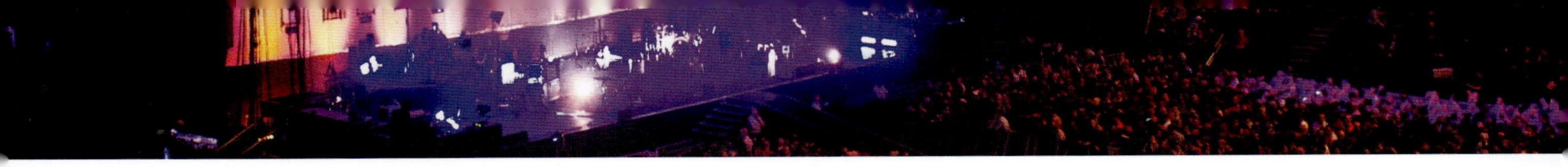

ISO stands for 'International Organisation for Standardisation'. ISO attaches itself to lots of different things. It's used to standardise certain products or certain parts of products across the world. You have ISO for products such as glass or wood and in this case, photography.

ISO in photography is the sensitivity your light sensor is to light. Basically you can make your camera more or less sensitive to light using the ISO settings.

You will see it displayed on your cameras as ISO 100 or ISO 400 and so on. The lower the number, such as ISO 100, the more light you will need and less noise the image will have. The higher the number, ISO 1600 for example, you won't need as much light but there will be more noise in the image.

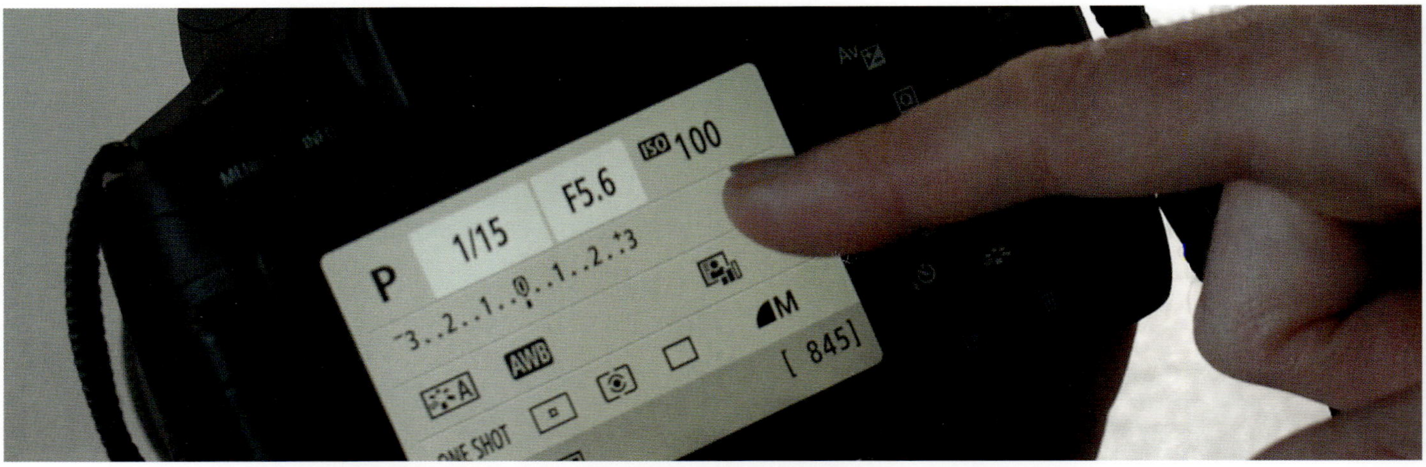

Now let's look at what noise is. Look at this picture (*right*).

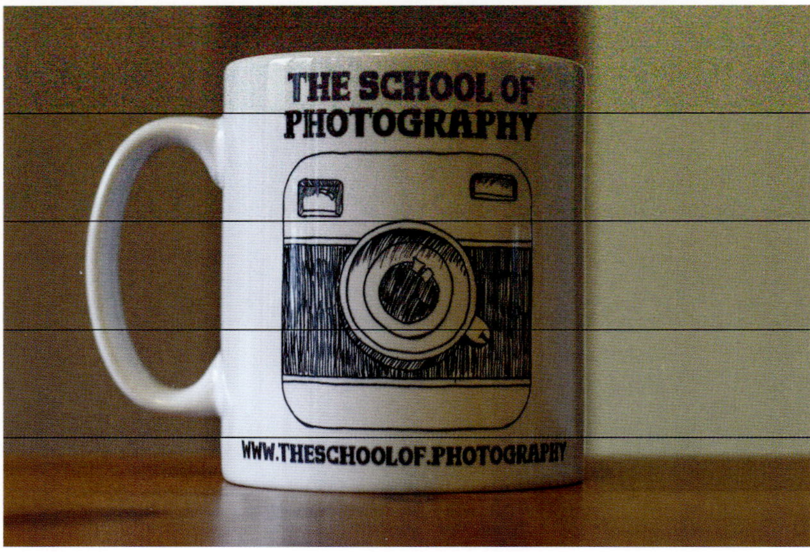

ISO 25600 (H2)
1/1000 second @ *f* 4

ISO 6400
1/250 second @ *f* 4

ISO 1600
1/60 second @ *f* 4

ISO 400
1/15 second @ *f* 4

ISO 100
1/4 second @ *f* 4

It's one picture taken on several different ISO settings. Down at the bottom you've got ISO 100 and at the top you have ISO 25,600. If you look at both sections you can see that the top one (ISO 25600) is very speckled; that's what noise is.

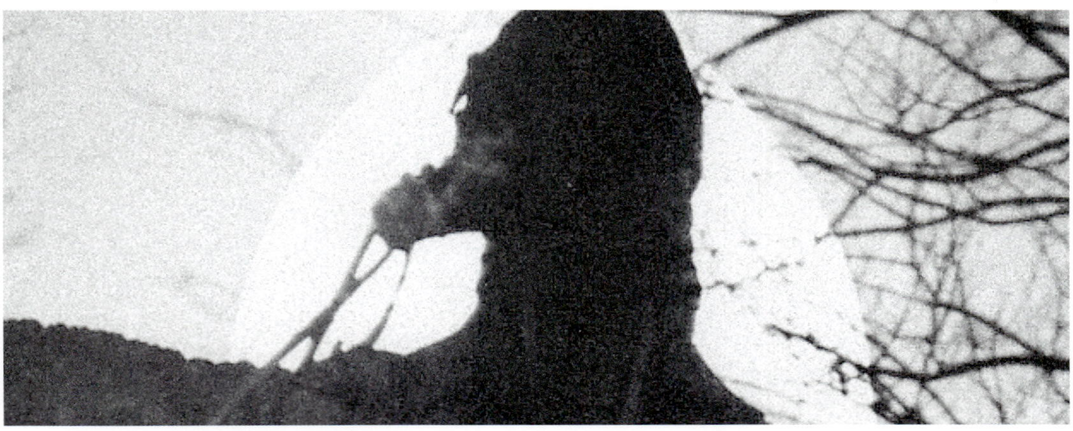

Noise used to be called grain in the days of film photography, but in the digital age it's called noise and it doesn't look as good.

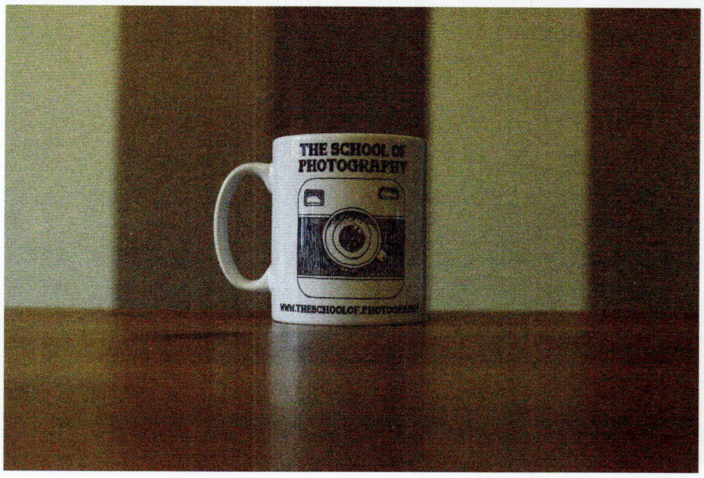

Here is the ISO 25,600 picture. It's really noisy, the colours are broken and the image looks soft and very dull.

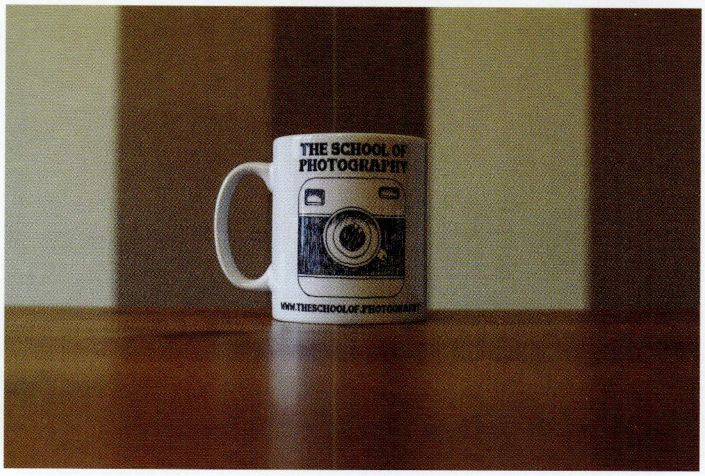

If we look at the same image taken at ISO 100, you cannot see any of that noise. It's nice and clear, the colours are vibrant and there are no dots.

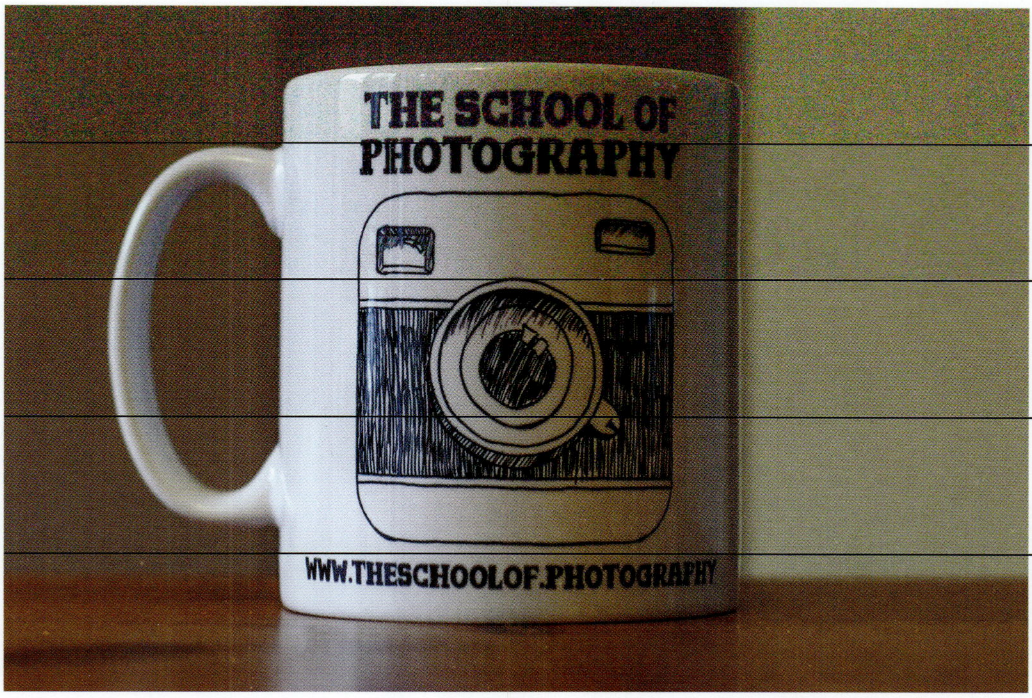

ISO 25600 (H2)

1/1000 second @ *f* 4

ISO 6400

1/250 second @ *f* 4

ISO 1600

1/60 second @ *f* 4

ISO 400

1/15 second @ *f* 4

ISO 100

1/4 second @ *f* 4

Look at the shutter speed time, that's the numbers where it states '1/1000 second'. Look at the one that says ISO 100, that has been taken at ¼ of a second. If you look at the one that has been taken at ISO 25,600, that has been taken at 1/1000th of a second. We will cover shutter speeds in much more detail later on in this course, but in a nutshell that means the high ISO shot has been exposed to a lot less light and the ISO 100 has been exposed to a lot more light.

Because I didn't let in a lot of light on the top image, the high ISO setting has captured the light extremely quickly, which means it hasn't captured all of the detail, it has just captured as much as it could within that time and filled in the gaps as best as it can. That's what's creating the noise.

As a comparison, think of when you're listening to the radio. When you're near to the radio station's antenna, you can hear it quite clearly, the further away you get, the sound starts to crackle and break. This is because the radio doesn't have as much detail to play you so it fills in the gaps with noise.

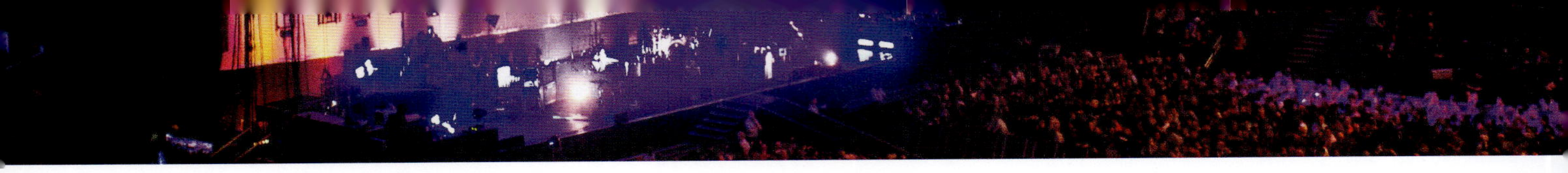

So when would you use different ISO Settings? With post-processing these days, you can add the grain effect into your images. So ideally, what you need to do is capture as much detail as possible in each picture you take - which means having a low ISO. If you have got a lot of light, for example outside on a sunny day, you can use ISO 100 as you have a lot of light available and this will give you the best quality image.

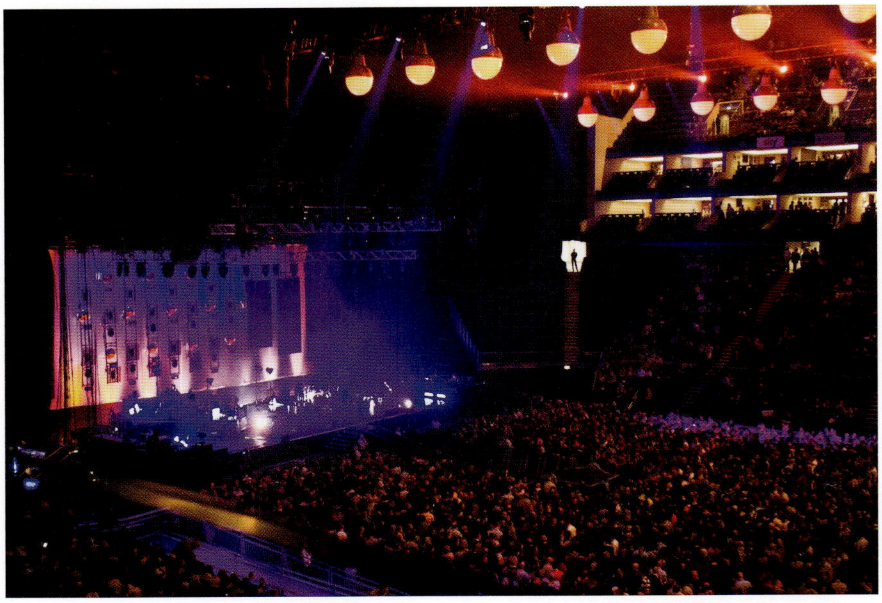

You would use a high ISO when you haven't got much available light, for example inside a concert. Or a restaurant at night when you don't want to use the flash. Flash could distract and bleach out features in the face, so a high ISO will get the shot for you but the trade-off for that will be noise.

ISO Settings

Before I set you the ISO task I want to show you where the ISO settings are on your cameras. Again, this is a guide for common cameras, don't worry if you don't have a Canon or a Nikon, it's pretty similar on all makes of camera. Simply refer to your camera manual under ISO settings if you get stuck.

Canon

- On a Canon, press the button marked ISO (on top or at the back of the camera)
- Then turn the dial to select what ISO sensitivity setting you want, then press SET.

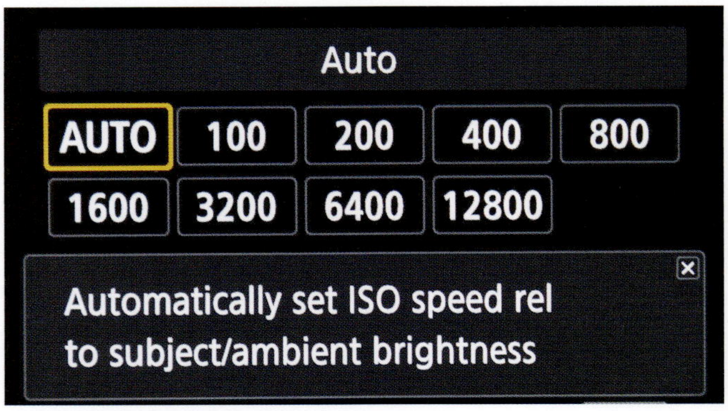

For the next task you may also want to use a two second timer to avoid camera shake.

- Press the drive button on your Canon (*pictured left, showing multiple squares*).
- Then select 2 second self timer from the options, then press SET.

Nikon

- Press the menu button and select the camera icon (*highlighted green*).
- Then go across and keep going down until you find the ISO sensitivity settings > Press OK
- Make sure Auto ISO sensitivity Settings (*highlighted yellow*) is off.
- Press the shutter release to go back to the main screen.

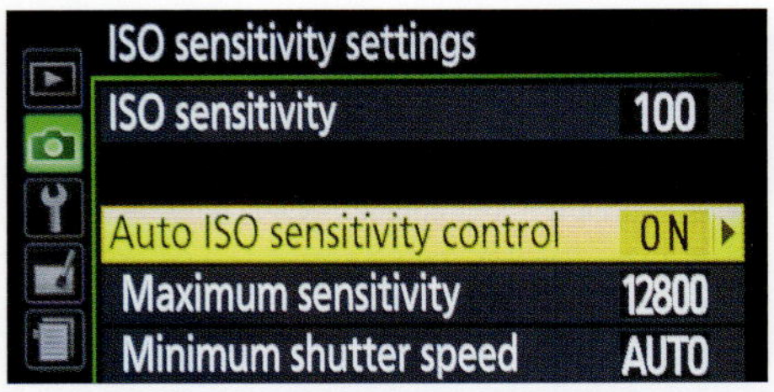

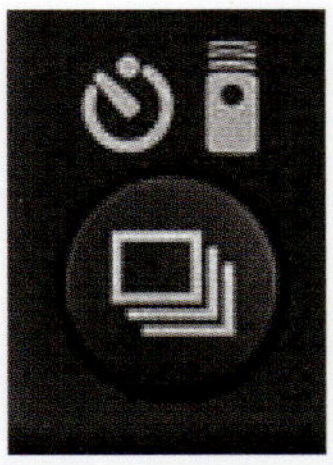

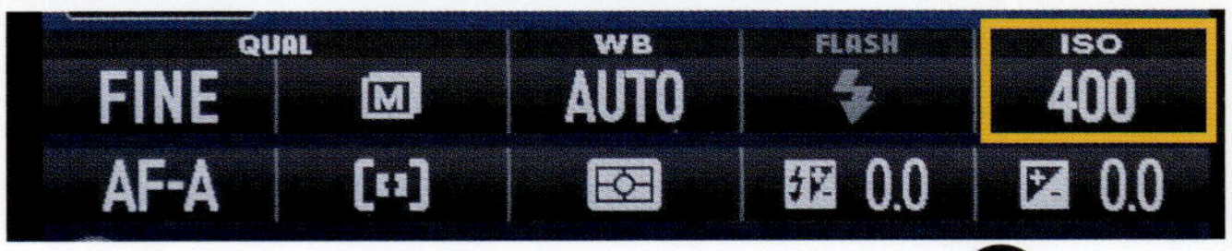

- To change the ISO now, just press the *i* button.
- Go left and right until you get to the ISO setting (*highlighted in yellow box*)
- Press OK and now you should be able to change the ISO sensitivity settings.
- To activate your 2 second timer, press the drive button (*above right*) and then choose the 2 or 10 second timer option.

Task

- Rest your camera on a table or put it on a tripod to keep it still during the exposures and do this task inside.
- Set your camera to its "P" setting and change the ISO setting manually.
- Take 2 pictures of the same object. Take one picture at your lowest ISO and take one at your highest ISO setting.
- Then transfer them onto your computer or zoom in on the camera screen and see the difference between the 2 shots.

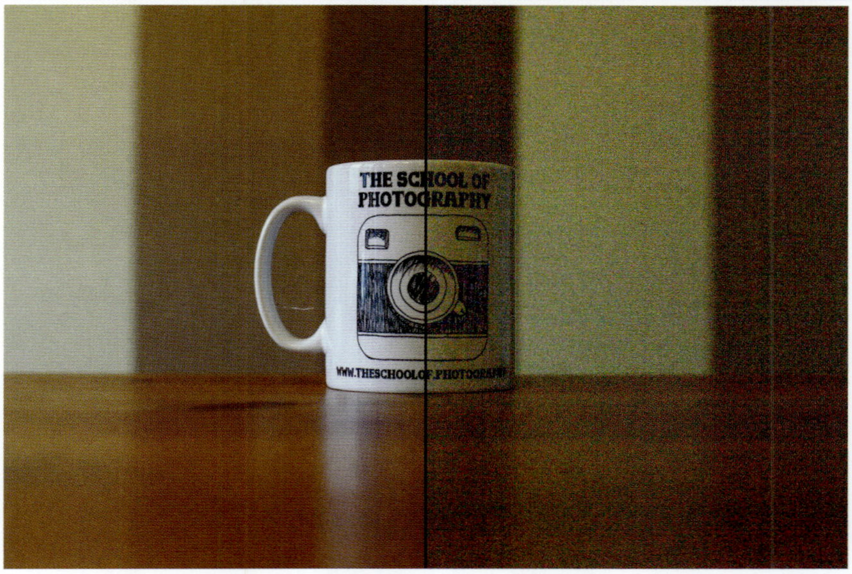

ISO 100 ISO 25600

I hope you can see the difference between the 2 images. All I wanted you to do there was be able to change the ISO manually and recognise within your own pictures when you have noise.

So you use ISO to make your camera more sensitive to light. Ideally you would want to set the ISO at 100 all the time to get no noise in your image, but for that you would always need lots of light and as we know, photography doesn't work like that. So ISO comes into play mainly in low light situations where you don't want to use the flash and you're hand-holding the camera.

We are going do a lot more on controlling and balancing exposures with ISO later on in the book. Remember that learning is layered – one step at a time - and if we do it one step at a time you're going to retain that information better. So, for now, your main focus is to know what ISO is, how to change it on your cameras, and to recognise that high ISO creates noise in your image.

Let's recap:

Your ISO setting is how sensitive you make your camera to light. A low number will require more light, and higher number will require less light.

A disadvantage of a higher ISO is noise in your image, with the advantage being you can take pictures in low light situations without using the flash or getting camera shake.

When you've practiced with this, move on to the next chapter.

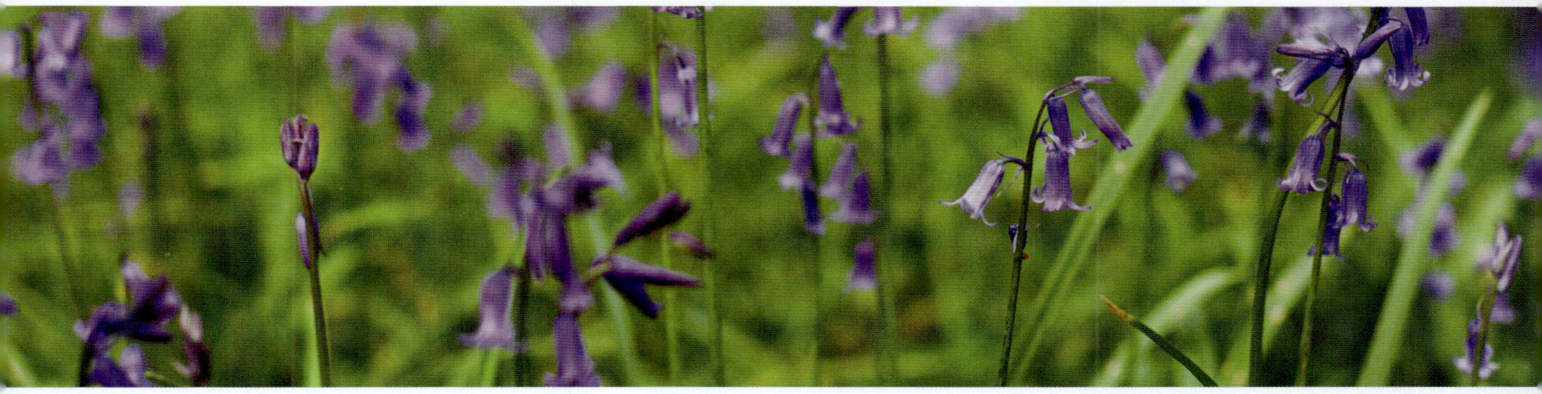

Apertures and Depth of Field

Chapter 9

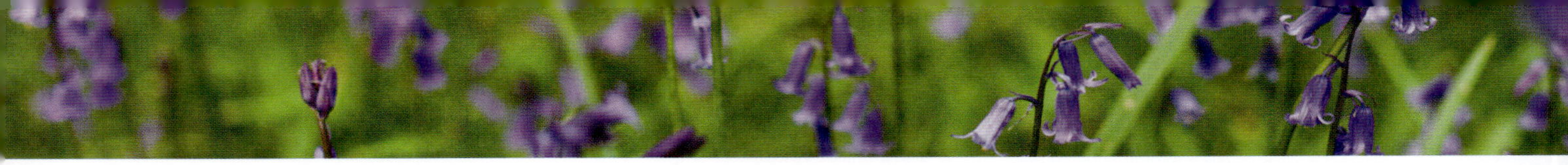

In this chapter, we are going to talk about Apertures and Depth of Field in Photography. Before we get started on that I want you to answer this question.

What is an exposure, in Photography?

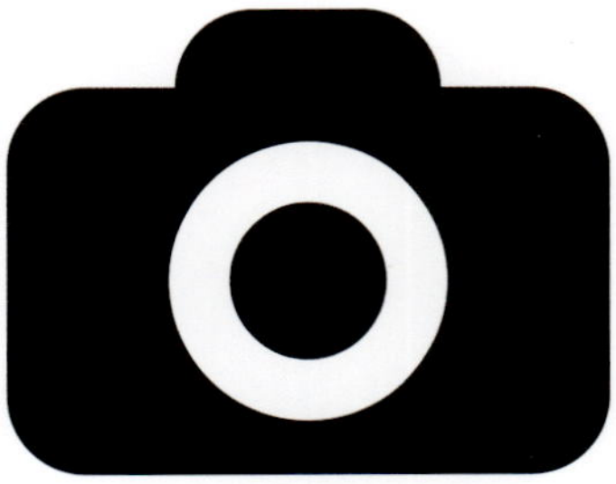

Write down what you think the answer to that question is.

Answer

I ask that question because sometimes people say it's the amount of time you expose for, or it's when the camera takes a picture and theses are partly true.

An exposure in photography is the amount of light you expose your light sensor to in your camera. It's not just the time you expose for, it's the amount of light you let into your camera. Sometimes people can get a bit confused with that so I want to establish that first.

An exposure in Photography is made up of two things, the first being your aperture and the other being your shutter speed. So, you can have an exposure of 1/60th second at f8 (highlighted red) - f8 being the aperture and apertures are what we are going to look at in this chapter.

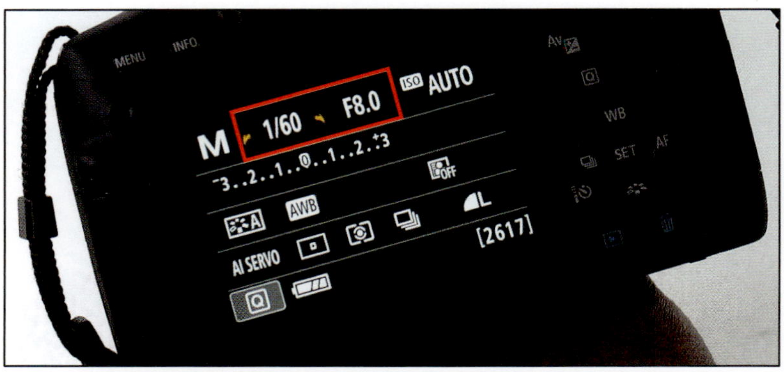

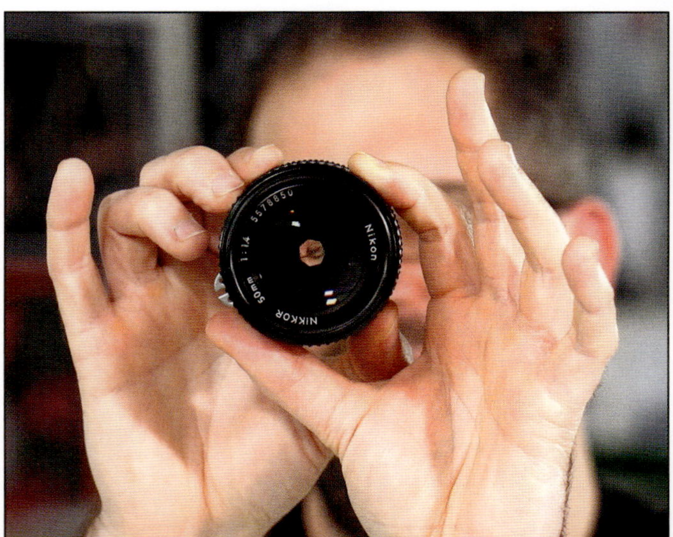

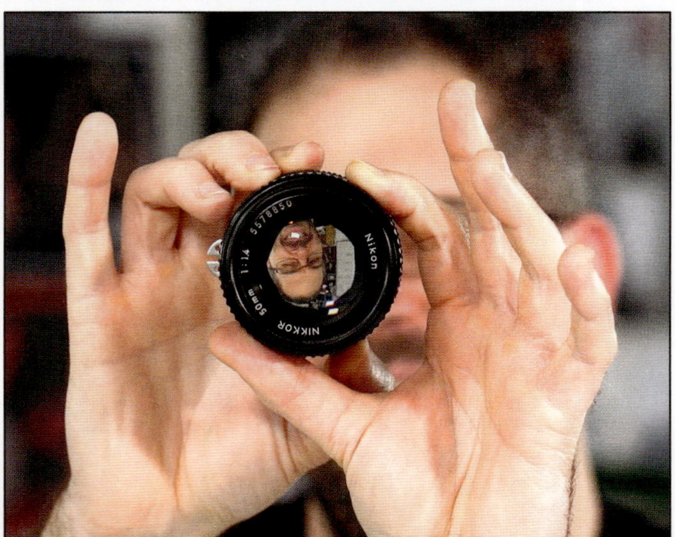

Using an old lens, I can manually show you how the aperture looks in the lens. The left picture being a small aperture and the right being a big or wide aperture. An aperture is held within the camera lens and is basically a hole inside that lens which you can increase or decrease to allow in more or less light, just like the pupil in your eye. When it's bright, your pupil goes really small to block the light and when its dark, your pupil goes big and lets in more light.

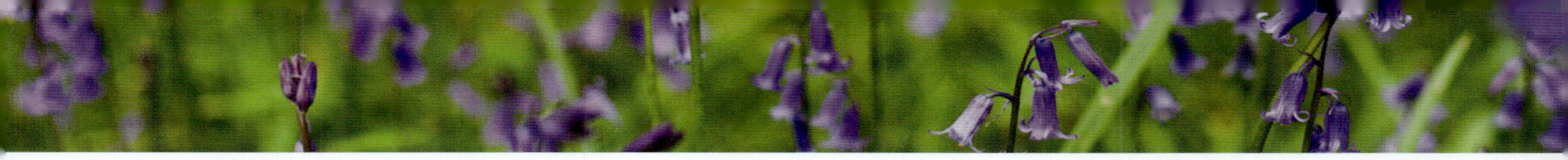

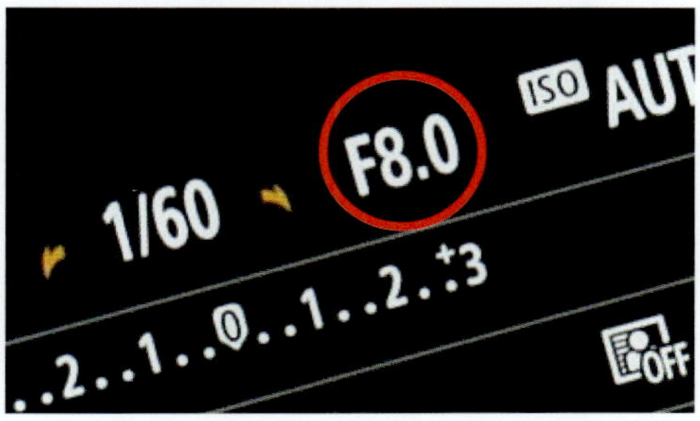

Apertures are identified by a series of numbers with the letter F in front of them. You might have seen them on your cameras, showing f8 or f5.6 and so on. The F stands for Focal Ratio.

Let's look at a typical aperture sequence found on an SLR Camera.

Here's a graph showing a series of number below the apertures.

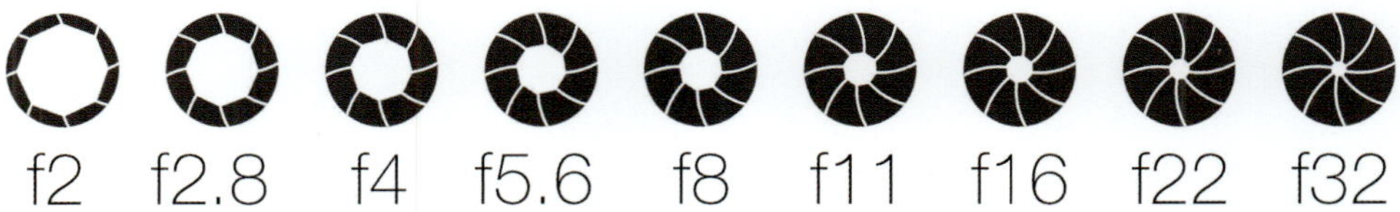

The lower the number, the bigger the hole, and the bigger the number, the smaller the hole. That's the first confusing thing to try and get your head round – it's back to front! The particular F numbers above are really important. You really need to learn these numbers and we'll talk about why that is as this chapter progresses.

You'll find on your cameras numbers in-between those (examples in red), they are called 1/3 stops and I would recommend that you ignore them for now and only use these particular f numbers until you are more confident with apertures and F stops.

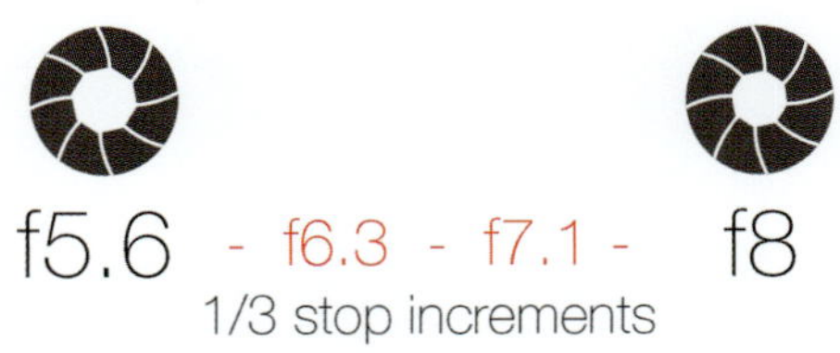

Task

For now, just as little warm up, I'm going to get you to use your Aperture Priority setting on your cameras, its either called AV or A. Your AV or A setting is where you tell the camera what aperture you want to shoot at and the camera will decide the rest for you. The camera will set the shutter speed and ISO for you, if you have your ISO on auto, to give you the correct exposure to light.

Take a few pictures using different apertures. I just want you to see what happens and I want you to be a bit more comfortable in the Aperture Priority setting. Again, below is a guide on how to do this on common cameras, if you get stuck refer to your camera's manual under Aperture Priority.

Canon

- On a canon, turn your wheel to Av (Aperture Priority) and when you turn the dial on top of the camera, your F number will change.

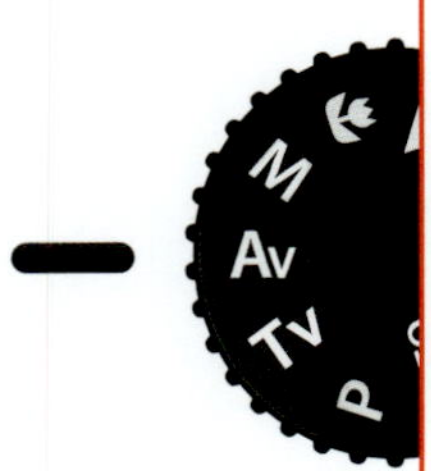

- Make sure your ISO is on Auto. Your camera will now change the shutter speed and ISO to correctly exposure for the the F number.

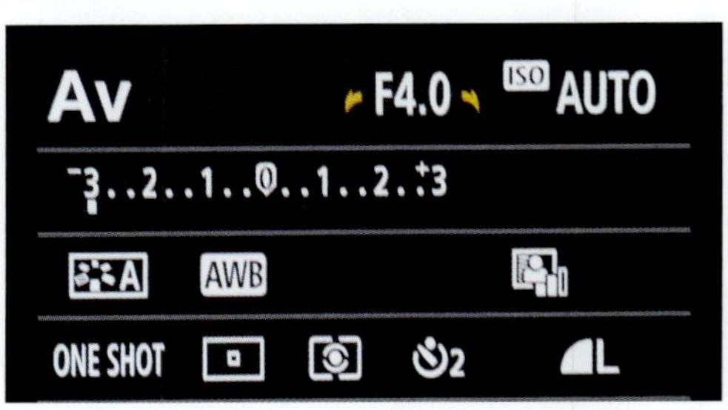

Nikon

- On a Nikon, turn your wheel to A (Aperture priority).
- Then, turn the dial on the back or front of the camera
- You should see the F number changing.
- Make sure your ISO is on Auto.

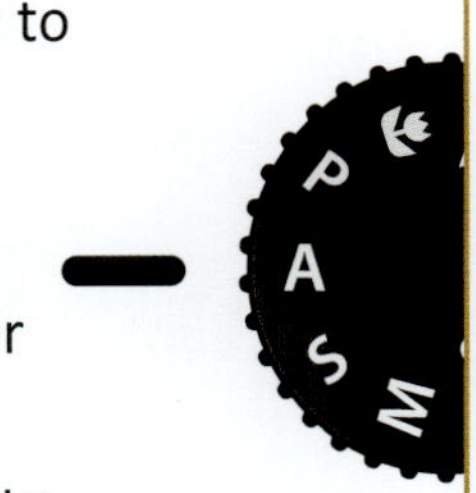

Your camera will now change the shutter speed and ISO to correctly exposure for the F number.

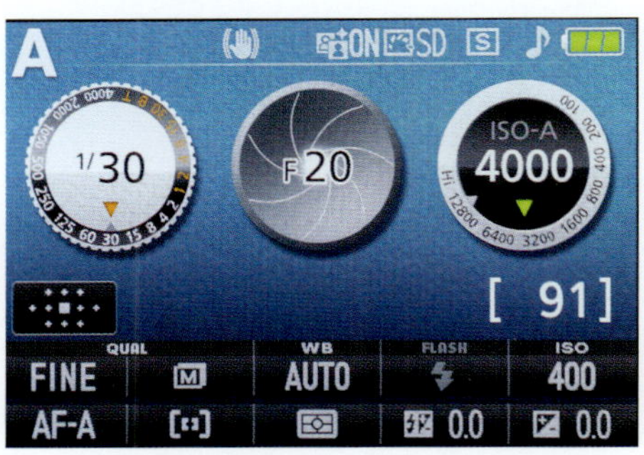

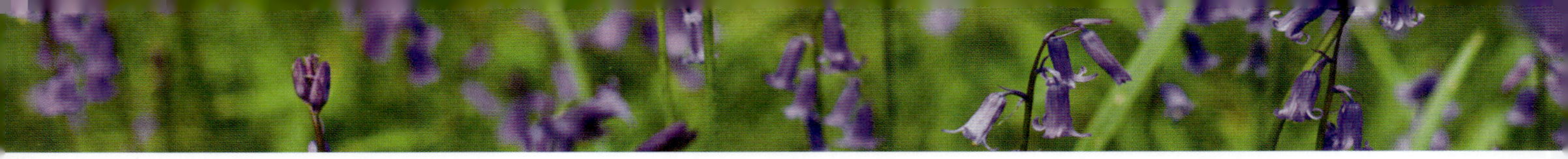

Now for some maths!

When you're balancing light coming into your camera, you need to know some mathematics I'm afraid - it's just part of Photography. I'm going to give you a quick question. Here's a picture showing f4, f5.6 and f8.

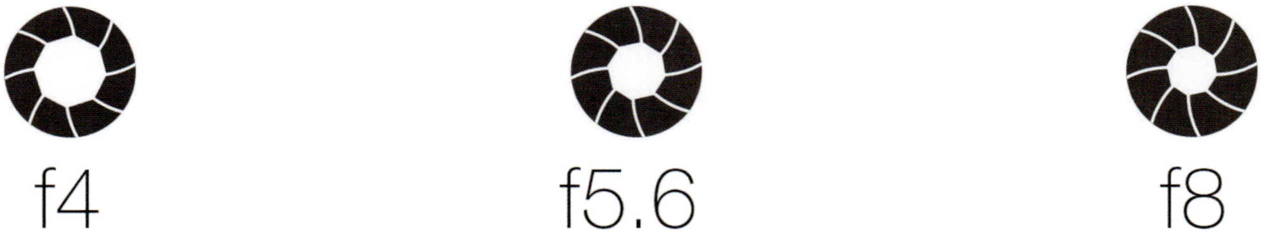

When you go from f4 to f5.6 you are reducing the amount of light. You can see that quite clearly as the hole is getting smaller.

How much, in a percentage, is the light being reduced by?

You're just having a guess for now, but it's more simple that you think!

Answer

Here's your answer. If you're going from f4 to f5.6 you are reducing the light by 50%. You're halving the amount of light. If you go from 5.6 to f8 you are halving the amount of light again. If you go the other way, f8 to f5.6, you're doubling the amount of light. This is one of the reasons why these numbers are so important and why the 1/3 of stops are not so important at this stage of your learning.

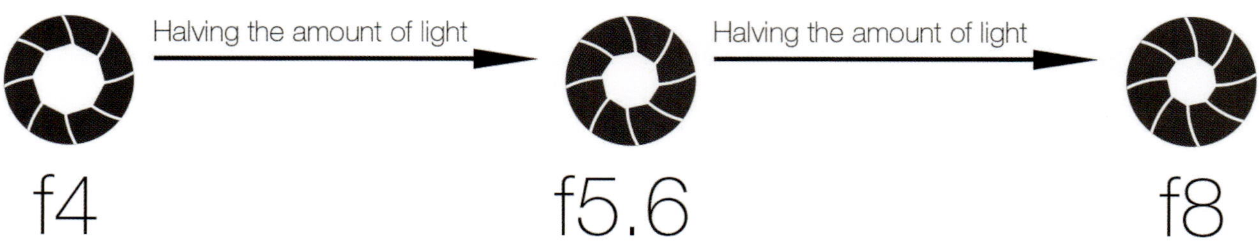

Also by going from these numbers, f4 to f5.6, you are going 1 stop down. If you go from f5.6 to f8 you are going another stop down. This is when it starts to get complicated, but try to simplify it in your head by associating it with light not numbers for now. Is the amount of light you let into the camera more or less than before? If it's more light you're stopping up, if its less you are stopping down.

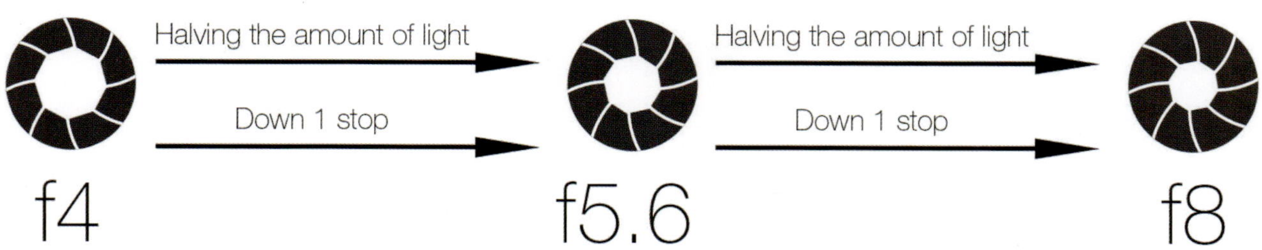

This is important to know as it's a professional term and eventually, knowing your stops will make your balancing of exposures very easy. For instance, if a shot is too dark, it's common to say that shot needs to be a stop brighter, which basically means double the amount of light coming into the camera. You also use stops in shutter speeds, ISO and post-processing programs, so getting used to them is really important to gain full control of your exposures. It will take time and practice but will be worth it in the end!

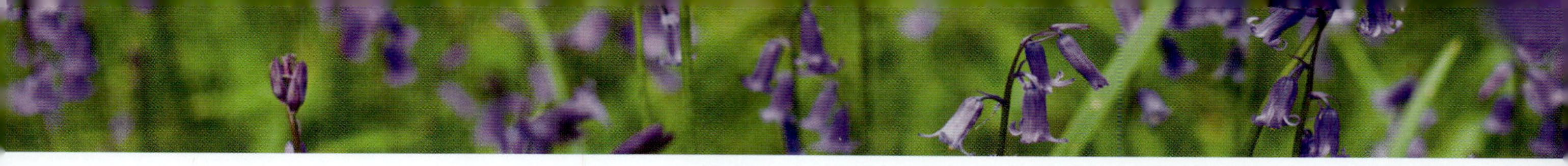

Here's another picture just to reinforce this. If we start at f4 and go to f11, we are going 3 stops down and what that actually means is you're reducing the light by half, half again and half again.

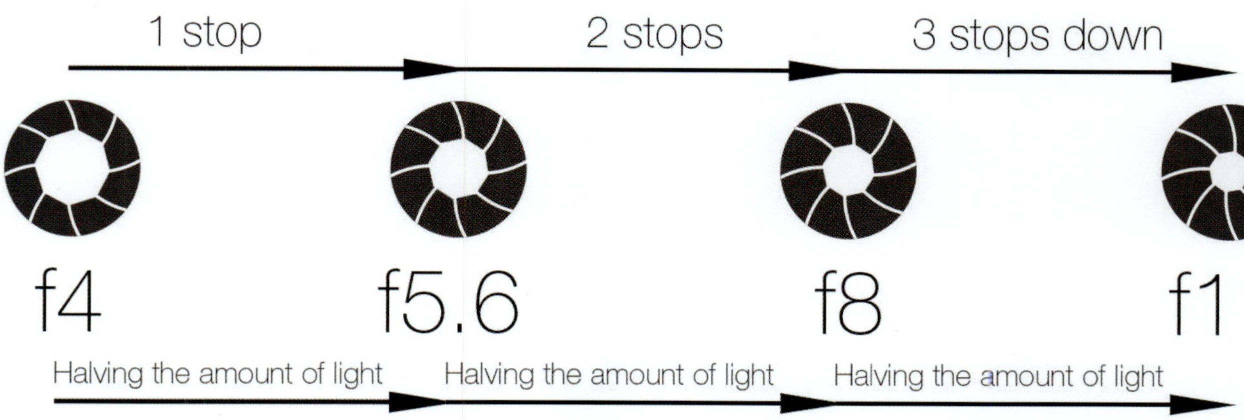

Let's go back to the aperture sequence. The wider the aperture, the more light you're letting in, the smaller the aperture, the less light you're letting in. The wider the aperture the less 'Depth of Field' you get, the smaller the aperture the more Depth of Field you get.

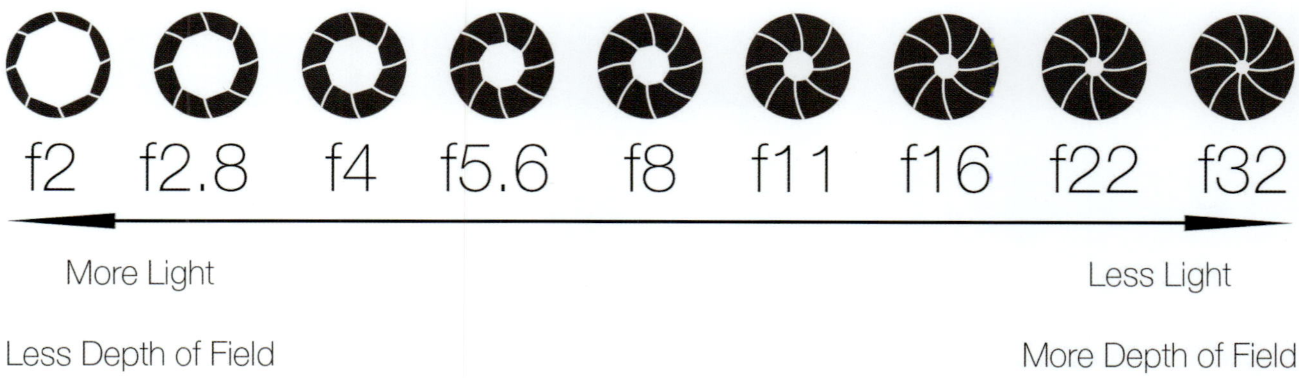

Here's another question

What is an depth of field, in Photography?

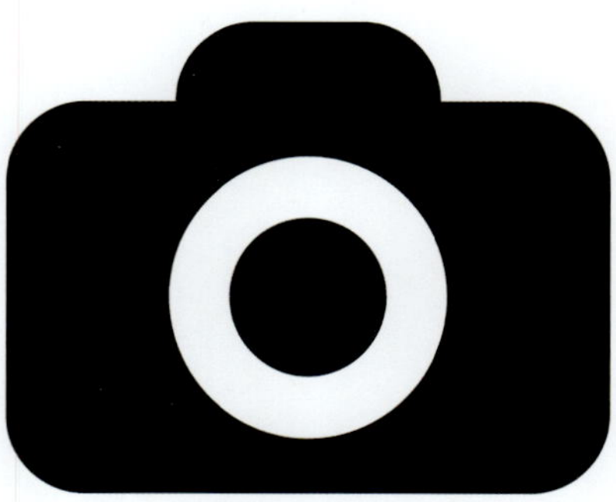

Write down what you think the answer is.

Answer

Depth of field is the amount of distance in an image that is sharp. I ask the question because a lot of people think it's what's in focus and it's not. Your focus point is your focus point. Depth of field is the distance around your focus point that is sharp.

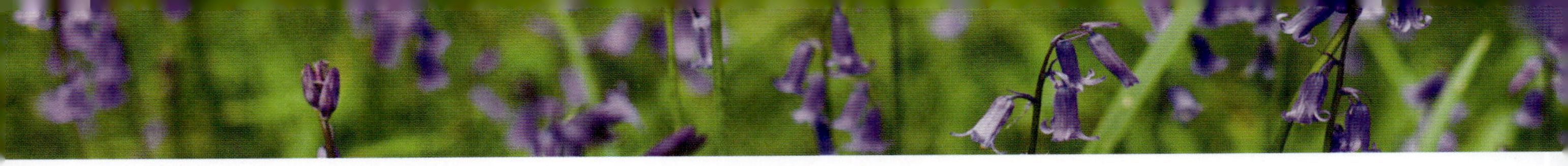

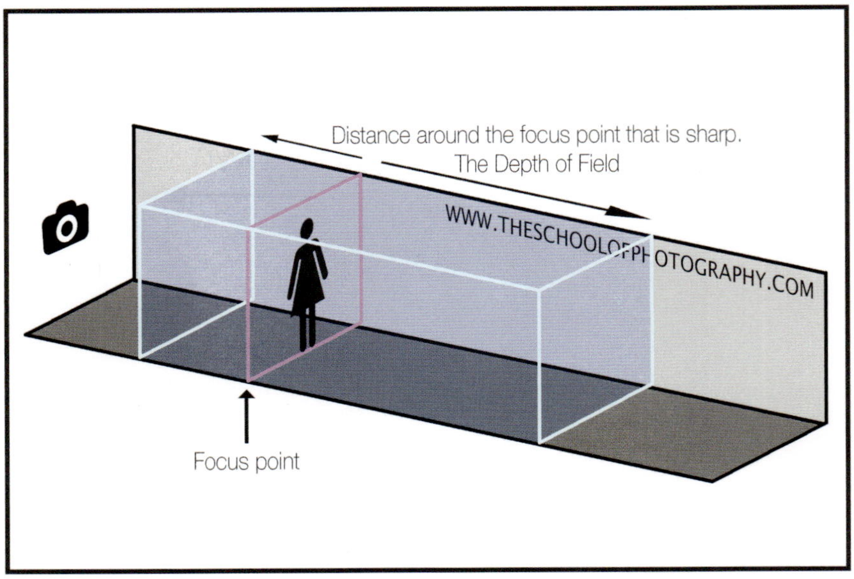

The purple square represents the focus point, and the shaded area is the depth of field around that focus point.

Depth of Field is controlled by 3 things in photography. The first thing is the aperture. Again, the smaller the aperture, the longer the depth of field. The bigger the aperture, the shallower the depth of field.

f2.8

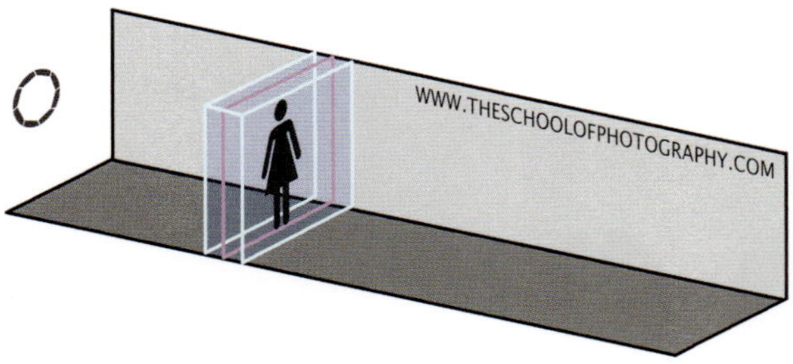

This illustration is representing f2.8. A big aperture like this gives a shallow depth of field. A very short distance around your focus point will be sharp, the rest will be blurred.

f5.6

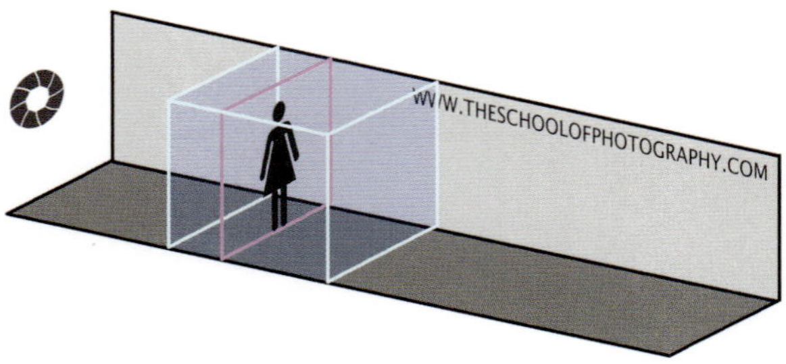

Then this one is representing f5.6, a medium size aperture. You can see the focus point is the same, it's on the person, but the distance around her that is sharp has increased. The 'depth of field' has increased.

f16

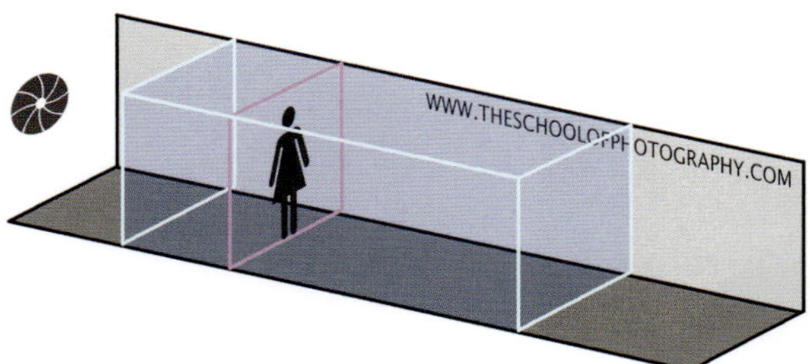

This illustration is representing f16 which is a small aperture. A small aperture will give you a long depth of field. More distance, around your focus point, will be sharp.

Task

Control 'Depth of Field' using Apertures

This task is to get you used to working with apertures and to get you to physically see the effect they have on an image. Setting your camera as per the below instructions have been covered in previous chapters, so please refer back if you need to.

- Put your camera on its Aperture Priority setting (AV or A)
- Put your ISO on Auto
- Make sure your AF point is set to centre frame
- Put your camera's lens on a focal length of around 35 - 50mm
- You also need set your camera up on a tripod and have it set to its 2 second timer or use a remote trigger so the camera stays in the same place and doesn't move during exposures.

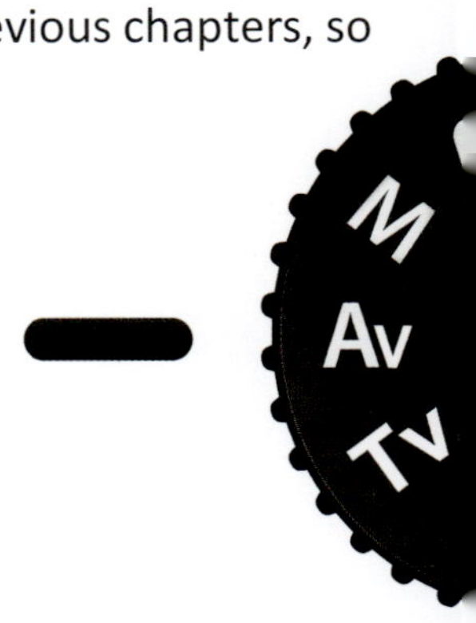

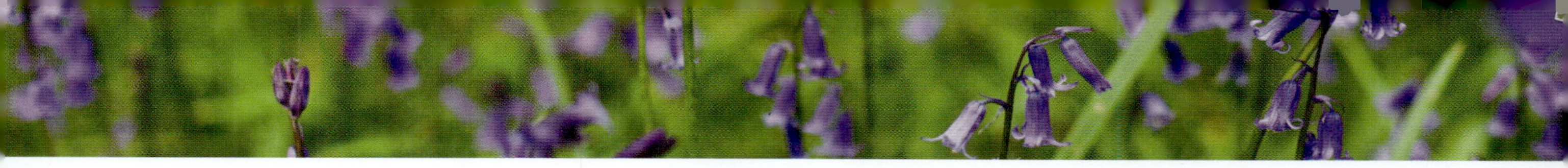

Control 'Depth of Field' using Apertures

Task

- Find a long wall or fence that has a lot of distance and make sure there's a lot of light, daytime is fine.
- Look down the fence/wall at an angle and find a focus point. Make sure that your focus point stays the same in each shot, and that your camera is firmly on the tripod as it needs to be dead still.
- Then take shots going through your apertures in the numbers mentioned previously in this chapter. NB. Different lenses may not have all the numbers shown so simply use the ones you have on your lens.
- Then compare the shots to see the depth of field change, it's best to view them on a computer screen.

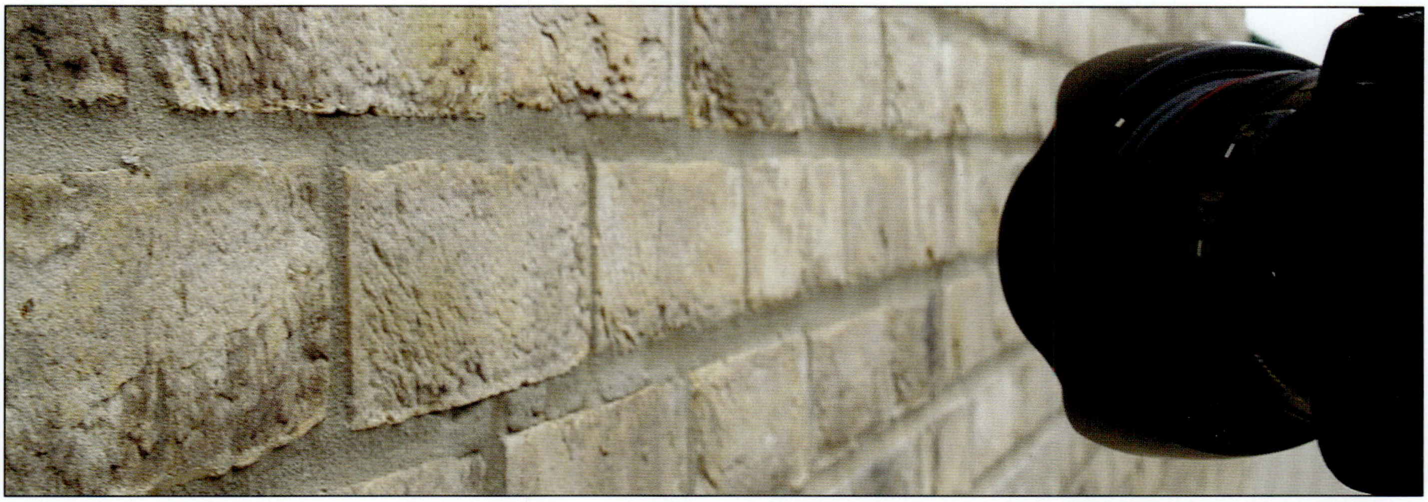

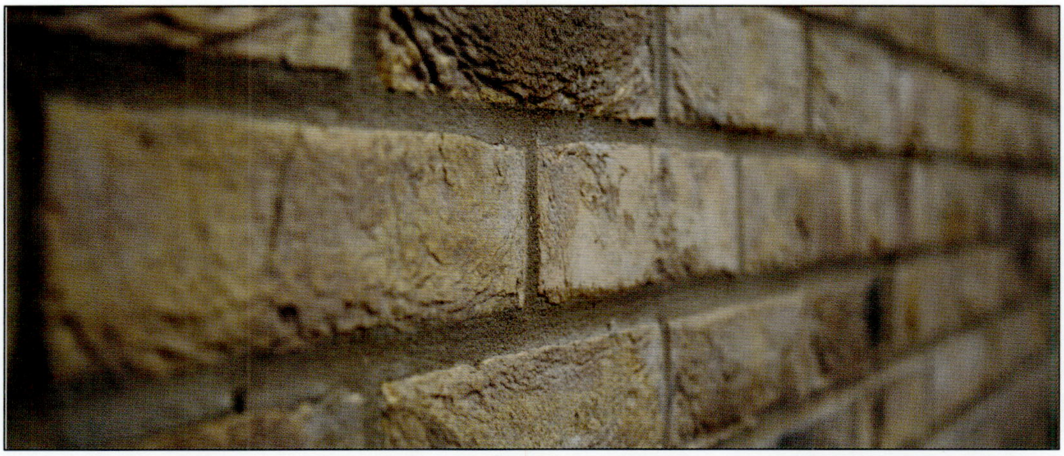

f4 (shallow depth of field)

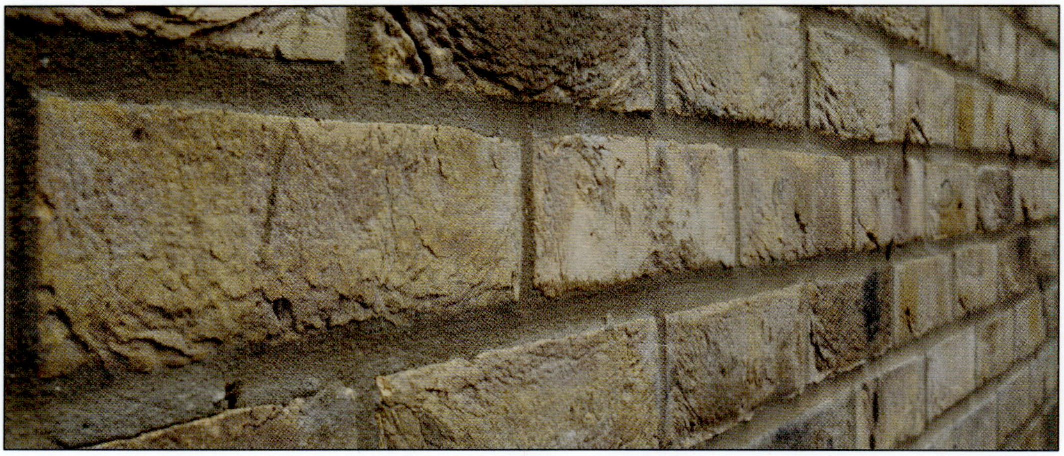

f22 (Long depth of field)

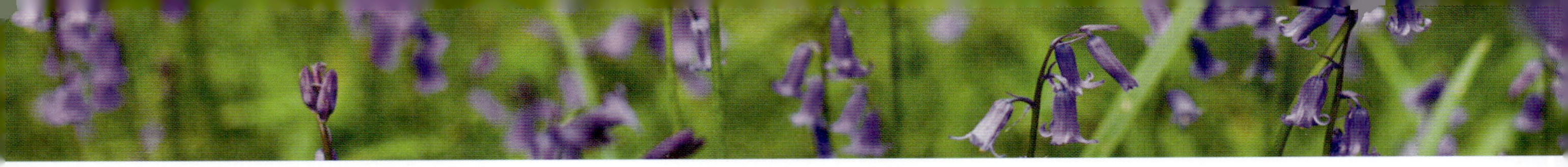

Example: Notice the difference in the depth of field between all of the shots.

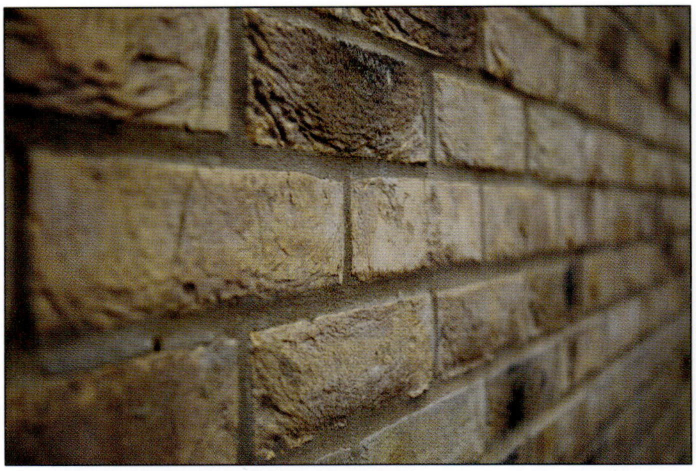

f4 (shallow depth of field)

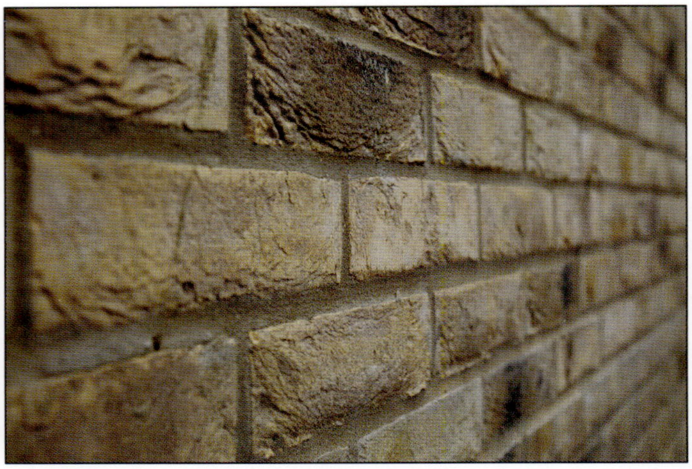

f5.6

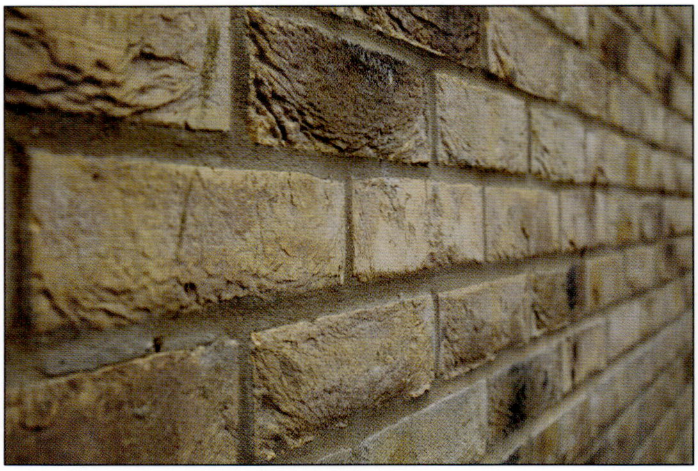

f8

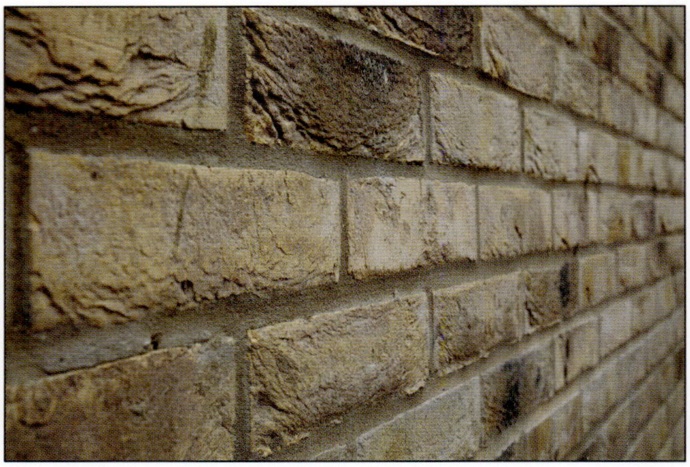

f11

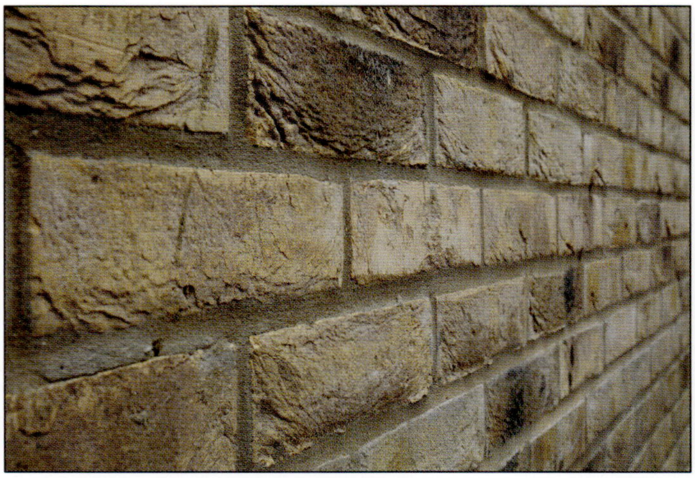

f16

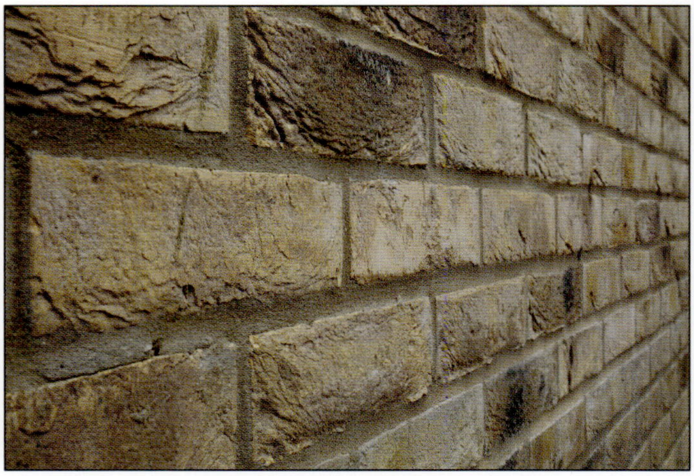

f22 (Long depth of field)

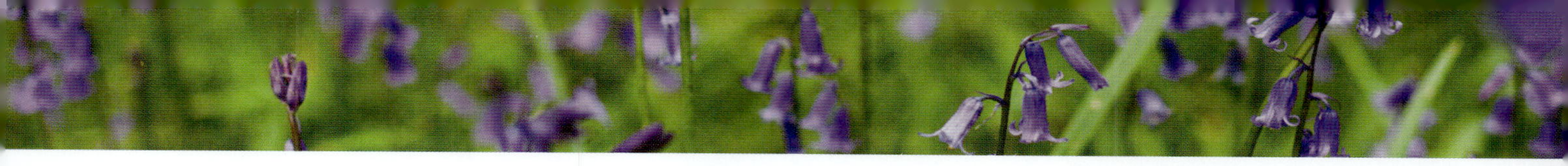

There are another 2 elements that will control your depth of field. One of them being the focal length that you use. We've already done a whole section on lenses and focal lengths, refer back to that chapter if you need to, but in short it is how zoomed in or zoomed out you are.

It's really simple to understand. The more zoomed in you are, the shallower the depth of field you can create. The more zoomed out you are, the longer the depth of field you can create.

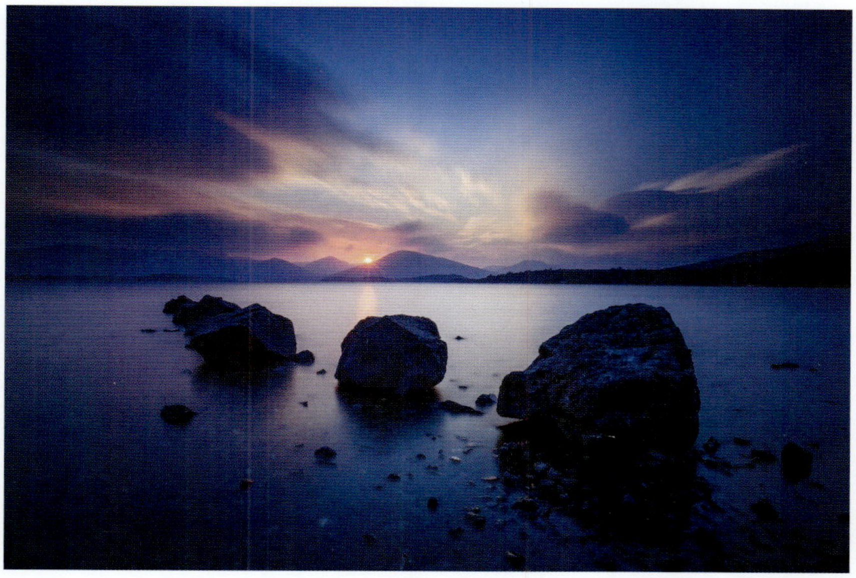

A way to prove this is to think of landscape shots which are normally taken at wide angles, zoomed out; they are sharp from the foreground to the background which shows a long Depth of Field.

Whereas portrait shots are generally zoomed in more which helps make the background blurry giving it a shallow depth of field.

Task

Control 'Depth of Field' using the lens's Focal Length

- Keep your camera on the same settings as before but this time put your camera's aperture on f5.6.
- Zoom out as far as your lens can and take a picture of the same fence/wall.
- Then zoom in as far as you can and take the same picture with the same aperture.
- Compare the 2 shots.

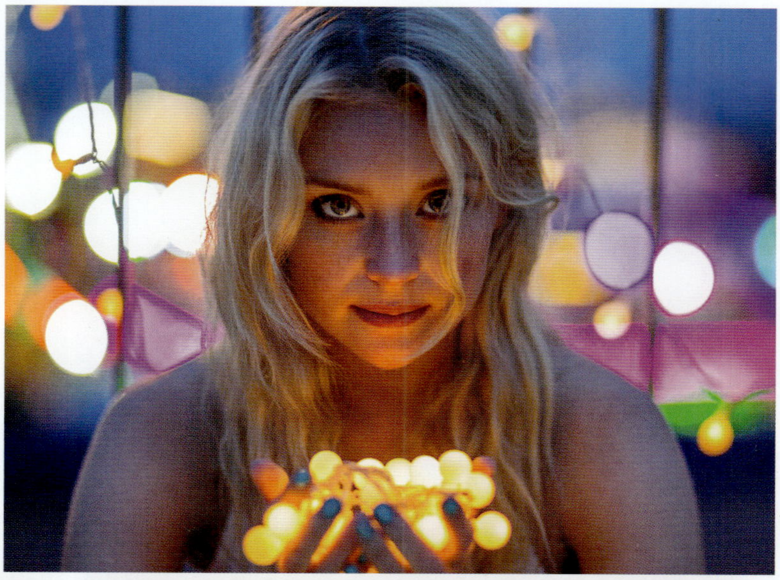

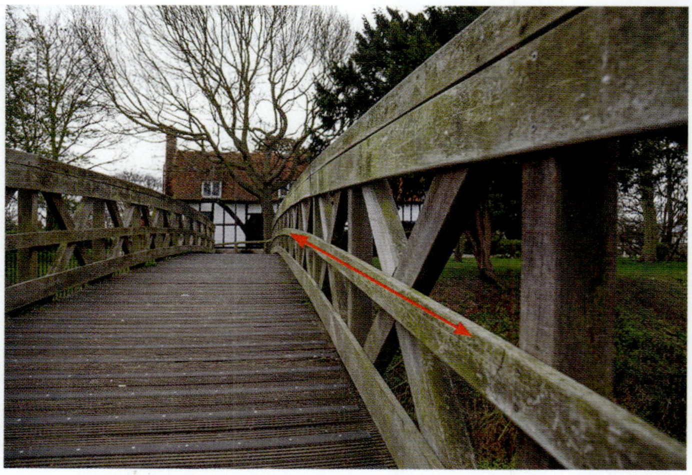

Focal Length 24mm - f5.6

- Wide angle
- Long Depth of Field (symbolised by red arrow)

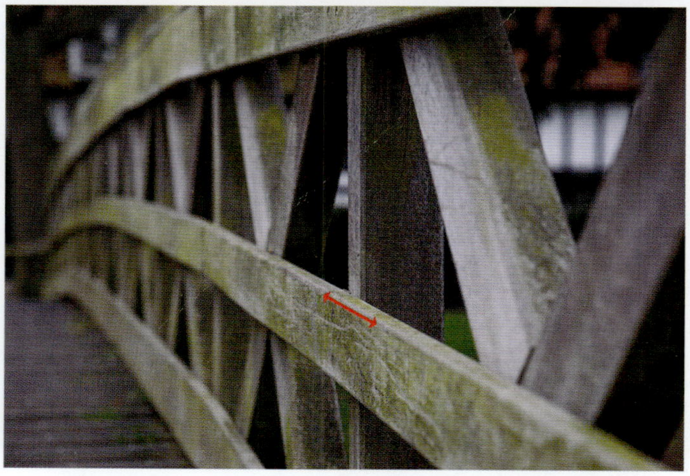

Focal Length 105mm - f5.6

- Zoomed in
- Shallow Depth of Field

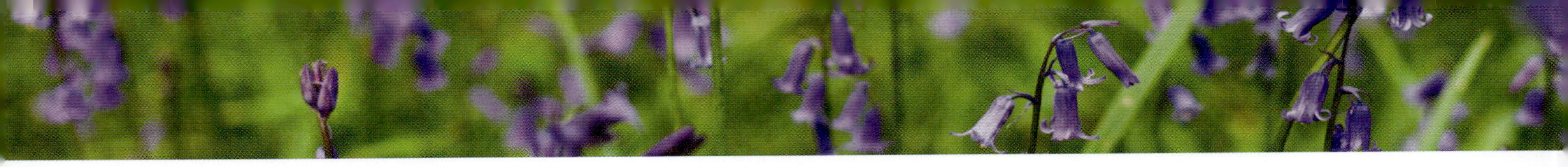

The third thing that controls depth of field is the distance of your focus point from your lens. If your focus point is close to your lens you will get a shallower depth of field. If your focus point is far away from your lens, you'll get a longer depth of field.

Here's a couple of examples:

Both of these pictures were taken with an aperture of f2.8 and a focal length of 50mm. The only thing that's different is the distance of the focus point.

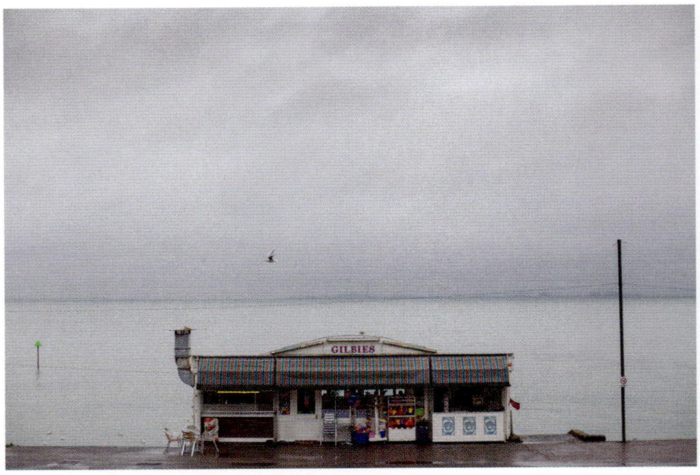

- The focus point is in the distance.
- Gives a longer depth of field.

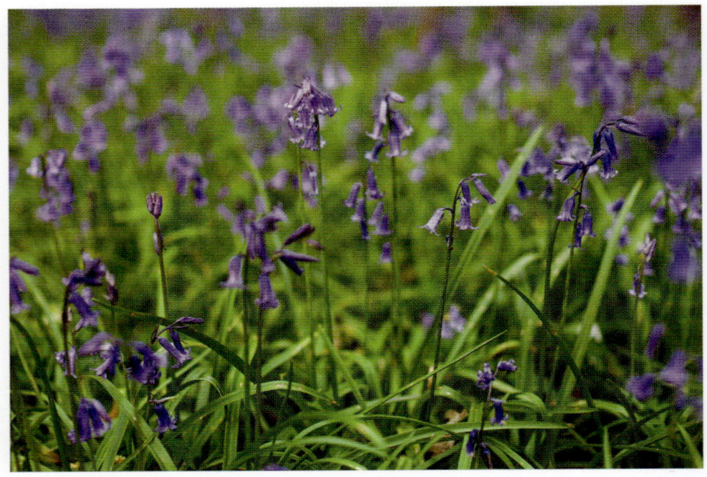

- The focus point is close to the lens.
- Gives a shallower depth of field.

Task

Control 'Depth of Field' using the distance of focus point from your lens

- Keep your camera on the same settings as before but set the lens' focal length to 50mm.
- Keeping your camera on a tripod, take a picture of the same fence/wall and make sure you are as close as you can but still keeping it in focus.
- Then walk backwards a few steps so that the focus point is now further away and take another shot.
- Compare the two images.

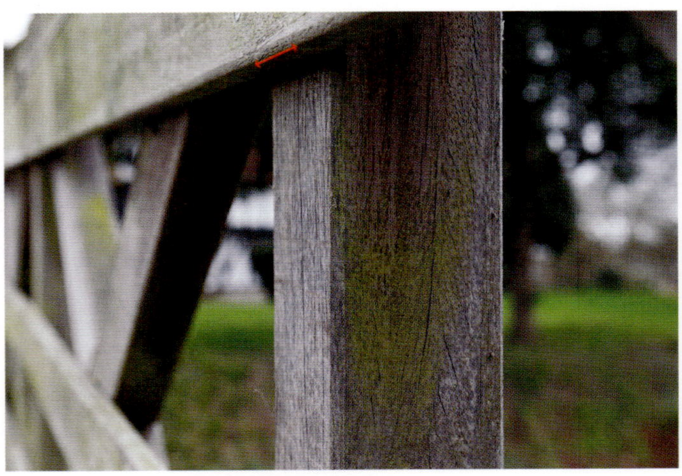

- Focal Length 50mm
- Aperture f5.6
- Focus point is close to the lens.
- Gives a shallower depth of field. (symbolised by red arrow)

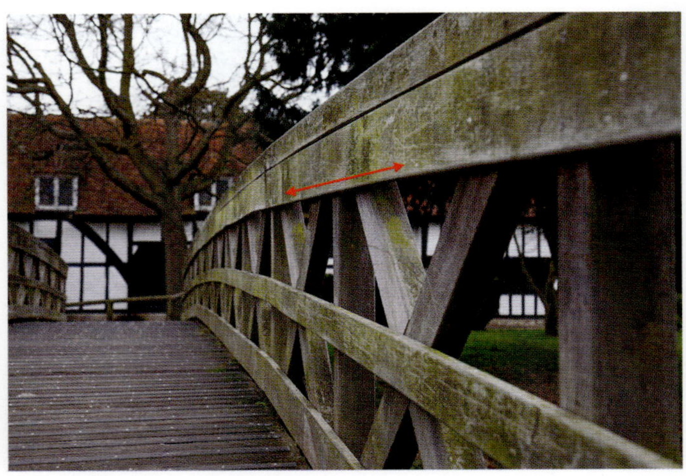

- Focal Length 50mm
- Aperture f5.6
- Focus point is in the distance.
- Gives a longer depth of field.

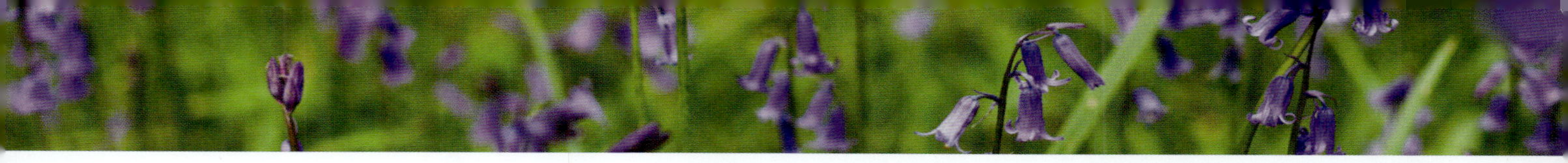

Let's look at some examples of controlling depth of field. These 2 shots were taken 30secs apart but both give totally different visual results.

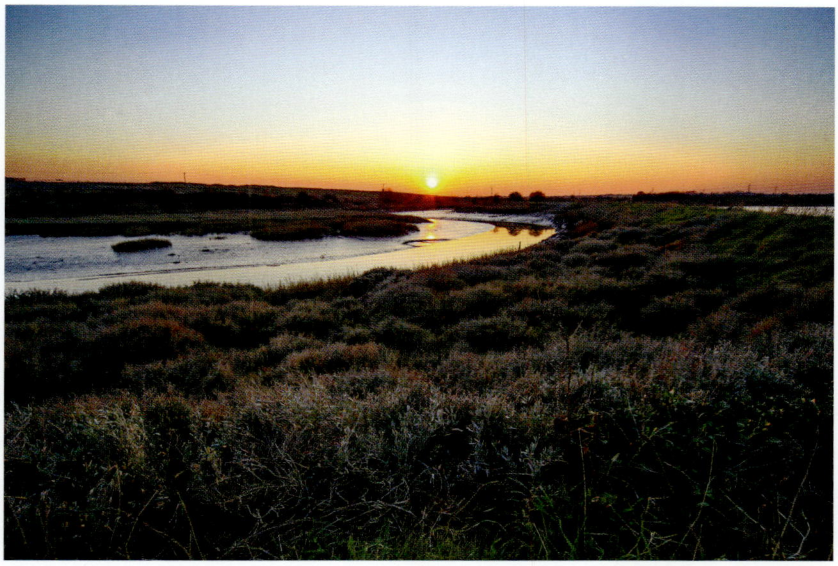

This picture was taken using a wide angle, the focus point was in the distance and the aperture used was F16. What you can see is the whole picture from the foreground to the background is sharp, it shows a long depth of field.

Long D.O.F.
- f16
- Focal length 16mm
- Focus point far away

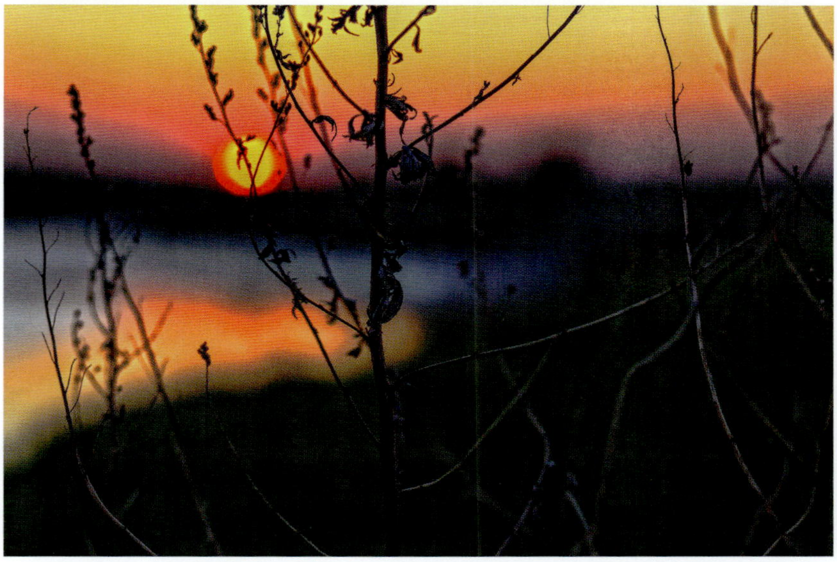

This picture was taken with a focal length of 85mm, an aperture of f2.8 and the focus point is really close to the lens. You can see it has given a really shallow depth of field.

Shallow D.O.F.
- f2.8
- Focal length 85mm
- Focus point close to lens

At this point in your learning you can now start to take more control of your imagery by combining your knowledge learnt. In the photo below I have demonstrated a combination of the different techniques you've learnt so far.

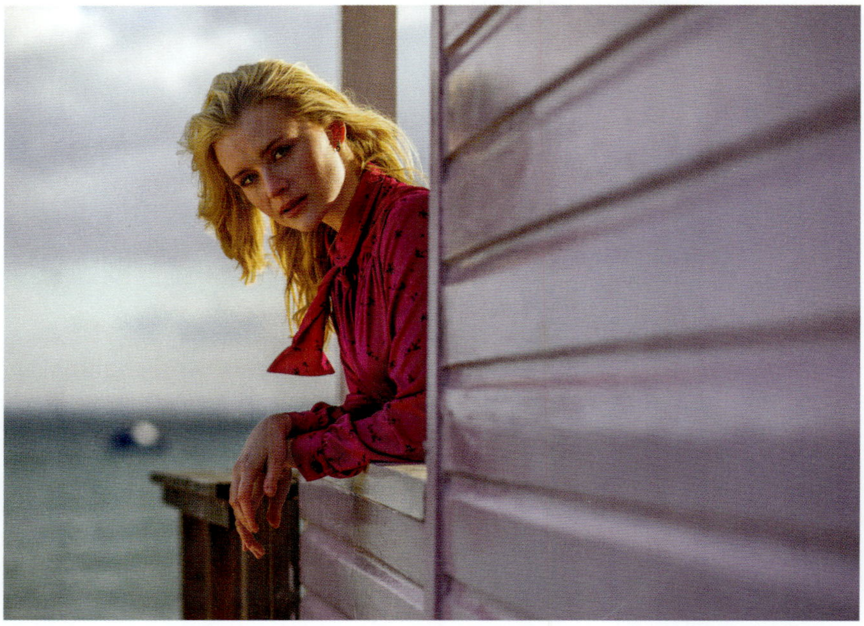

- The focal length was 85mm and the aperture used was f2.8 – This was to give me a shallow depth of field.
- I focused on the face, then - whilst holding the focus - reframed to get the focus point where I wanted it to be.
- I've used a composition where the slats of the beach hut lead you into the model (leading lines).
- As it was a bright day I used an ISO of 100 to give me as little noise as possible.

I have also used lighting and shutter speed techniques which we will get to later in the book.

Try to realise how many techniques you are now using in combination to get your shots.

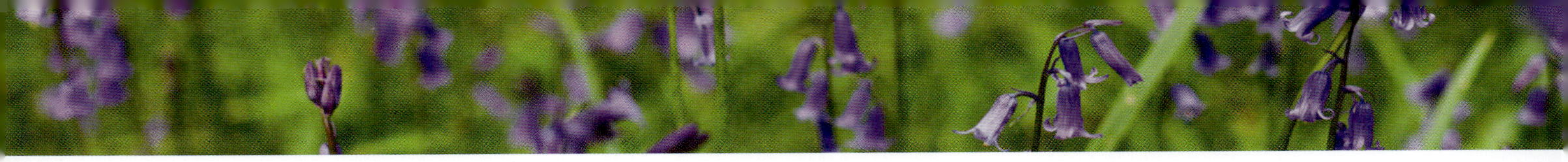

Let's recap on this chapter of Apertures and Depth of Field.

- An aperture is a hole in your lens. The bigger the hole the more light is let in, the smaller the hole the less light is let in, just like the pupil in your eye.
- Apertures are displayed as a series of numbers with the letter F in front of them.
- Try to remember the aperture sequence we've spoken about, which indicate whole stops, and ignore the in-between numbers which are called 1/3 stops for now.

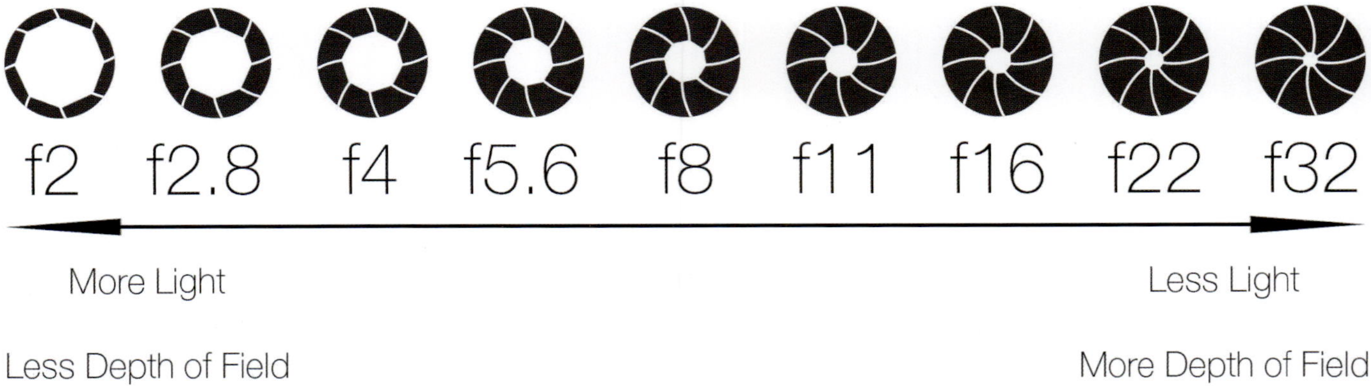

- The A or AV setting on your camera is called Aperture Priority. On this setting you can control the aperture and let the camera do the rest.
- When you go from 1 aperture to the next you are halving or doubling the light, this is why you stick to the aperture sequence I have given you; it will be the same on every camera, everywhere.
- The higher the F number the smaller the aperture, the lower the F number the larger the aperture.
- Going from one number to the next is called a stop, if you're letting in more light, it's called a stop up. If you're letting in less light it's called a stop down. Whilst you're learning, the best thing to do is think about the amount of light that you need first (do you need more or less light) then attached the number afterwards.
- Depth of field is the amount of distance that is sharp around your focus point.
- There are 3 things that control depth of field. The main one being the aperture. A big aperture such as f2.8 will give you a shallow depth of field. A small aperture, such as f16 will give you a long depth of field.
- Your focal length also controls depth of field, the more zoomed out you are, the more depth of field you'll get – such as a landscape. The more zoomed in you are, the shallower depth of field you'll get – such as a portrait.
- The distance of your focus point also controls depth of field. The closer the focus point, the shallower the depth of field. The further away your focus point, the longer depth of field.

To view a video tutorial on panning and slow sync flash go to www.theschoolofphotography.com and type aperture in the search bar.

Shutter Speeds

Chapter 10

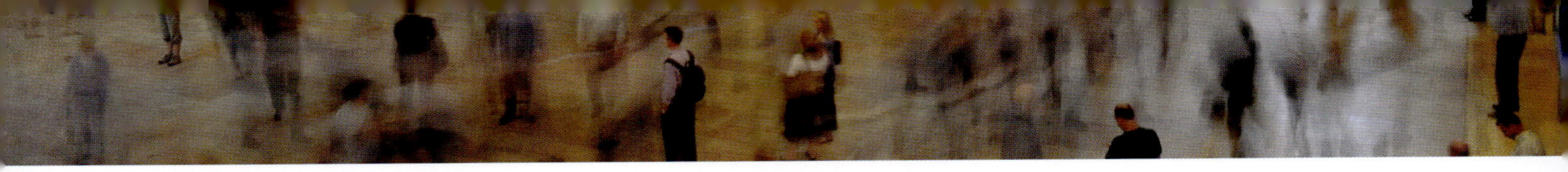

In this chapter, we're going to look at shutter speeds, but before we do I want to recap on what exposure is in photography. An exposure is the amount of light you expose your digital sensor to. An exposure is made up of an aperture, what we've looked at in the previous chapter, and a shutter speed setting. For example, 1/60th of a second at f8. The aperture is the F number. A shutter's job is to let light into the camera over a period of time.

The camera body houses the shutter - below are two pictures showing a shutter open and closed.

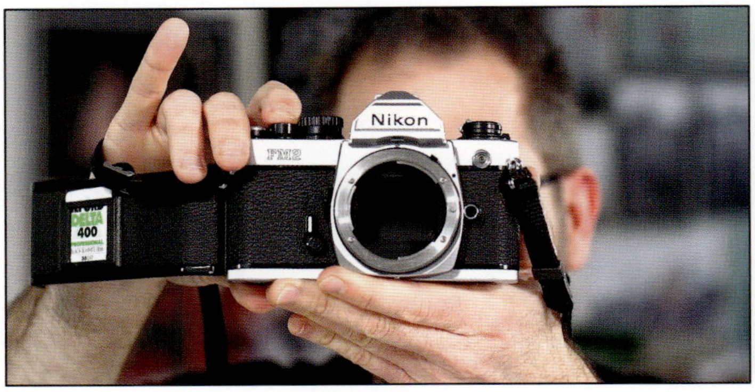

Shutter closed

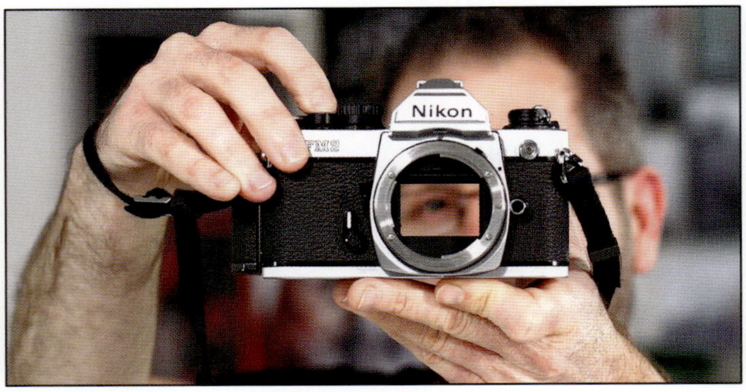

Shutter open

Task

Before we get started, I want you to set your camera to the S or the TV setting (shutter speed priority) and change your shutter speed by turning the dial on your camera. Put your ISO on Auto and take a few shots on different shutter speeds. This is just to get you used to the setting and see the difference in the shots. In this setting you set the shutter speed and your camera will change the aperture and ISO automatically to give a correct exposure (if you have your ISO on Auto).

Again, below is a guide on how to do this on common cameras, if you get stuck refer to your camera's manual under Shutter Speed Priority.

Canon

- Turn your wheel to the Tv position.
- Make sure your ISO is on Auto.
- Move the dial on top of your camera to change the shutter speed. You should see the shutter speed number changing.

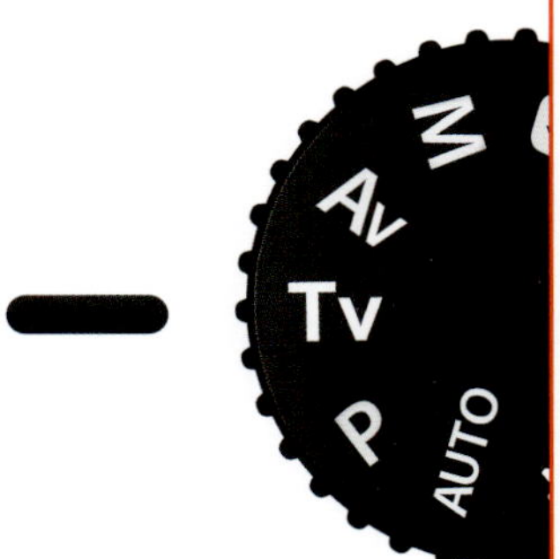

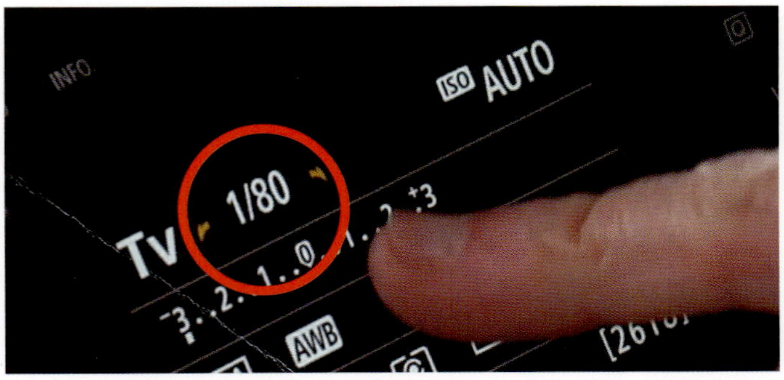

Nikon

- Turn your wheel to the S position.
- Again, make sure your ISO is on Auto for this task.
- Then move the dial at the back or front of your camera to change the shutter speed. You should see the shutter speed number changing.

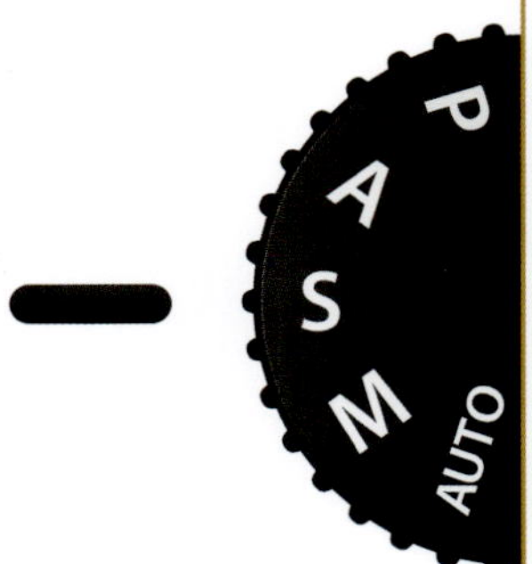

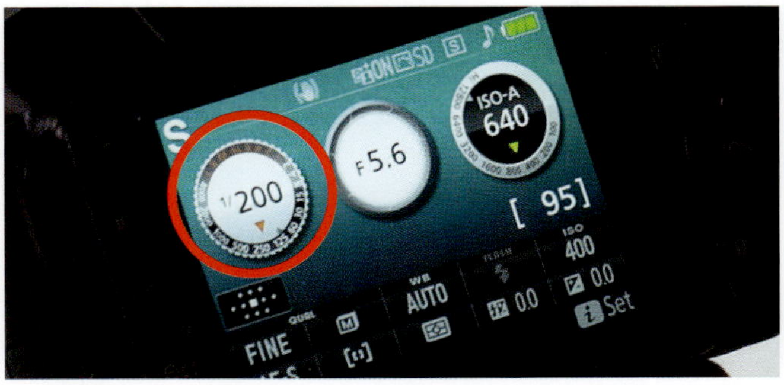

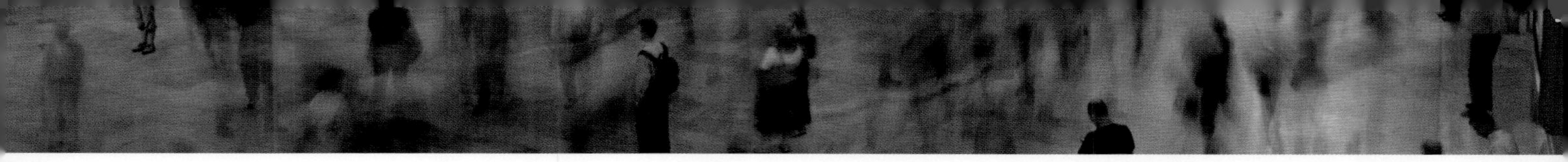

The easiest way to think about shutter speeds is to think about them mathematically as fractions. Here's a whole second.

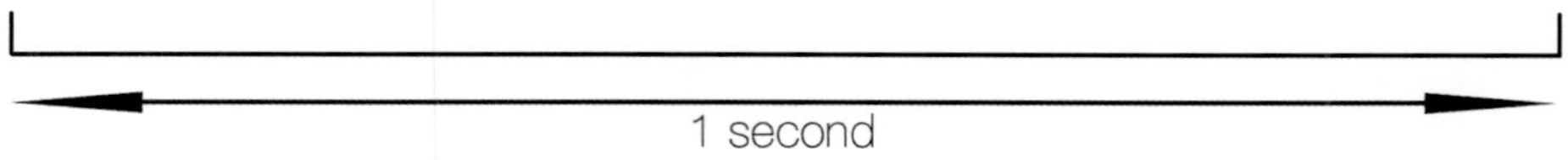

If we split that second in half, we have ½ a second each side, if we split that again it becomes ¼ of a second, half again, 1/8 of a second etc. A shutter speed is a fraction of a second or whole seconds.

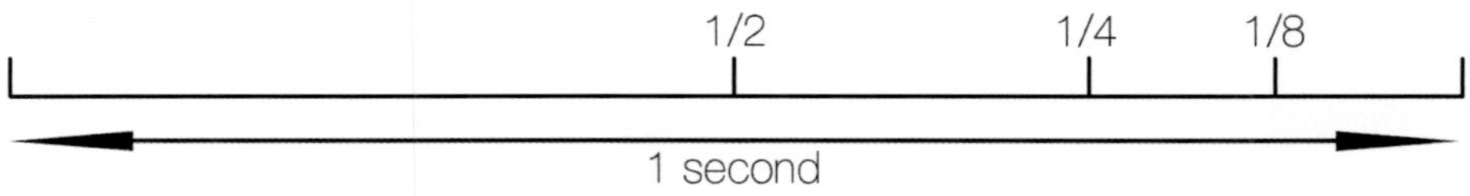

Here is a typical shutter sequence found on SLR cameras. What you can see here is 1 second, ½ sec, ¼ second, 1/8th of a second, 15th and so on. At 1 second you're letting in more light (this is a slow shutter speed) and at 1/1000th of a second, you're letting in a less light (this is a fast shutter speed).

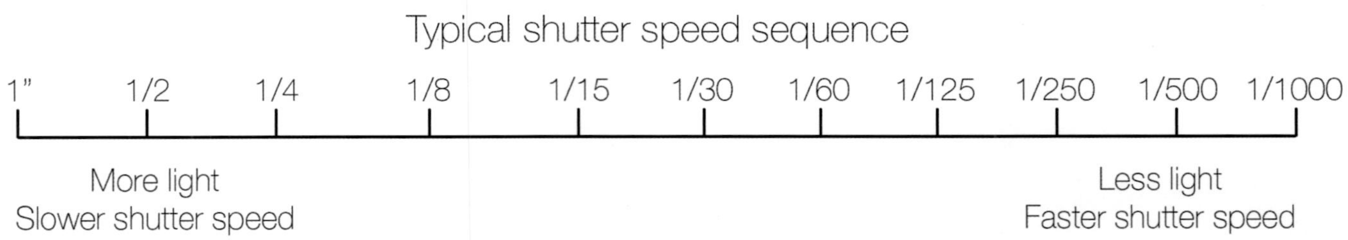

Now those good at maths might be looking at the shutter speed sequence and thinking something is wrong in a few places. You can see it goes 1 sec, ½ a second, ¼ of a second, 1/8th of a second, and these are all halving. But then it jumps to 1/15th of a second which doesn't make sense because half of 1/8th is 1/16th.

This is again another confusing thing that photography does. It's because if you jump from 1/8th to 1/16th it becomes harder to work out the next half fractions. It's changed it to 1/15th to make it easier to half again. So you go from 1/15th to 1/30th to 1/60th and there you can see it changes again for the same reason. You go to 1/125th instead of 1/120th because it makes it easier to half and half again.

Now you might be thinking 'the numbers are doubling but you're saying halving'. I'm saying halving because when it comes to exposure, it's about light and it's really important to understand that. So I'm actually referring to the light, its halving the amount of light coming onto the camera. We'll be coming back to this and putting it into practice a bit later so don't worry too much if it's confusing you for now.

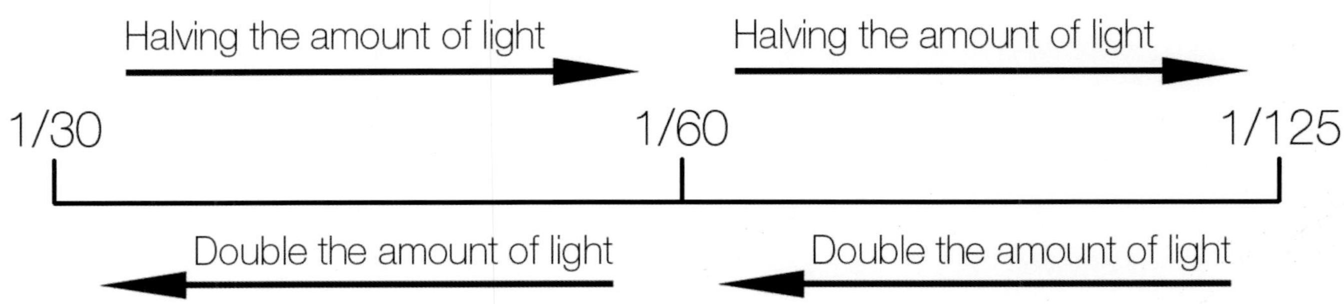

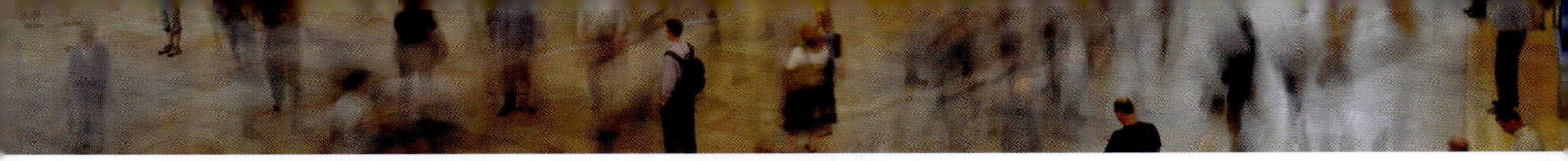

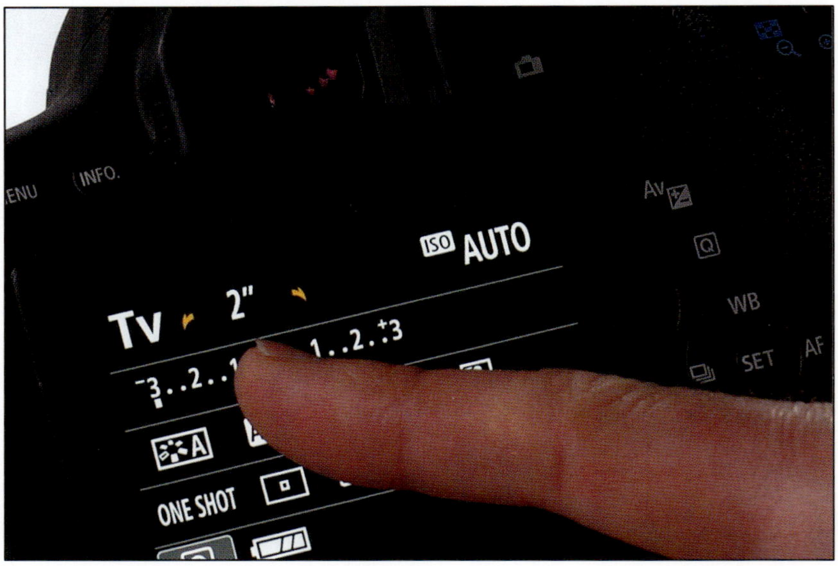

The way shutter speeds are displayed on cameras can also be quite confusing as different camera models show these settings in different ways. Let's take **1/60th of a second** to start with, on most cameras it will be displayed as **1/60** but on some cameras it can be displayed as just **60**. Then when you go from fractions of a second into seconds you will see a number displayed with the quote symbol: "

So if you see 1" that means 1 second if you see 2" it means 2 seconds etc.

On some cameras, you might see ½ second displayed as the half fraction, which makes sense. But on other cameras you will see half a second displayed as 0"5 which means 0.5 seconds. This can be really confusing but the basic rule is when you see a number followed by a " you are in seconds, not fractions of a second. When you see zero followed by a " you are in zero point something. So the camera can show 0"5, which is 0.5 seconds, 0"3 which is 0.3 seconds and so on.

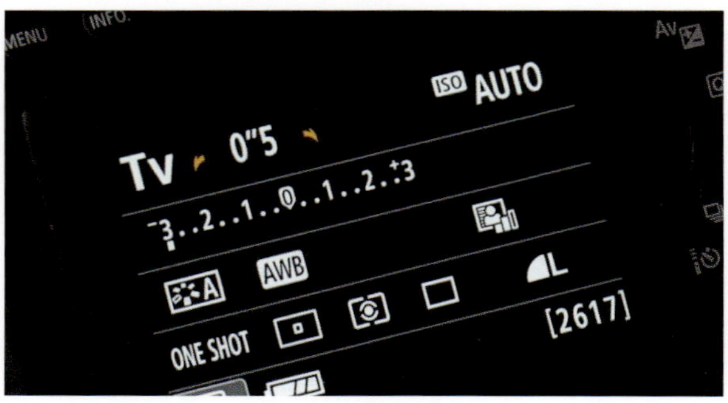

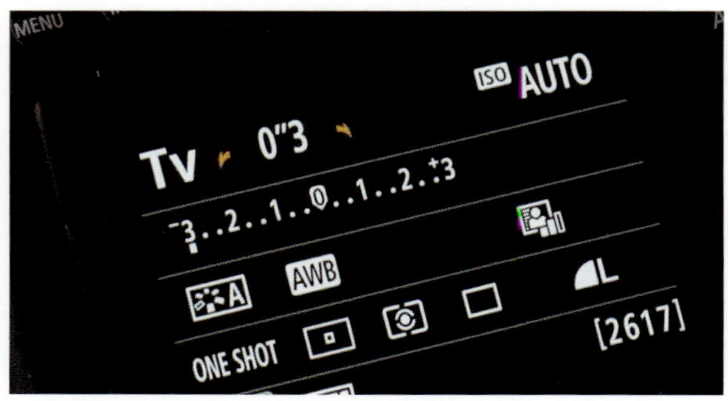

Ok, so if you haven't had enough of maths yet, I've got some more for you. If you remember in the Aperture chapter, we talked about stops. A stop in photography is either halving or doubling the amount of light. The same thing happens with shutter speeds. Have a look at this picture:

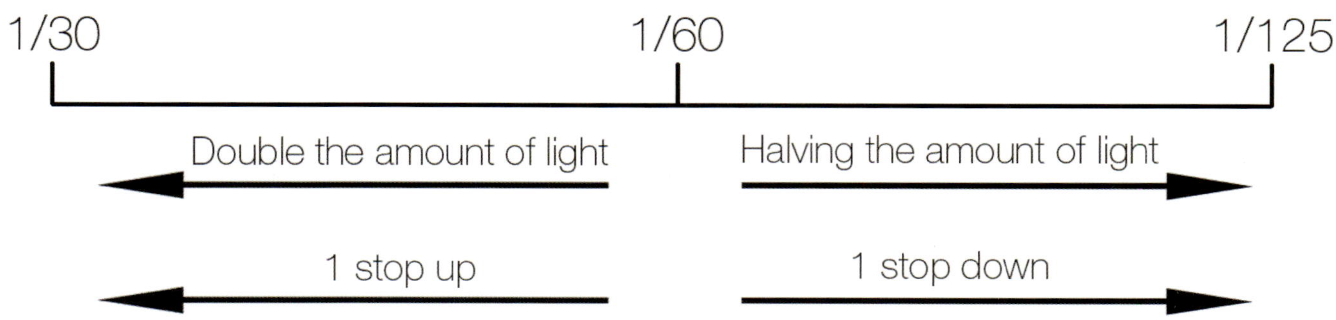

We have 1/60th of a sec on the middle. If we double the amount of light, we go to 1/30th of a second and if we half the amount of light, we go to 1/125th of a second. It gets confusing again because the number is decreasing but the light is increasing, as with aperture numbers, it's all opposite.

When I was learning photography as a young photography student in the 1990's, all this really did confuse me, all these numbers and maths. But I came to the conclusion that photography is back to front, the numbers are simply back to front to what actually happens to the light. If you start to think like that it may help you to understand exposure better.

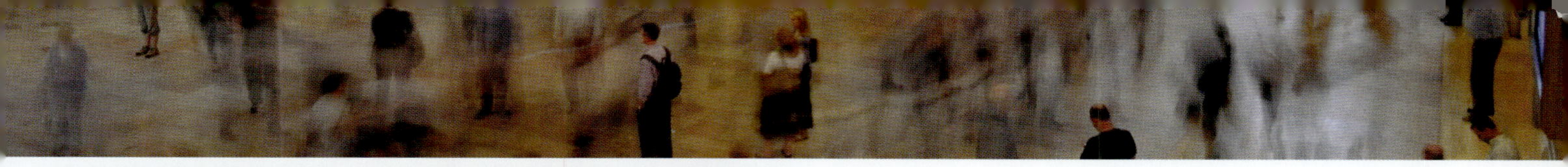

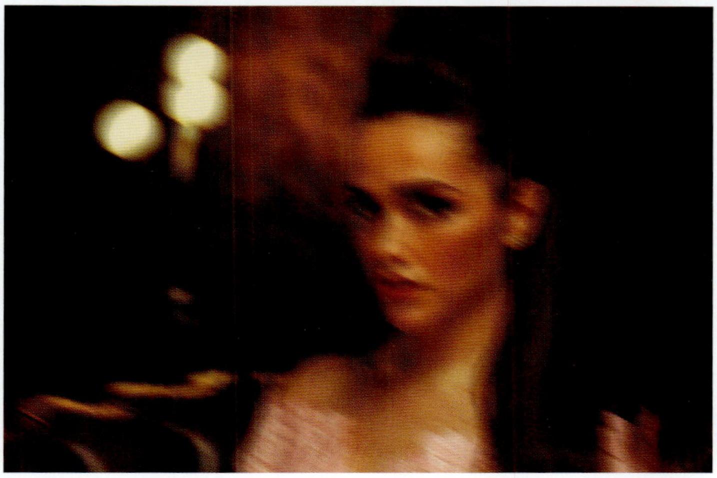

Camera Shake

If you go below $1/60^{th}$ of a sec when you are hand-holding your camera, you're likely to get what is called camera shake; this means the image will blur. Higher focal lengths (zoomed in) will also increase the likelihood of camera shake. To avoid this, use faster shutter speeds or a tripod.

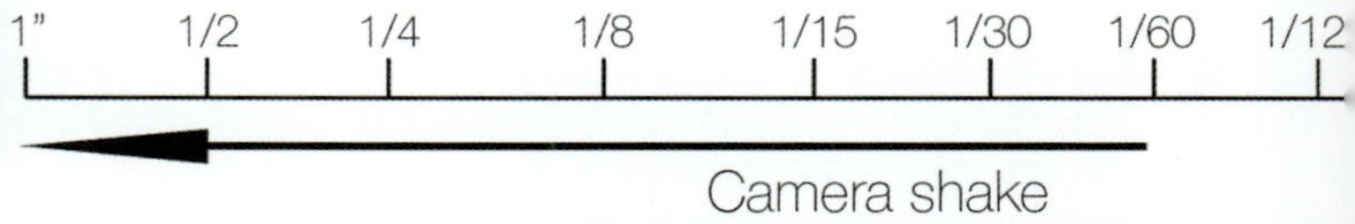

When you go above $1/125^{th}$ of a second, you're creating faster shutter speeds.

Faster shutter speeds are used to freeze the action.

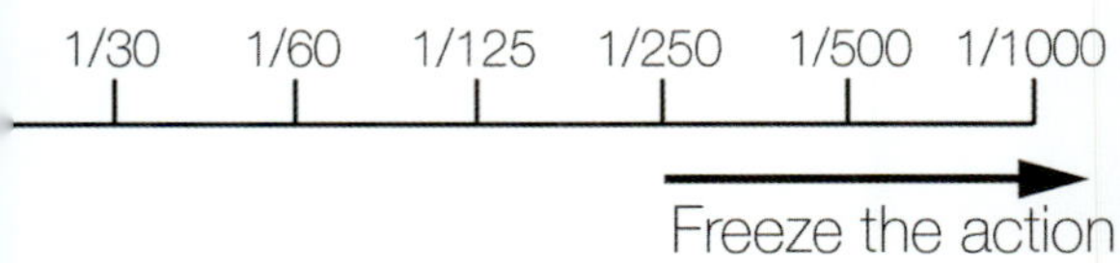

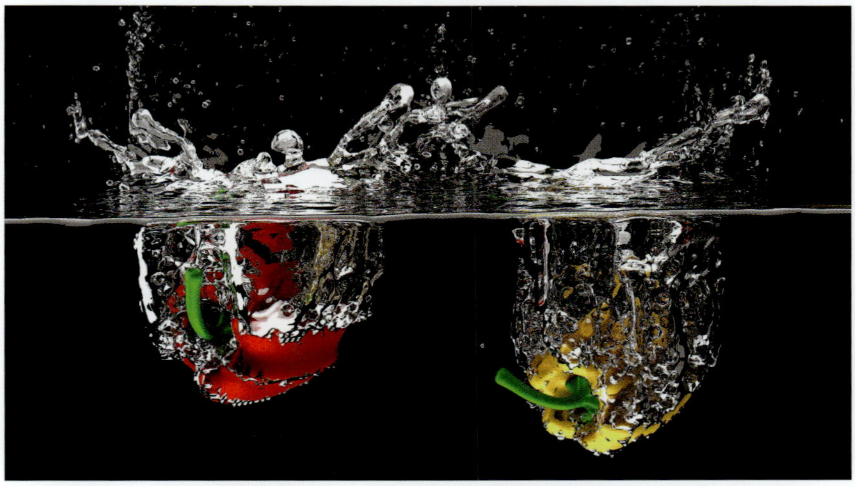

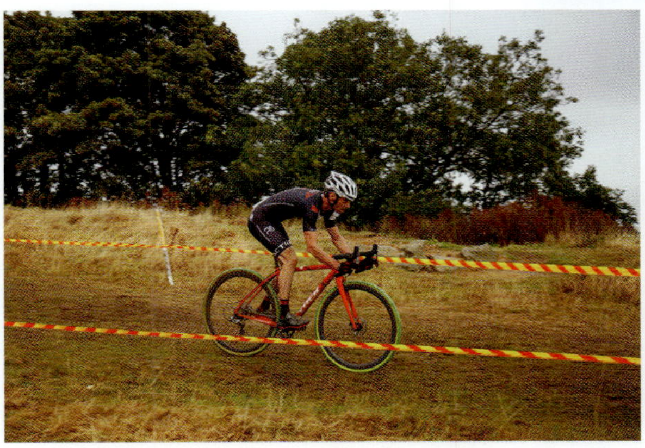

1/500th Second - f2.8 - ISO 100

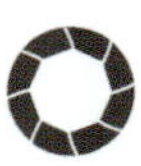

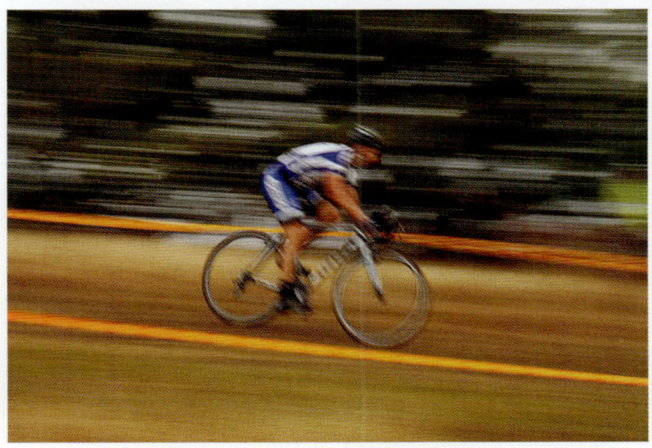

1/8th Second - f22 - ISO 100

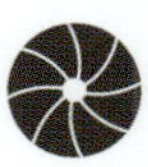

On the left we have an image taken at $1/500^{th}$ of a second and on the right, we have one that was taken at $1/8^{th}$ of a second.

As you can see, the one on the left is nice and sharp, the action has been frozen and that's because the shutter speed is faster. The one on the right is blurred (camera shake). This is because the photo has been taken at a slower shutter speed – the light entered the camera at a slower rate whilst the camera was moving.

Also, notice here that the aperture has changed, the one on the left is a wider aperture, the one on the right is a smaller aperture and that's to balance out the amount of light coming into your camera. As you let less light in with the shutter speed, you need to let more light in with the aperture and visa versa. We will cover this balancing of exposure in more detail later on, I just want you to notice it for now.

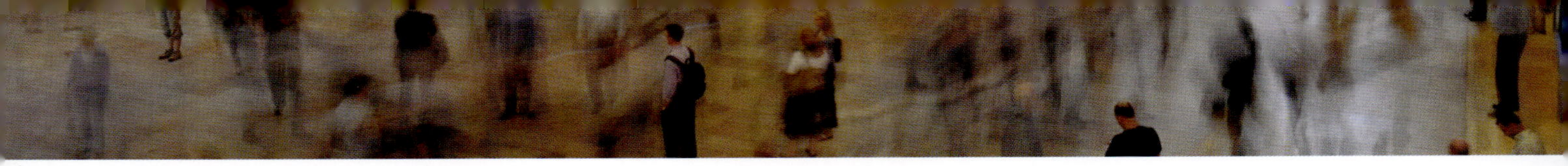

Task

Let's look at some more examples, here are 4 pictures that have all been taken using a creative use of shutter speeds.

Which ones do you think have been taken with a longer shutter speed and what ones have been taken with a faster shutter speed, and how can you tell?

Jot down some notes.

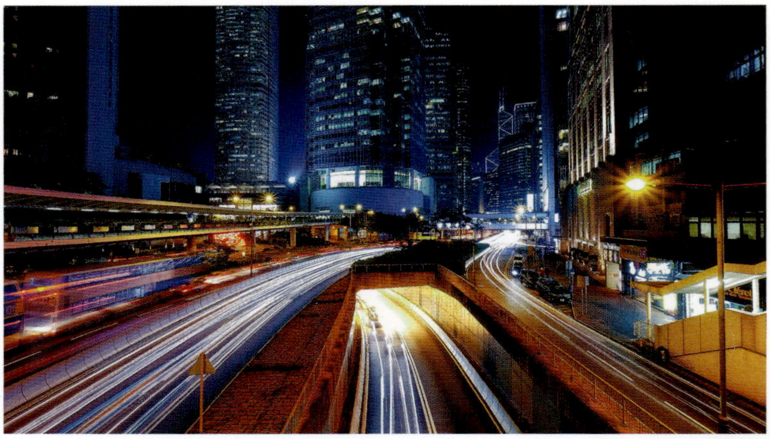

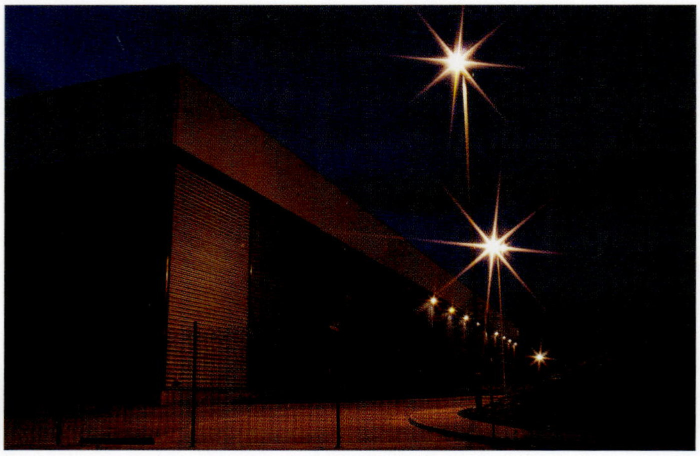

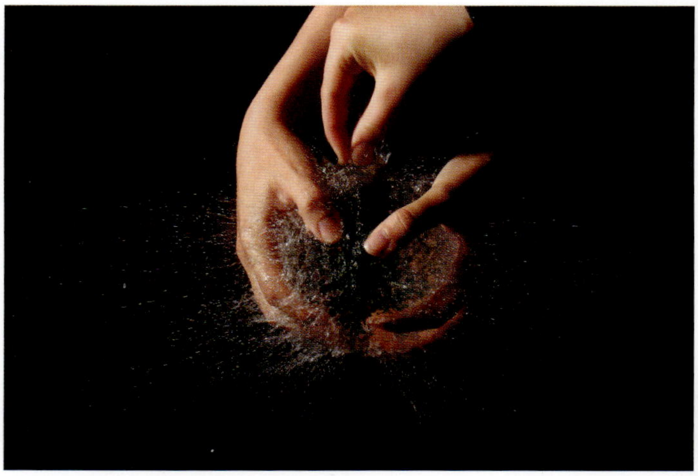

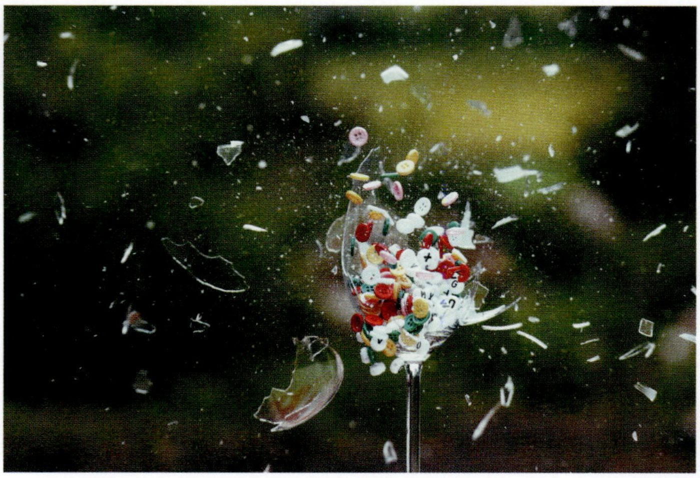

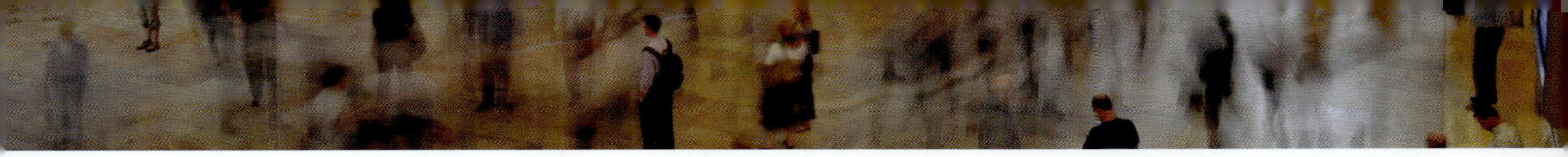

I think you'll agree that these 2 pictures (top of page) have been taken with a faster shutter speed. You can see that because the action in the images have been frozen – the water balloon has been frozen in time. You can only do this using a fast shutter speed.

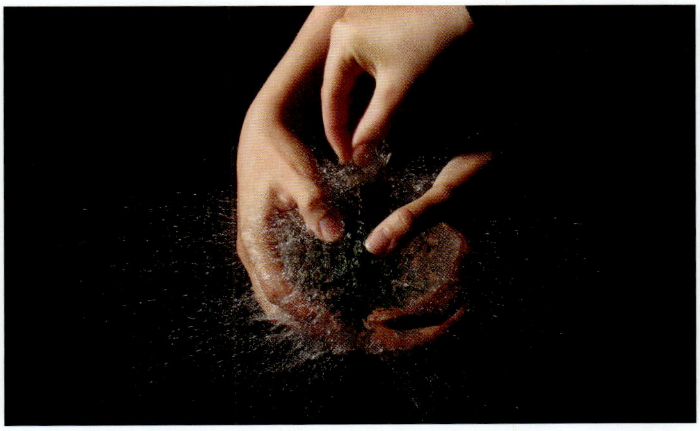

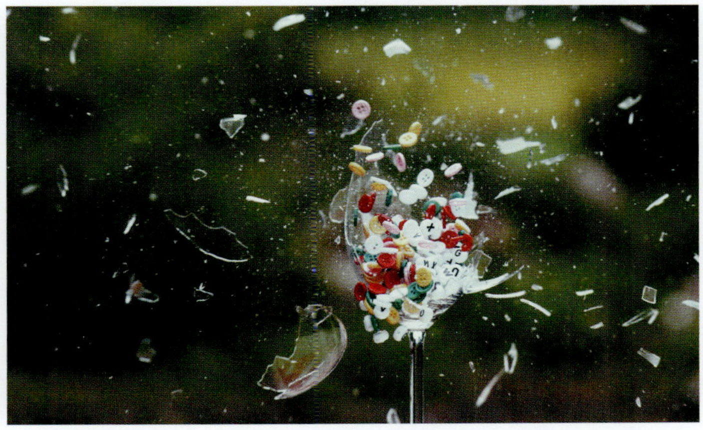

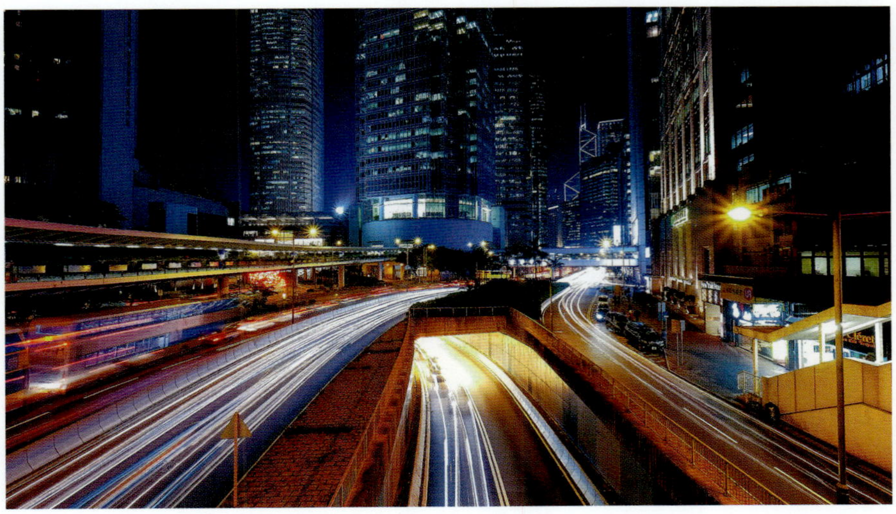

Then you have this one of a road. This picture has been taken using a longer shutter speed. You can see this because the road is dead still but the cars are moving. The lights on the cars travel through the frame as they are the only things moving within the scene.

The reason you can see only the cars moving is because this picture has been taken using a tripod.

When you take a picture with a slow shutter speed, on a tripod, everything that is still, stays still, and everything that moves, blurs - in this case the car lights.

This one here is a bit of trick question because there's nothing in this image that's moving however this shot has been taken using a slow shutter speed.

You can tell this is a long exposure because of the way the street lights have formed a star formation. When you do a long exposure and there are lights in the scene, for example street lights, they bleed out into your exposure and create this lovely star effect.

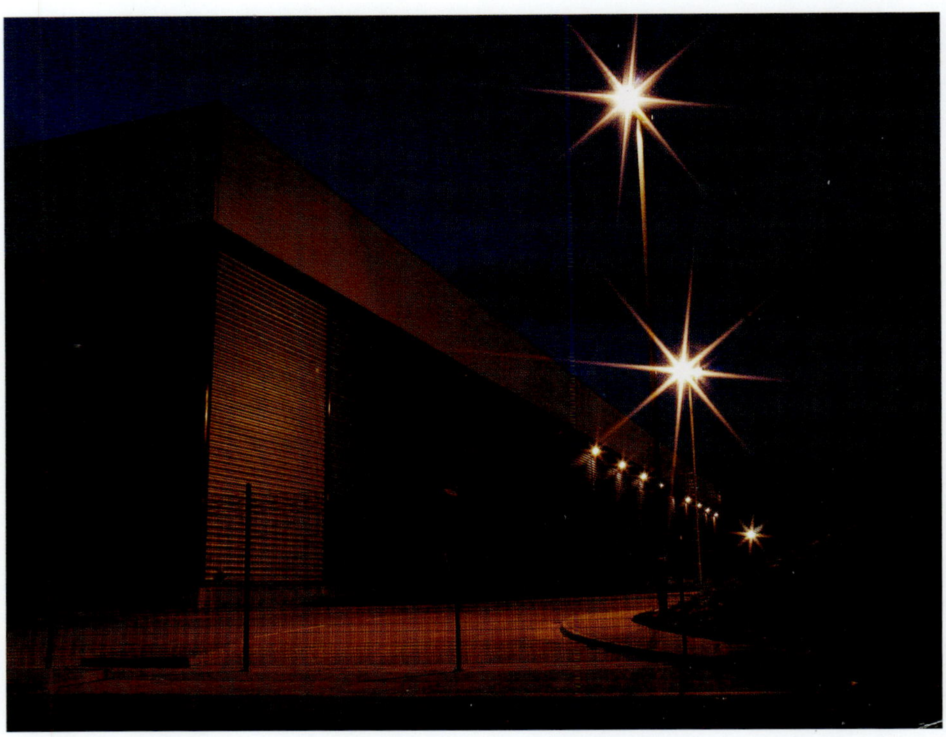

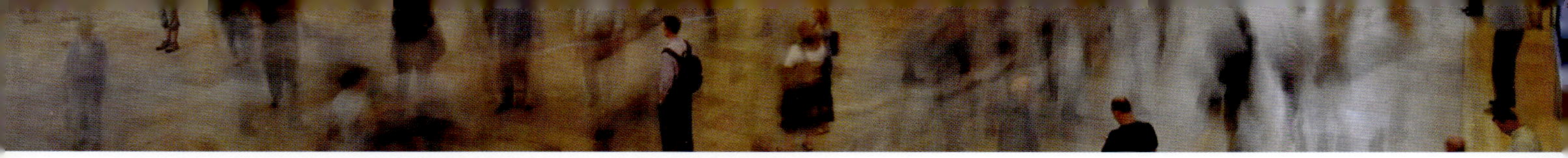

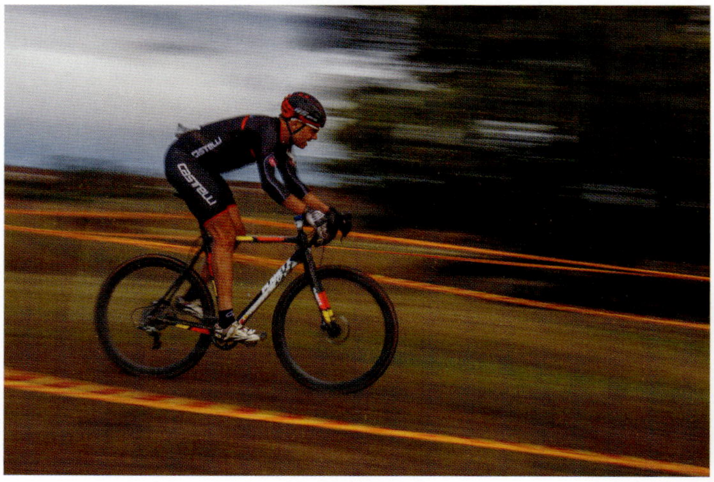

Here's another example of how you can use shutter speeds to get good effects *(left)*. This is called panning. In panning you follow the moving object with your camera which keeps the moving object still, whilst the background blurs.

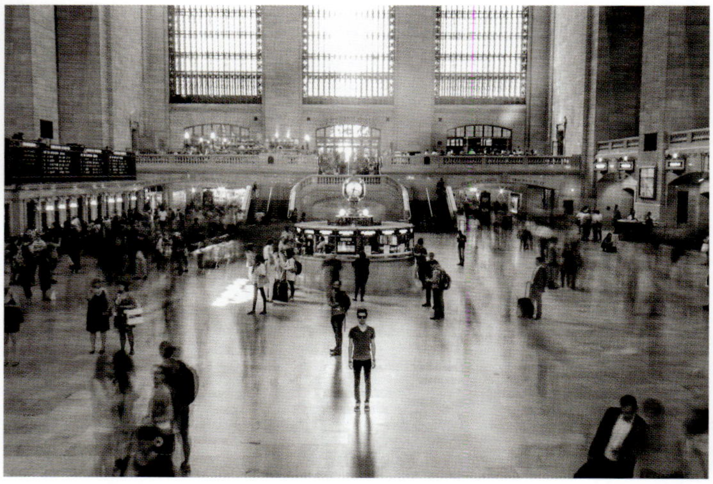

Here's another example of how to use shutter speeds (*right*). This shot is a long exposure but the person who is clear has stood still and everyone is moving around them. Again anything moving has become blurred and anything still has stayed sharp.

Task

Set your cameras to the S or TV setting. Then, because we are going to be shooting moving objects, we're going to change the focus mode so it can track moving subjects. We're also going to change the shoot mode to continuous shooting to make sure we get the shot.
Again, below is a guide on how to do this on common cameras. Simply refer to your camera manual under 'Continuous servo' or 'AI Servo' and 'Drive modes'.

Canon

To change the focusing mode on a Canon:

- press the Q button
- select the 'One Shot' area on the screen
- select AI servo.

To change the shooting mode:

- press Q again then go over to the square symbol that says 'Single Shooting'
- Select 'Continuous Shooting'.

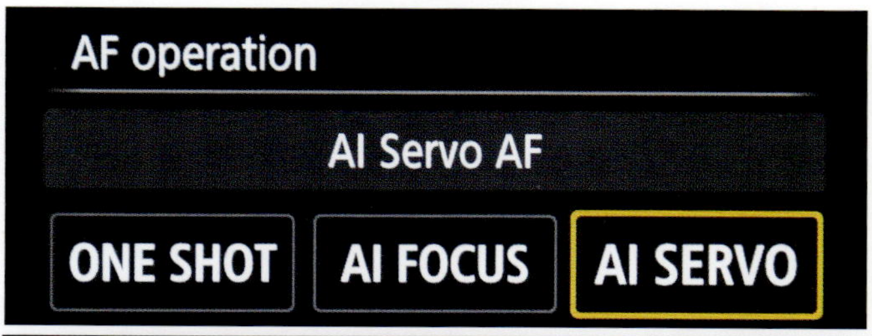

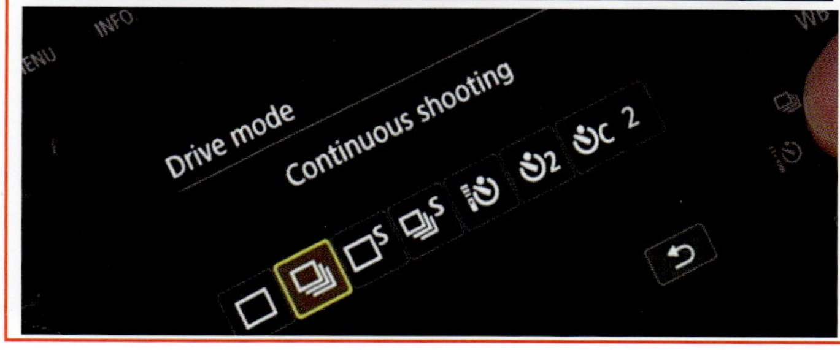

Nikon

- Press the *i* button
- Go to 'Focus mode'. Select AF-C.
- Then press the shooting mode button and select 'Continuous'.

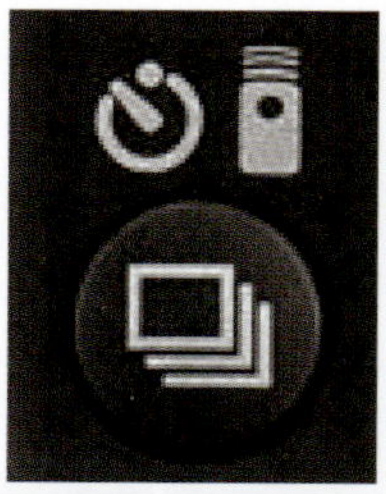

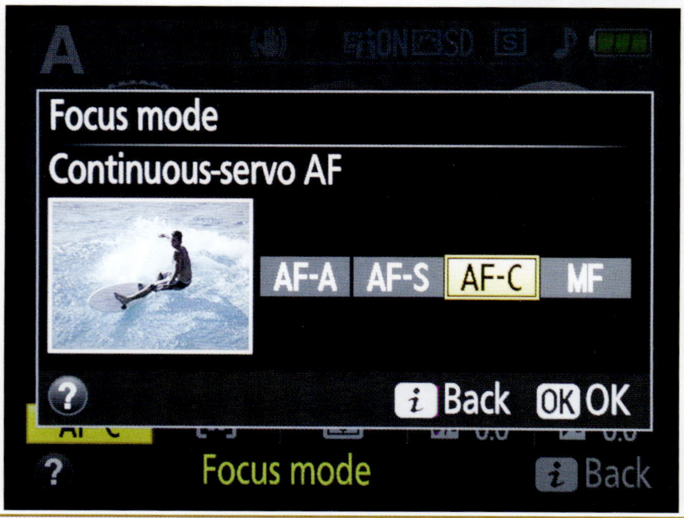

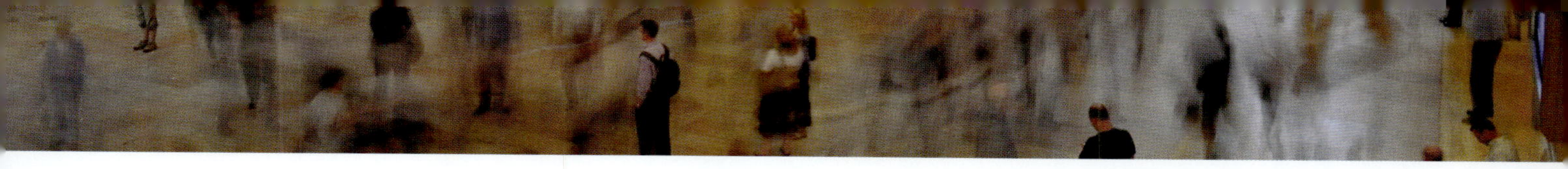

Task

Control the movement in your shots

Ok, the first task is very simple. I want you to freeze the action of something moving. This could be someone running, car moving, mountain bikes etc.

- Change the focus mode and drive mode as mentioned in previous page.
- Put your ISO on Auto.
- Make sure your focus point is set to centre frame (as shown in previous chapter).
- Take a shot of the moving subject/s using the shutter speeds below.
- Compare the shots to see which shutter speeds have frozen the moving subject.

In this task I just want you to see the effect a shutter speed has on a moving object and get you working around your camera so you can start to control shutter speeds.

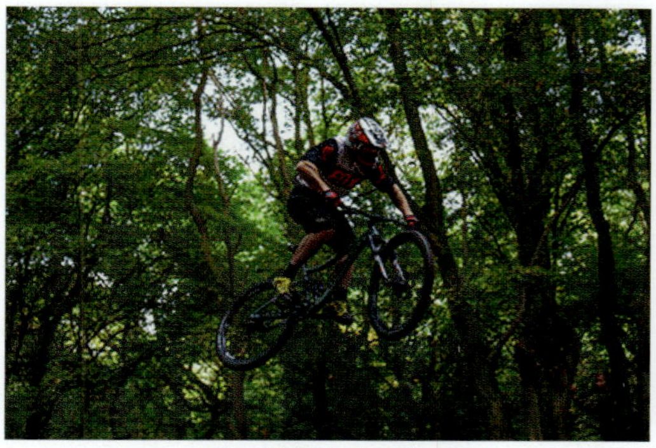

1/500th

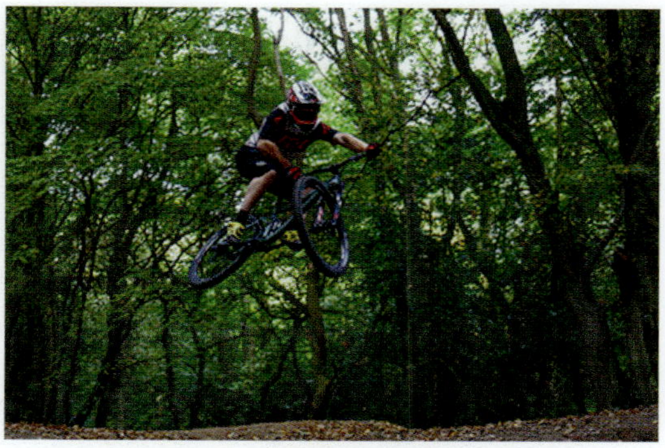

1/250th

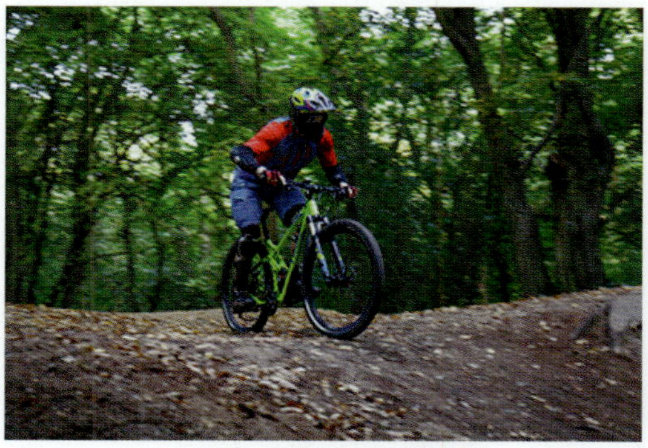

1/125th

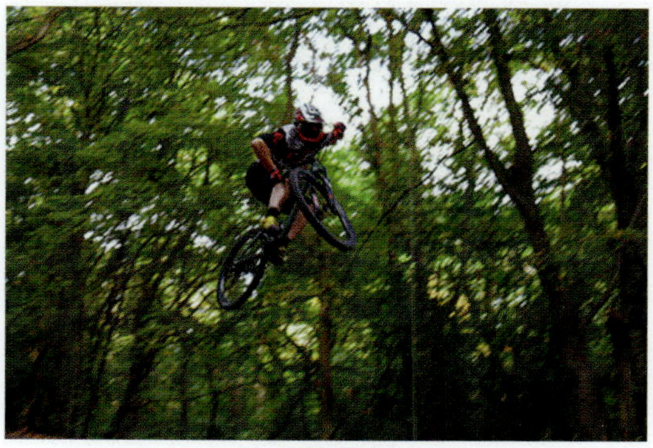

1/60th

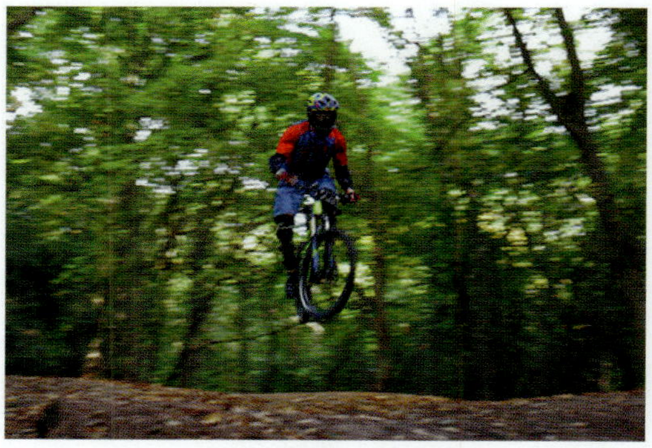

1/30th

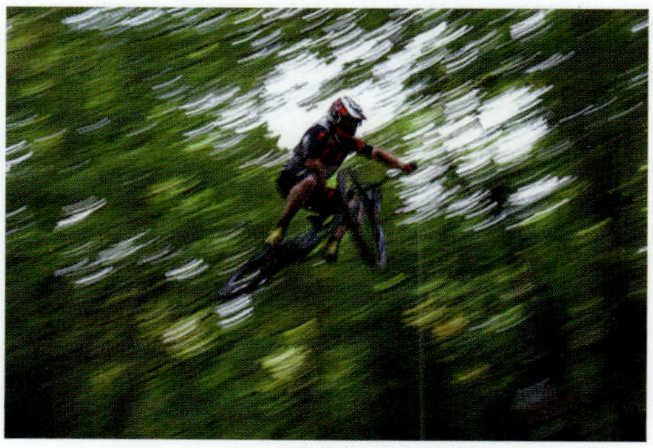

1/15th

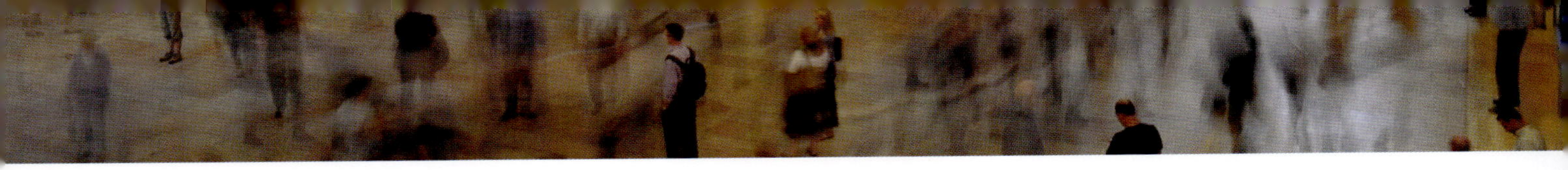

So hopefully you had fun with that, as I said before it's just to get you working with your shutter speed settings and getting you to recognise the effect shutter speeds can have on moving objects.

Task

Panning – Setting up your tripod

The next task I want you to try is a technique called panning.

You're going to need a tripod for this and make sure your camera is solid on your tripod. If your camera isn't solidly on your tripod, this task will not work. Make sure the lens points away from you and a handle comes towards you as shown right.

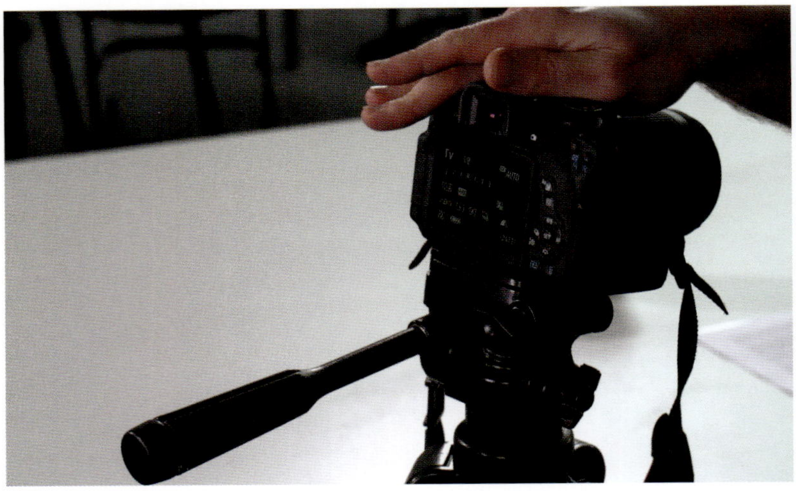

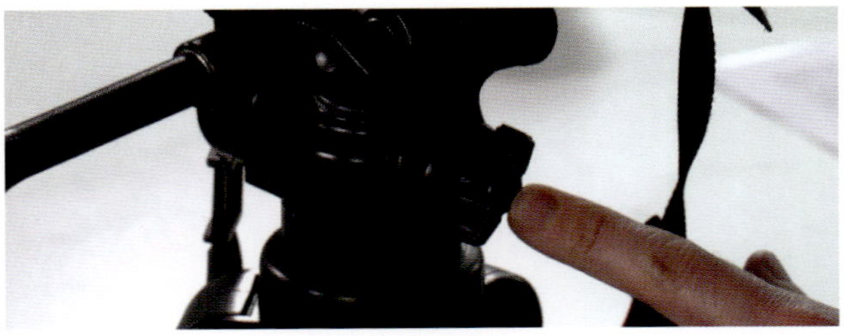

On the tripod, loosen what's called the 'pan lock'. It's usually located on the side of most tripods (*shown left*).

Once loosened, you should be able to pan left and right freely.

Panning

Panning is where you move the camera at the same speed as a moving object. The visual effect achieved is the moving subject still and the background blurred. It creates a sense of speed. Getting set up for panning isn't too hard, getting your camera to move at the same speed as the moving subject is the difficult bit!

Take pictures of a moving subject, someone walking, riding a bike etc. and try to keep them still in the image whilst the background blurs. First start this task using a tripod, then try it hand-held.

- Set your camera to $1/8^{th}$ of a second.
- Make sure your focus point is centre frame and your ISO is on Auto as in the previous task.
- Focus on the subject and hold the focus by half-pressing the shutter button down, as shown in the focusing chapter.
- Pan the camera on the tripod so it moves at the same speed as subject, then take the shot. Getting this right first time will be rare so keep practicing until you get it.
- You can also do this task hand held so if using a tripod becomes difficult, try it hand held instead.

Then try the same thing again at different shutter speeds. There is no 'one setting fits all' with panning. Objects moving at different speeds will require different shutter speeds to get the desired effect.

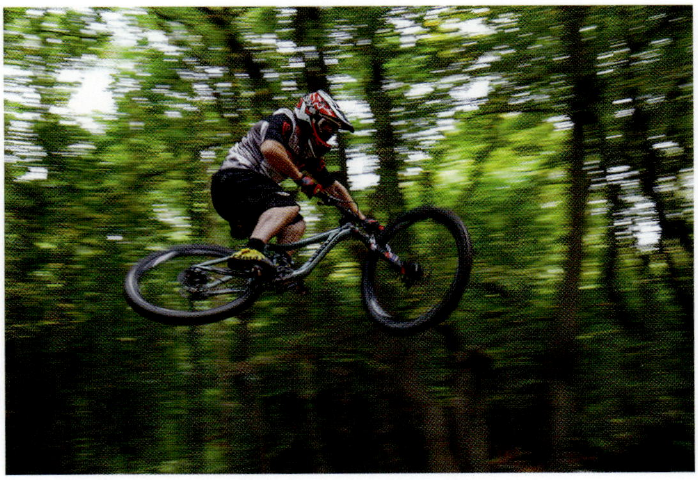

1/60th Second

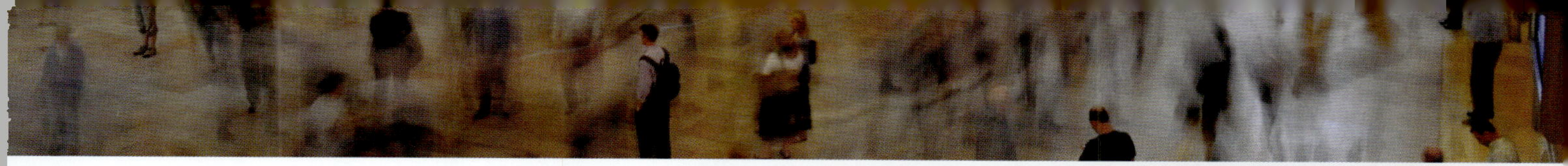

1/15th Second

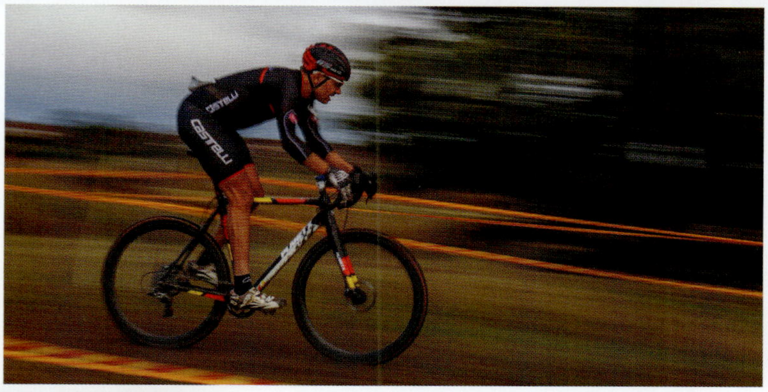

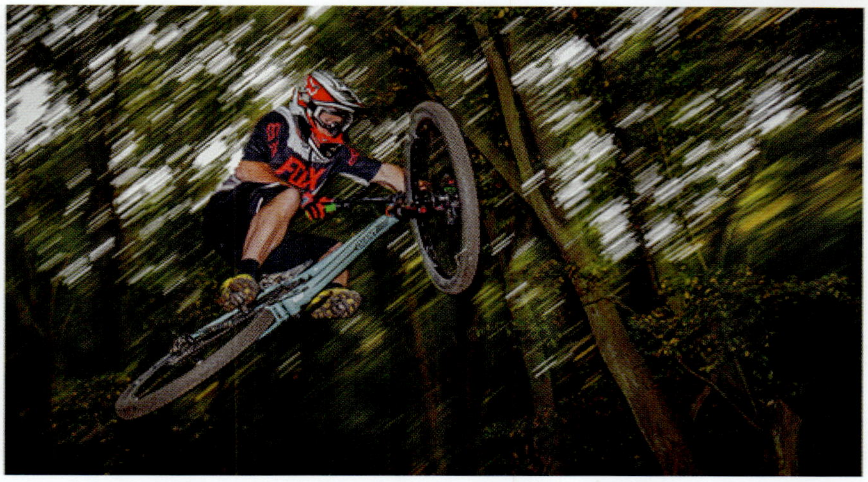

1/15th Second with Flash

This picture shows the same technique but a burst of flash has gone off during the exposure. This is a technique called Slow Sync Flash. Simply pop up your flash or use a flashgun to get this effect.

To view a video tutorial on panning and slow sync flash go to www.theschoolofphotography.com and type slow sync flash in the search bar.

So there is your panning task, a really good technique - lots of fun to try, but quite hard to master.

Faster moving objects will need a faster shutter and you can't actually judge that until you are in situ working. So give that a go, practice your panning technique then we'll look at some more stuff you can do with shutter speeds.

Task

Here are some more tasks you can do to push your use of shutter speeds further. You can do these with your kids, your friends or family and they're just really fun activities to do whilst learning shutter speeds.

The first task is to give a model wings! Firstly, set your camera up on a tripod and turn it to Tv/S mode with your ISO on auto.

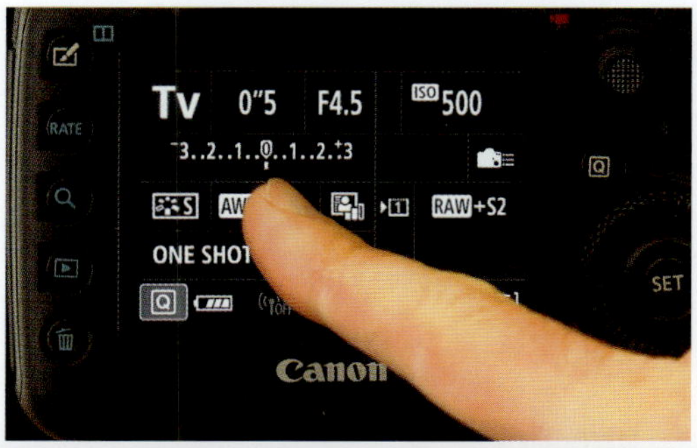

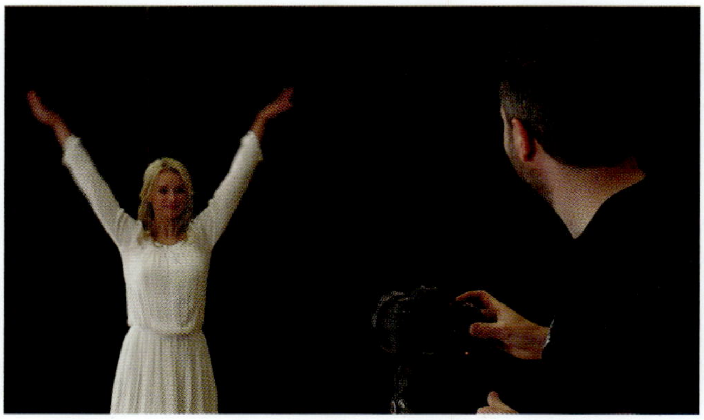

Get your model to move their arms up and down by their side whilst you take the shot. Start at half a second, then experiment to get the shot. Go up to 1 second, 2 seconds, or use quicker shutter speeds if you want to instead, it's up to you.

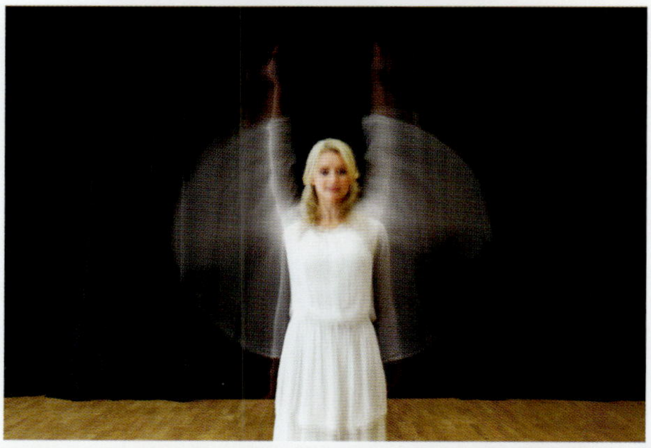

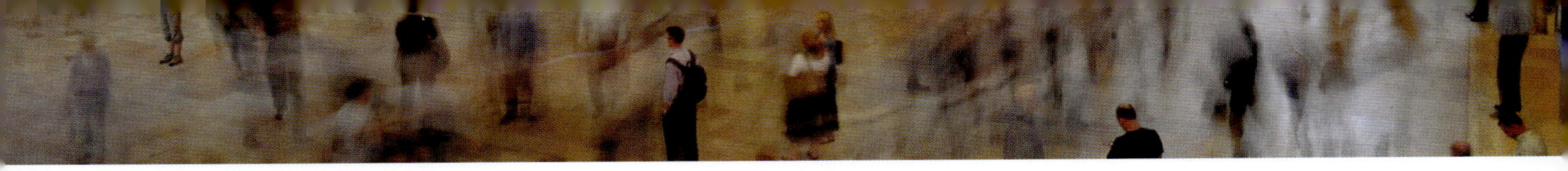

Task

You can also use slow shutter speeds whilst zooming in and out. Set your shutter speed to ½ of a second put the focus point in the middle of the eyes. Take a shot whilst zooming in or out. This will create a really weird surreal effect and is great fun to do!

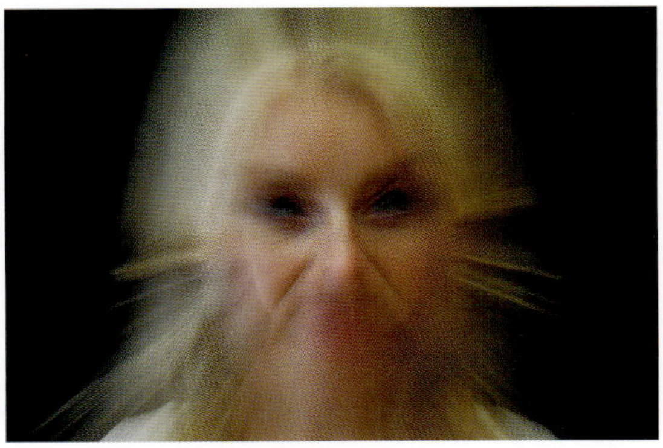

Zooming in

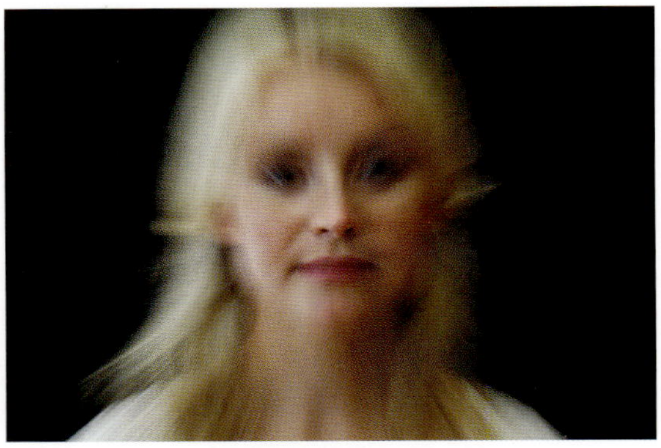

Zooming out

You can also add some flash into the shot. If you have a flash gun, this will work really well, but you can also use your pop up flash too. Simply do the same as the above but with your flash popped up or your flash gun on.

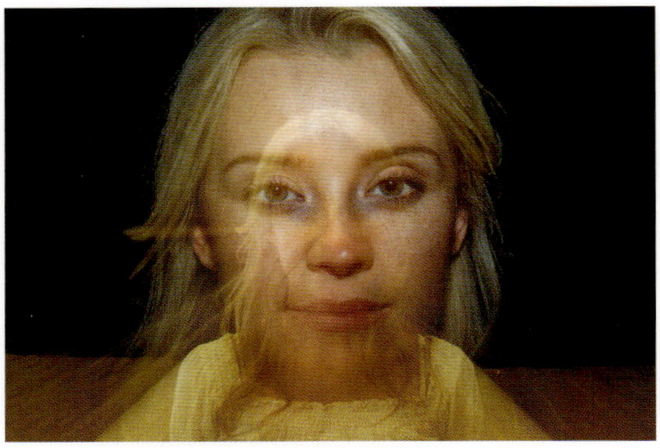

Zooming in with flash

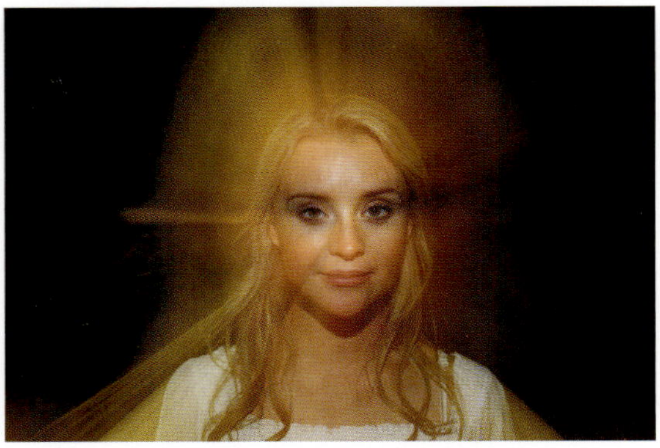

Zooming out with flash

The next task involves water balloons!

- As before, make sure you're on Tv or S for shutter speed priority, and set your ISO to auto.
- To capture the water balloon bursting, you need to set your shutter speed to 1/250th of a second or faster.
- Have your drive mode on continuous shooting.
- Put the focus point where the balloon is going to burst, then switch to manual focus on your lens to hold the focus on that spot. If you don't do this, it's likely the camera will try to auto focus on different parts of the scene as the balloon bursts.
- Start taking shots just before the balloon bursts and you should catch it.

It might take a few attempts, but it's a great task to do on a sunny day.

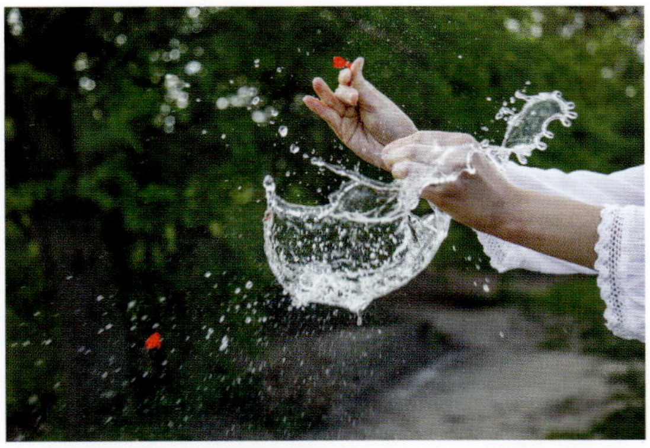

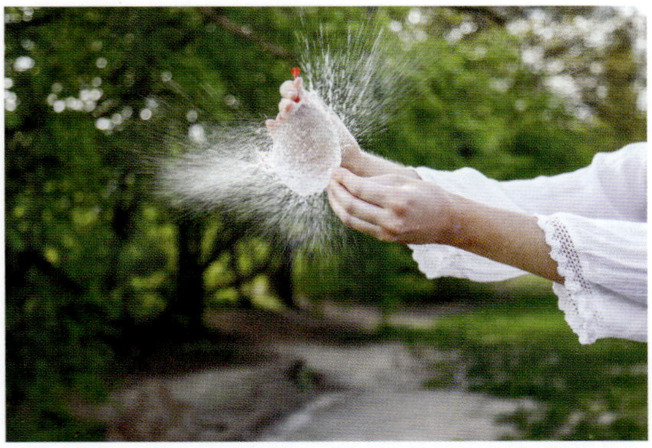

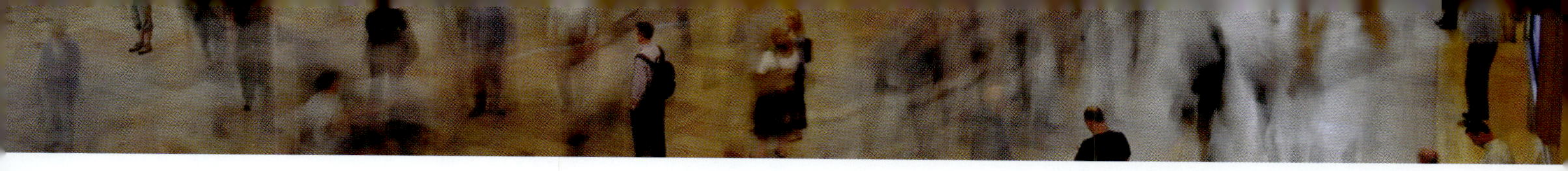

Once you've done all that, you've just started to take control over your shutter speeds. To challenge your skills further, make images that show a creative use of shutter speeds. What else can you do with these techniques? This will really cement the learning and you'll have some fun whilst doing it.

And don't forget, we always like to see students' work here at The School of Photography. So, if you want to show us yours, tag your best shots on social media #theschoolofphotography.

Have a good practice with those tasks and when you're ready, I'll see you in the next chapter.

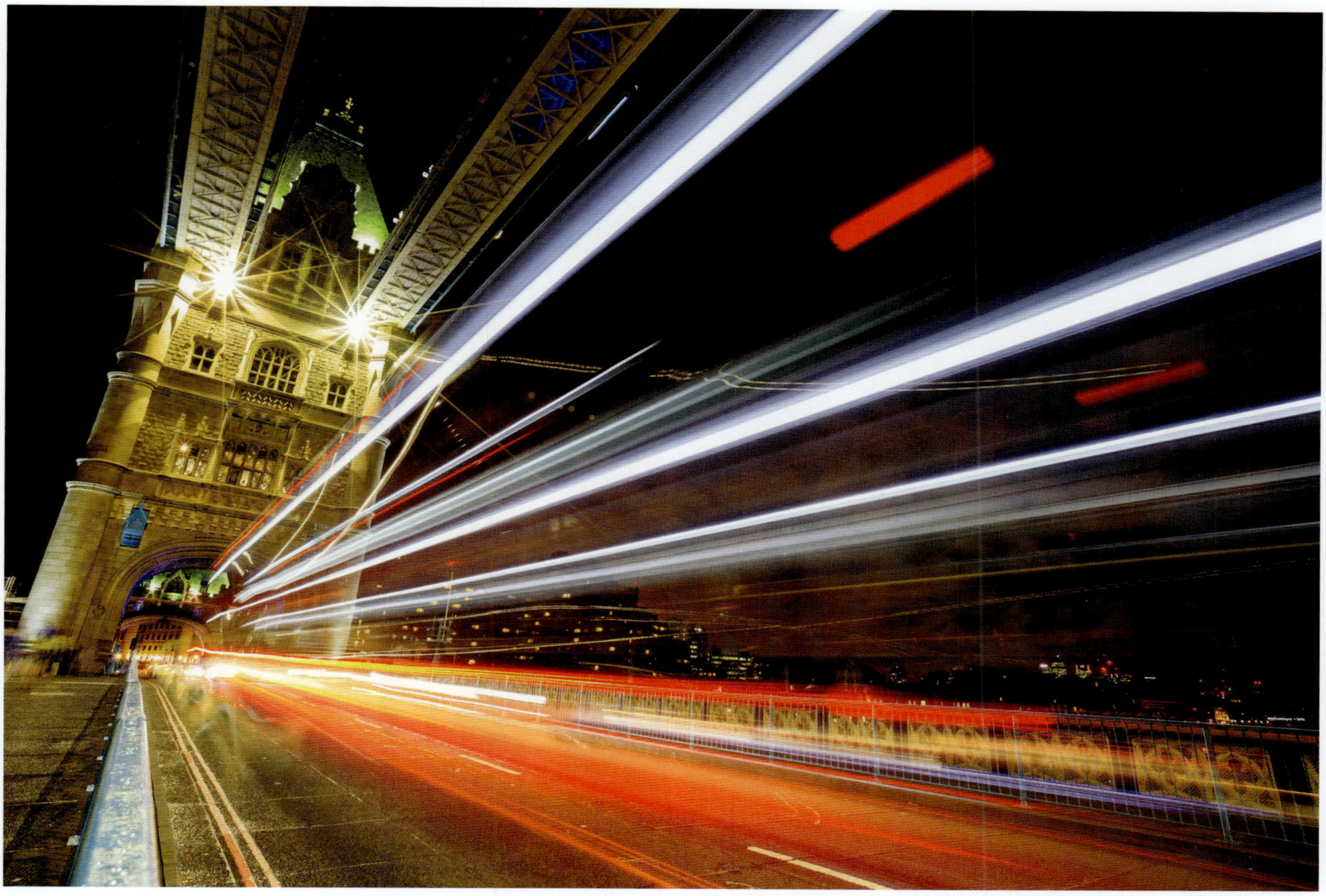

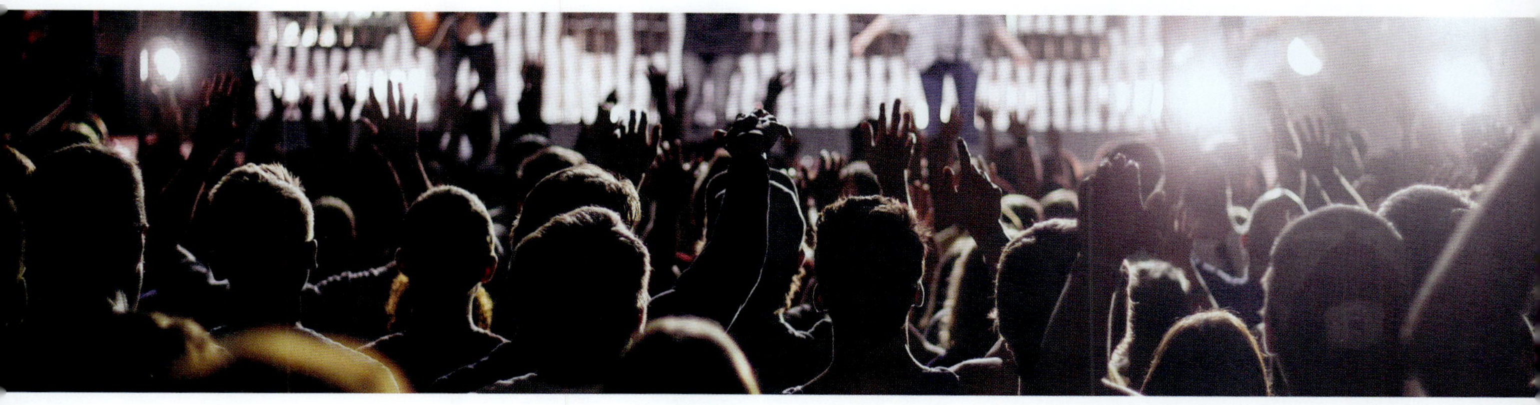

Balancing Exposures

Chapter 11

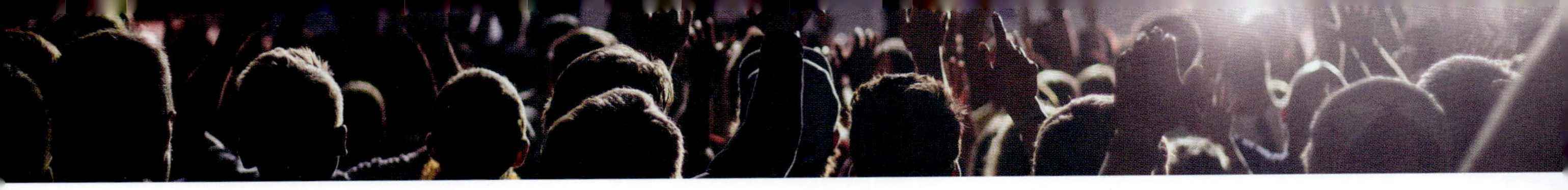

In this chapter, we're going to start putting things together and look at how we balance exposures to create different visual effects.

We've learnt about apertures, we've learnt about shutter speeds and we've learnt about ISO. Now we're going to look at how we balance exposure as this is what makes a photographer to someone who just picks up a camera and goes 'click'.

A photographer will be able to balance light coming into the camera to get a certain visual effect.

Remember that an exposure in photography is letting in an amount of light. An exposure to light is made up of your aperture and your shutter speed. You are doubling or halving the amount of light when changing your shutters speeds or apertures. These are called stops. Don't forget that you should be using the particular aperture sequence that I showed you earlier in the book.

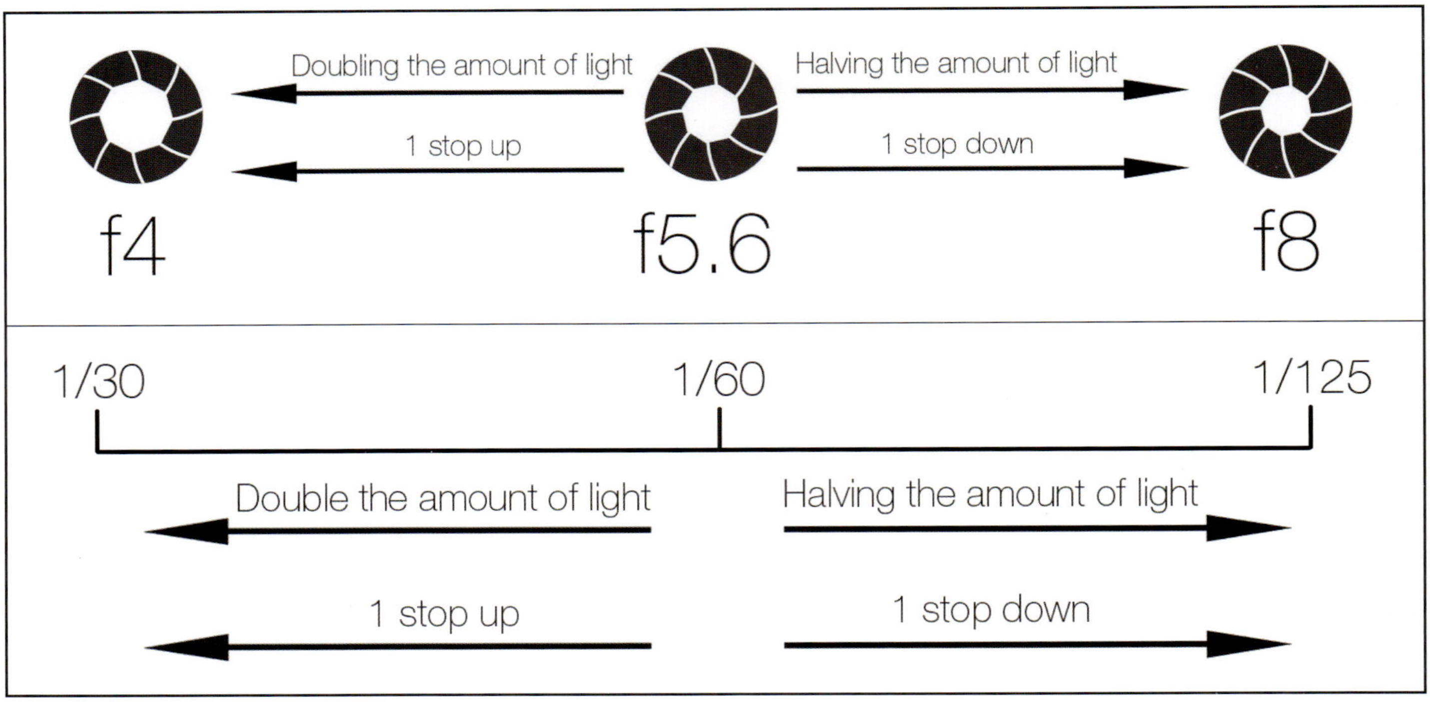

Your job as a photographer is to balance light via the shutter speed and aperture to get the visual effect that you want. To help you understand this, I want you to imagine light as weight and this scale representing the exposure of an image. The left part being the light let through the aperture and the right part being the light let in via the shutter.

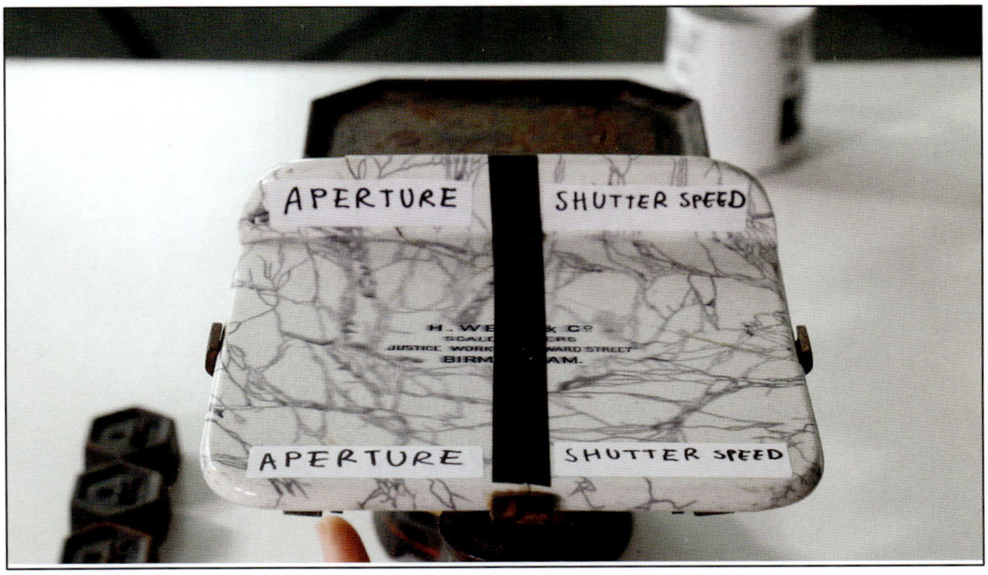

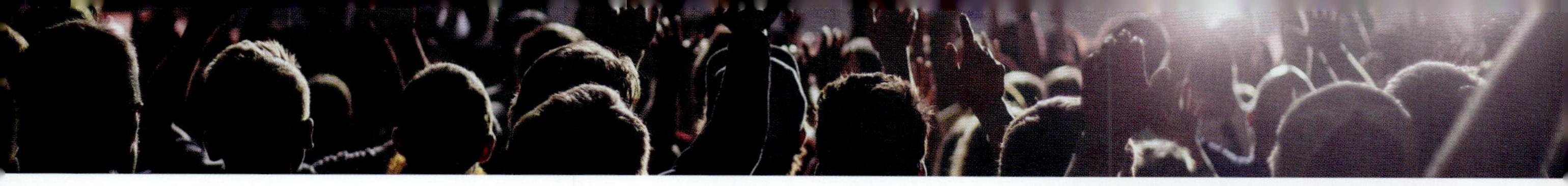

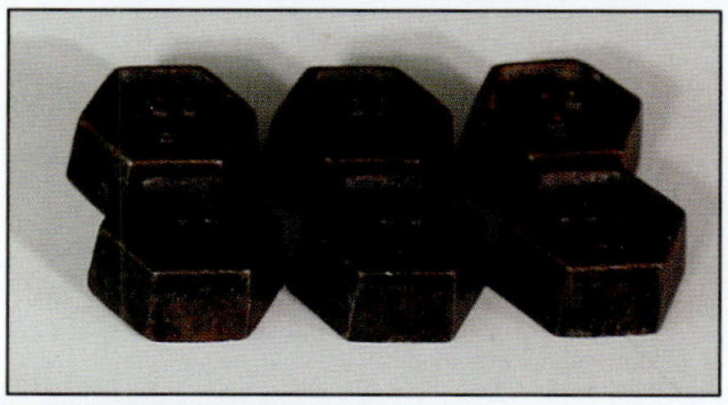

The three weights on the right represent the correct exposure (amount of light) I need, 600g in this case.

In auto mode, your camera will try to put the light into your camera as evenly as it can.

In this case we have 300 grams on the aperture and 300 grams on the shutter speed.

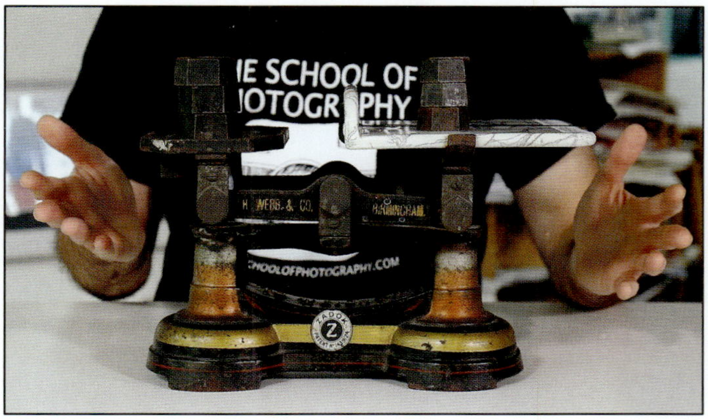

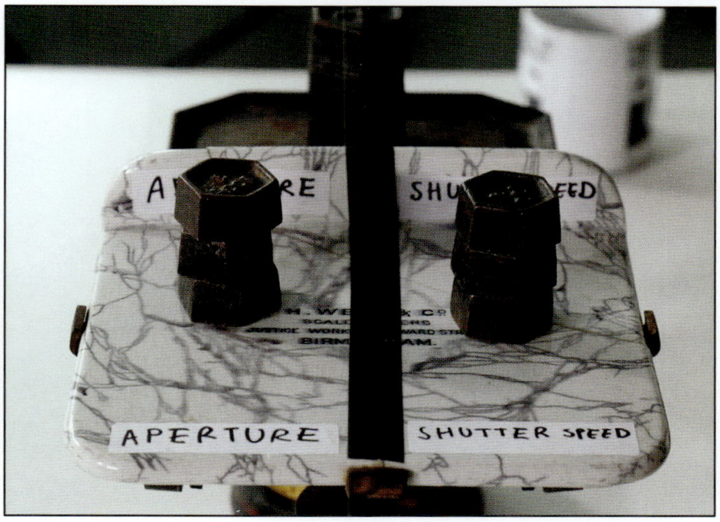

Now, as a photographer, 'you' should be taking control of the light. We've only got 600 grams of weight to play with (our available light) and let's say I want to create a shallow depth of field look. For this you will need a wide aperture.

A wide aperture is going to let a lot of light into the camera, so to compensate for this, we need to let in less light through the shutter speed to give us the same exposure to light as before (600 grams).

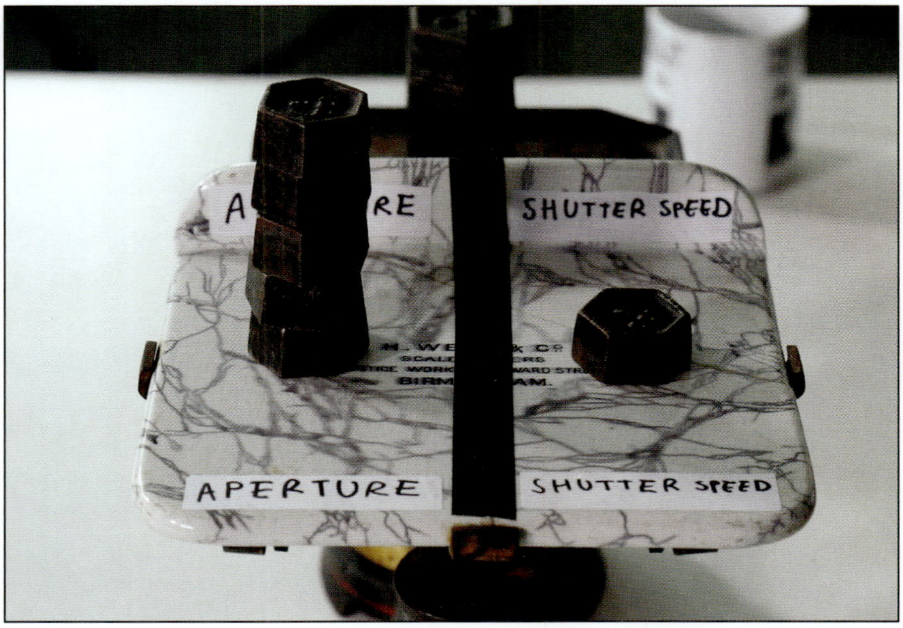

Therefore, 500g has gone on the aperture and to compensate, only 100g on the shutter speed side.

This is now equal to the correct exposure (600g) but giving a totally different visual effect.

Auto mode	**Taking control to get a shallow DOF look**
300g > Aperture	500g > Aperture
+	+
300g > Shutter Speed	100g > Shutter Speed
= 600g	= 600g

Same exposure to light – Two different visual effects

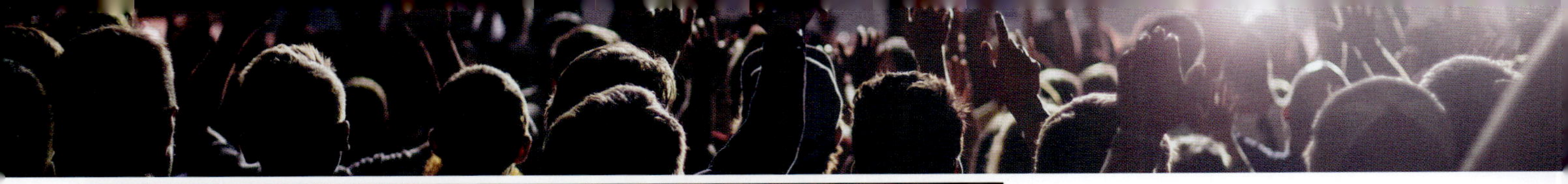

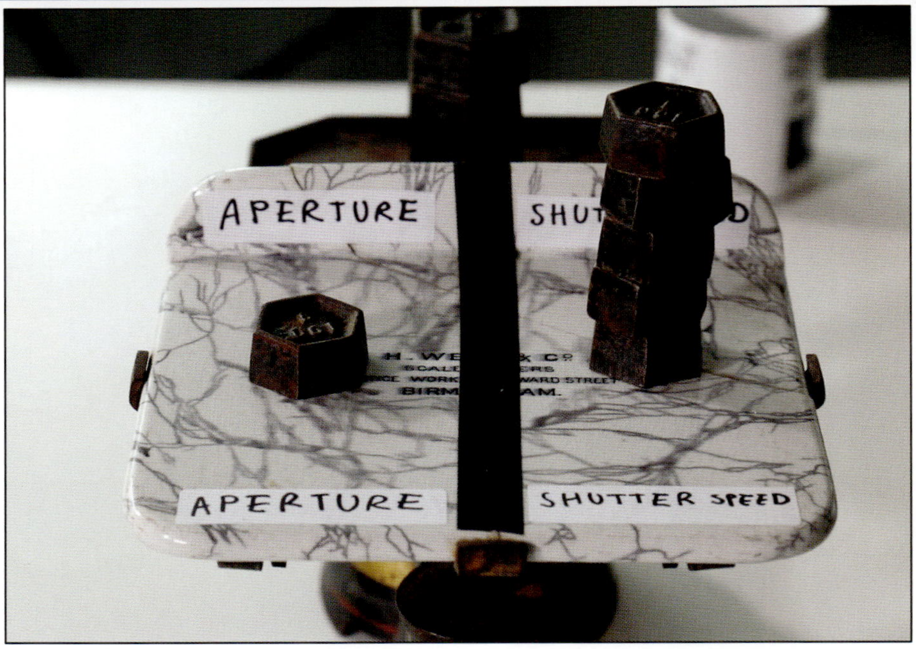

Now let's say I want to create a sense of movement in a photo. For this, we'll need a slower shutter speed, and therefore most of our available light (600g) is going to come through the shutter speed.

To balance the exposure, I need to let most of the light through via the shutter speed, 500g, and to compensate only a small amount of light via the aperture, 100g. This is the correct exposure again, but again a completely different visual effect.

Auto mode	Shallow DOF look	Creating Movement
300g > Aperture	500g > Aperture	100g > Aperture
+	+	+
300g > Shutter Speed	100g > Shutter Speed	500g > Shutter Speed
= 600g	= 600g	= 600g

Same exposure to light – Three different visual effects

Another way to show you this balancing of exposure is to use water to show you how the shutter speed changes when you change the aperture.

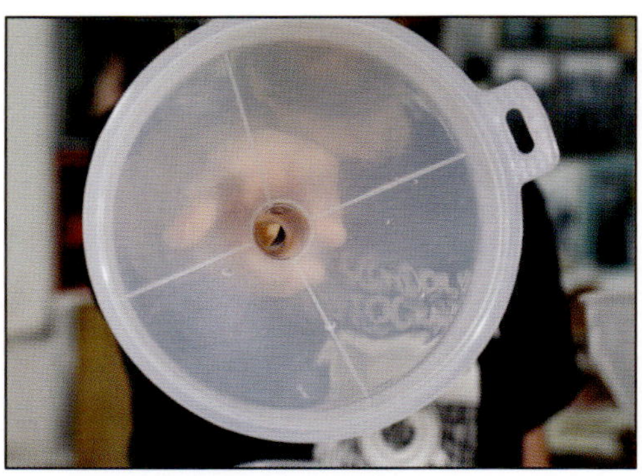

On the left, I have a very wide funnel representing a wide aperture of f2.8.

On the right, I have a smaller funnel representing an aperture of f16.

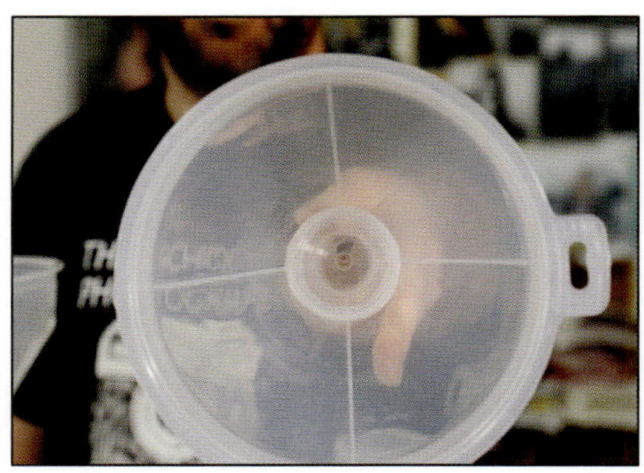

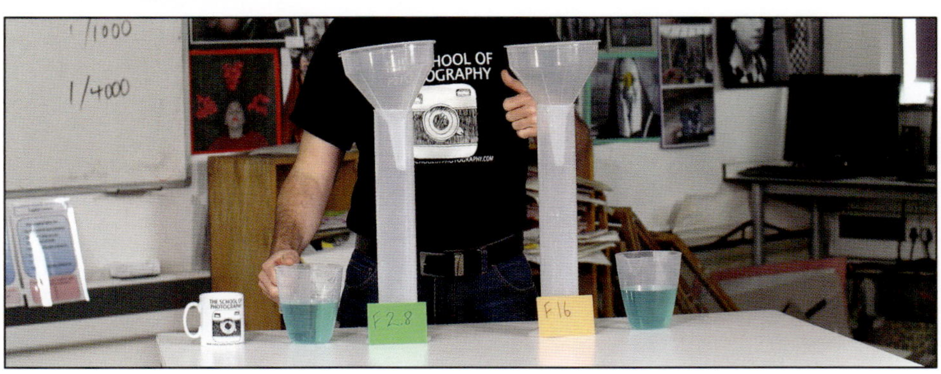

And here I have two jugs of 500ml of water which will represent the amount of available light.

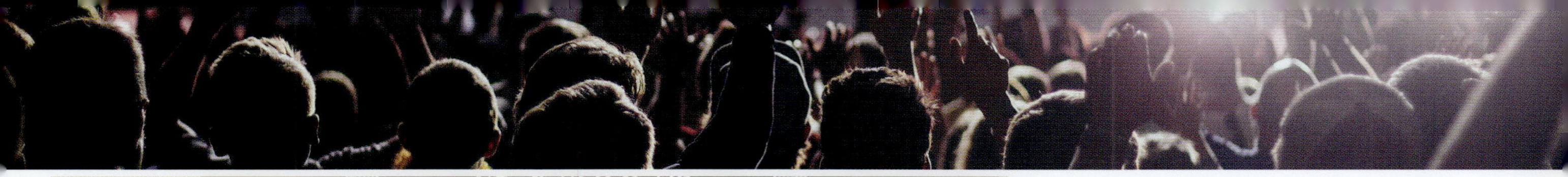

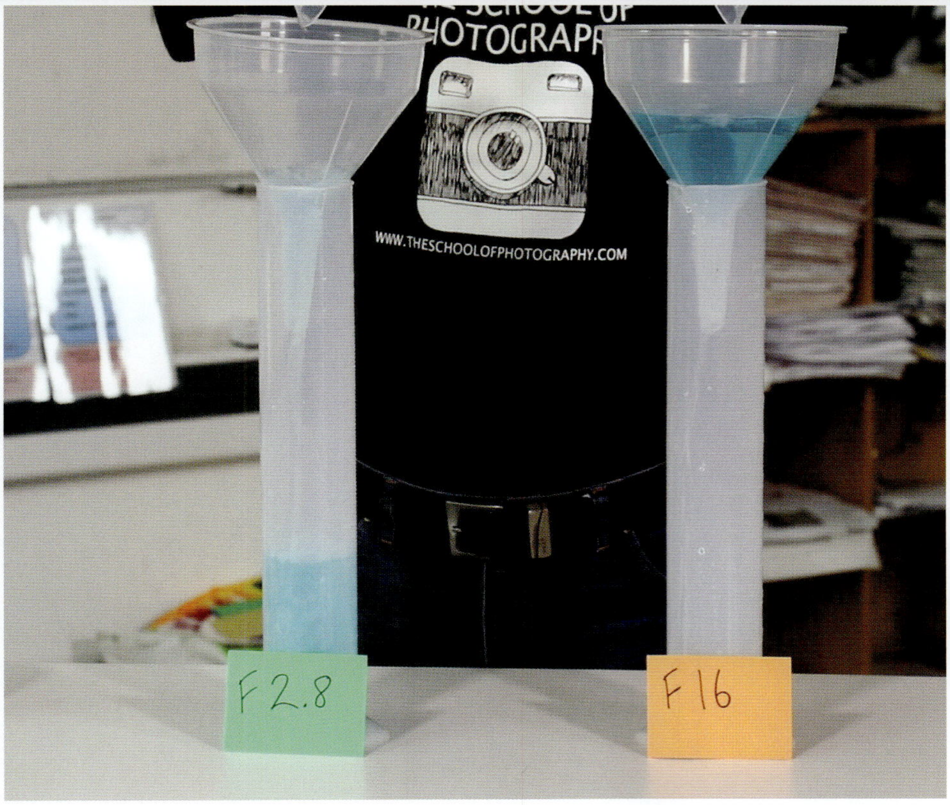

If I pour the water into the funnels at the same time, the time taken for the cylinders to fill up is different. This represents the shutter speed.

The water in the cylinder on the left (the wide aperture) has let in the water (light) very quickly. This means that the shutter speed for the wide aperture needs to be fast.

However, the water going into the cylinder on the right (the small aperture) has let in the water very slowly. This means that the shutter speed for the small aperture needs to be long.

Now I'm going to give you a maths test! I want to do this just to cement this knowledge of how to balance exposure. It might seem hard and difficult at first, but once you get it, I promise it will all sink in and make things a lot better for you in the future.

So, in true maths lesson style, here's a question:

An exposure for a shot of a person is 1/60th @ f8. This is the correct amount of light the camera needs for the current lighting conditions. In auto mode, this is the exposure the camera is showing.

But as a photographer, I want to control the visual effect of the image. I want to create a 'shallow depth of field' so the background goes blurry, so I change the aperture to **f2.8.**

What does the shutter speed need to be, to expose the camera to the same amount of light?

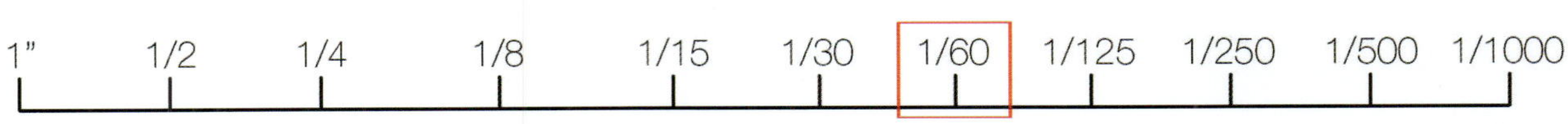

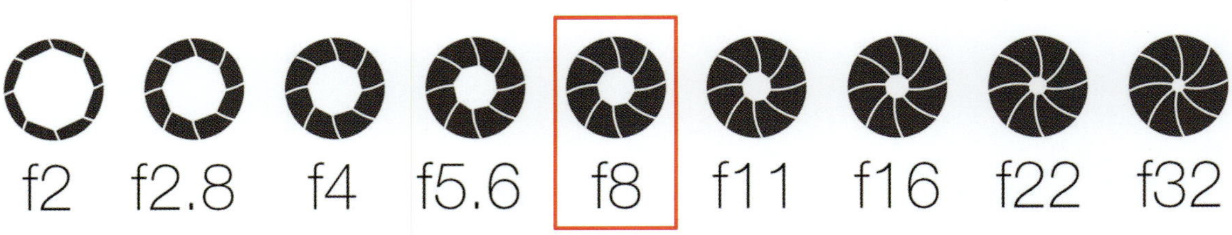

Remember, this is a balancing act. By changing the aperture from f8 to f2.8, I have increased the amount of light entering the camera, and therefore must compensate with the shutter speed. Take a few minutes to think about this, then write down an answer on your notepad.

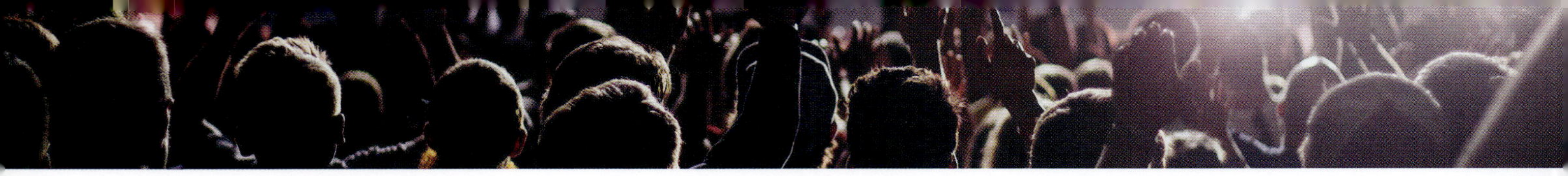

Here's how you should have worked it out. Remember, the balancing act, remember the scales.

We started on f8, that's what the camera gave us to start with. I wanted a shallow depth of field and for that you need a wide aperture, so I went from f8 to f2.8. That is 3 stops brighter, I've increased the light via the aperture by 3 stops.

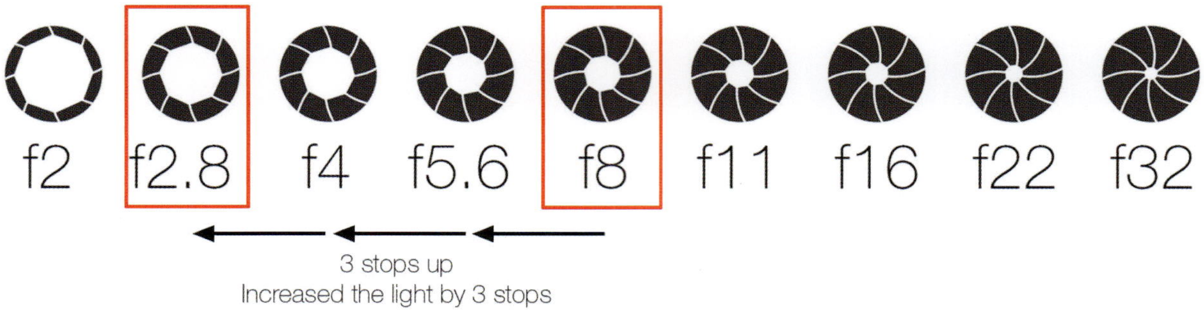

So, I need to make it 3 stops darker via the shutter speed to balance out the light. If I don't, I'll get an over-exposed shot.

The original shutter speed was 1/60th of a second and I need to go 3 stops darker. I go to 1/125th, that's one stop darker, 1/250th, that's 2 stops darker and 1/500th of a second which is 3 stops darker. I've now balanced out the exposure to give me the same amount of light. The correct answer is **1/500th of a second**.

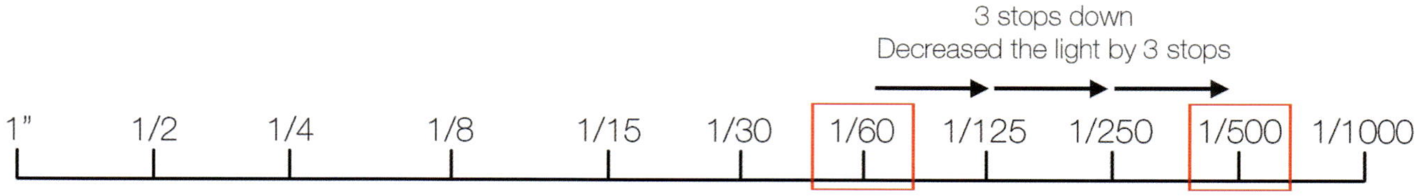

Both of those exposures are letting in the same amount of light but they are giving 2 totally different visual effects. Let's do another question as I know you've not had enough yet!

Let's keep to the original exposure with this next question - 1/60th @ f8. This is the camera just giving an automatic exposure.

This time, however, I want to create a sense of movement so I set the shutter speed to 1/15th of a second which will give me that blurred look.

What does the aperture need to be to expose the camera to the same amount of light?

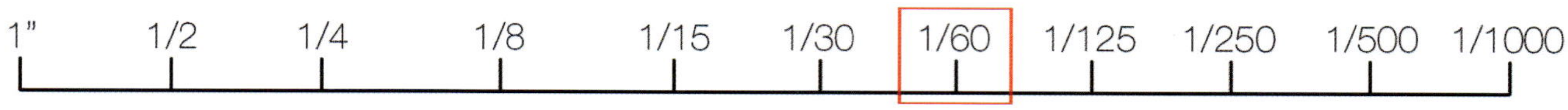

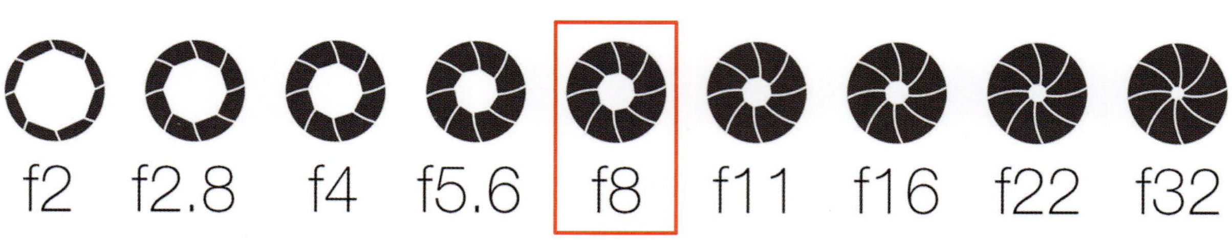

Refer to the aperture and shutter speed sequences, then write down an answer in your notebook.

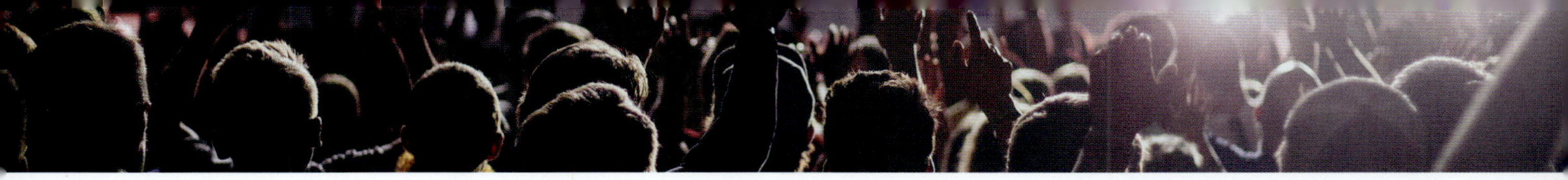

Answer

Let's go through the answer. The original exposure was 1/60th at f8. I have moved the shutter speed from 1/60th to 1/15th which is 2 stops brighter.

The original aperture was f8 so I need to balance the light by making the aperture 2 stops darker. So, I go to f11, which is one stop darker, then to f16 which is two stops darker.

So the answer is f16.

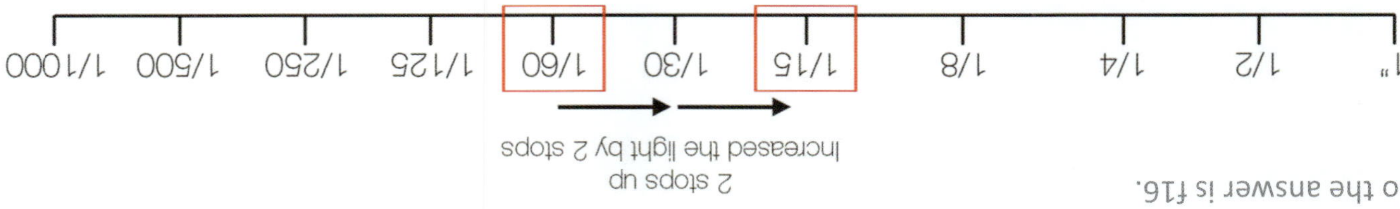

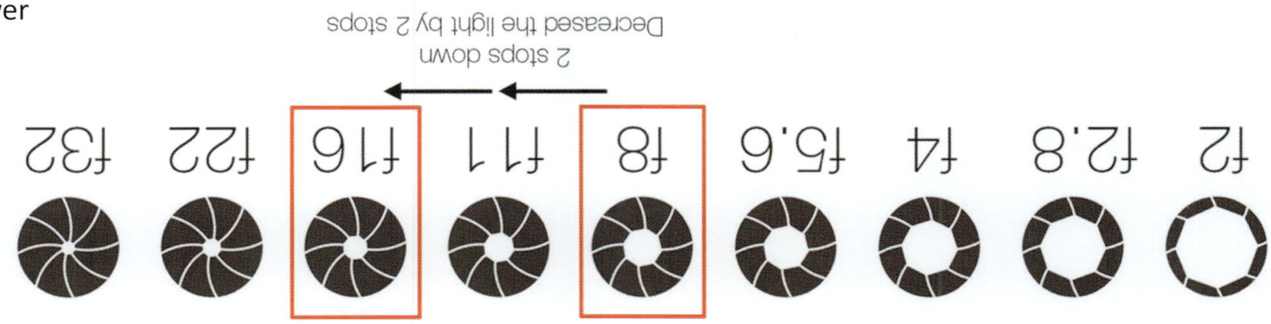

Now hopefully you should be getting there but just in case here's one more. I want you to correct these exposures below to give the same amount of light. The base exposure is 125th of a second a tf5.6.

Base exposure – 1/125th @ f5.6

___ @ f16

1/500th @ ___

On the first one I've changed the aperture to f16 so you need to change the shutter speed to balance it out to give the same amount of light. The second one I've changed the shutter speed to 1/500th of a second, so you need to change the aperture to give the same amount of light as the base exposure.

Have a think and write your answers in your note book.

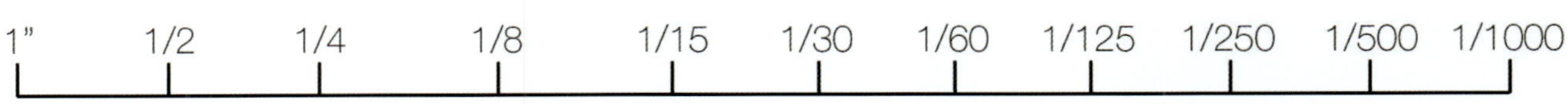

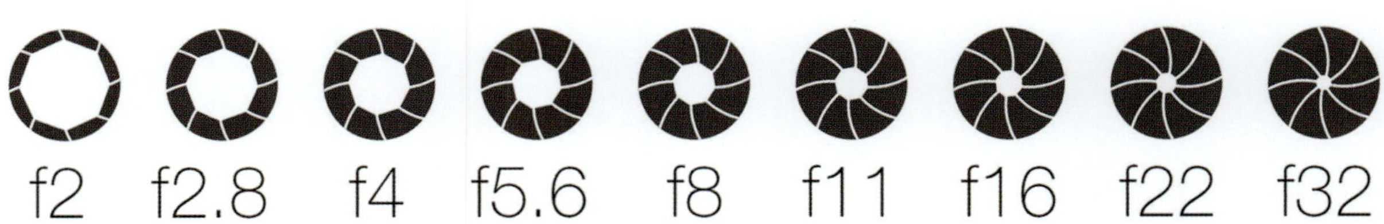

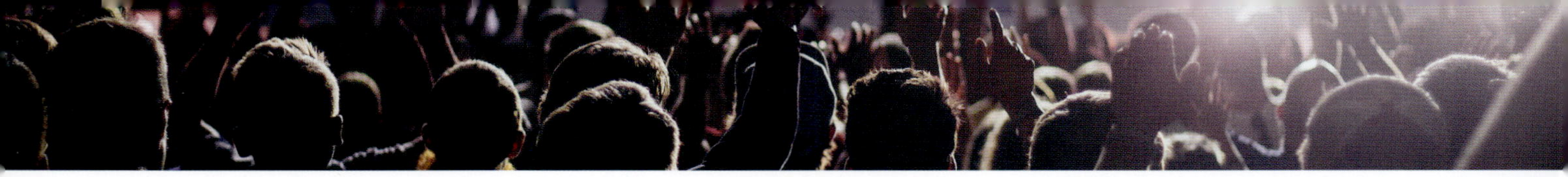

The first answer is 1/15th of a second and the next one is f2.8. Hopefully you got those right that time, if you didn't, I recommend you read back over the last few pages until you understand it.

Base exposure – 1/125th @ f5.6

1/15th @ f16

1/500th @ f2.8

All these exposures let in the same amount of light into the camera.

However, each one will give a different image effect.

Photographers control the visual effects of their image by balancing light. This is really important to know. Balancing exposures for different visual effects is what makes you a photographer from someone who just snaps away in auto. Now I'm going to set you a task to get you out there and practising in fully manual mode.

Task

Use fully manual mode to control the visual effects of your photographs

- Take two pictures of the same thing showing two different visual effects.
- Twist the dial at the top to the 'M' position.
- Set your ISO to 400. If it's a very bright day set the ISO to 100.
- Set your camera up on a tripod and use a remote trigger or 2 second timer.
- Expose each picture correctly by making sure your exposure meter is on 0 for each shot. You do this by changing the shutter speed and aperture.

On the next page is a guide to how to expose for shots in fully manual mode on popular cameras. Most other cameras work very similar and if you get stuck simply refer to your cameras manual under 'manual mode'.

Try to create the following effects:
- Long Depth of Field and Shallow Depth of Field.
- Motion blur and a Still shot.

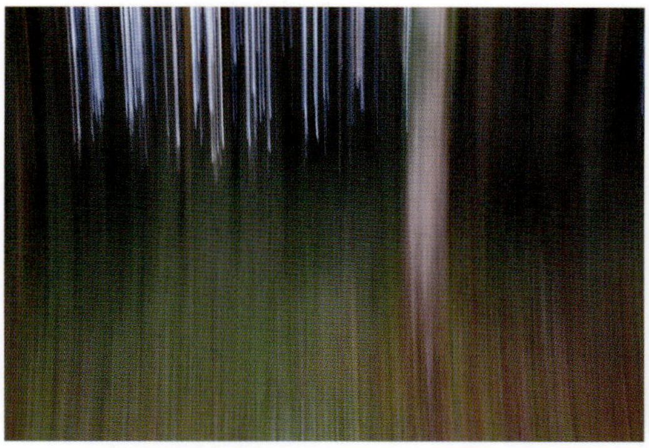

f8 - 1/2 sec - ISO 400

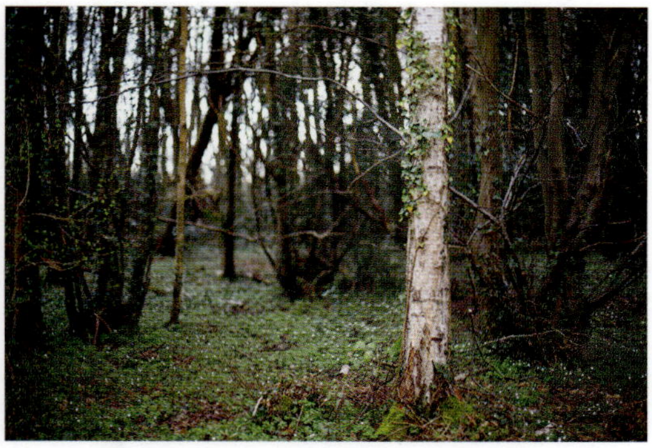

f1.4 - 1/60th - ISO 400

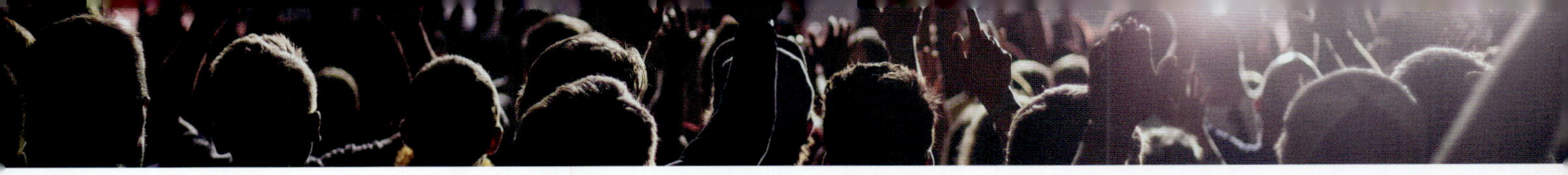

Nikon

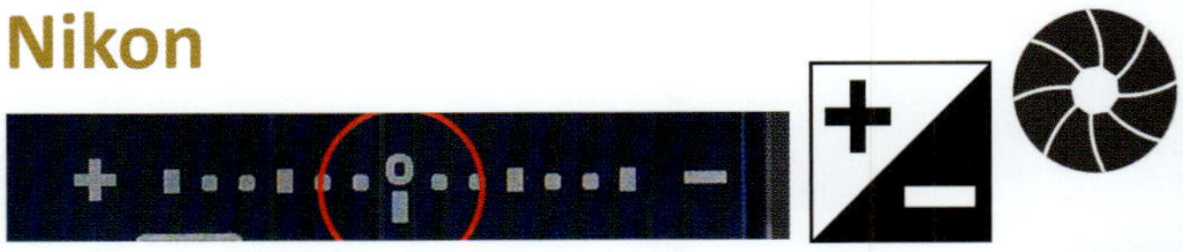

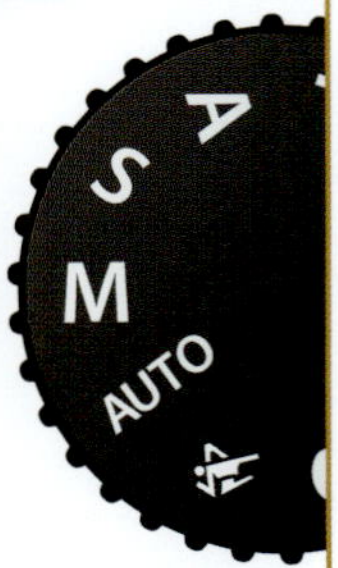

- Make sure you take your ISO off auto, then set it to 400 or 100 if it's a very bright day.
- Twist the dial on the back to change the shutter speed.
- To change the aperture, hold down the Exposure Compensation button (+/- button) or the button with the aperture symbol whilst twisting the same dial. You should see the meter on your screen change. Some cameras have a second circular dial on the front to change the aperture.
- Keep changing the shutter speed or the aperture until the meter reaches the centre '0' (pictured above).

Canon

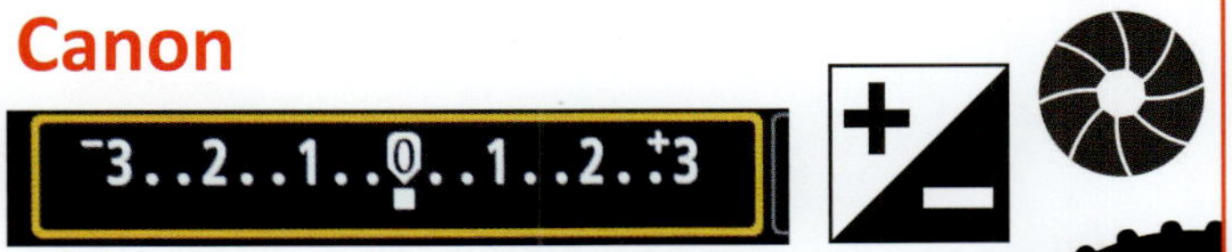

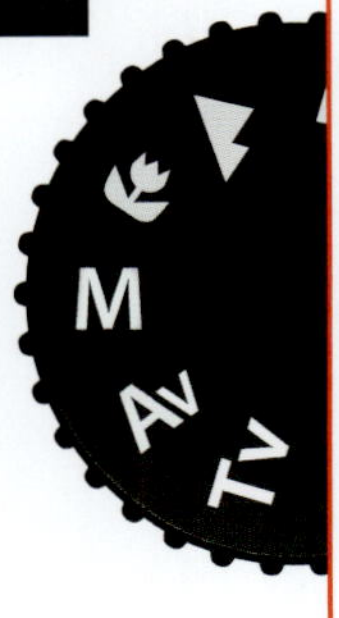

- To manually change your shutter speed, twist the dial on the top of your camera
- To change the aperture, press and hold the AV button (+/- button) whilst twisting the dial on top.
  Some canon cameras have a second circular dial on the back to change the aperture.

When in the 'M' mode, if you press the shutter half way down, you'll take a meter reading (the camera will measure the light available). The camera's light meter (Highlighted red and yellow above) will show a dot/line going into – numbers or + numbers. This is your meter reading.
If the dot is in the + numbers you are currently over exposed, if the dot is in the – numbers you under exposed.
You need to change the aperture and/or shutter speed accordingly to get that dot onto 0. When the meter reading is 0 you are correctly exposed for the shot.

Examples
In the example below, I've panned upwards on my tripod whilst taking the shot at a slower shutter speed. The slower shutter speed has blurred the shot whereas the faster one hasn't.

Same amount of light – Two different visual effects

To view a video tutorial on getting this blurred look go to www.theschoolofphotography.com and type ICM in the search bar.

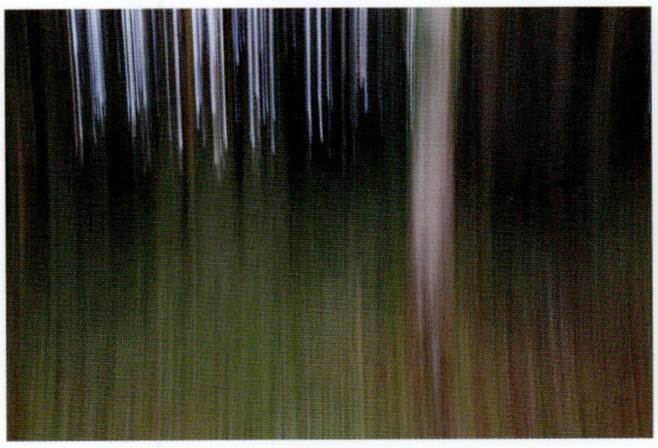
f8 - 1/2 sec - ISO 400

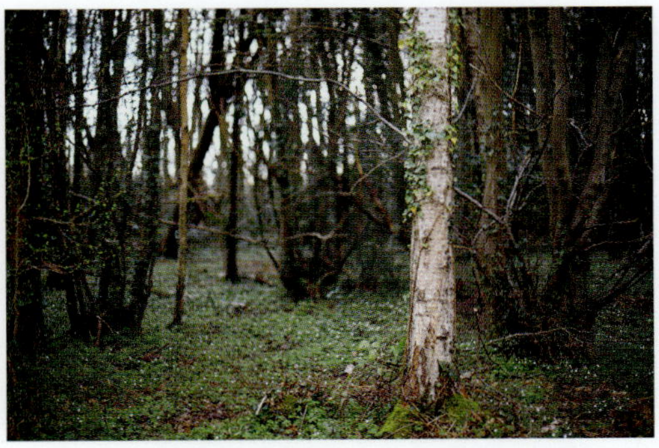
f1.4 - 1/60th - ISO 400

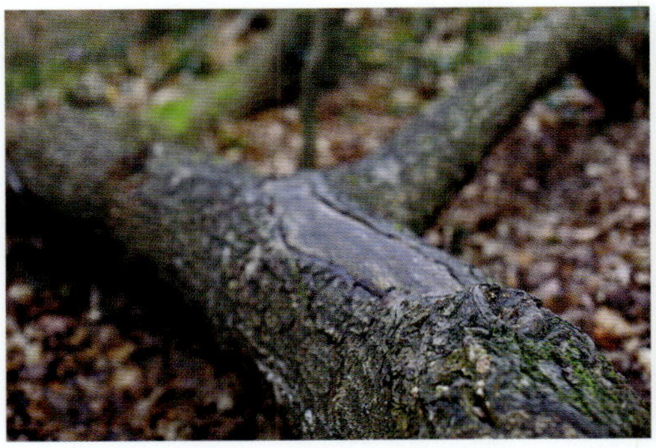
f2.8 - 1/60th - ISO 400

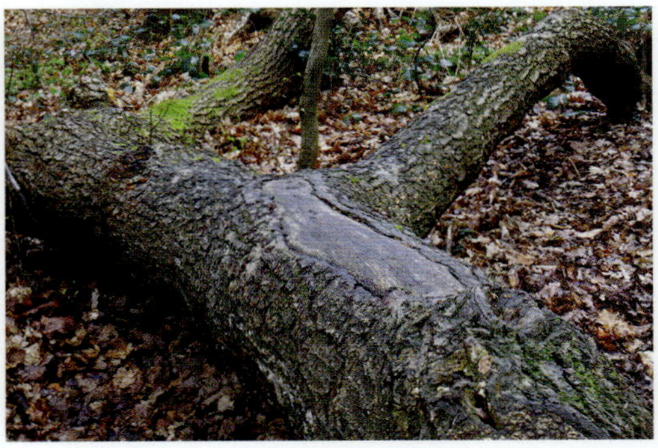
f22 - 1" - ISO 400

In this example I have changed the aperture in the two shots to give me a shallow DOF in one shot and a long DOF in the other.
Same amount of light – Two different visual effects

In photography, you should always start with the visual effect you want to achieve, e.g. if you want to create a sense of motion blur, you know you will need a slow shutter so you start there and work the rest of the exposure around that. Keep practicing this task until you have full control over the visual effects of your photography.

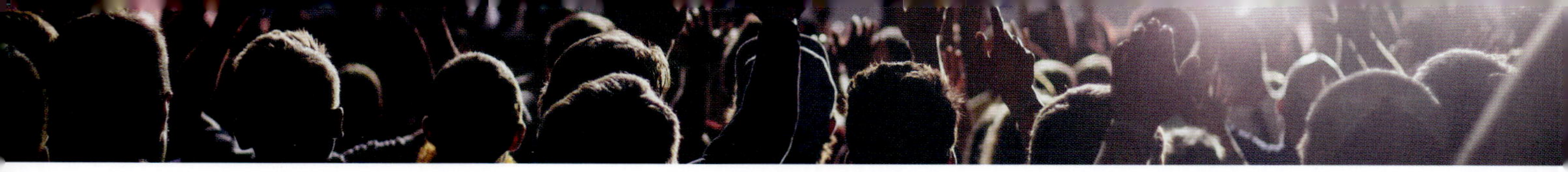

I hope you've had a good practice with that, it's a really good task to help you understand that balance of light. Now let's talk about where ISO fits into to all of this because ISO also affects the exposure.

Now when you're doing any shoot, as stated before, your starting point is deciding what image effect you want. For instance, do you want to create a shallow Depth of Field? If so, a wide aperture is needed (example below).

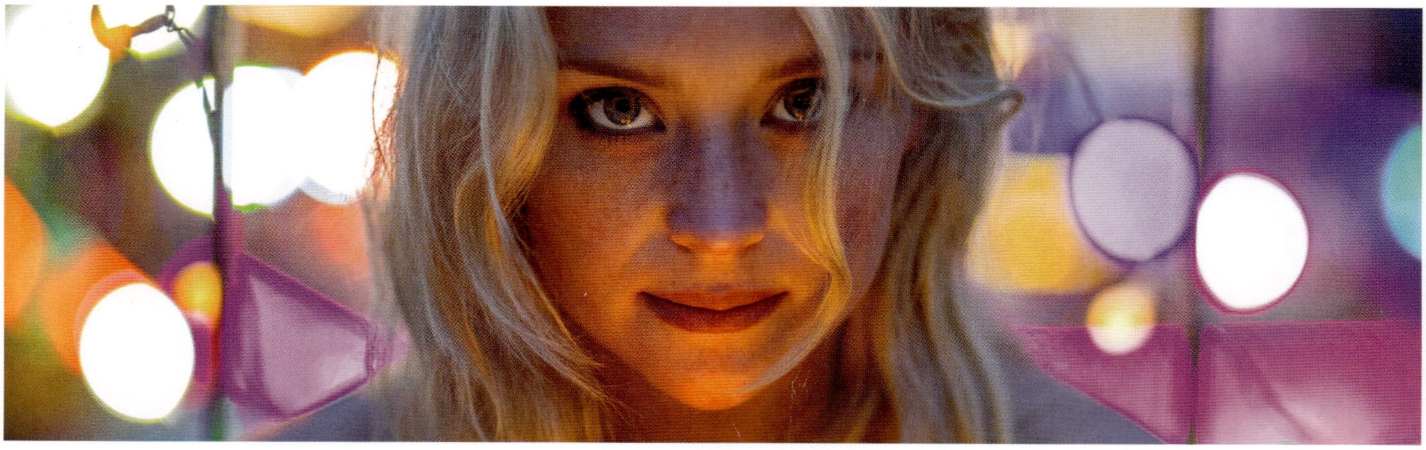

Or do you want car lights streaking of into the distance? For that you need to use slow shutter speeds (example below). These are the things that give you the image effect.

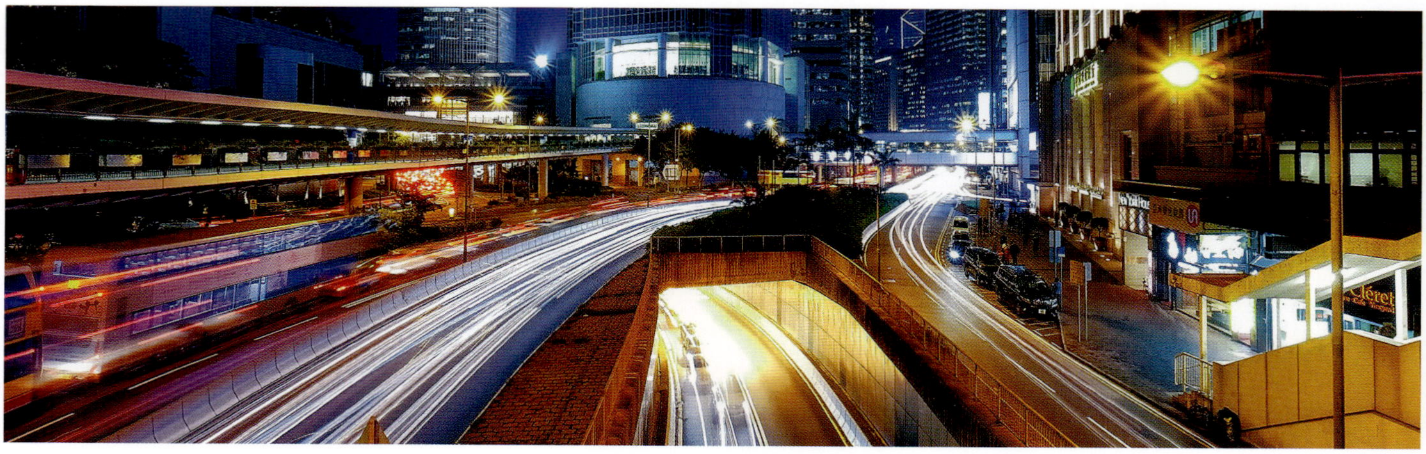

So where does ISO fit into all of this?

The ISO doesn't make the cars streak of into the distance, a slow shutter speed does that. The ISO doesn't create a shallow DOF, your aperture does that.

As shown in your ISO chapter, ideally you want as low an ISO as possible in all your shots as this will reduce noise and give you a finer quality image. But the real world doesn't work like that. You might be inside, outside, cloudy day etc. So, you need to think about what ISO setting you need after you've thought about what image effect you want.

Always start with what image effect you want first and work your exposure settings around that.

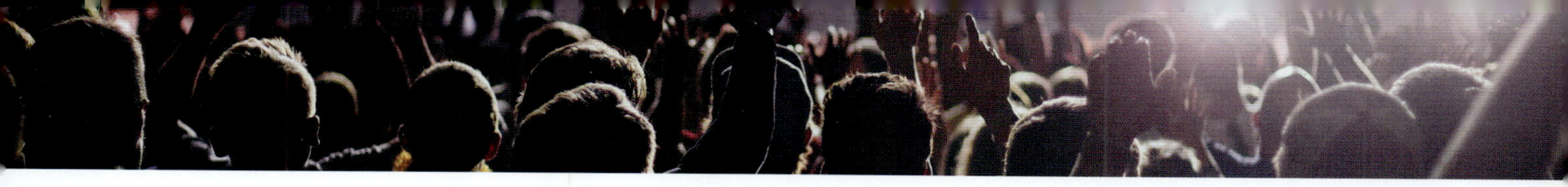

If you're in a low light situation, let's say you're inside a building, and you want to take pictures of people; you're hand holding the camera and the image effect that you want is nice, sharp people with no blurring.

For this you need a fast shutter speed, so this is your starting point. A shutter speed of 1/125th second will be fine here. Then you might set your widest aperture to let in as much light as possible, let's say f4. So, in this situation your settings to get that image effect is 1/125th second @ f4.

That still might not let in enough light to enable you to use a low ISO. So in this case you will need to up the ISO to make the camera more sensitive to light. This will enable you can get a shot with a faster shutter speed in low light. The trade off for this though, is that you will get some noise in your image - but, you will get a sharp picture.

You're limited to the light you have available in photography and that's that. There's nothing you can do about it, you have to just control it coming into your camera as best you can. Think back to the first chapter of this book - Photography is about controlling light.

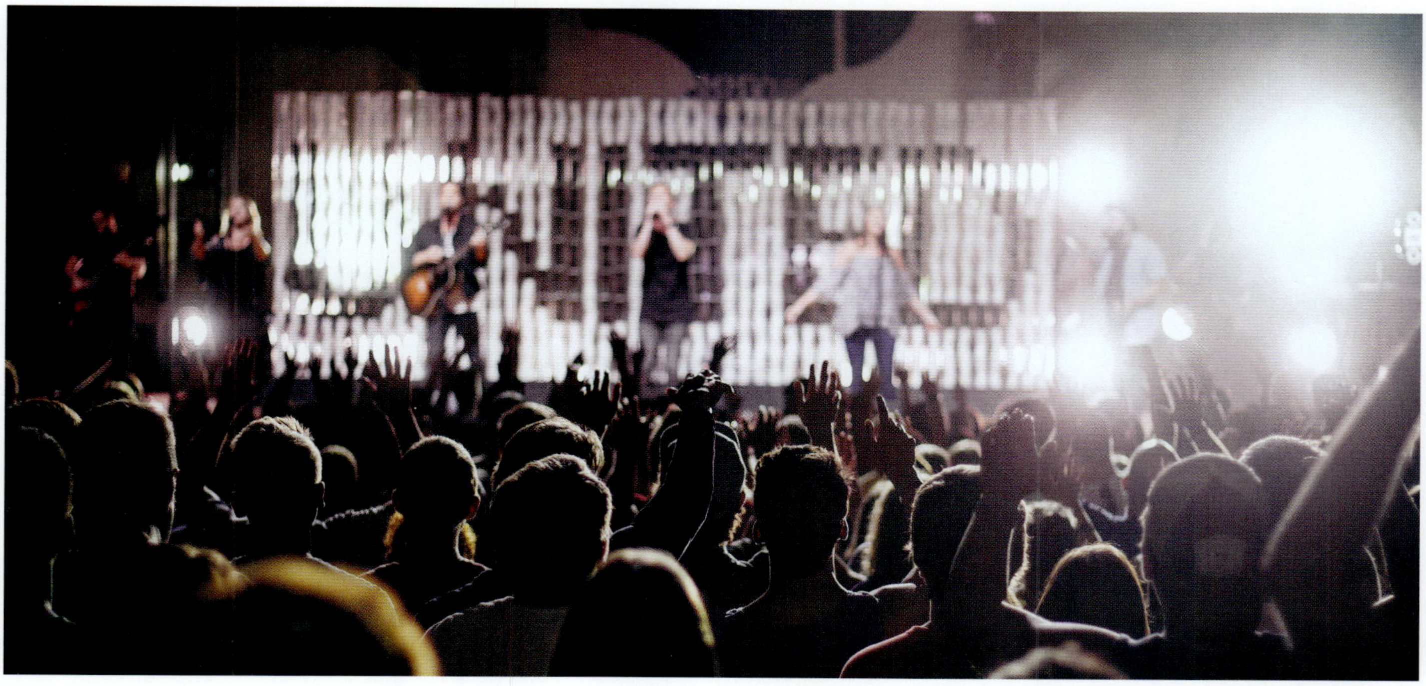

1/125th Second – f4 – ISO 1600

Above is a perfect example of this. A low light situation, but you want to capture the scene without any movement. You use a shutter speed of 1/125th sec, you use your lens' widest aperture, in this case f4. There is not enough light to use a low ISO so you up the ISO to 1600 to make the camera more sensitive to light instead. In this situation you are able to freeze movement in low light by increasing the camera's ISO setting. The trade off for this however is the image will have noise.

I know that balancing exposures can be quite complicated to get your head round and I recommend that if you haven't quite got it, read this chapter again, get out there with your camera and use it in fully manual mode. Control the image effect that you want. Sometimes it's much better to just give it a go and get practicing with it. Once you're good with all of that, move onto the next chapter.

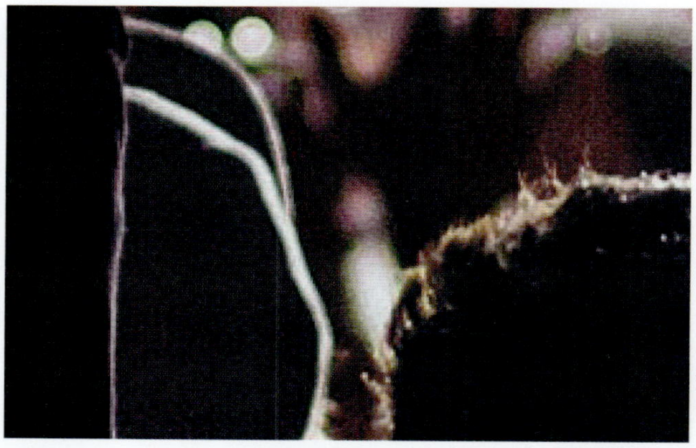

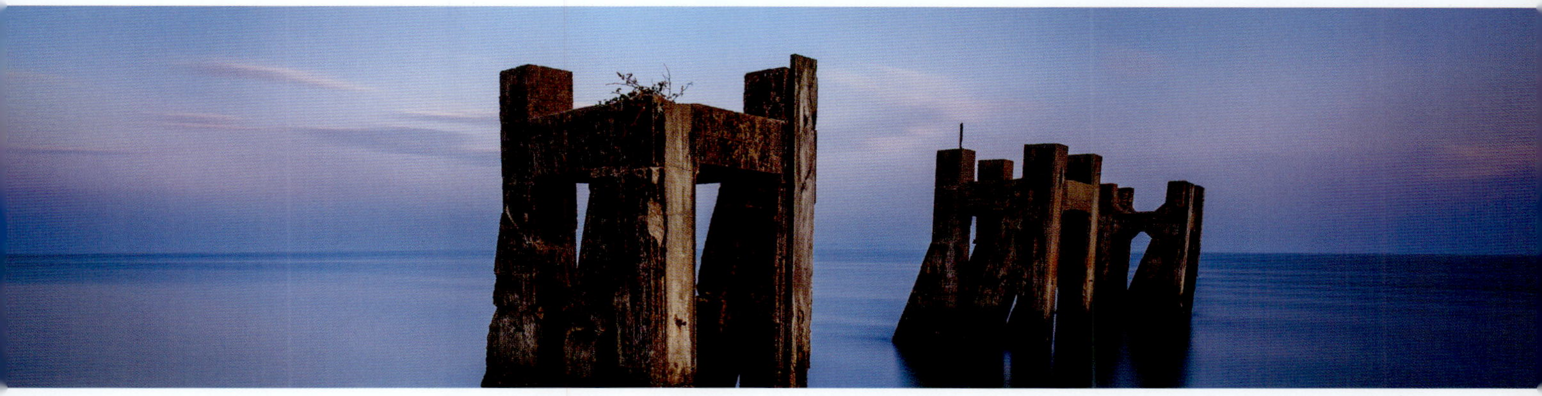

Resolution

Chapter 12

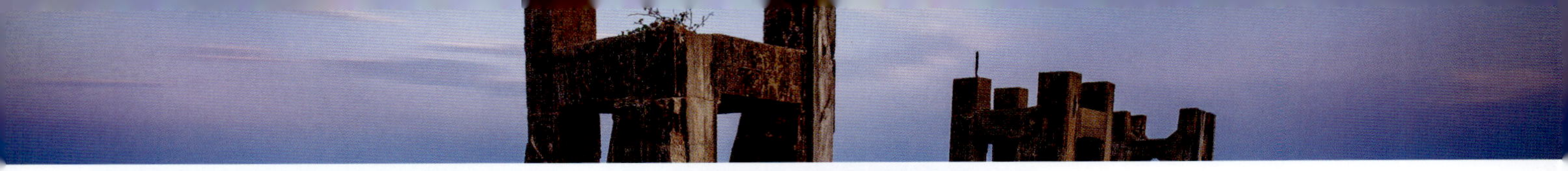

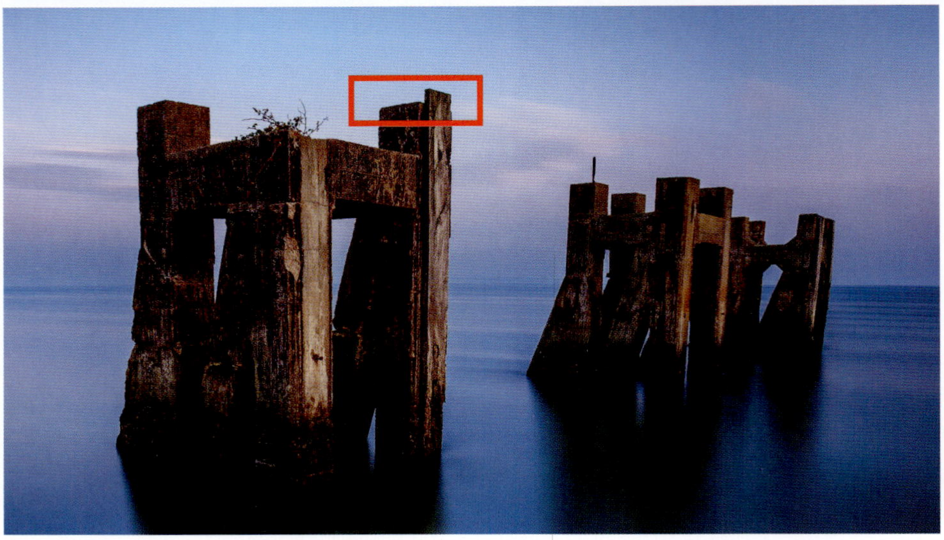

This chapter is about resolution, what it is and how it can benefit you as a photographer.

Resolution, or sometimes called the image res, is the amount of pixels an image has. A pixel is the smallest part of a digital image. If you've ever zoomed in on an image, you will have seen that the image turns into lots of little squares – those squares are the pixels.

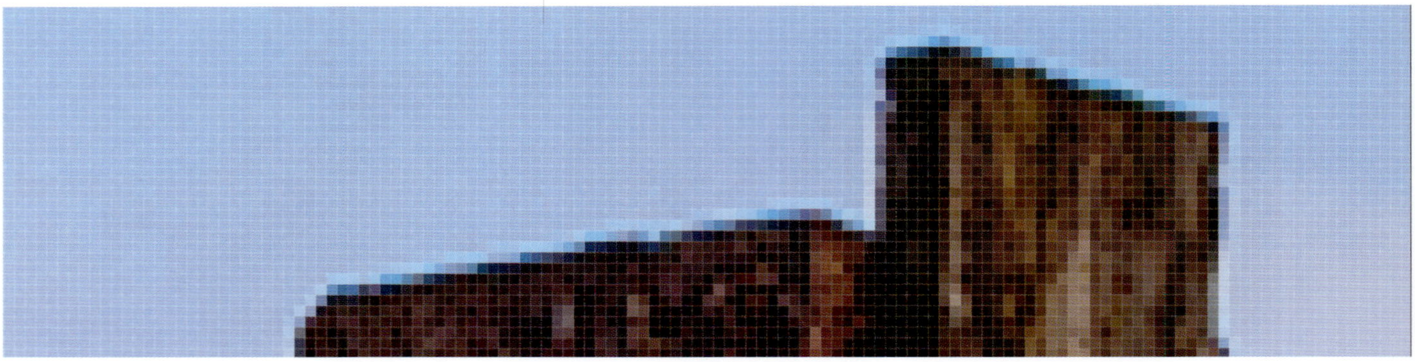

The resolution of an image is the total amount of pixels within it. Resolution comes into effect when you want to print big images. To get big prints you need a high res image. For instance, if you going to print a 10x15 inch print, you're going to need your camera set to it's highest resolution as you're going to want as many pixels as possible in the image.

If you're never going to print a picture and it's just, for example, for an internet auction site, then you will just need a low-resolution image. There's more about that further on in this chapter, but first let's have a look at what a low-resolution image looks like against a high resolution image.

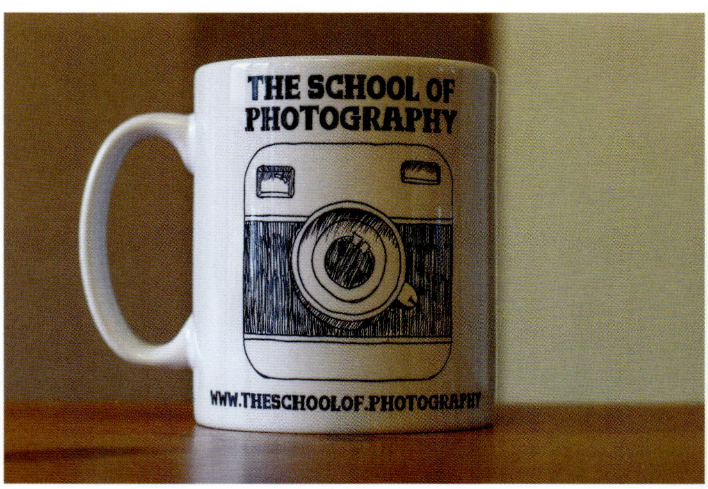

High resolution

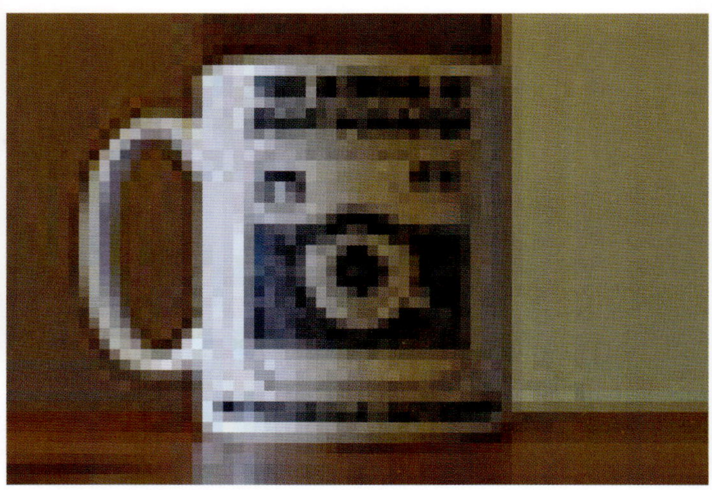

Low resolution
(pixelated image)

Here we have 2 images of the same picture, one has been taken with a high resolution and the other has been adjusted so it has a very low resolution. You can see the low resolution is very blurry. This is what's called a pixelated image.

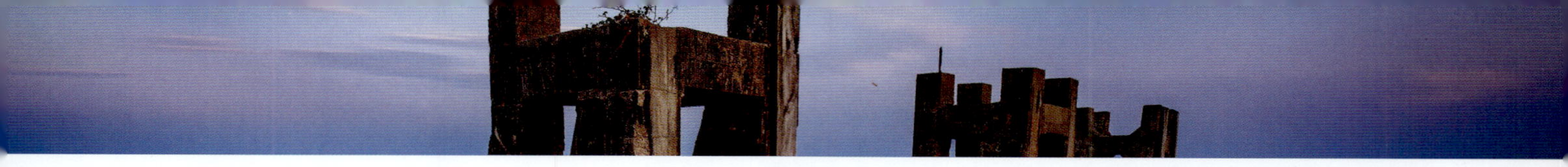

Here are the file sizes of two images taken at different resolutions. The High Res image has a file size of nearly 8 Megabytes whereas the Low Res image is just over 1MB (or 1,000 Kilobytes). To put that into context you can get roughly 8 low res images for your 1 high res image.

A high res image can stretch out more, which means it can print much bigger. Also, the higher the res, the more pixels you have to play with, so if you need to crop into it, it should still enlarge ok to print.

Name	Type	Size
High Res.jpg	JPG File	7,704 KB
Low Res.jpg	JPG File	1,131 KB

Now you might be thinking "I'll just take all my images at high res just in case". Well there is a downside to that. It will clog up your camera card quickly, it could use up more of your computer hard disk and, if you're going to be emailing or uploading to websites, it's going to take a lot longer for images to be sent.

That's where low res images come into effect. When you want to upload to websites, share images via emails or just use less room on your hard drive, it's better to use low res images.

Resolution is quite simply the amount of pixels an image has, the higher the res – the more pixels, better for printing big prints and cropping into the image. The lower the res, the less pixels - better for uploading and emailing.

If you have the fastest computer you could ever want and as much space on your hard drive as you need, then in theory you could just leave your resolution on high, unless you are going to be emailing your pictures to other people.

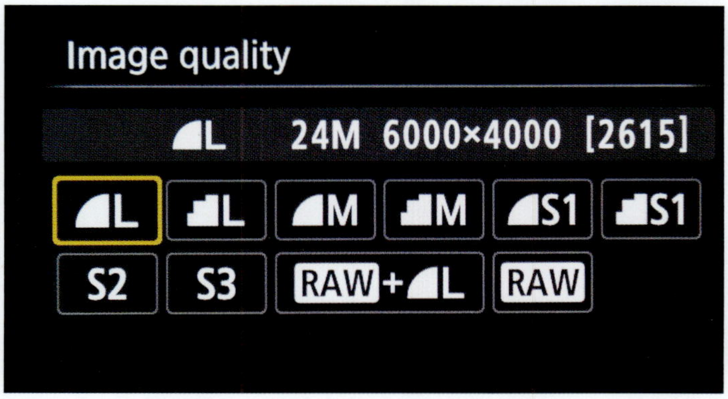

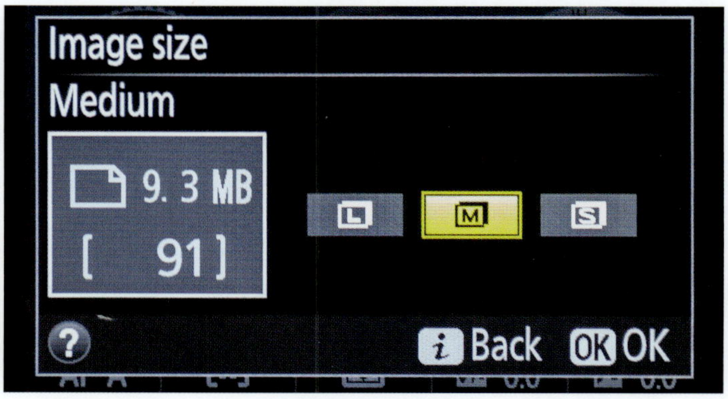

The confusion can come on your camera settings. Some camera settings will have resolution displayed as L M S which means Large, Medium, Small. Other cameras will have it displayed as their megapixels, so you might see something like 8M or 12M etc. Some cameras show both.

A Mega Pixel is 1 million pixels. So to put this into context, if your camera can take 24 Mega pixels, your image will have 24 million pixels within it.

Some cameras will display the file size as well – for instance 10 Megabytes (MB). It all sounds confusing and quite honestly, it is. It's just down to the different camera brands all doing different things. Try to figure out the way in which your camera displays resolution. This information will be in your camera's manual.

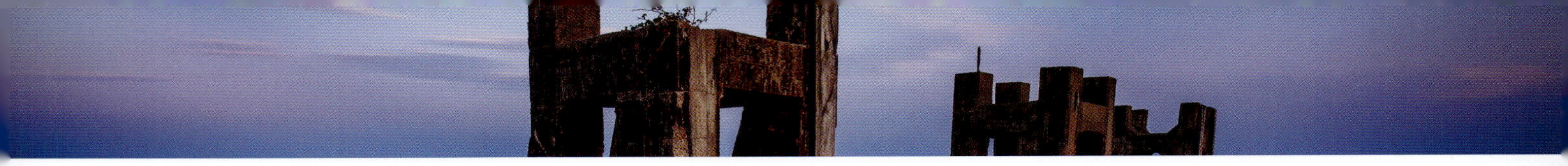

Just to confuse you even more, cameras have something called Jpeg quality, sometimes called Image quality. So you have your image size (the resolution of your image) and your image quality or Jpeg quality. Some cameras will show smooth arch and jagged arch symbols like this:

A smooth arch means a high-quality Jpeg. A jagged arch means a low quality Jpeg. Other cameras will say Fine, Norm, Med and Low (below).

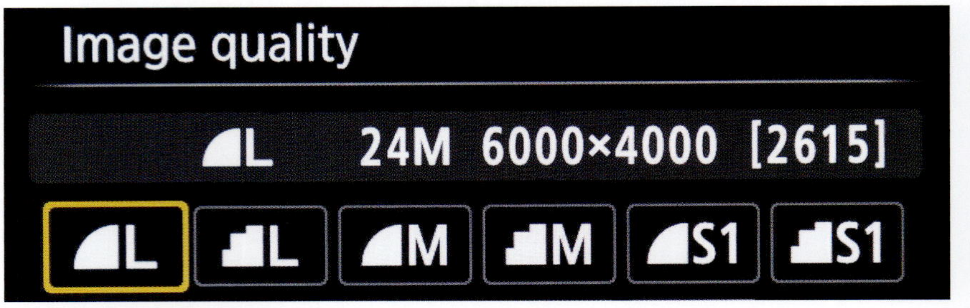

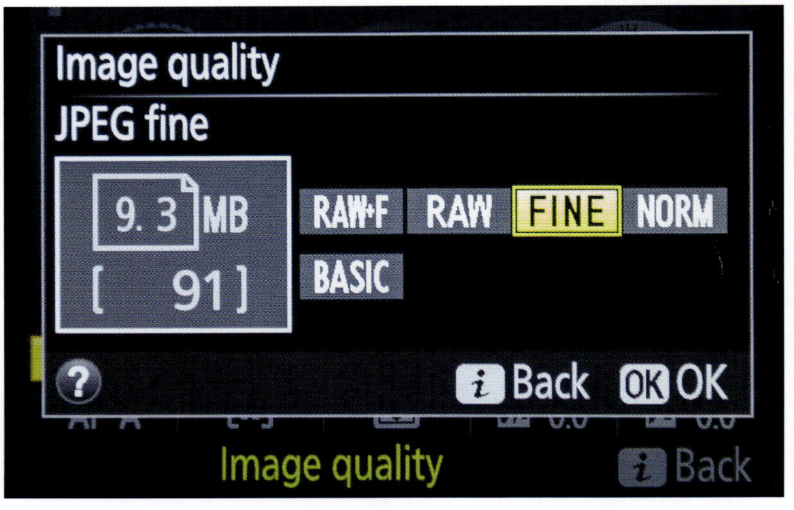

There's more about Jpegs later on in this chapter but for now my advice is to leave the Jpeg quality on the smooth arch or fine setting. The only reason you would put it on a lower setting is if you are going to be taking several images to be sent via the internet.

I want to refer to this table stating the resolution (amount of pixels) needed for a particular print size.

At the top is 0.5mp and for those of us that remember, this was the resolution of the first ever camera phones. On your phone screen, they looked great but try to print them or enlarge them and they looked terrible!

Next we have 2mp. With a 2mp image, you can print a 3x5 inch print and it will look perfect. If you go to the bottom of the table, 10mp plus, here you have enough pixels to print a 13x17inch image.

Resolution needed for various print sizes		
Resolution		Max print size
0.5 megapixels		N/A
2 megapixels		3x5 in.
4 megapixels		5x7 in.
6 megapixels		8x10 in.
8 megapixels		11x14 in.
10+ megapixels		13x17 in.

Let's put this into context – how many times are you going to want to print an image that is bigger than 13x17in? If you're doing final prints that are for art or for Clients then you will want the highest res possible, but if you're doing holiday snaps and you know that you're not going to print them larger than 8x10in, you only need to have your camera set to 6mp, and on most new cameras, that is lower than its smallest setting.

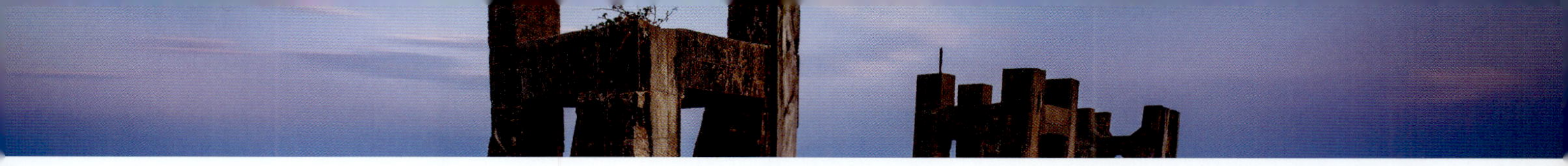

Get familiar with your camera's image size and quality settings

Task

This task is to get you used to where the resolution settings are and getting you to figure out what image sizes your camera is going to produce.

Again, below I'm going to show you how to do this on common cameras, other makes will be very similar or simply look up 'Image Quality' or 'Resolution' in your camera's manual.

- Set your camera to P
- Put your ISO on Auto
- Put your camera on tripod and use a remote trigger or two second timer to make sure your camera stays still during the exposures.
- Work in Jpeg, not RAW. We'll cover RAW later in this Book, it's important you get your photography correct first before we look at RAW files. RAW files are for post-processing so we'll stick to shooting in Jpeg while we are learning.
- Take 2 shots of the same thing, 1 at the lowest resolution and 1 at your highest res.
- Then transfer the 2 images onto a computer and zoom to view the images in more detail. I want you to see the difference between where the high res image breaks and looks pixelated, to where the low-res image breaks and looks pixelated.

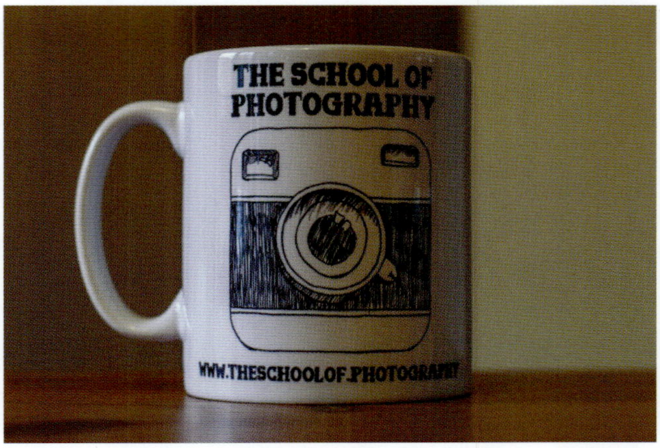

High Res

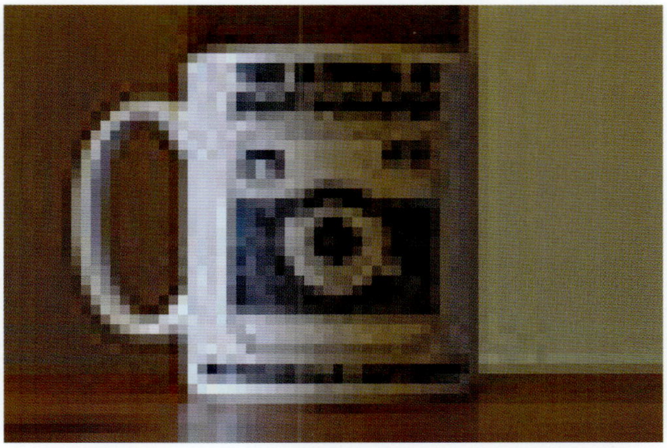

Low Res

Canon

- Press the MENU button and scroll with your dial until you find image quality.
- In the image quality menu, you'll see the selection of L M S that was mentioned earlier.

Take one photo using the L setting, then another using the lowest S setting.

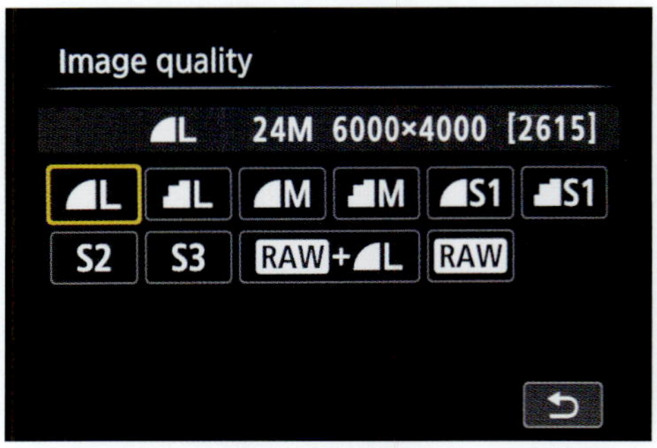

Nikon

To change the resolution on a Nikon:

- Press the button then select 'Image quality' and press 'OK'.
- Select JPEG FINE
- Press the button again and select 'Image size'

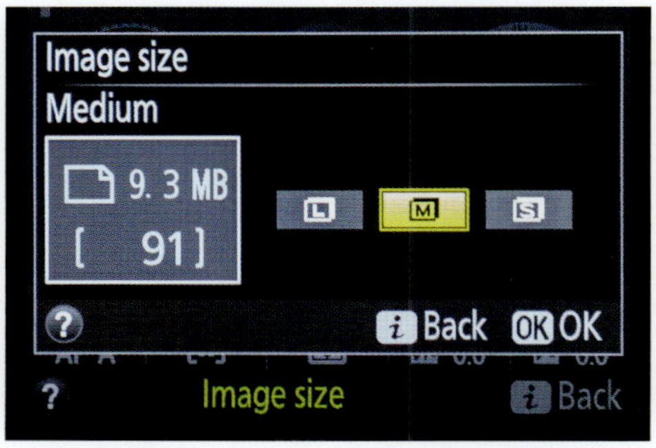

Select L to take one picture on your highest resolution and S to take one on your smallest.

Example

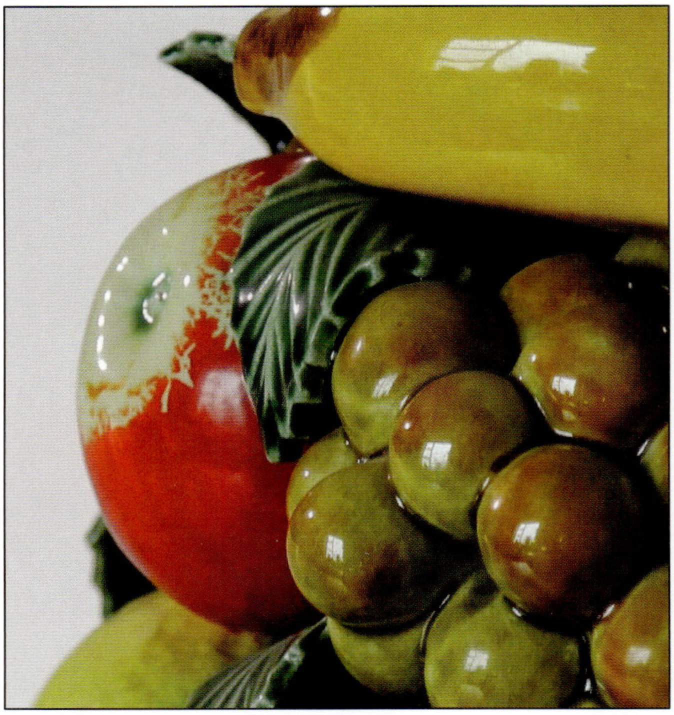

- Taken at a high resolution
- Picture is clear even when zoomed in

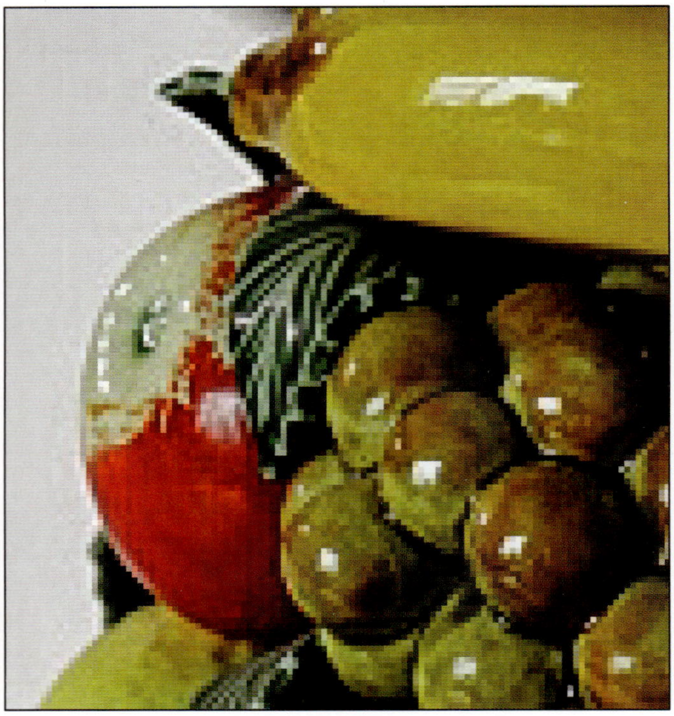

- Same picture taken with a low resolution
- Picture is soft when zoomed in. It has become pixelated.

So hopefully you're getting a bit more comfortable with the resolution settings on your camera. The next thing to learn is something called PPI. PPI stands for Pixels Per Inch.

I'm sure things are getting quite confusing now what with PPIs, Pixels, Resolutions etc, but please don't worry. PPI is something you don't need to worry about too much unless you're working with external print labs or building a website where you need images to be a particular size and resolution. However, I do feel it's important to go through this as it might be something that you've come across or will come across in the future.

If you have an image 10 inches wide and its resolution is 72 PPI. It will mean that there are 72 pixels within a straight line of 1 inch of the image (*above*).

On screen it will look fine, as 72ppi is the optimum screen resolution. If the image has more than 72ppi, you will not see any difference. If the image has less than this, it will become pixelated.

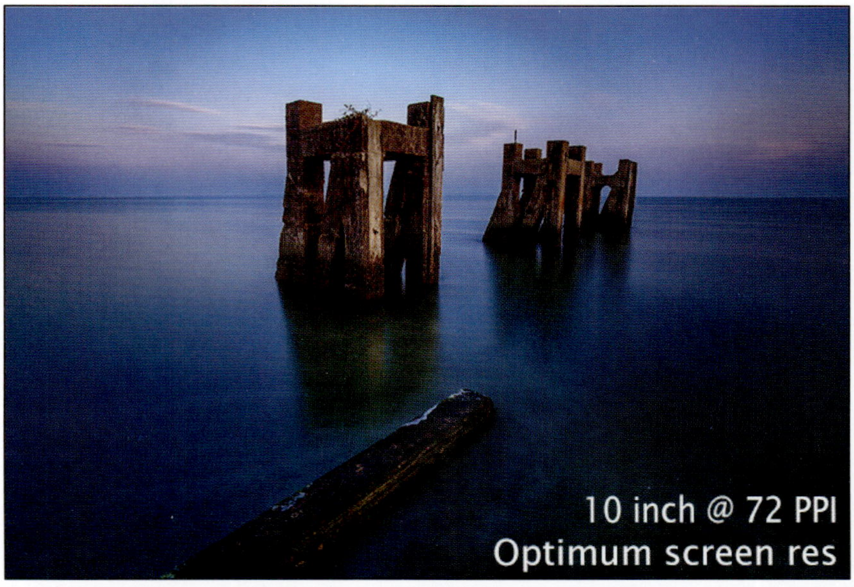

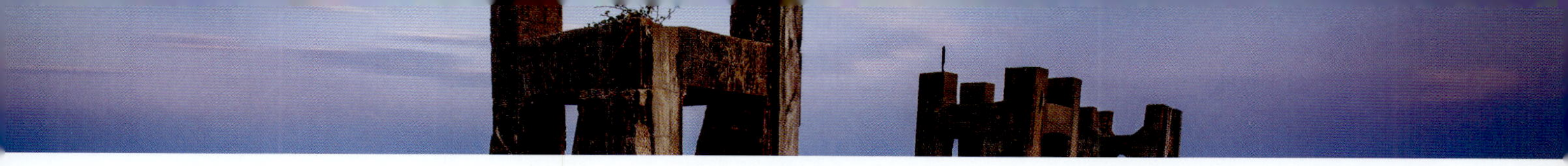

If you try to print an image with 72ppi it will look like this (pixelated).

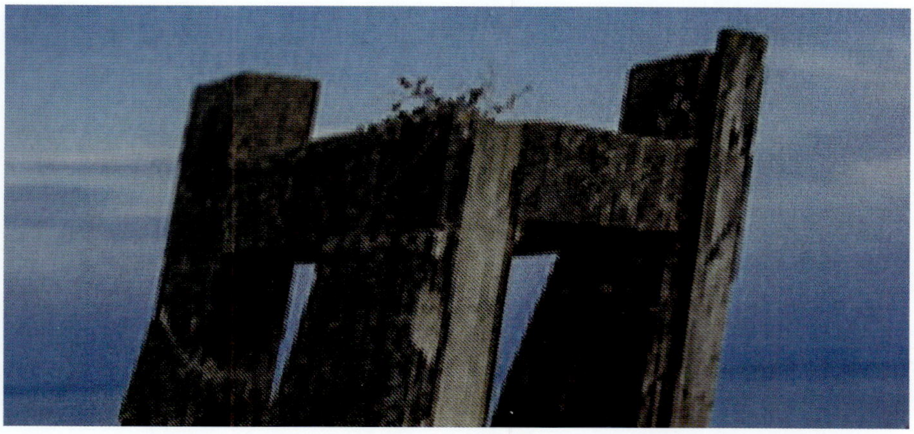

A print printed at a resolution of 72ppi (pixels per inch)

To get a print looking perfect it needs to at least 300 PPI like this:

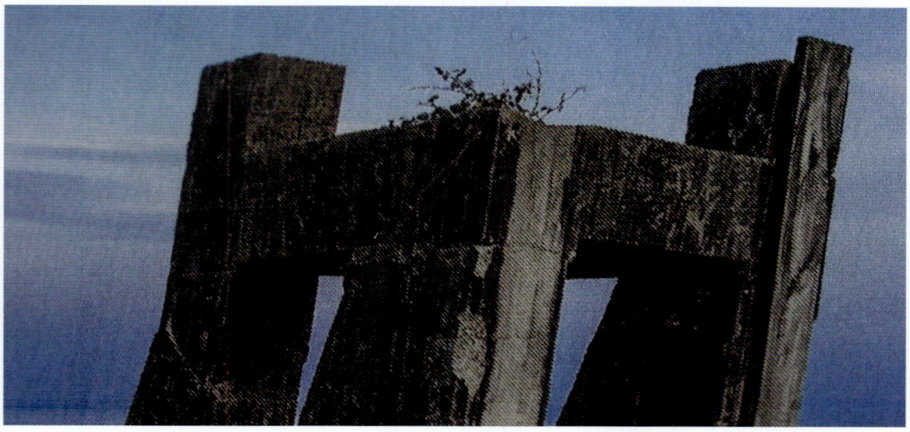

A print printed at a resolution of 300ppi

The optimum print resolution is 300ppi. If the image has more than this, you will not see it. If the image has less than this, it will become pixelated.

I know it sounds confusing but that's pretty much all you need to know. For an image to look good on screen it needs to have at least 72 pixels within one inch and for a picture to look good in print it needs to have at least 300 pixels within one inch. The reason it needs to be higher in print is because your eye sees a lot more that a screen can project.

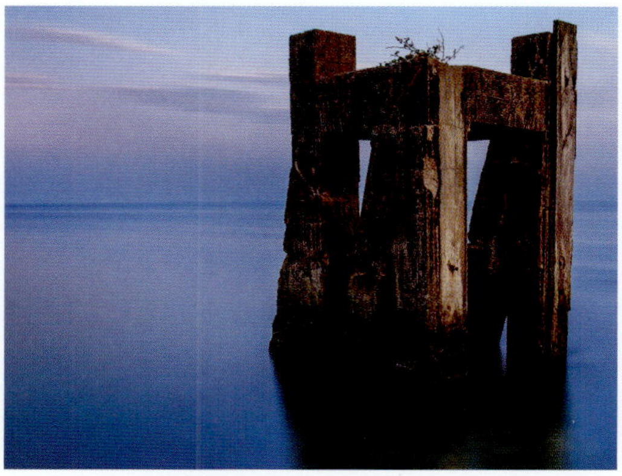

Lets recap:

- Resolution is the amount of pixels your image has.
- A pixel is the smallest part of a digital image – 1 square.
- High res images are good for printing big or cropping.
- Low res images are good for internet and emailing.
- High res images will have a bigger file size and will take up more space on your camera card and PC whereas low res images will have a smaller file size and take up less space.
- Camera settings around resolution differ from brand to brand – get to know your camera models' way of doing things.
- A Megapixel is 1 million pixels.
- Leave your Jpeg or Image quality to its highest setting.
- PPI – mean Pixels Per Inch and your minimum screen res should be 72 PPI, your minimum print res should be 300 PPI

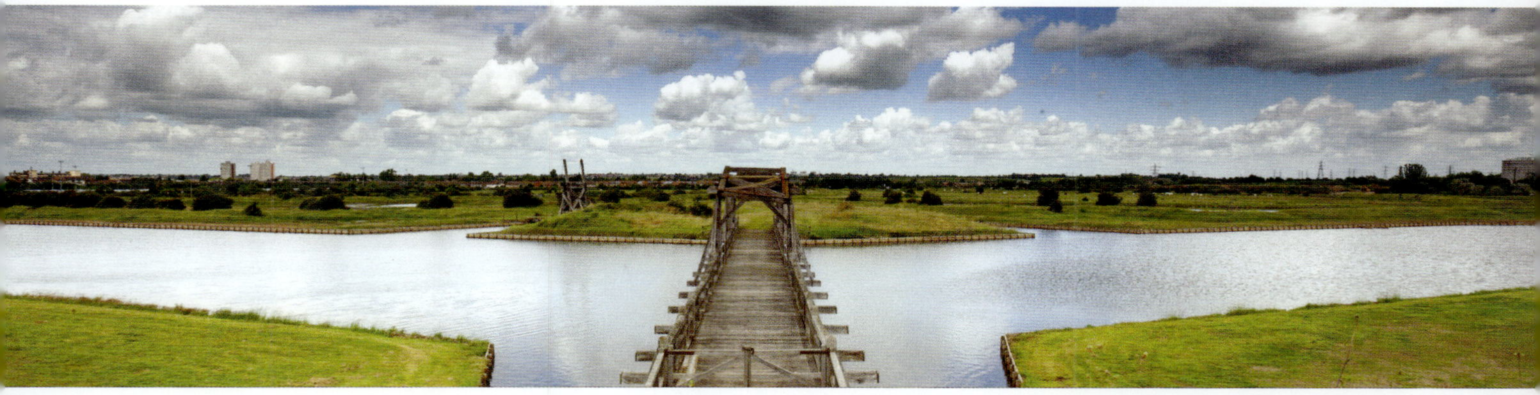

Understanding Light and White Balance

Chapter 13

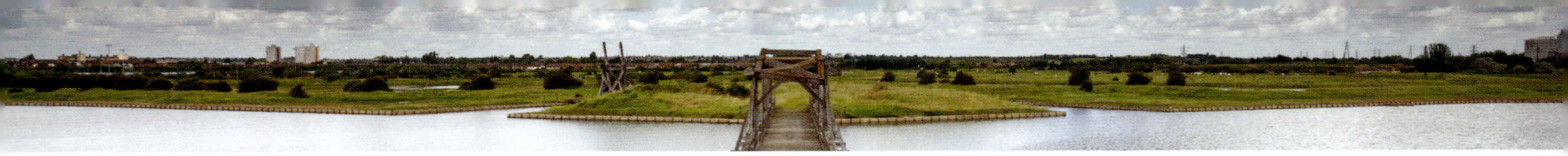

This chapter is going to be looking at light. Photography is all about the control of light and here you'll get a better understanding of how light works with photography.

To get us started I want you to answer this question:

Where does light come from?

That sounds like a really simple question. But I want you to think about that and I want you to **name as many types of light sources as you can.**

For example, you can say car lights is a source of light, a street lamp is a source of light and so on. I want you to write down as many examples you can think of.

Answer

Hopefully you have got lots of examples written down. Common answers I get are:

- Flood lights	- Street lamp	- Strip lighting	- Daylight
- Incandescent	- Car headlights	- Halogen light	- L.E.D
- Luminescent	- Neon lights	- Studio flash	- Flash
- Plasma lamp	- Fireworks	- Lanterns	- Torch
- Light from TV	- Fluorescent	- Sun	- Candle
- Oil lamps	- Lamps	- Moonlight	- Light Bulb
- Lasers	- Lightning	- Starlight	- Fire

The fact is there are lots of different light sources available to us, and knowing the effect they have on a picture can really help you out. I'm now going to put these different light sources into 3 groups. Natural Light, Flash Lighting, and Artificial light. Then, look at the variations of light under these headings.

Natural Light

Under Natural Light you have daylight at noon, which will give you a pure white light.

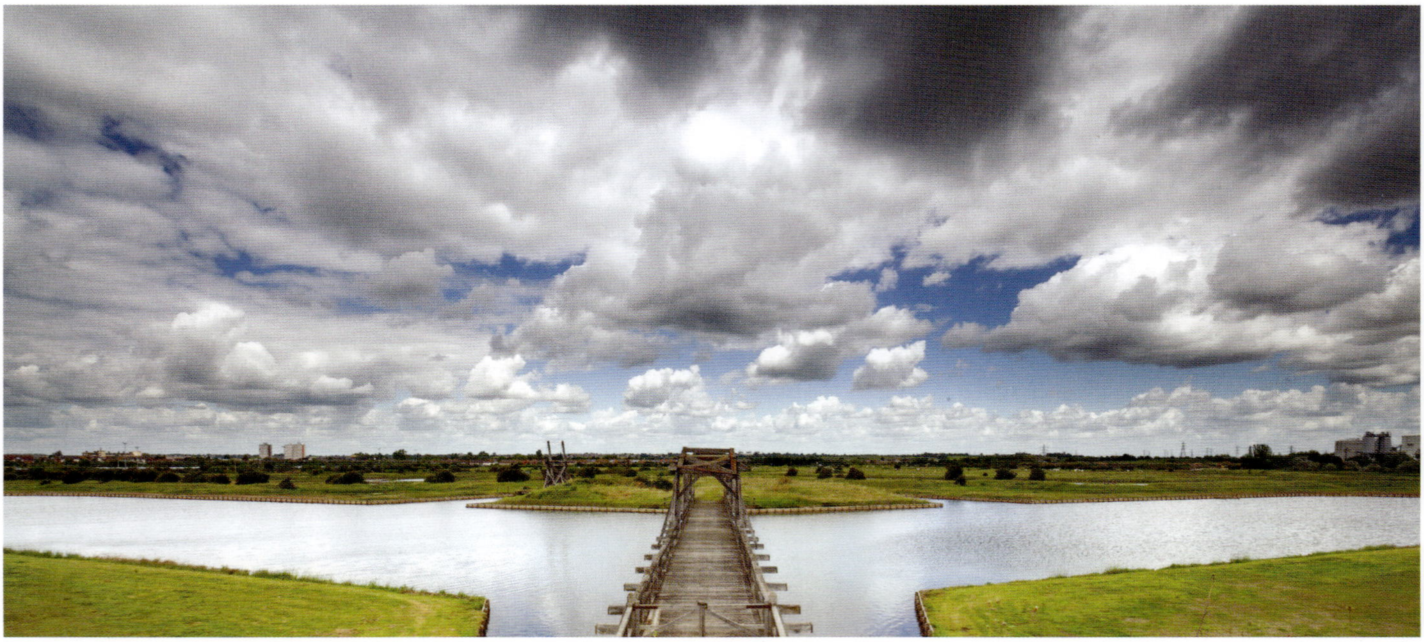

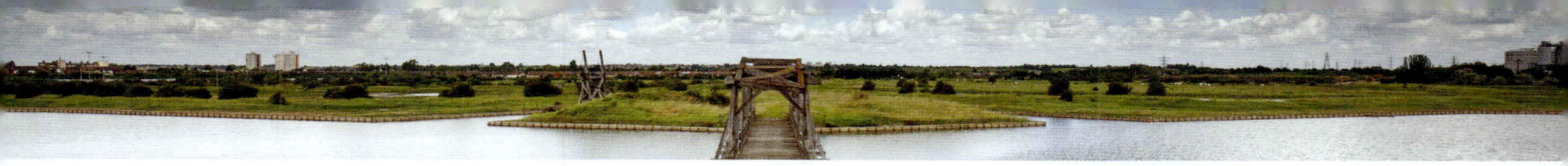

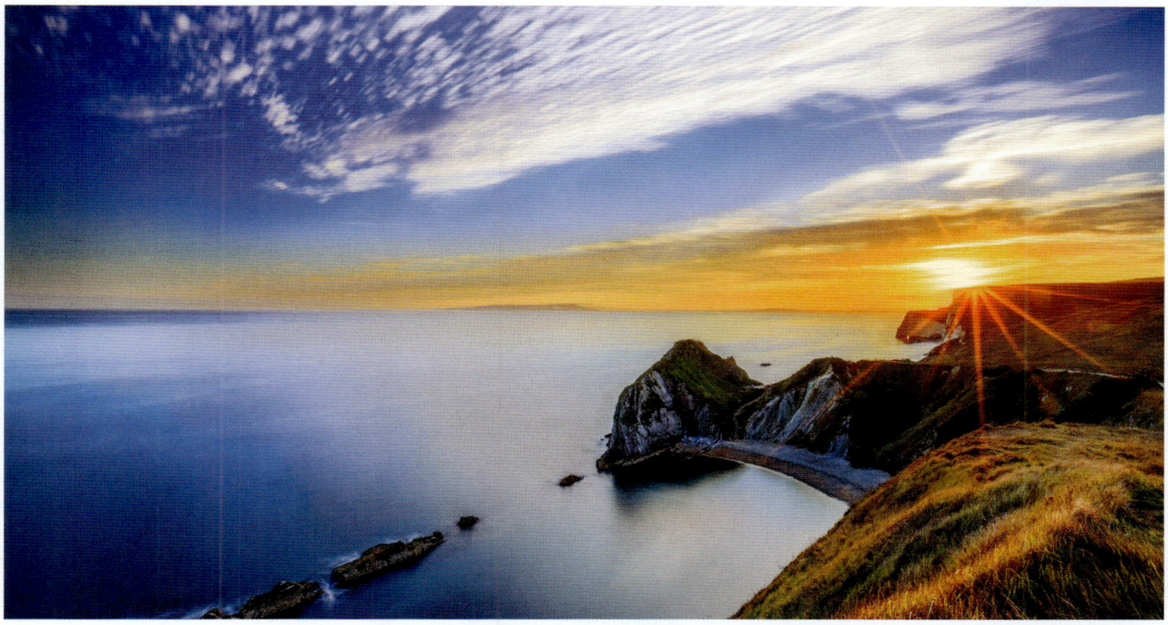

You have sunsets and sunrises, which give you orange light.

You have a cloudy day, which will add blues into the light.

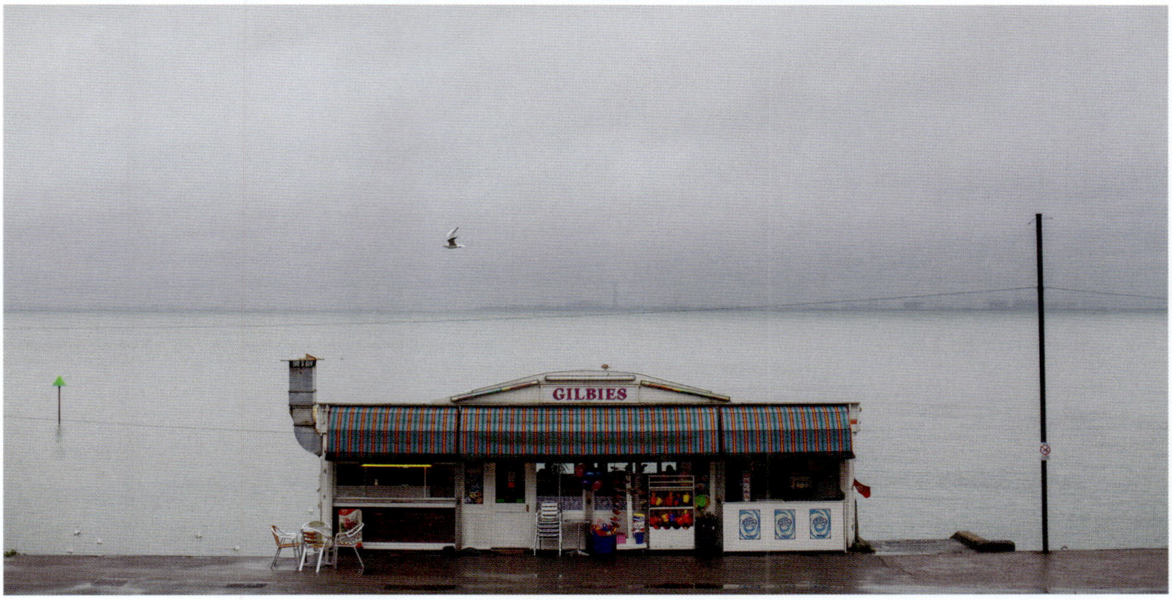

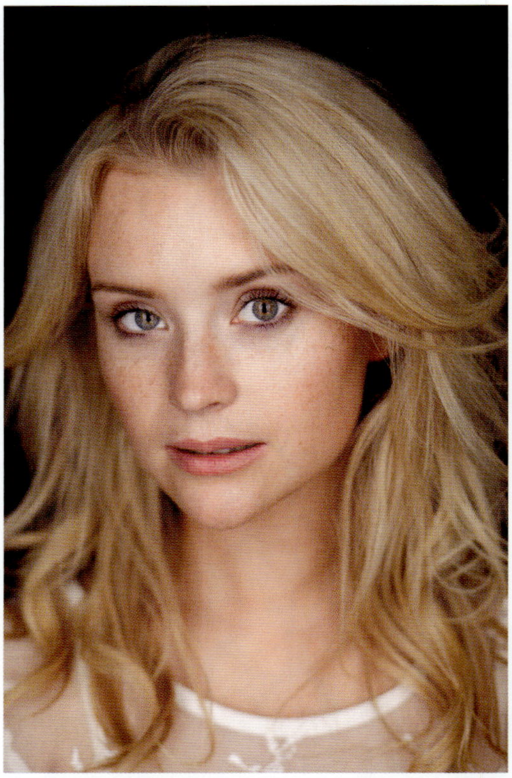

Flash Light

Under Flash, you get studio lighting for a more controlled look (*left*). Or flash guns which are a good portable light source (*below*).

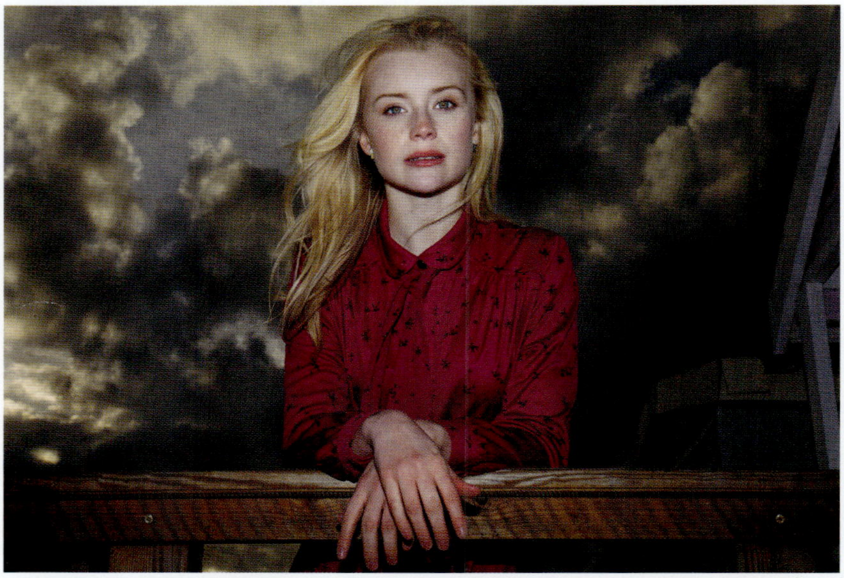

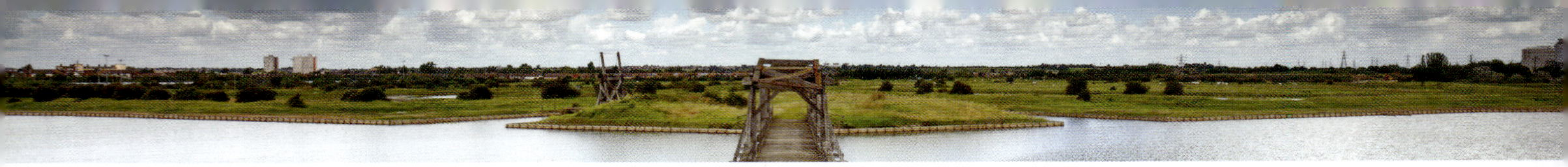

Artificial Light

Under artificial light you get something called Tungsten lighting, which will give you an orange light, commonly found in the old light bulbs (*right*). You also get Fluorescent lights which give off a green cast (*below*).

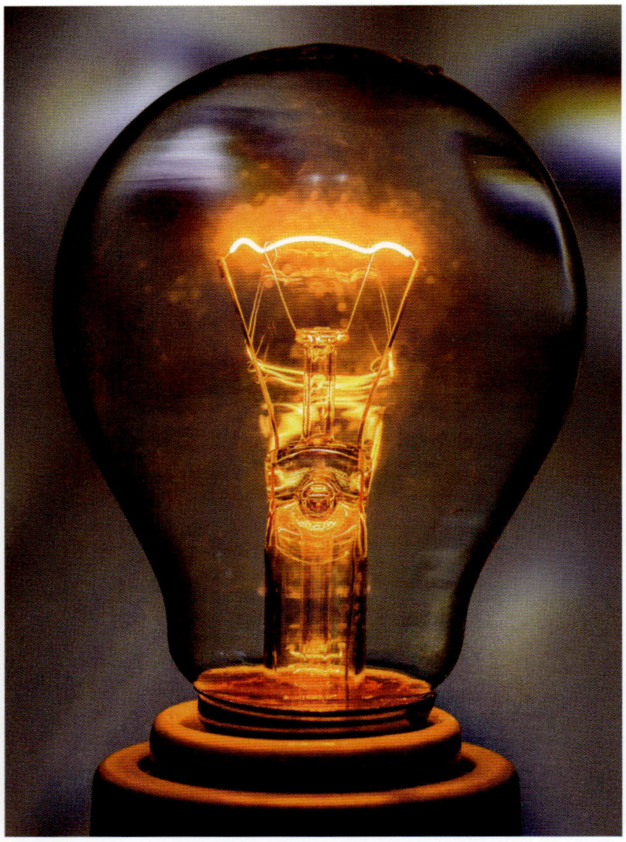

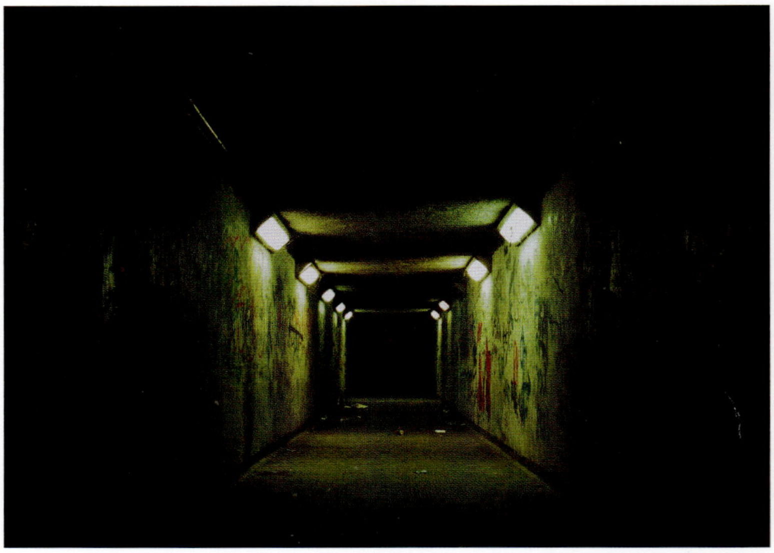

And street lights which are generally a yellow/orange colour (*right*).

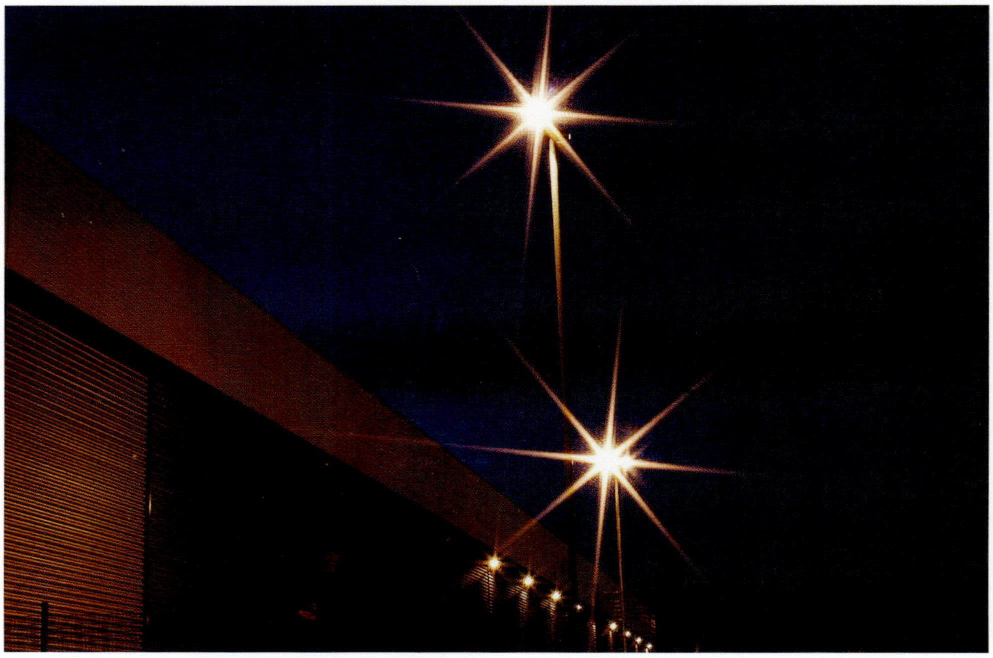

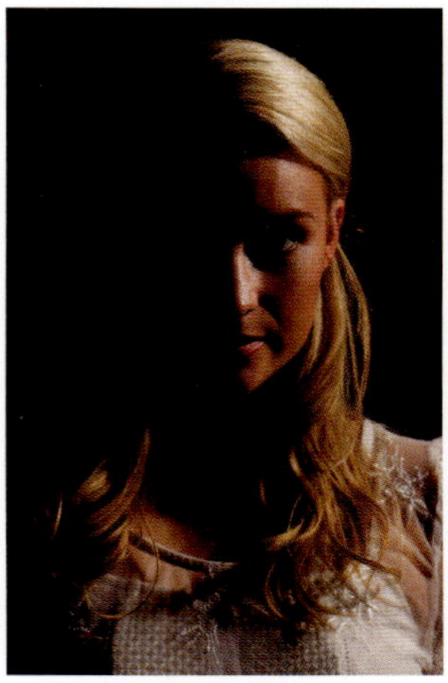

Hard light

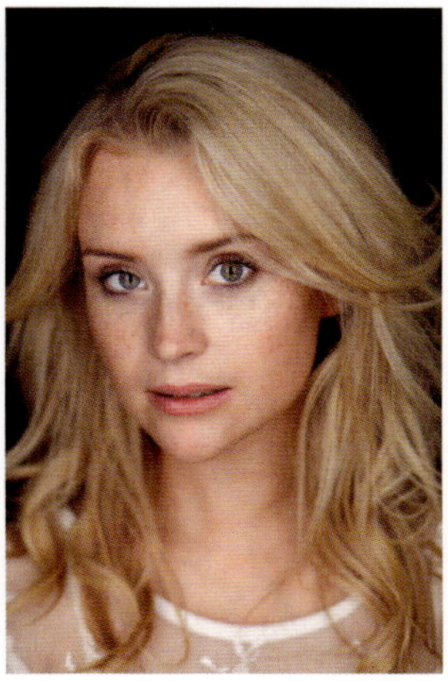

Soft light

There are loads of different types of light and each one will give you a different look; and it doesn't end there because under every light source you can get different effects of light.

This basically breaks down into two sections - hard light and soft light.

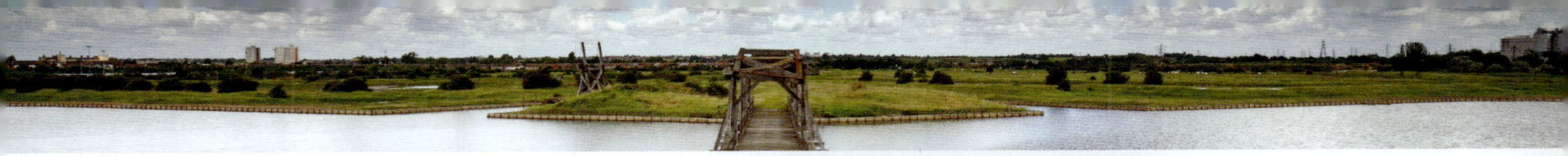

Hard Light

Hard light is created by direct light. This means the light is coming direct from the light source and hitting the object.

Examples of hard light would be a sunny day or a flash on a camera and the effect it will show is strong shadows, shining skin etc.

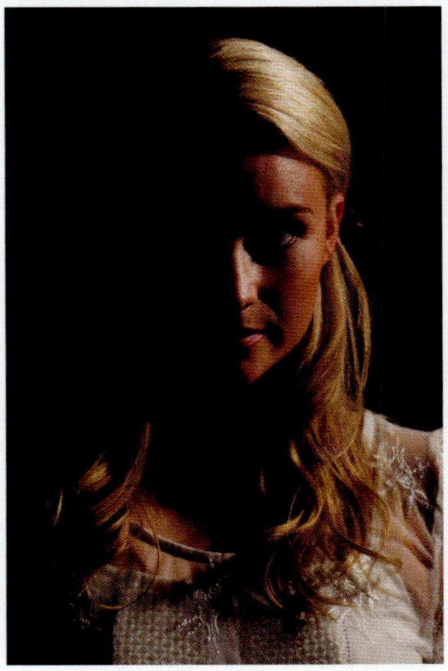

Hard light
Direct from source

Soft Light

Soft light can be created in two separate ways. One is by reflected light where light reflects off a surface and hits the subject.

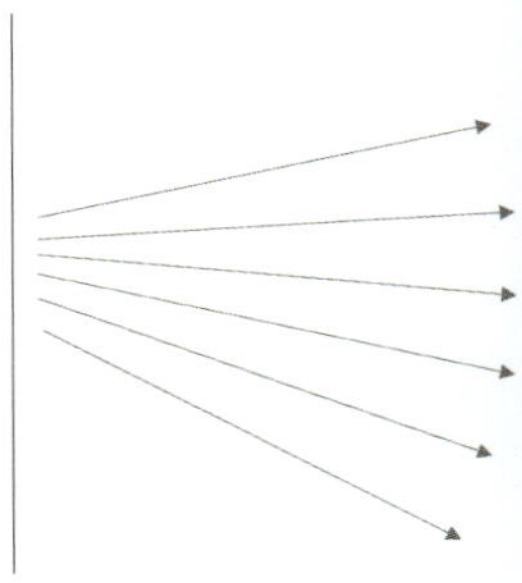

Soft light
Reflected off white surface

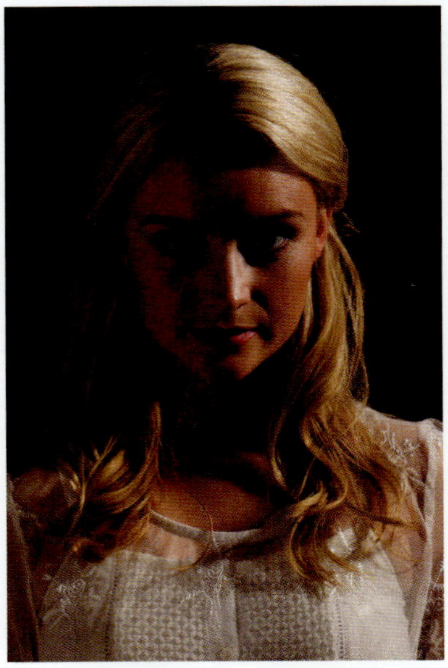

Hard light
Direct from source

Another type of soft light is called diffused light. That's created when light travels through something.

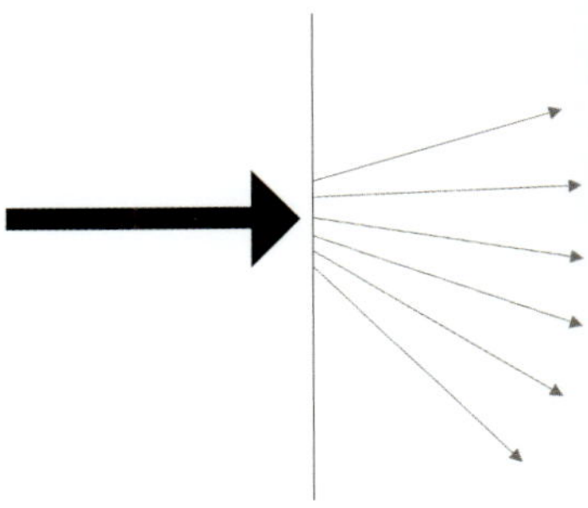

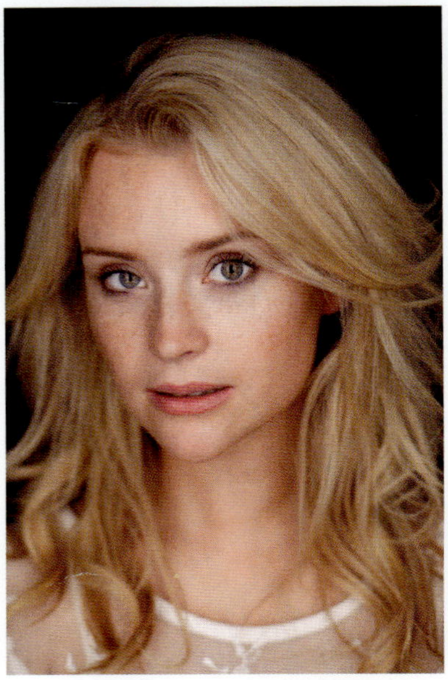

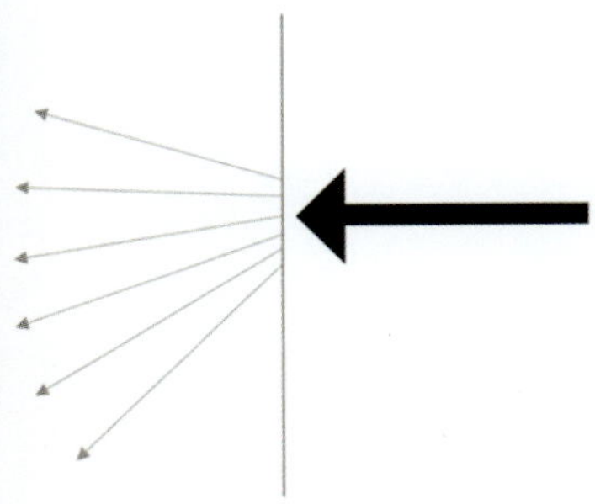

Soft light - Diffused
Light travelling through something

As you can see, there are loads of different types of light that can give you all sorts of effects in your photography. **Recognise what type of light you have available or what type of effect you want before you start shooting.** That little bit of planning will really help you out.

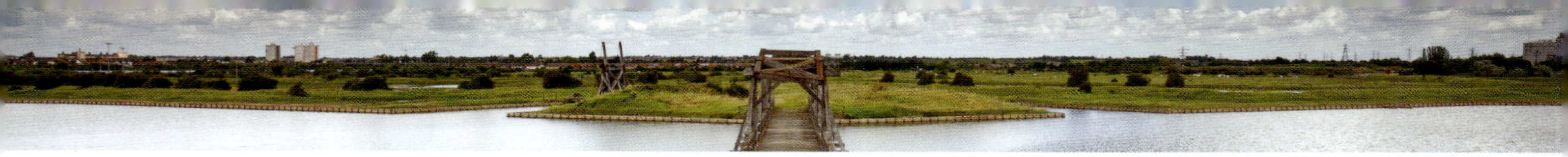

White Balance

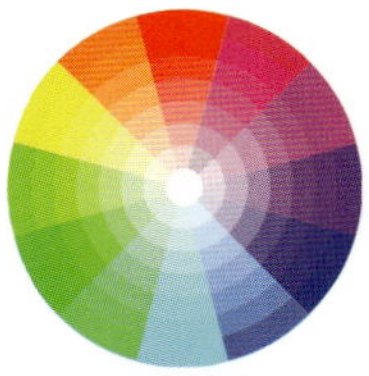

White balance is all to do with controlling the colour of your light. The easiest way to describe white balance is by way of colour temperature. Colour temperature is a way of measuring the colour of the light source. Here is a White Balance table.

White Balance Settings			
Light Source	Colour of light	Colour Temp (approx.)	Symbol on camera
Shade		7000 K	
Cloudy		6000 K	
Flash		5500 K	
Daylight – Noon		5200 K	
Florescent		4000 K	
Tungsten		3200 K	

On the right of this table are the common symbols you will see on your camera. Under colour temperature there are numbers and those numbers refer to the colour of the light, the K stands for Kelvin. In short, the higher the number, the bluer the light, the lower the number the more orange the light is.

These numbers are something you don't really have to get involved with too much, but what you do have to know is what colour certain light sources produce.

If you hold a piece of white paper in bright daylight, it looks white. When you come inside i.e. a classroom/office lit by strip lights, to your eye that piece of paper is still white.

That is because your brain adjusts to say that this is a white piece of paper. Cameras don't work like that, cameras actually see the colour of light that is being emitted.

For example, a cloudy day will give you a bluer light.

Cloudy		6000 K	

The sunshine symbol represents daylight at noon. That is pure white light, when the sun is highest in the sky.

Daylight – Noon		5200 K	

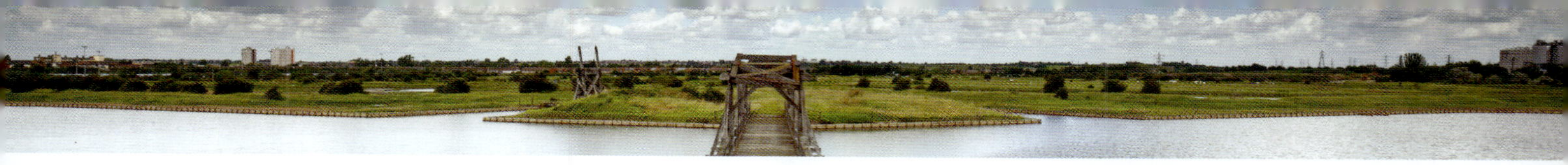

Then you go to fluorescent lighting which is a bit more green.

Florescent		4000 K	

And then you have a light bulb symbol, that's called Tungsten Light, and emits an orange colour.

Tungsten		3200 K	

Tungsten is on the periodic table, it's a metal. It's that little bit of metal that runs through an older type light bulb and when electricity is passed through it, it glows orange.

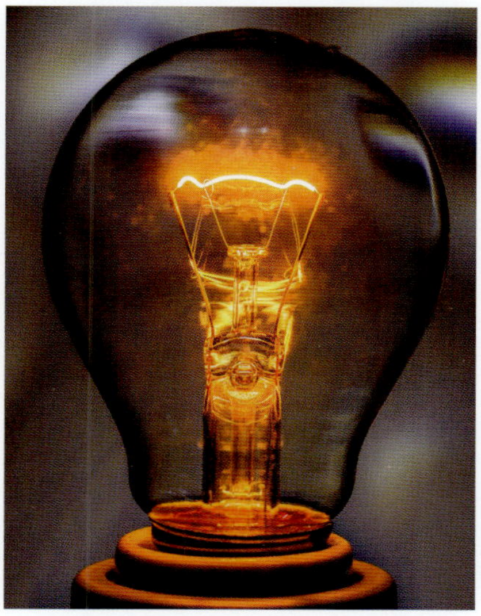

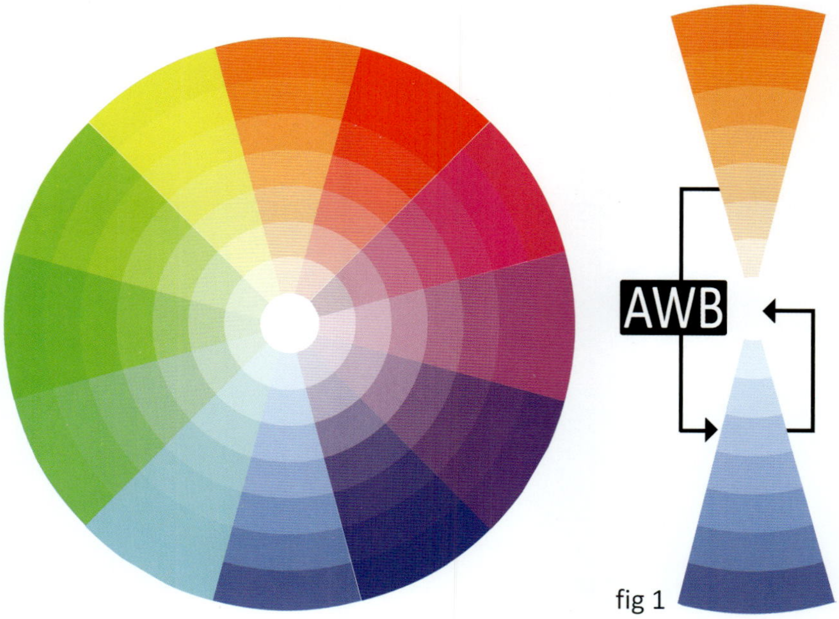

fig 1

Auto White Balance

Auto White Balance, or AWB, does a pretty good job most of the time, but I want to show you how Auto White Balance works via a colour wheel.

Imagine you're inside a restaurant which is being lit by tungsten light bulbs and it's an orange light being emitted. On Auto white balance, the camera sees the orange light and adds the colour opposite on the colour wheel, in this case blue, into the image in equal measure. The same amount of blue cancels out the orange and brings the light in the scene to white. See fig 1.
So AWB balances the light as best as it can back to white.

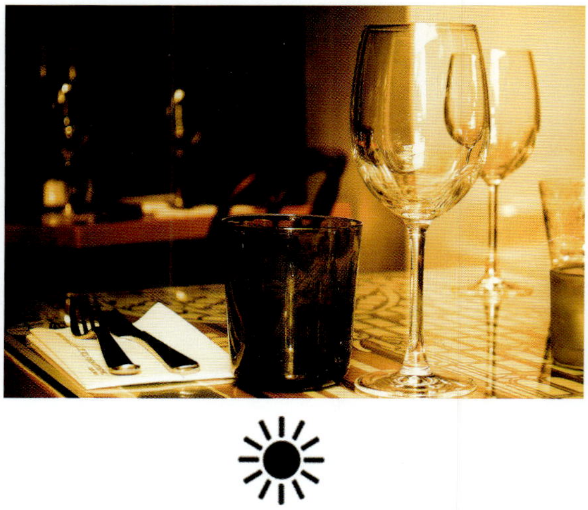

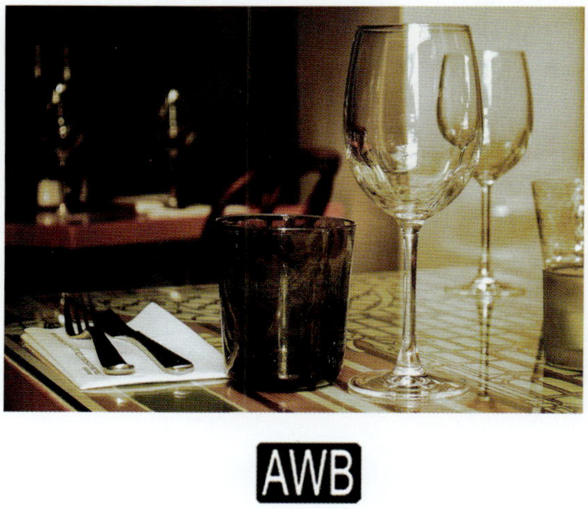

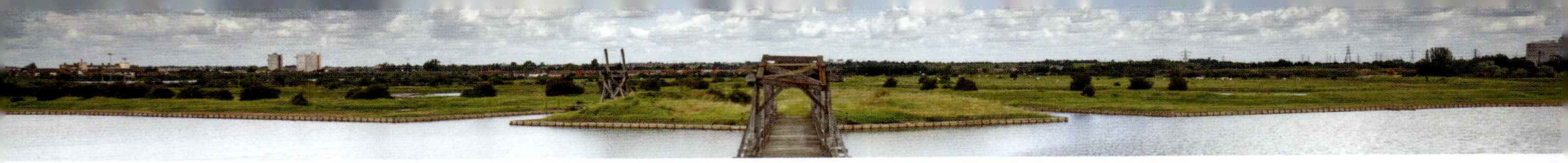

Opposite colours on the colour wheel will cancel each other out - this is how Auto White Balance works on your camera. Here's another example.

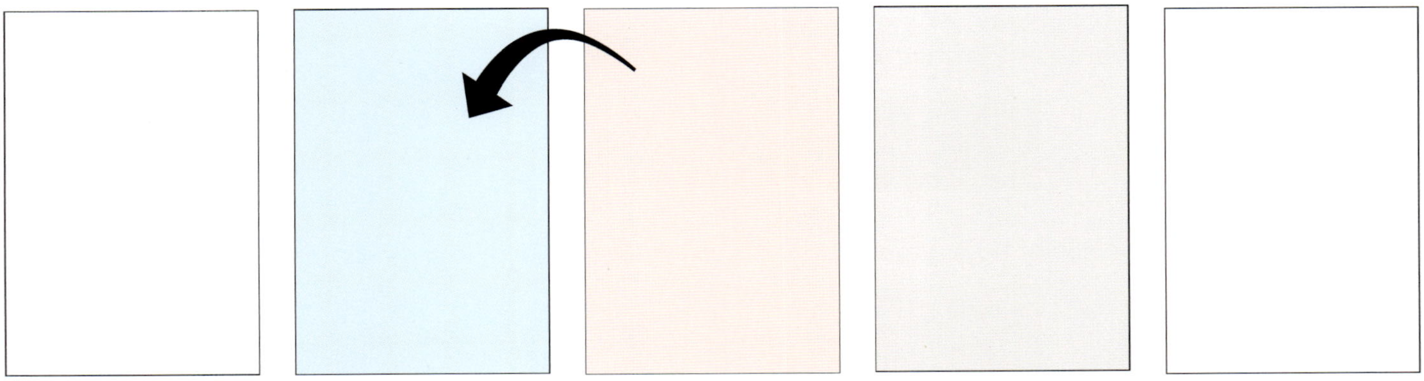

We start with a blank piece of paper – pure white.

Then I've added a blue cast over the paper.

If I overlay the exact shade of orange that's opposite on the colour wheel...

...it cancels out the blue, making it grey or what's called 'Neutral Density'.

Then, to make it pure white again, all you do is brighten it up. This is what your camera is doing in AWB.

So, what if you like the orange glow of the light bulb, or what if the AWB is not doing a good job? This can happen in situations where you have a mixture of light sources. This is where 'you' take control and tell the camera what light source you are shooting under.

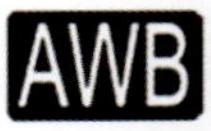

Look at this picture here of some light bulbs. This is the colour given on Auto White Balance. The oranges have been turned back to pure white as best they can.

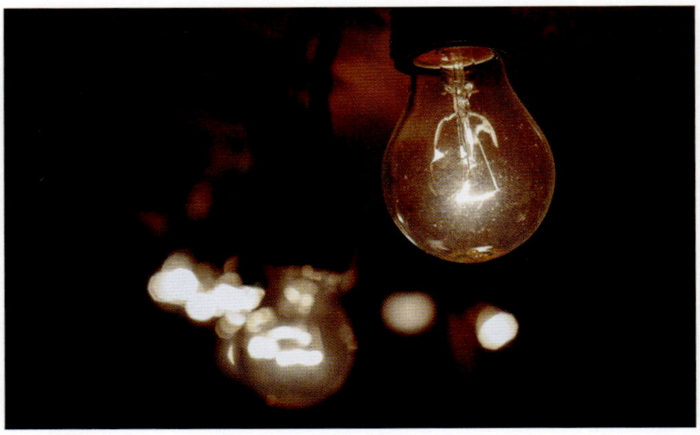

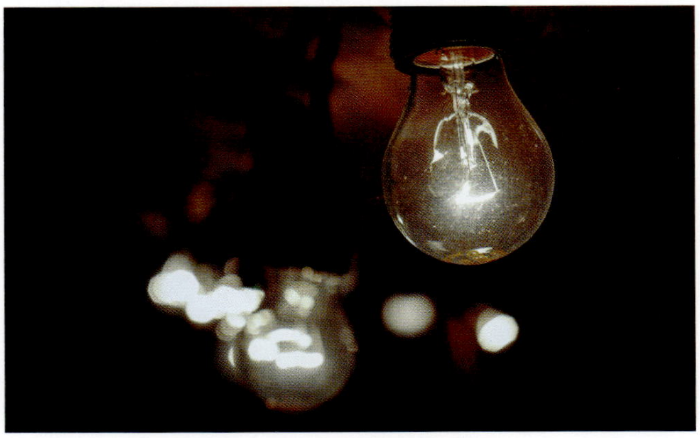

To make sure the oranges go white, you set your camera's white balance to tungsten. The camera will then specifically look for tungsten light and turn it back to white.

If you want to show colours as true, you set the camera's white balance to daylight. In this setting, the camera doesn't add any colour to your shot and shows the true colour of the light source.

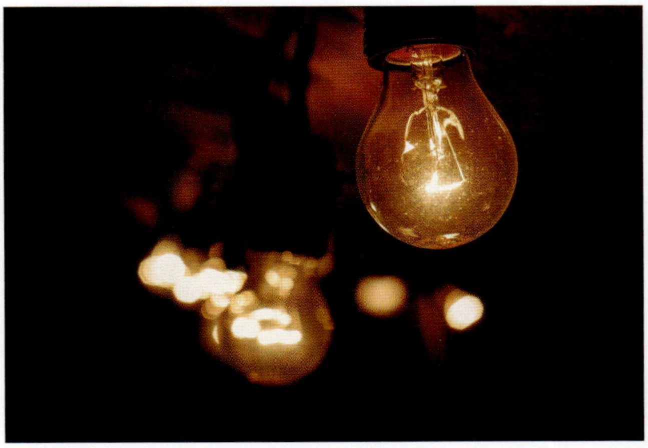

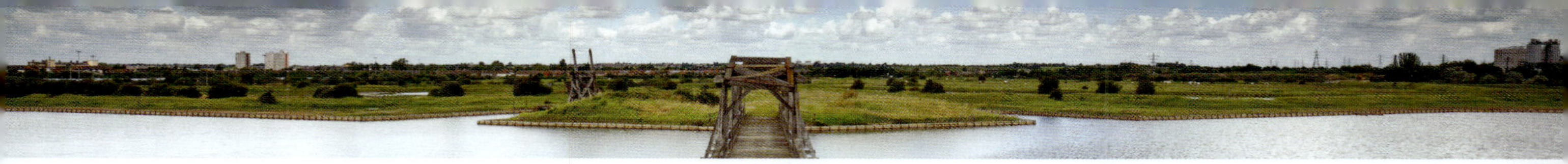

Knowing about colour temperature can help you obscure or intensify the colour of your shots to get different effects.

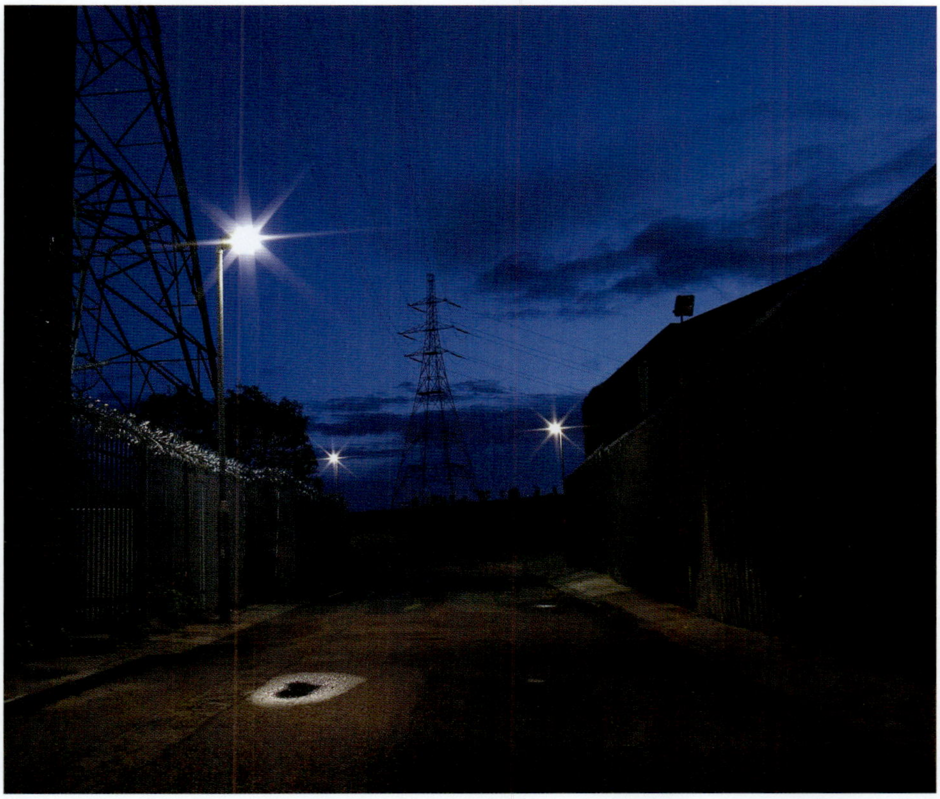

Here's a picture of an alleyway with street lighting and the sun has just gone down. This picture has been balanced to Tungsten light. You can see this because it's turned everything that would be orange, like the street lights, to white.

The sky also looks a lot bluer than it would do normally and that's because the camera has added blue to the shot to cancel out the orange - there wasn't any orange in the sky to cancel out which is why it's made the sky look bluer.

This picture has been balanced to daylight, no colour has been added by the camera. This is giving you a true representation of what the street lights look like, You can see that they are orange in colour and you can see how the light hitting the concrete and factory building also has an orange glow. Because the camera has been balanced to daylight, it is showing the realistic colours of the street lights.

If this was taken on AWB, the camera would have tried to turn those oranges back to white.

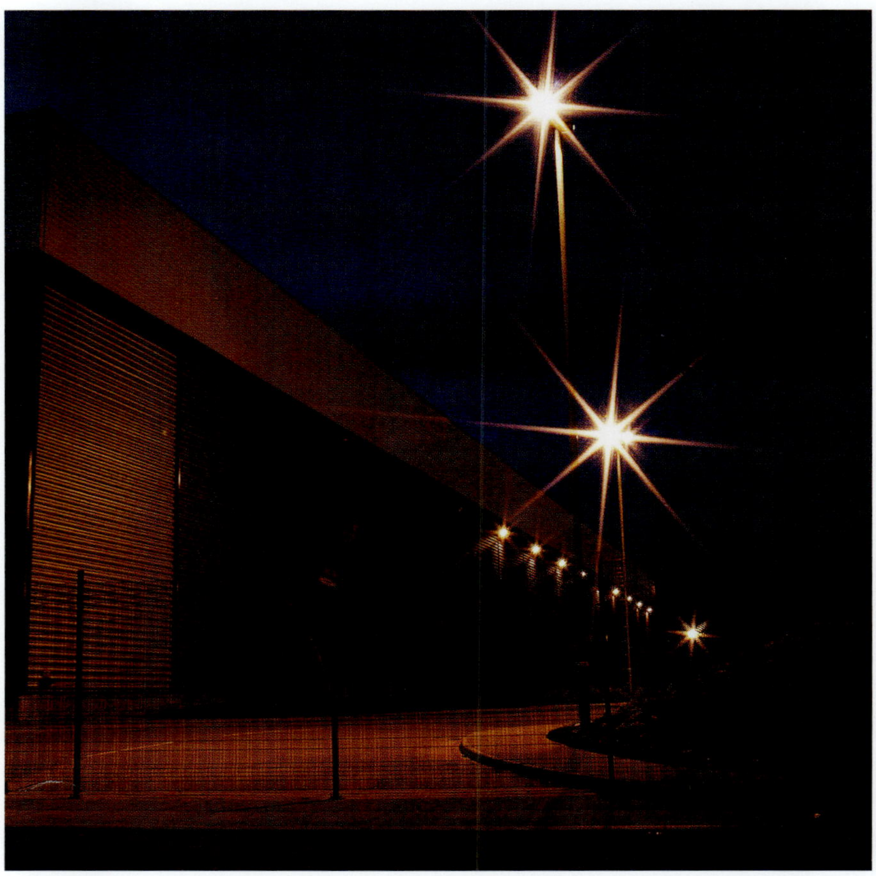

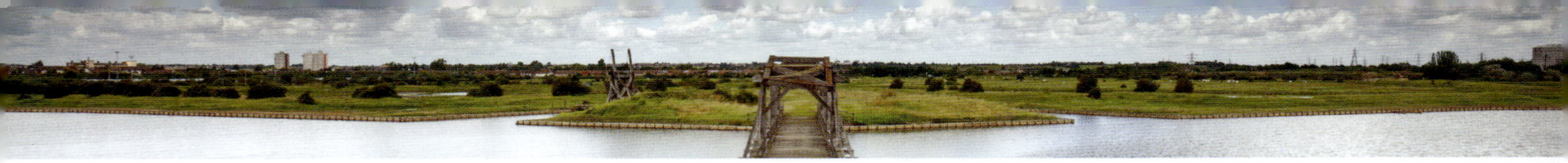

Task

Get familiar with white balance settings on your camera

Here are some tasks to get you working around your white balance settings so you can see the different effects you can have on an image when you control the white balance.

Here's how to change the white balance on common cameras, other cameras will be very similar, simply refer to your camera's manual under white balance if you get stuck.

Canon

- Put your camera onto 'P'.
- Press the 'WB' button. This will bring up the white balance menu.
- Select the white balance you want.

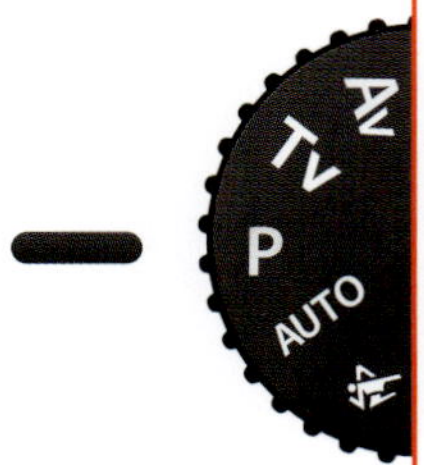

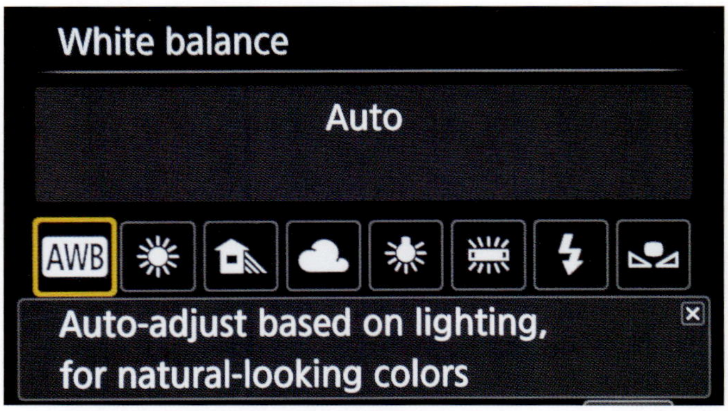

Nikon

- First, put your camera onto 'P' setting.
- Press the (i) button, and go to the White Balance setting.
- Select your white balance.
- Some Nikon cameras will have a WB button that you can press for easier access.

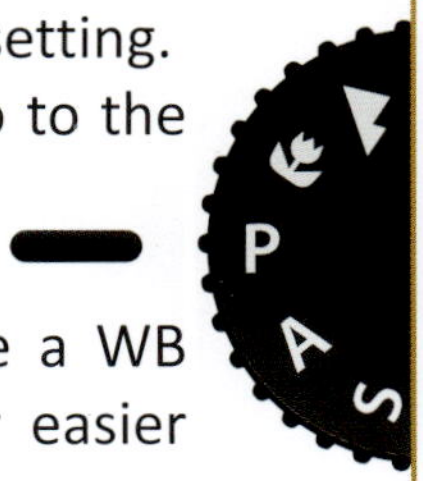

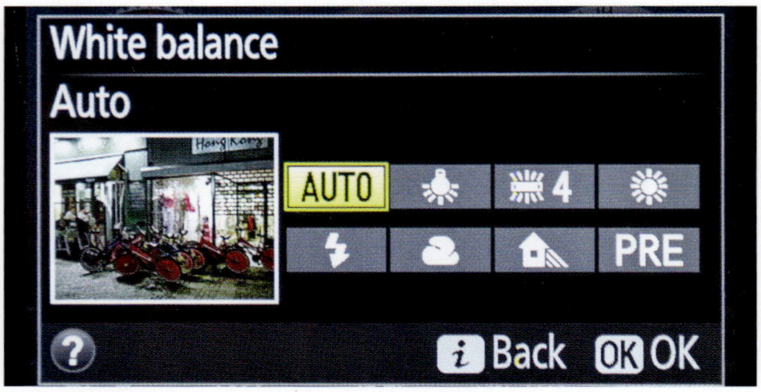

Task

Take pictures of the same scene in different white balance settings and answer the following: What colour is being added to the scene? What colour is being cancelled out from the scene?

- Set your camera to P
- Put your ISO on Auto and make sure you've set it to Jpeg.
- Go outside and make sure there is some sunlight.
- Take shots on different white balance settings and see the different colour cast that each picture has. Then make a note of what colour the camera has added to give that effect.

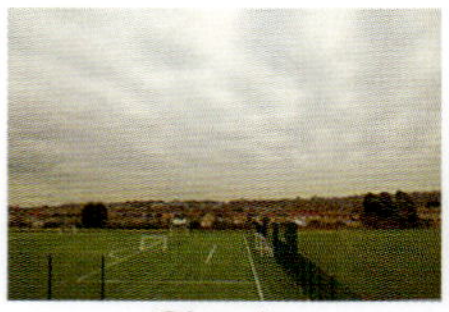
Shade

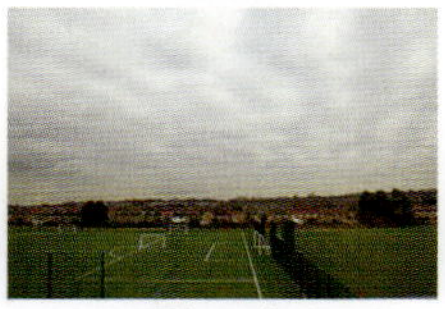
Cloudy

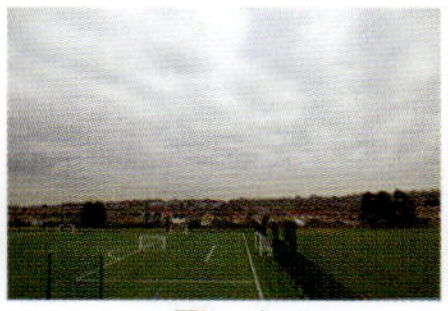
Flash

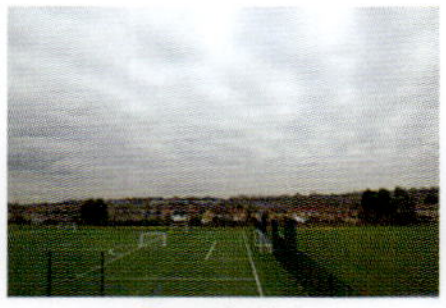
Daylight

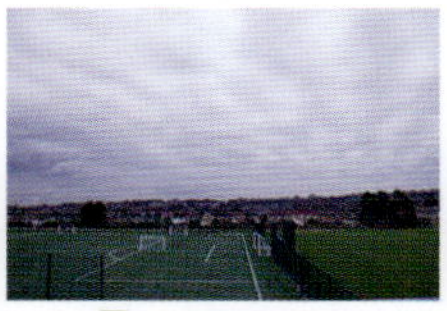
Fluorescent

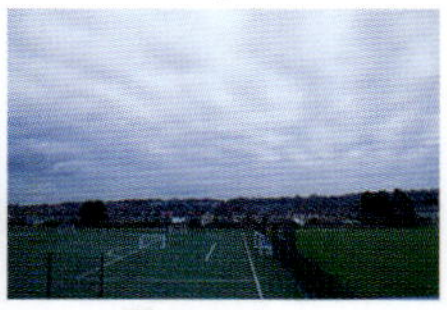
Tungsten

AWB

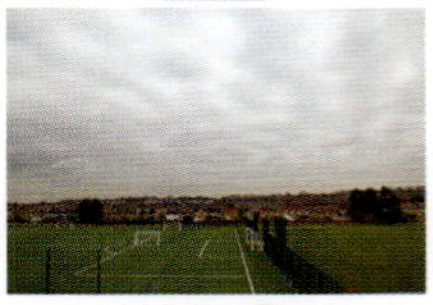
Auto White Balance

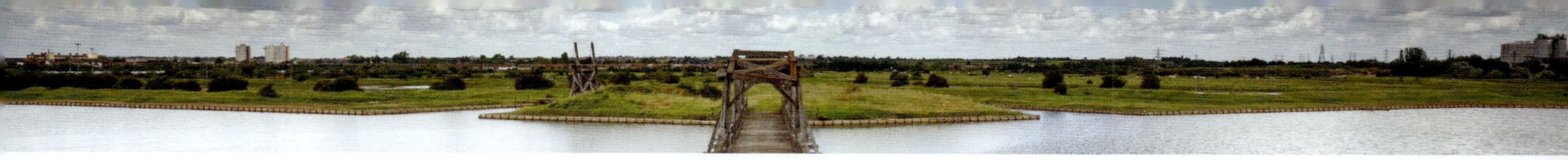

Task

Now practice your control of white balance

Take shots of urban night scenes where you have different types of light sources. Adjust your white balance accordingly to enhance or cancel out colours to get a desired visual effect.

You will need to use a tripod and a remote trigger or cable release, or put your camera on its 2 second timer to keep your camera still during the exposures.

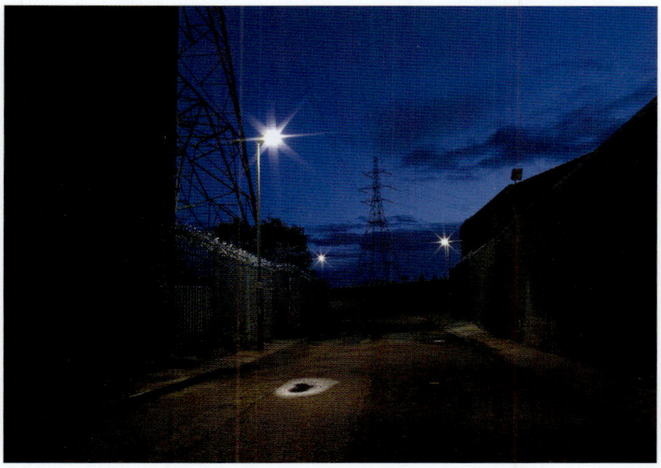

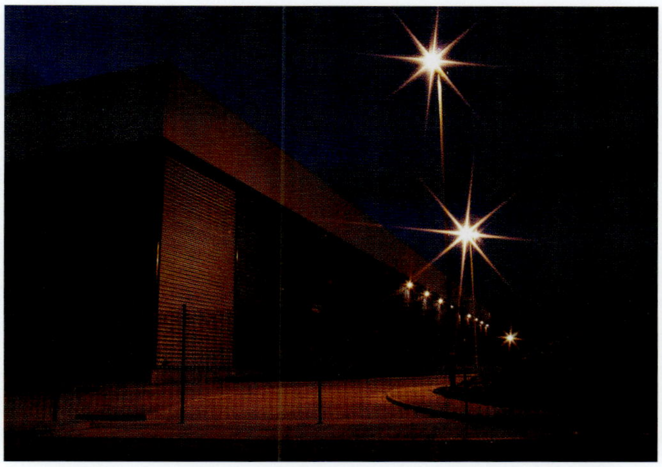

Let's recap on this chapter.

- There are lots of different types of light sources - Flash light, street light, light bulb etc. Knowing what effect they give a photograph will help you plan a good shoot.
- Light comes in many different colours. Your camera will try to turn those colours back to white if you leave it on Auto White Balance.
- In general, you get two different effects of light, one being hard, which is light coming directly from the source and hitting the object, and the other being soft which comes in two different variations, reflected light and diffused light.
- White balance can be set on your camera. You use white balance to cancel out colours that you don't want, or to capture colours as they are, you set your camera's white balance to daylight.

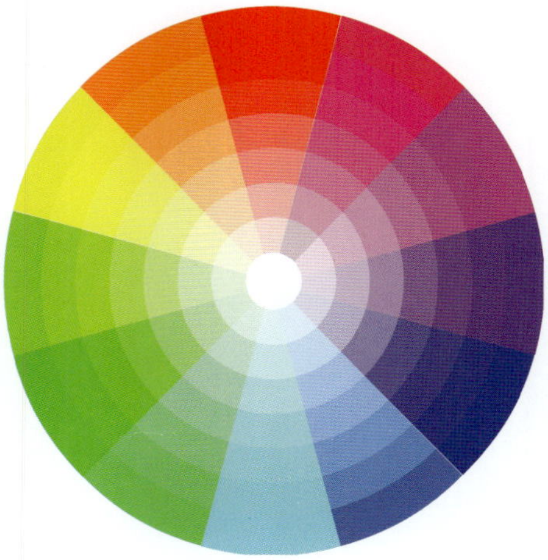

That's the end of this chapter, I hope you enjoy those tasks. When you're ready, move on to the next chapter.

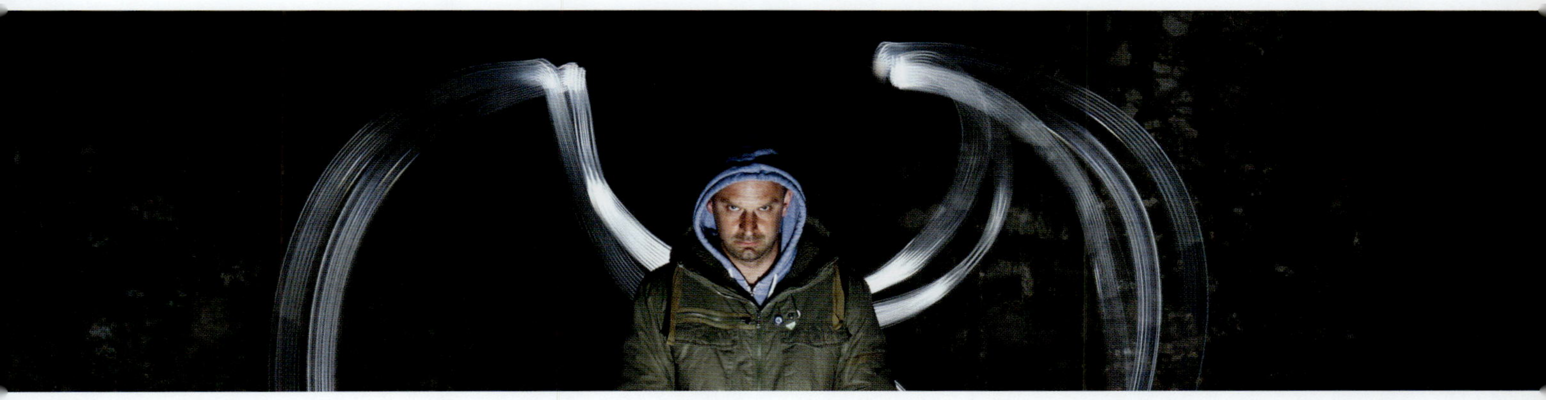

Painting with Light

Chapter 14

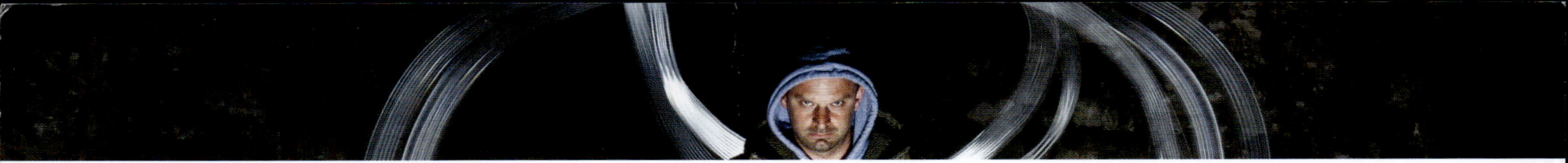

In this chapter, we are going to put together all of our knowledge and do what's called Light Painting. This is a really fun task and it just cements what we've learnt about controlling light. It's an extension task, but one you will really enjoy.

Before we start, I want you to look at the picture below and tell me how you think it's been created. Write down what you think the settings were, what equipment was used and so on.

Think about all the knowledge learnt during this book. **How would you recreate this shot?** Write an answer down and then read on.

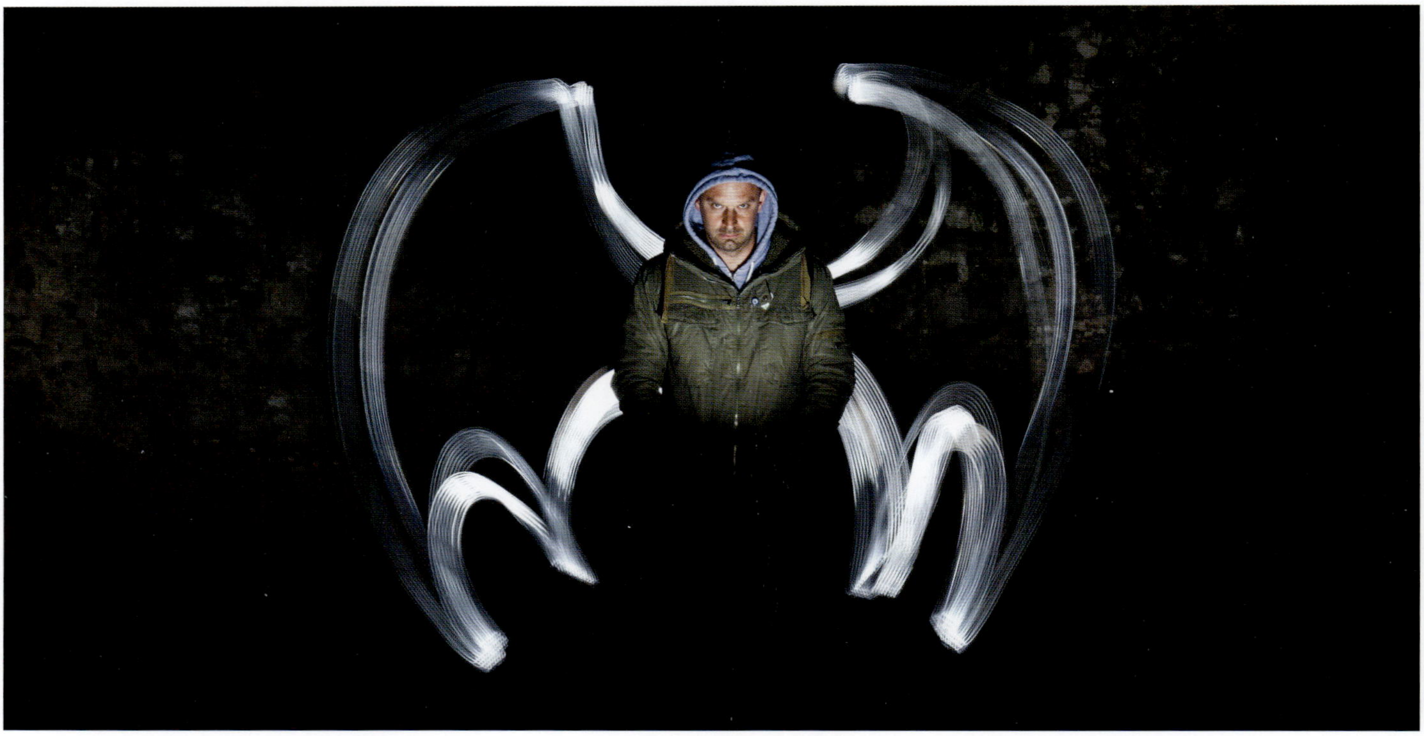

I hope you have some good stuff written down. I want you look at this picture now and do the same – **how do you think this picture has been taken?** Again, draw on the knowledge learnt in this book.

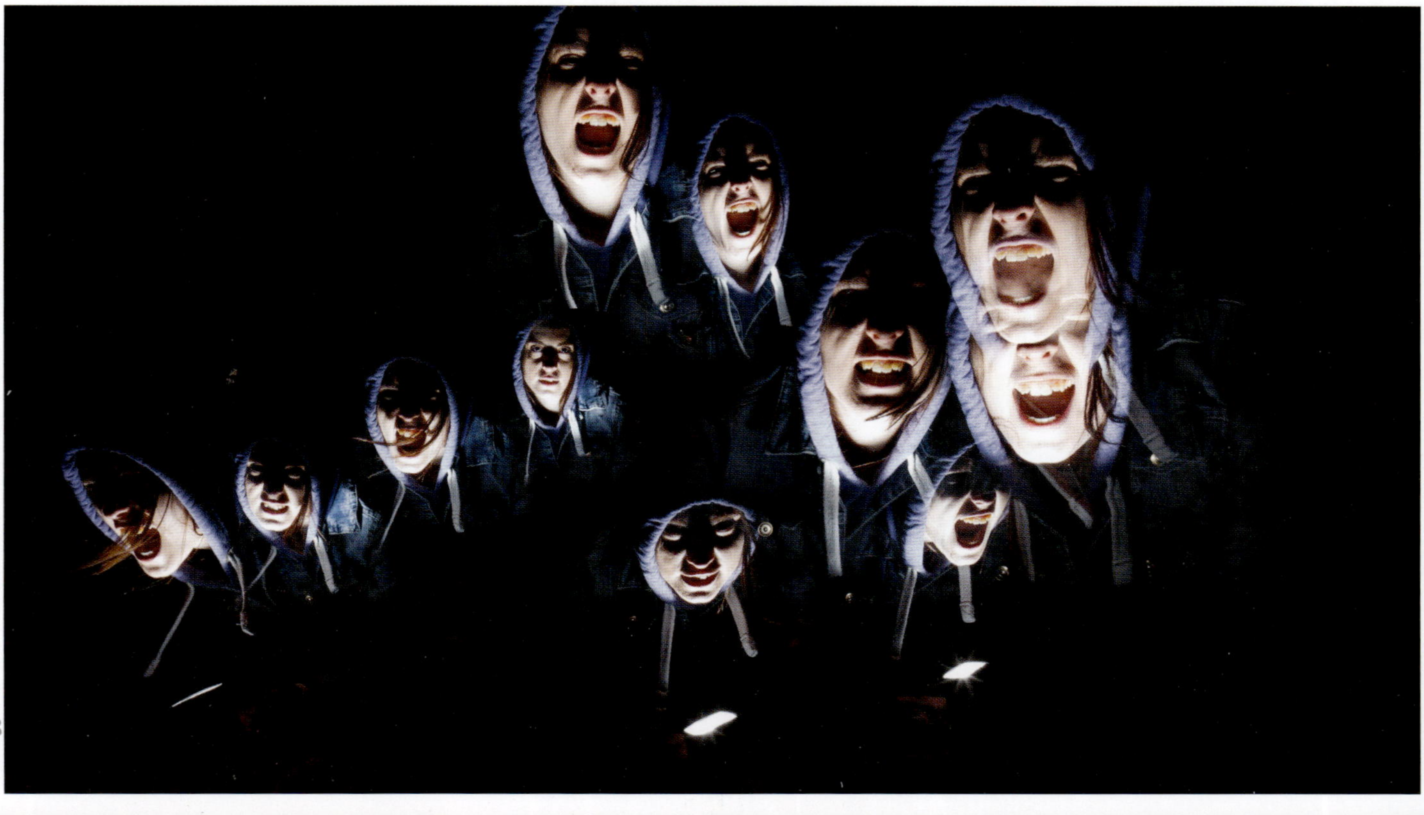

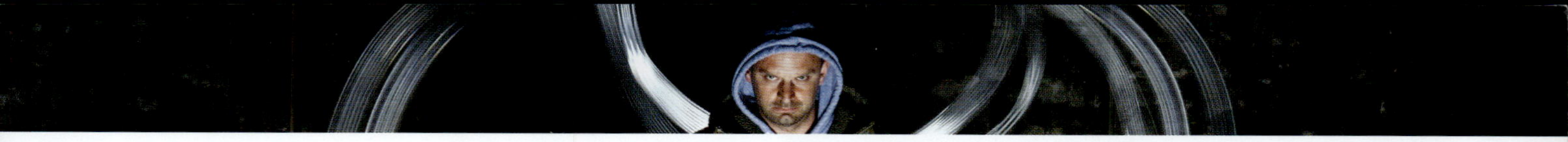

Ok so this is how they have been made. These are called long exposure shots, these particular type are called light paintings, and to create these shots you have to work in fully manual mode and need to know how to balance light correctly.

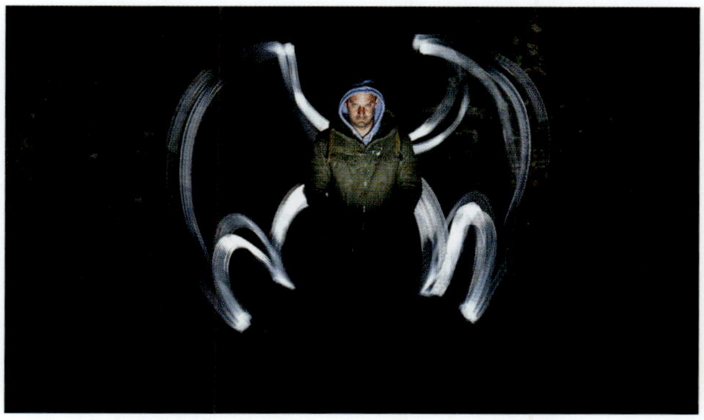

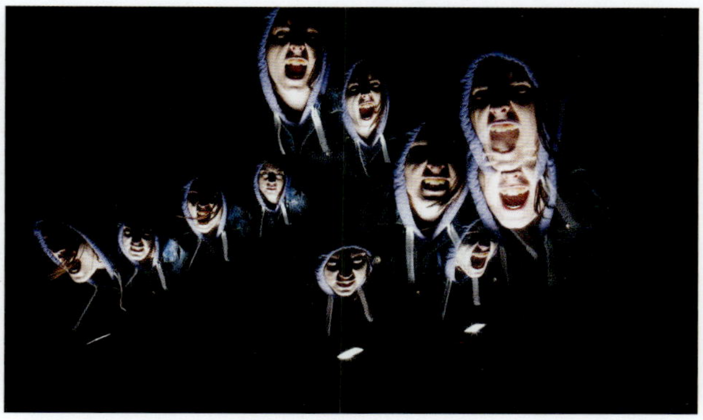

They were taken as one long exposure so this would have been around a 30 second shutter speed. Because you need to let light in slowly over a long period of time, the aperture would be small, around f22, and the ISO would have been around 100. You also have to use a tripod so that everything stays still except the moving lights.

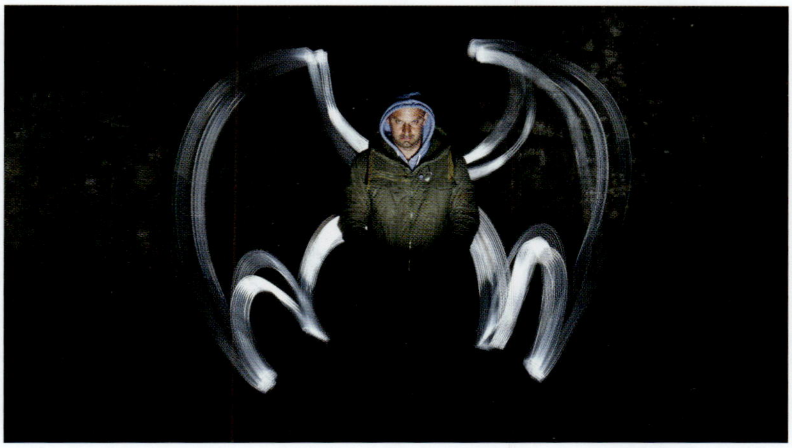

There are 2 people in this shot – one you can see and one you can't. The person you can see has been lit with a torch and stood still. The other person is behind them and created these batwings by drawing them in the air with an LED torch. The reason you can't see that person is because they were moving around and weren't lit by any light.

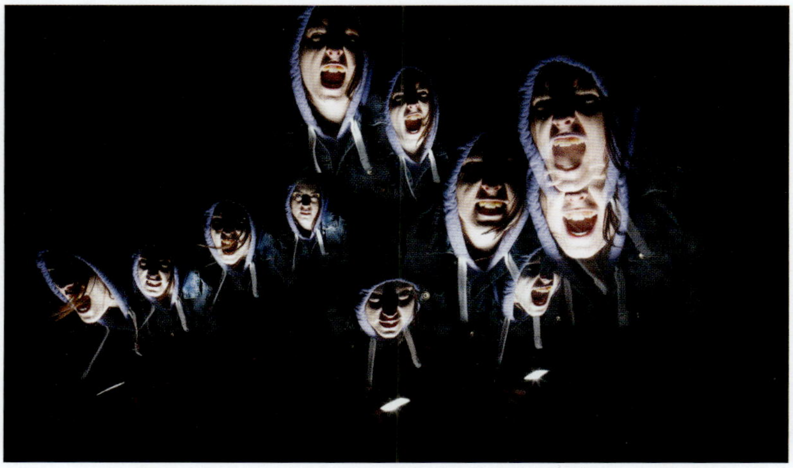

The second one again was a long exposure shot but during the exposure, a burst of flash has gone off to light the person's face. Then they have moved and another burst of flash goes off, they move again, another burst of flash and so on. You can also do this with a bright torch and just flash that on and off instead.

The reason you can only see the face and not the body is because no light hit the body, the light only hit the face.

You don't get shots like these right first time; you need to do a few test shots first, figure out if you need more or less light, then adjust settings and the process until you get the look you want. That's what makes it good practice and doing this task really helps you understand that control of light.

So to create shots like this, this is what you need:

- A small aperture
- A long exposure using the shutter speed
- Low ISO
- A tripod
- A bright torch and possibly a flash

The rest is to experiment and get creative.

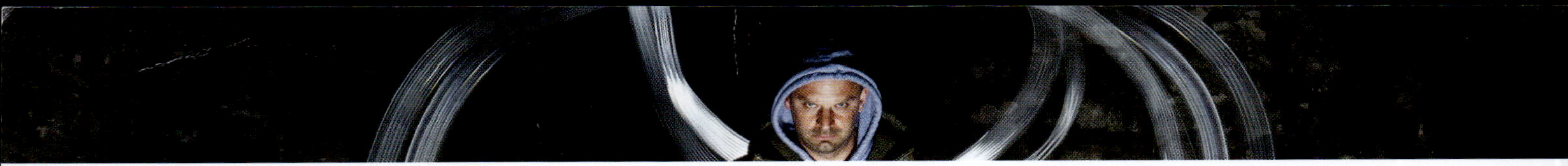

Task

Creating Light paintings

It's best to go outside at night to do this but you don't need to, you literally just need a dark room. It's important that wherever you do this, it's as dark as can be.

- Put your camera on a tripod
- Set it to manual mode (M)
- Set your shutter speed between 15 - 30 seconds (experiment for best results)
- Set the aperture to f22
- Set the ISO 100.
- As it's dark your camera may not be able to focus onto your subject. To solve this, use manual focus or light the subject with a torch and focus in on them.
- During the exposure use a torch to draw whatever you want or light whatever you want.
- Then it's just a big experiment to get different effects!

Give that a go and have some fun with it.

As always, we would love to see your attempts at this. So, if you want to show us, tag your best shots on social media #theschoolofphotography

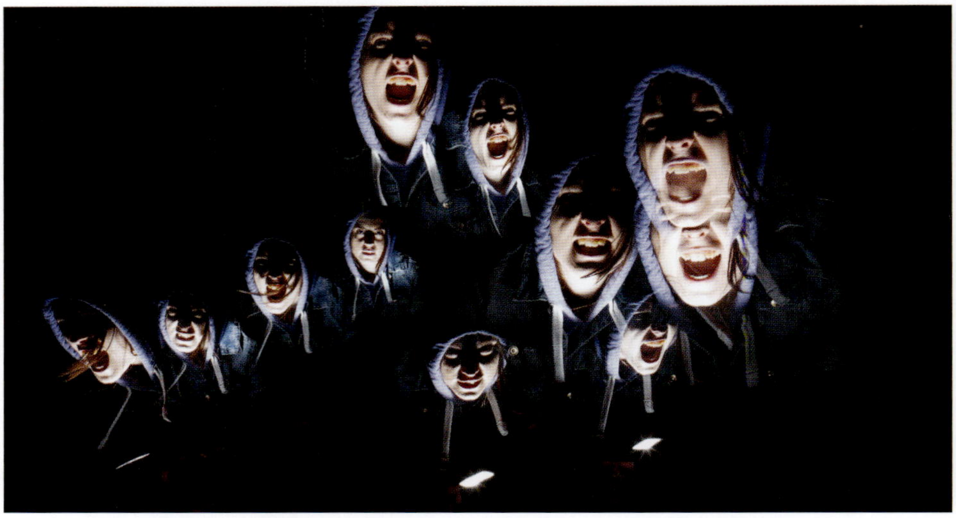

So when do you photograph in full manual mode?
Well it sounds obvious but you photograph in full manual when you want to take full control of everything. It's normally when your camera's light meter can't figure out what your intentions are because you're getting creative – like these light drawings.

Your camera hasn't got a clue what you're thinking when doing these types of shots so you have to take full control over the camera to get the desired shot.

If you just want to take control over the aperture and depth of field, you can use the A or AV setting. If you just want to control shutter speed effects, you can use the S or Tv setting. If you want full control over everything, you use fully manual and balance the light yourself.

Remember - ISO, apertures and shutter speeds can be balanced in stops. Your job as a photographer is to get that balance right for your desired effect.

That's this section over with – when you're ready, move onto the next chapter.

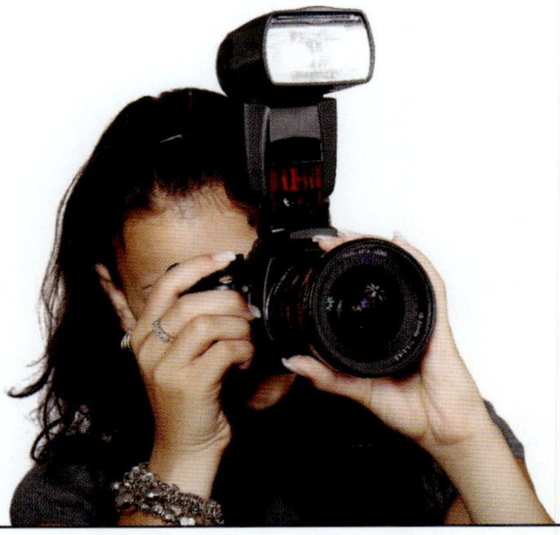

Balancing Exposures with Flash

Chapter 15

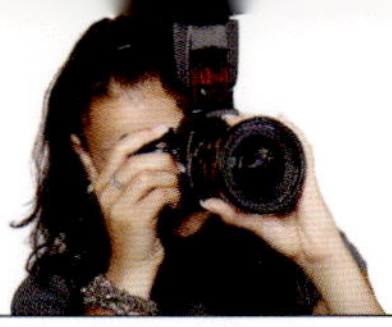

This section will expand on the balancing of exposures by introducing something called fill-in flash. Fill-in flash is normally used to fill in shadow areas of a person if shooting outside on a sunny day. You wouldn't normally think that you need to use a flash on a sunny day, but it really does help by filling in the shadow areas caused by bright sunlight. And, by using fill-in flash creatively, you can control the darkness of your background.

Here is an example of fill-in flash. The one on the left has been taken normally outside using the P setting on my camera. The one on the right again has been taken on the P setting but this time a flash gun has been added to the camera.

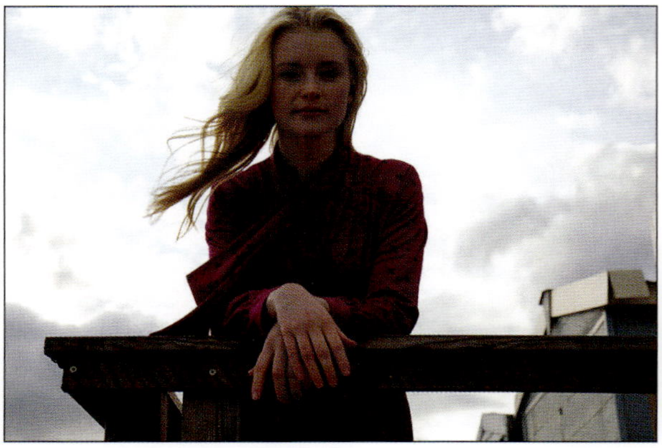

No flash

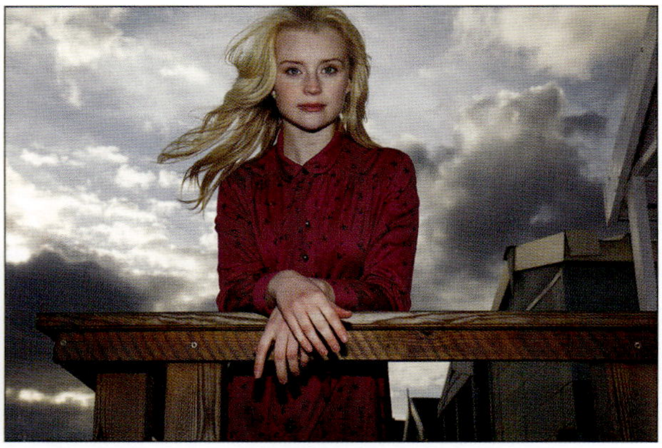

Fill in flash

This is the simplest use of a fill-in flash – you just add a flash gun or pop up your flash and shoot away whilst in the Program mode. You can see how much brighter it's made the face, it has filled in the shadow areas.

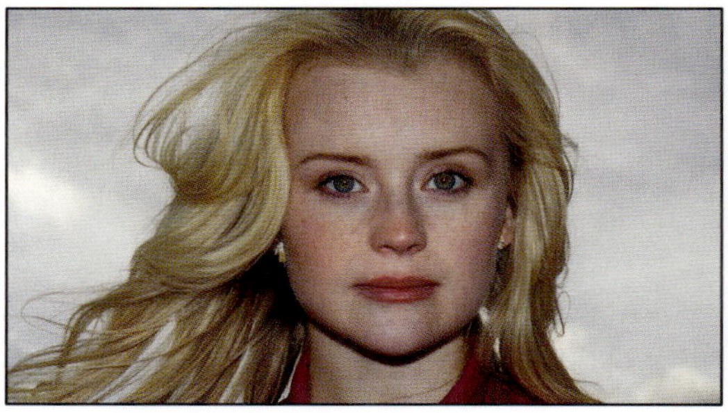

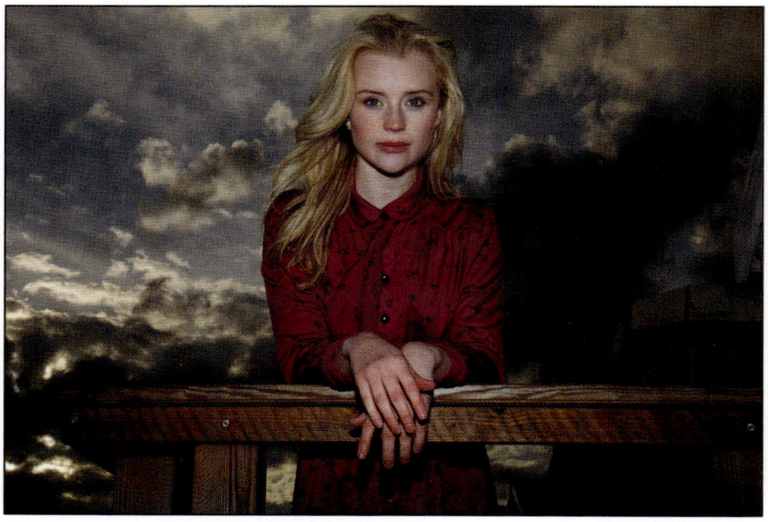

Here's another example. In this example I've underexposed the background to make it darker.

Below you can see the normal fill in flash picture against this one. The flash exposure, that's the exposure of the person, is exactly the same in both images but the background has been exposed differently.

You do this by combining your exposure compensation setting with your Flash Exposure Compensation setting.

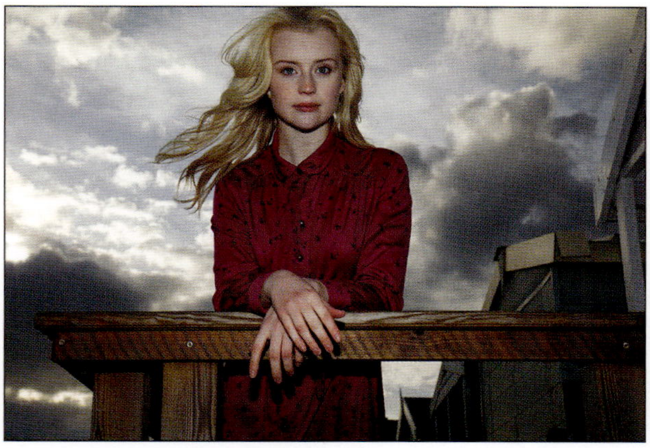

Fill in flash

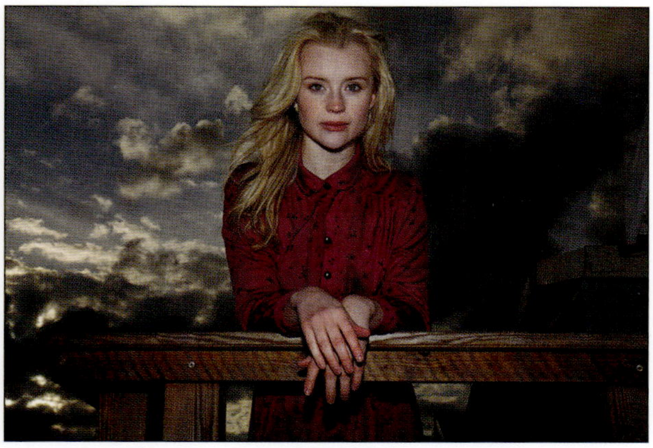

Fill in flash
Ambient light underexposed by 2 stops

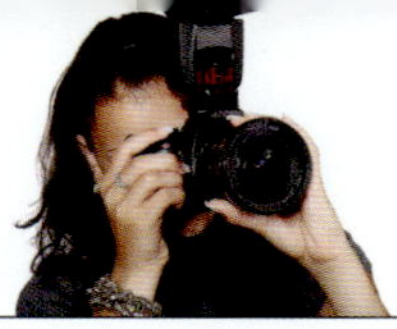

It gets a little complicated here, because what you're doing is thinking about 2 exposures at once. You're thinking about the flash exposure - the light hitting the subject - and your background exposure, which is called your 'ambient light' (the rest of the light in the scene - in our case the daylight).

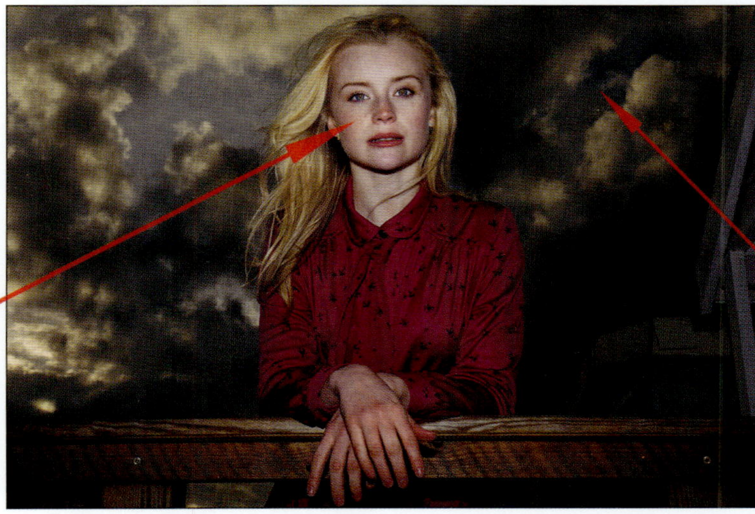

In the metering chapter, we did something called exposure compensation. This was when you could control the light coming into the camera to make a picture darker or lighter by holding down the plus and minus button and twisting the dial to minus 1,2 etc.

In the same way, this is how you control the exposure of your ambient light (your background light) whilst using fill in flash. You then use something called 'flash exposure compensation' to control the brightness of your flash. The technique is this - you under-expose the background whilst keeping the person exposed correctly via the flash.

Task

Get familiar with the camera settings

Here's how you use Exposure Compensation and Flash Exposure Compensation on common cameras. Look up these functions in your camera's manual if they are different.

Canon

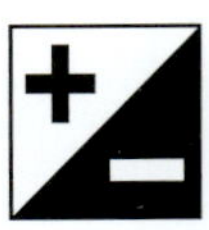

- Put your camera on 'P' mode.
- Press and hold the Exposure Compensation button and then twist the dial on the camera to -1, -2 etc to darken the ambient light (highlighted yellow)

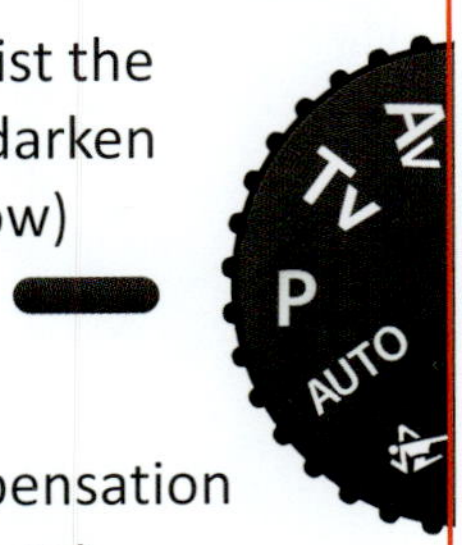

To change your flash exposure:

- press the 'Q' button.
- Go to the flash exposure compensation setting (highlighted red), press set.
- Increase the flash power to +1, +2 etc. Press set to confirm.

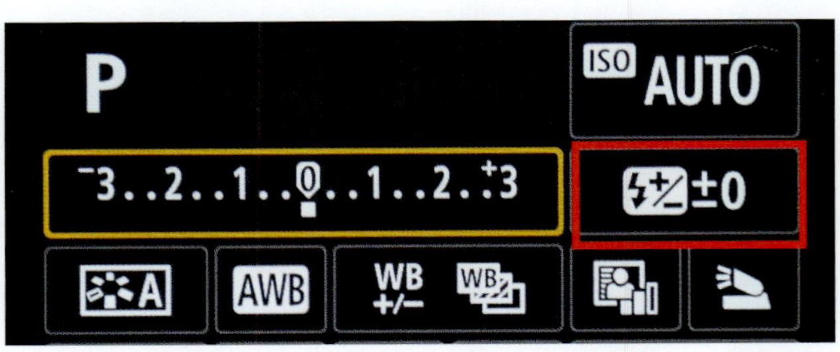

Nikon

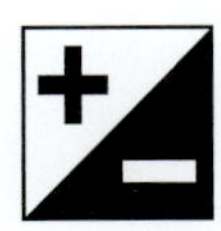

- Put your camera on 'P' mode.
- Press the *i* button.
- In the settings bar, you'll find Exposure compensation (highlighted yellow) and Flash Exposure Compensation (highlighted red).
- You can select either of these then press 'OK'.
- Change the level up and down accordingly.

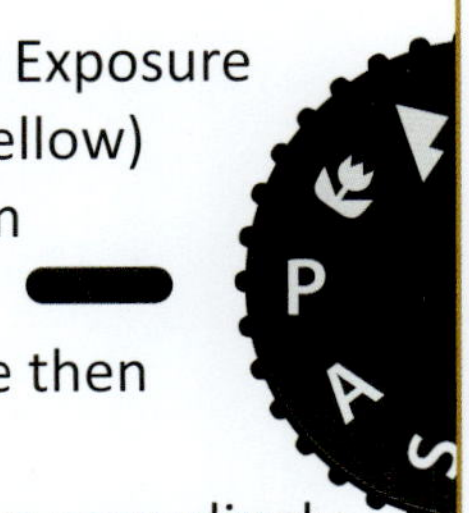

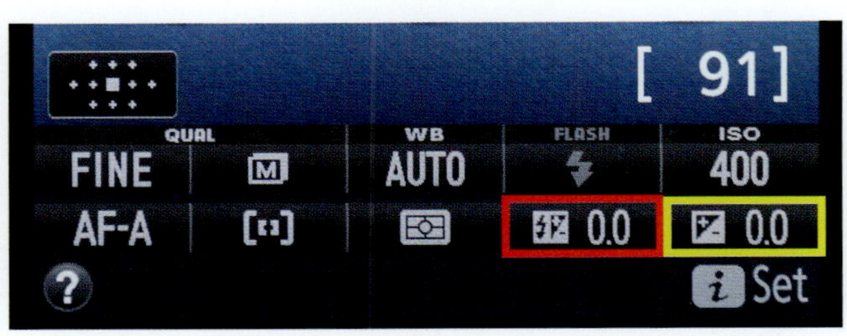

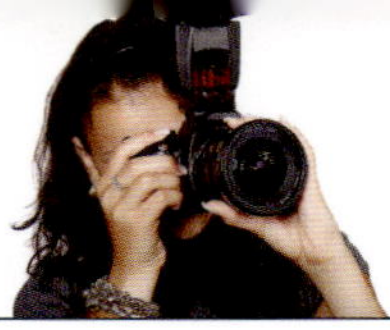

Task

Things to note

You can only use fill-in flash in close proximity to your subjects if using an on-board pop-up flash. Your pop-up flash will only reach a couple of meters in front of you in bright daylight.

However, If you're using a flash gun you're going to get a longer range. Also, on most flashguns you control the flash exposure compensation directly on the flash gun, not in the camera menu. Each flash gun works differently so look up flash exposure compensation in your flash manual for instructions on how to do this.

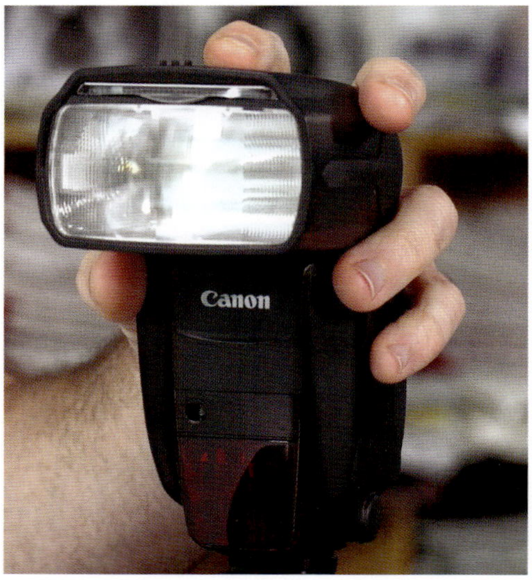

A common flash gun. (*left*)
This will slot onto the hot shoe of your camera.

On most flash guns you access the flash settings on the back of the gun, (*right*) not in the camera menu.

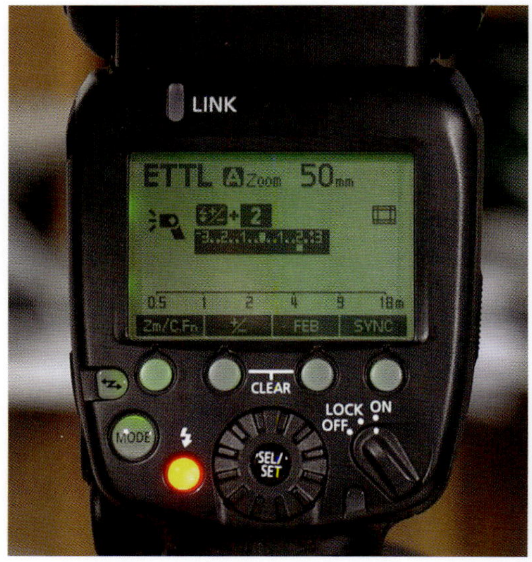

Go outside with a subject, preferably when it's sunny.

- Put your camera on the 'P' setting and ISO on 100.
- Take a shot of the model, with the sun behind them, without flash.
- Take another shot, but this time with your pop-up flash on, or your flash gun on its default setting (called ETTL).
- Then control the ambient light and the flash light to get different visual effects.
- Going down to -1 and -2 on the ambient light on your camera will make your background darker.
- Going +1 and +2 on your flash light will make the flash light brighter.

Take shots at different settings and compare the differences.

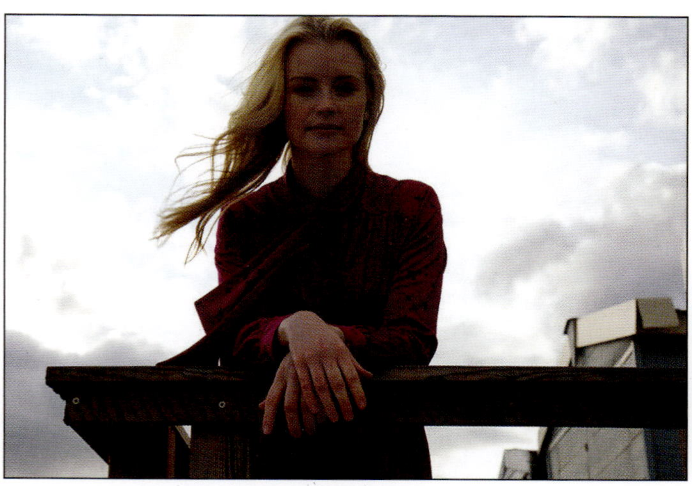

No flash

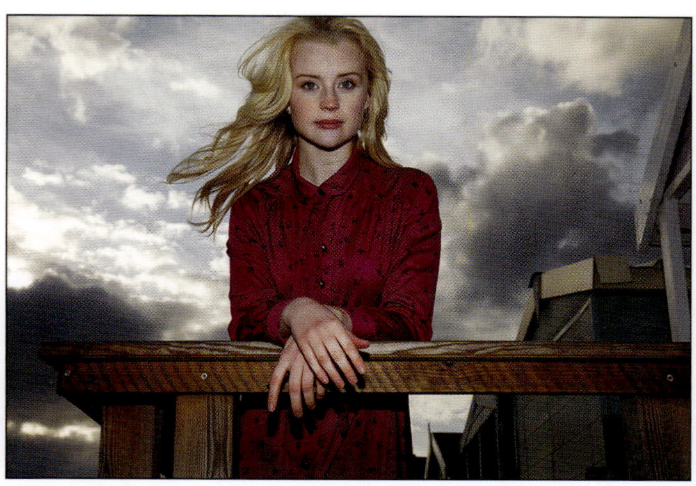

Fill in flash

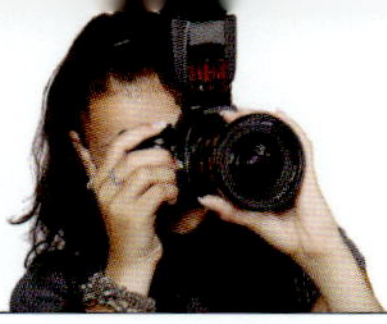

Examples

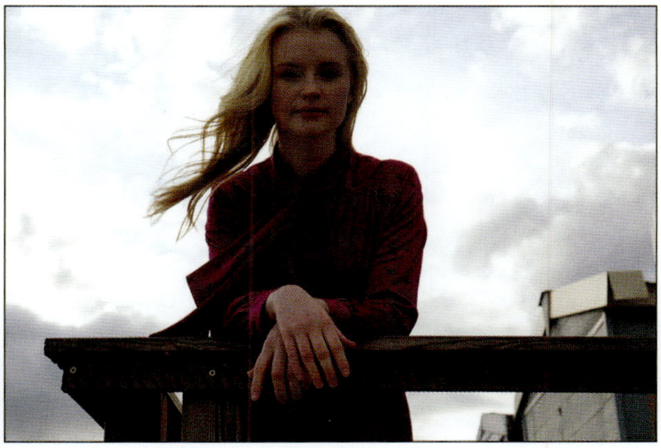

No flash

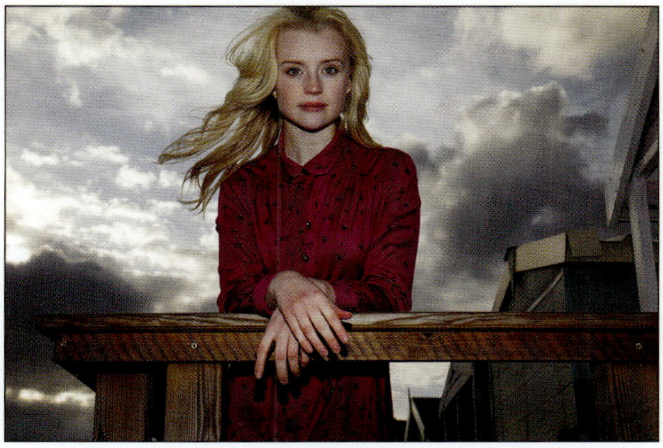

Fill in flash

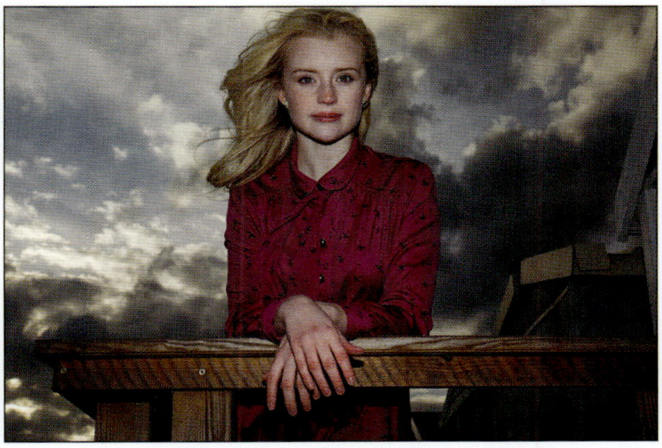

Fill in flash
Ambient light underexposed by 1 stop

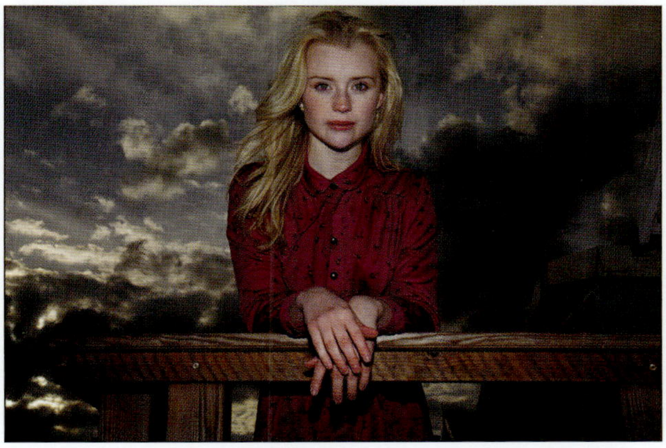

Fill in flash
Ambient light underexposed by 2 stops

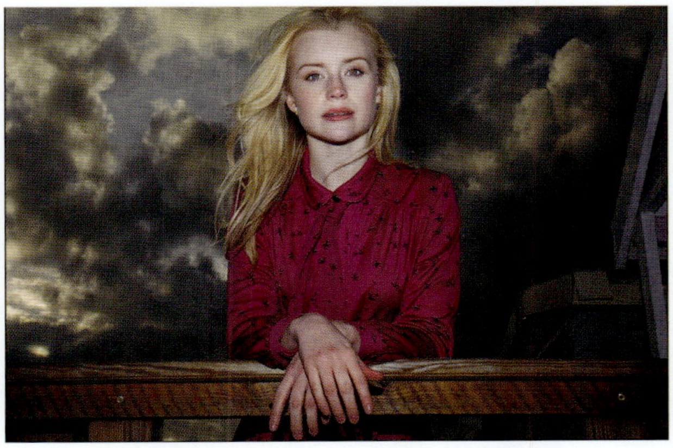

Flash over exposed by 1 stop
Ambient light underexposed by 2 stops

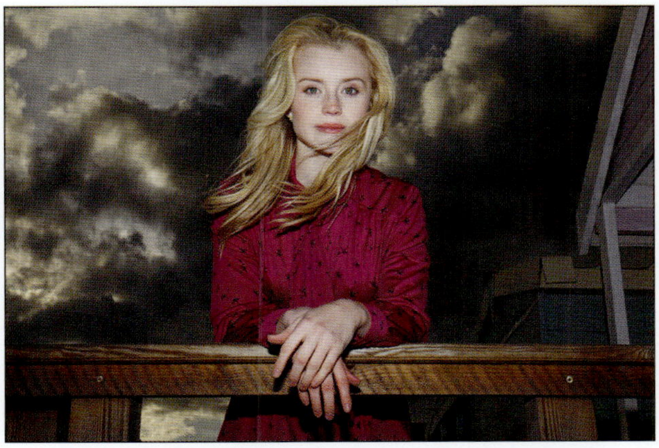

Flash over exposed by 2 stops
Ambient light underexposed by 2 stops

Let's recap on balancing exposures with fill-in flash.

- Fill-in flash is used to fill in shadow areas when shooting on a sunny day.
- By using fill in-flash in conjunction with exposure compensation, you can control how dark the background is.
- You can only use the fill-in flash in close proximity to your subject. This is dependent on the strength of your flash.
- You can use fill-in flash when shooting directly into the sun to give lens flare effects.

A great technique - particularly for portraiture. Have a good practice with that and read on when you're ready.

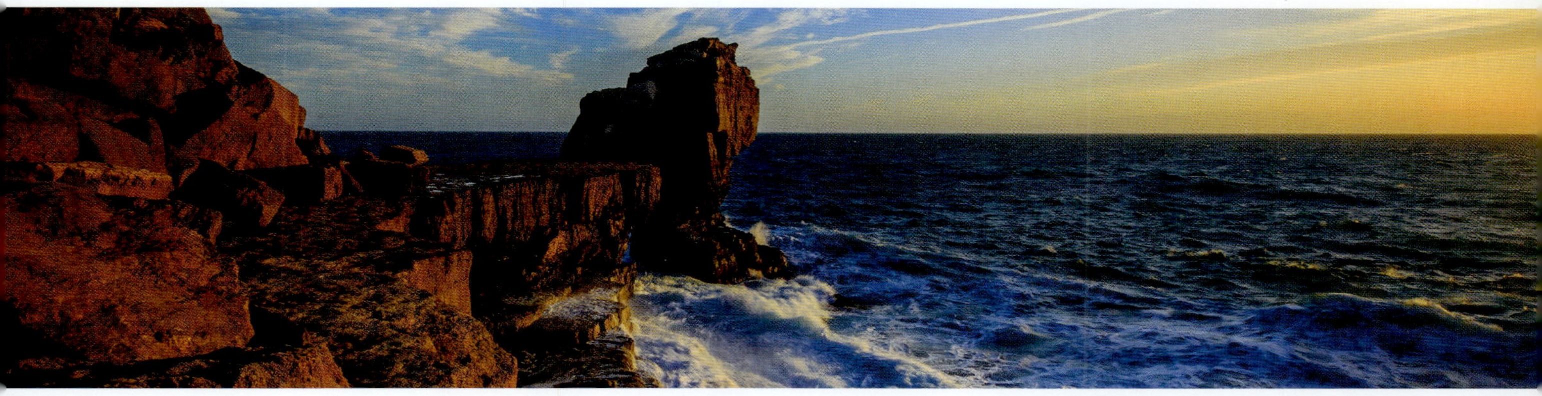

Post-production and Using Raw Files

Chapter 16

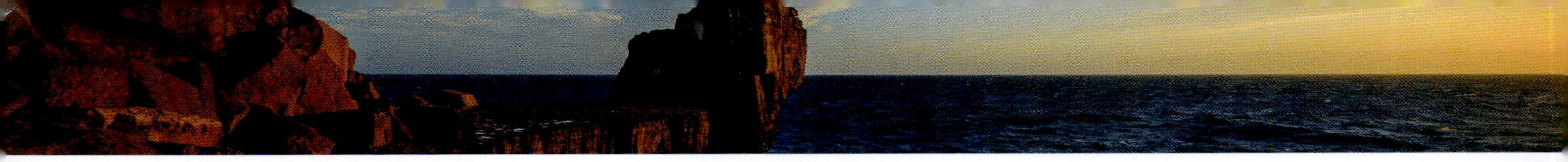

This chapter is about the post-processing of digital images and RAW files. Firstly, understand that every good image has been post-processed in some way.

Even before digital photography, prints had been enhanced. The sky could have been burnt in so you can see the clouds clearer or the foreground would have been dodged so it was brighter, faces were retouched on the negatives and so on.

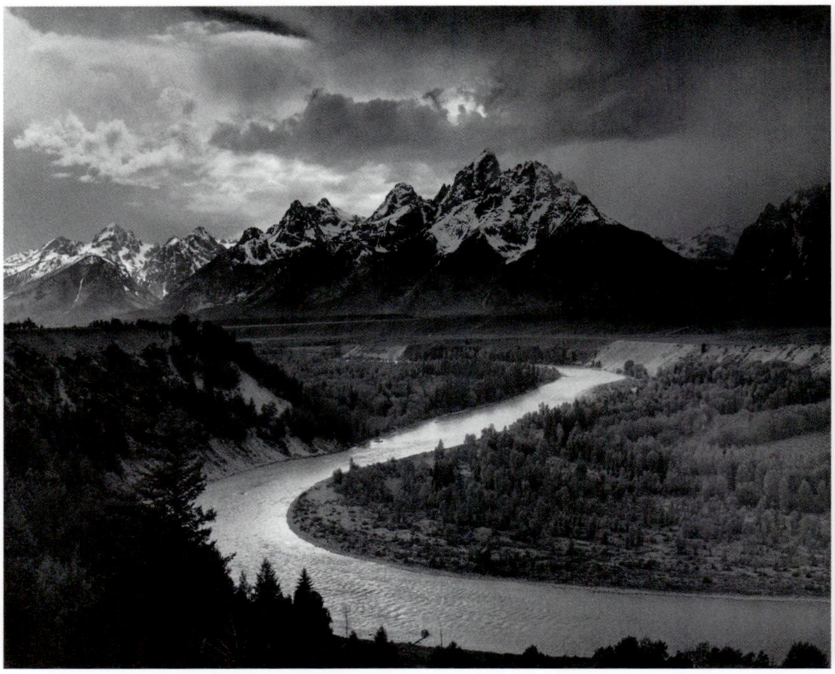

Ansel Adams. The Tetons and the Snake River, 1942.

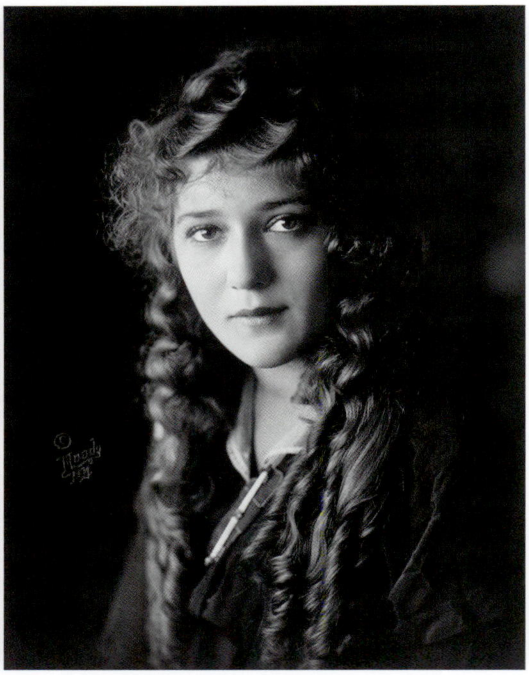

Mary Pickford, 1910

Now we do a very similar thing with digital files. Most images you see have been post-processed in some way and it's something you will need to learn. But, it's important to remember that your first stage is learning and controlling photographic techniques. Then, when you're confident with that, you learn about post-processing. Good post-processing will rarely recover a badly taken shot.

Let's understand what post-processing is. Post-processing is what you do to your picture, after you've taken it. These days that's done in a computer program. There are several computer programmes you can use to post process images; you can get free ones on the internet, you can get apps on your phone, or you can get paid ones.

Free Programs

There's a couple of free ones that are quite popular. One is called Pixlr.com. This is a good online photo manipulation tool but it's web-based meaning you use it through your browser and have to be on the internet to use it.

PIXLR

Another free program is called Gimp; this one can be downloaded directly from their website gimp.org and you install it like you would any program.

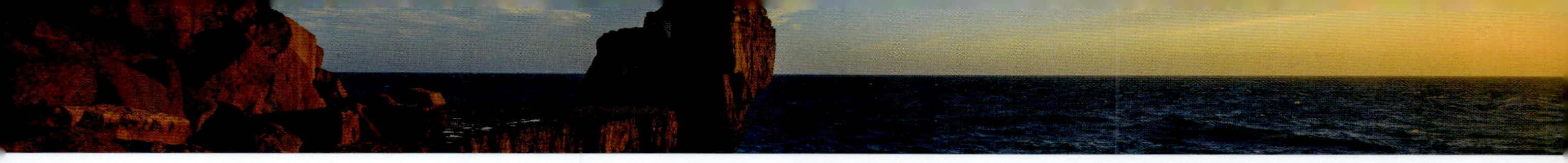

Paid Programs

You have Adobe Photoshop.

A really powerful photo manipulation tool mainly used by professionals.

You get Adobe photoshop Elements which is their cheaper version, its Adobe's entry level photoshop programme, designed to give you a taster of the full program.

You also get Adobe Lightroom. This program is not a photo manipulation tool like photoshop, it's designed to assist you in managing large quantities of digital images. It is a digital darkroom and image management system so you can import, process & export a batch of files all at once.

It's designed to work hand-in-hand with Photoshop. It's a really good programme, especially when you start working with RAW files.

There's also another good program called Affinity Photo by a company called Serif. This is a good option as it's a powerful program and it's cheaper than Photoshop.

In my examples I'm going to use the 2 most popular programs – Photoshop and Lightroom, and I'm going to show you how you can do a few simple things in these programs to make your images 10 times better.

But before we go into that I want to talk about what RAW and Jpeg files are and the differences between the two. There are the two main types of digital files that are produced when you take an image. You can either shoot in Raw or you can shoot in Jpeg.

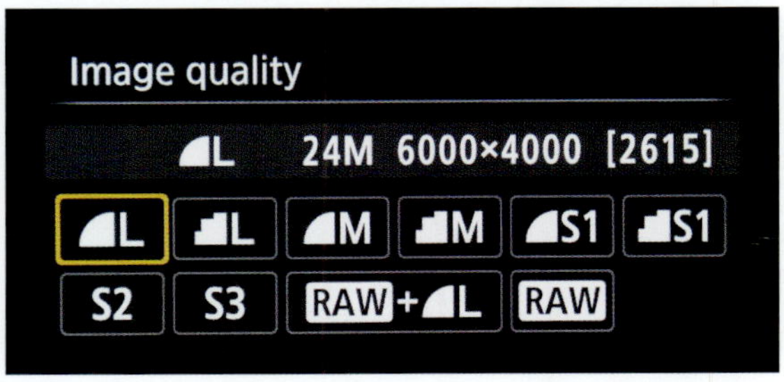

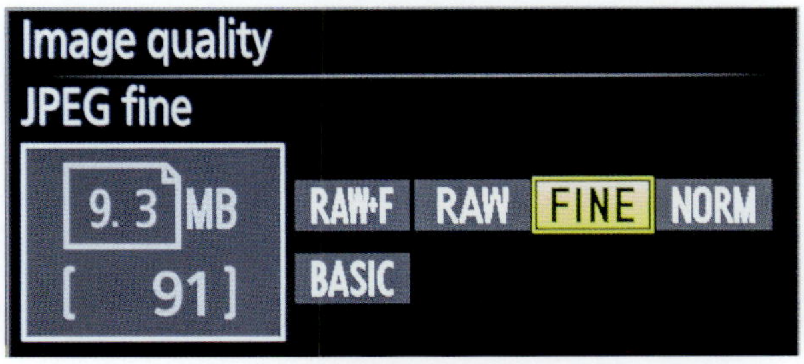

Raw Files

A RAW file preserves most of the information from the camera, it doesn't process it or compress it. It's like an old negative (right) if you remember them. You can't actually see the image from a negative and this is the same for Raw files. A negative needs to be processed in a darkroom with an enlarger, paper and chemicals before you can see the image.

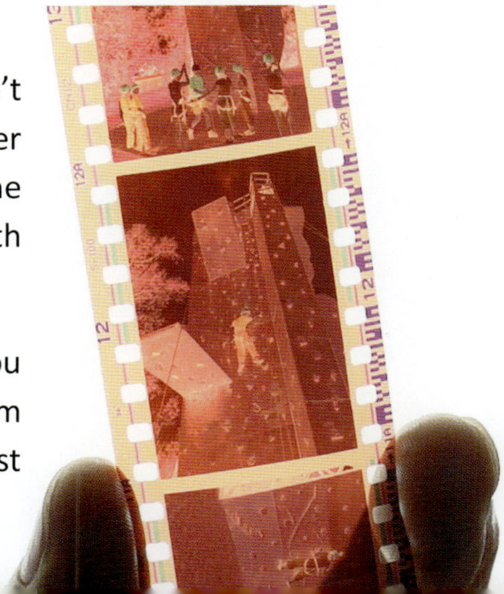

It's the same for a RAW file, you can't actually see a RAW file until you process it through a computer programme. The computer program effectively becomes what used to be the darkroom. The RAW file is just holding the information needed to produce a print, like a negative.

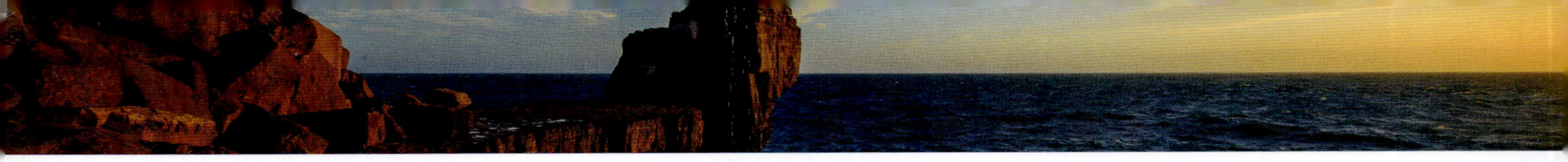

Jpeg Files

A Jpeg file is a visible image, you can see it on the screen, print it out and you can view it on any computer or device. A Jpeg is a compressed file, it's actually a code. The camera takes the RAW data and compresses it into a code. That code is then read by computers and opened up into an image again.

You have moderate information in a Jpeg files but you don't have as much as you would with a RAW file. What that means is you can't push a Jpeg as far in post-processing.

Let's say you want to make a Jpeg image brighter. You will only be able to brighten it by 1, possibly 1 ½ stops before you see visible degrading in the quality of the image.

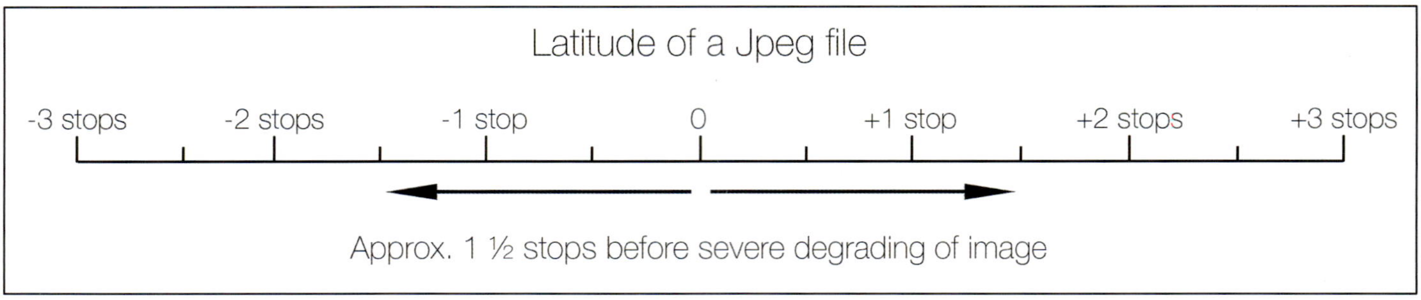

But with a RAW file you can push that to 2 or even 3 stops. This is what's called the latitude of the image. You have much more 'latitude' in a Raw file than a Jpeg file.

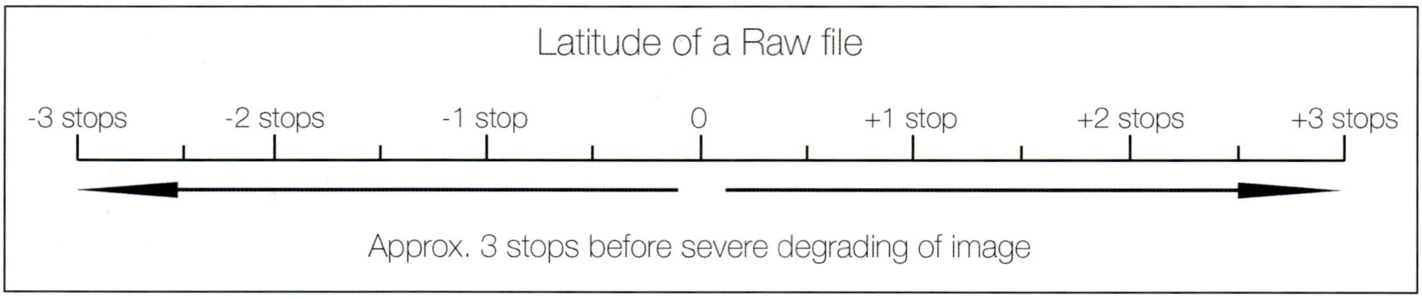

When you're shooting in Jpeg, your camera gives you a 'compressed' version of the RAW data. You will see this in the file size between a RAW and a Jpeg file.

Name	Size	Type
Original RAW file.dng	25,472 KB	DNG File
processed jpeg.jpg	5,877 KB	JPG File

On average a RAW file is 3-5 times the size of a Jpeg file. That's because there is a lot more information in the RAW file which is beneficial when you enhance them in digital programs.

Should you shoot in RAW or Jpeg?

This is a question I get asked a lot. Well, you should shoot in RAW only if you know what to do with that file in post-processing. Also, if you don't know how to control your depth of field, ISO, composition, shutter speed techniques and everything else you have learnt throughout this course, then you need to stick to Jpeg and get all that right first because all you will do is add another element of confusion into your learning process.

A Raw file won't get you a good image, your control of photography will do that.

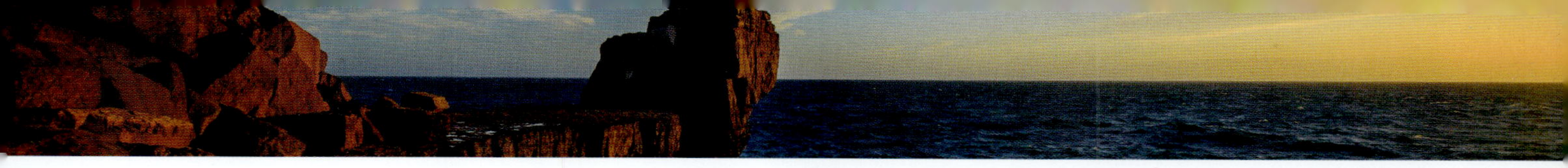

Processing a Raw File in Lightroom

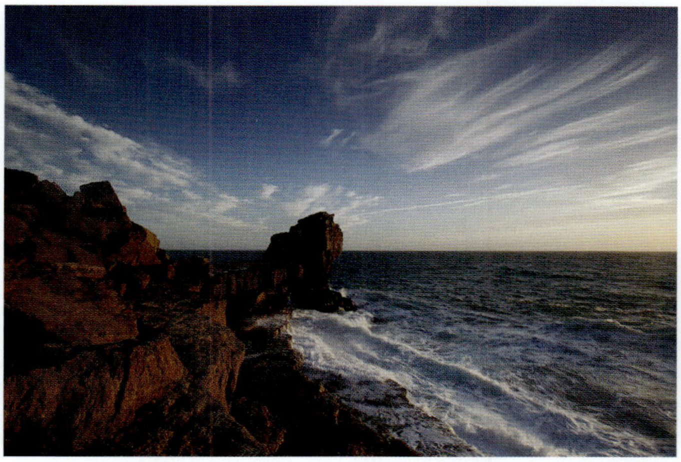

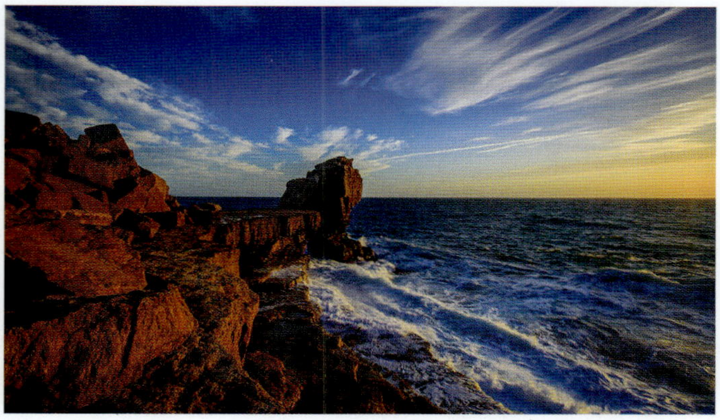

Original Raw file

Processed Raw file

Here's an example of what you can do with a Raw file in post-processing. For this, I used Lightroom to take an image from its RAW state into something much better with just a few steps.

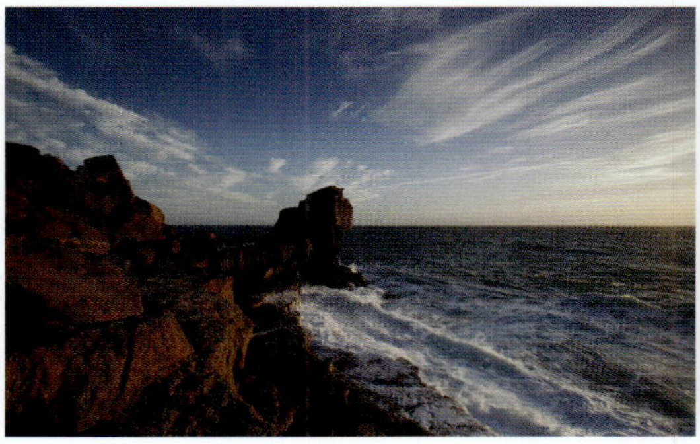

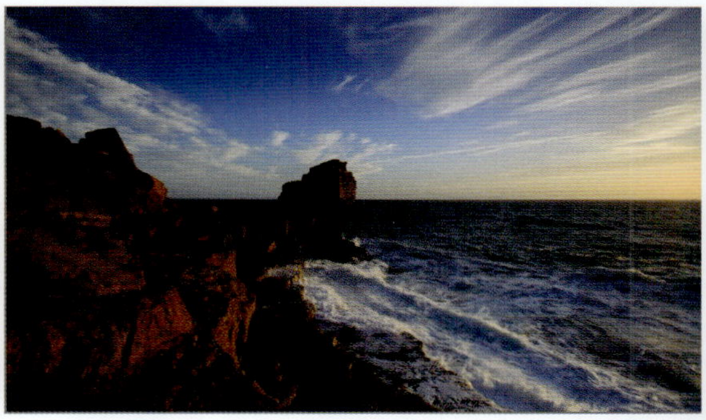

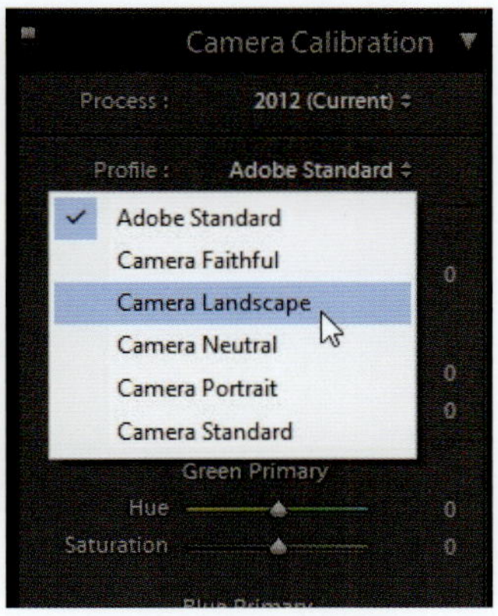

Firstly I changed the camera profile to 'Camera Landscape' as this is a landscape shot. This changes the colour saturation slightly as you can see (*above centre*).

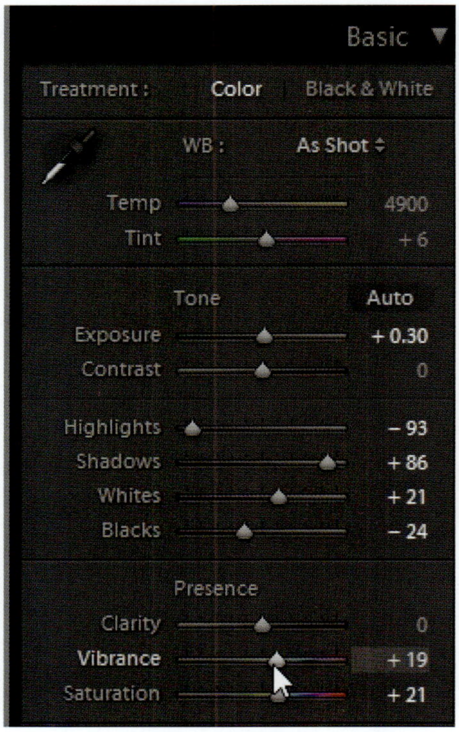

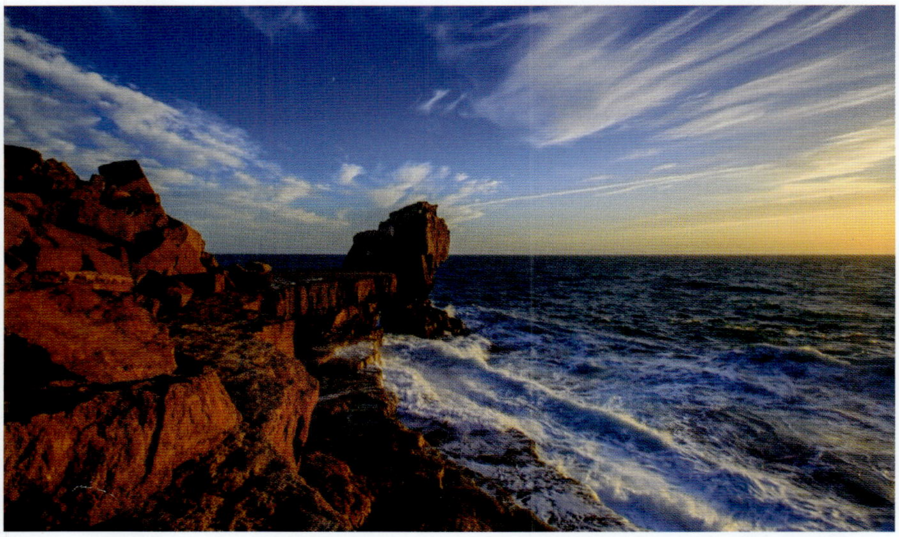

Next, I made some adjustments in the basic palette. I brightened the exposure, took down the highlights, brought up the shadows, and increased the saturation and vibrance.

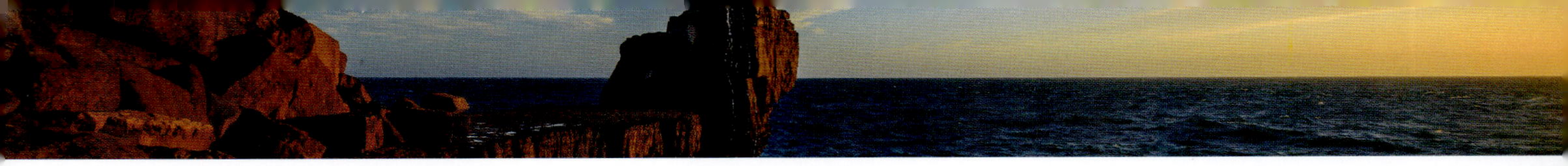

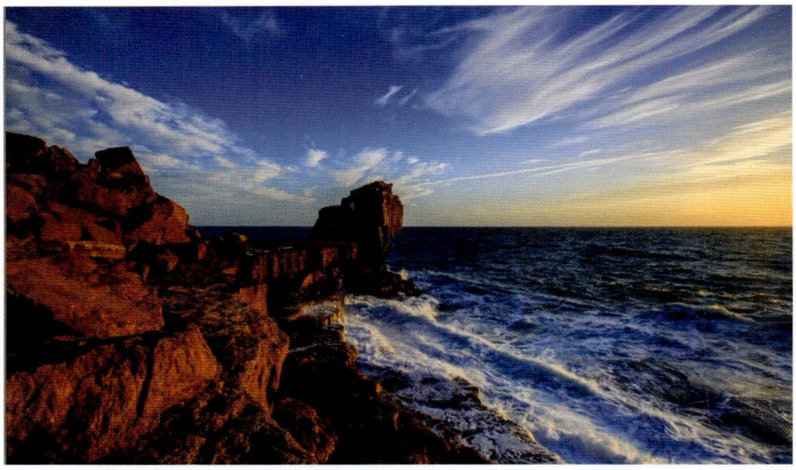

Next, I added a slight 'S' curve in the curves palette. This just increases the contrast slightly.

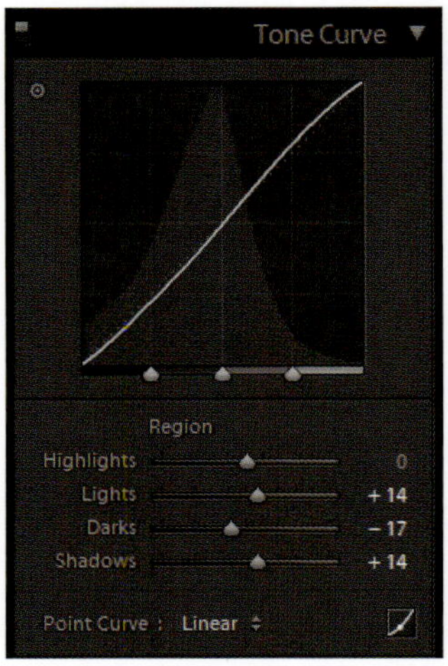

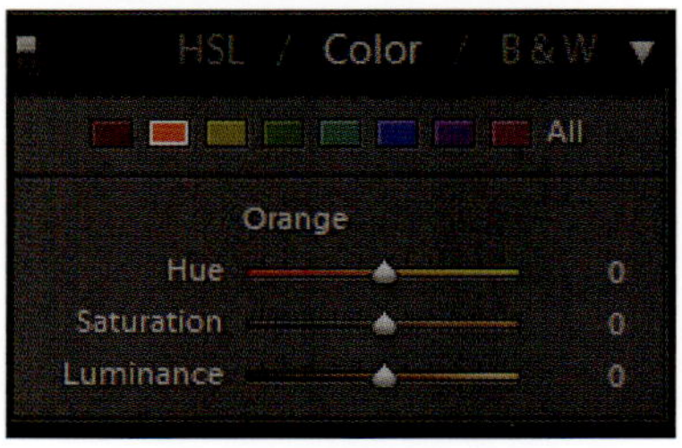

Then, I adjusted the colours individually, in the HSL/Colour palette. I increased the saturation and luminance of the blues, to bring out the sky more, and then I increased the saturation of the yellows, oranges, and reds to bring out the sunset colours.

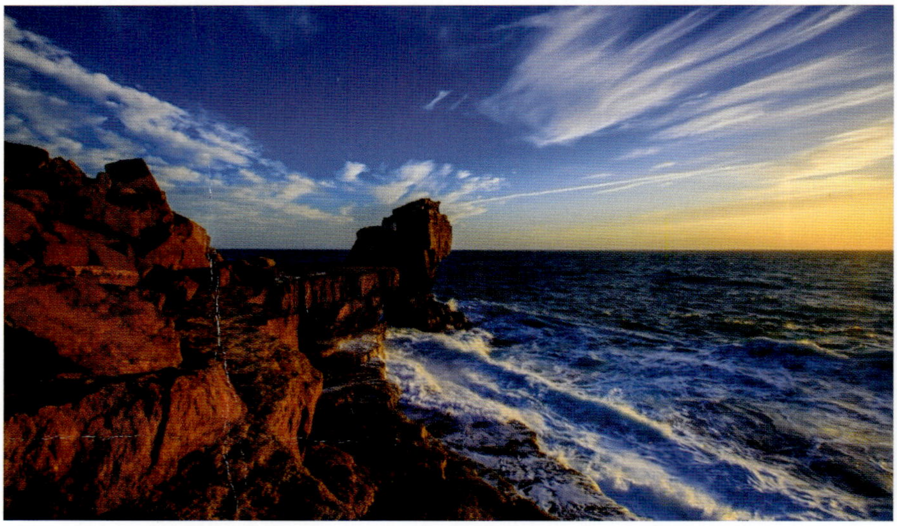

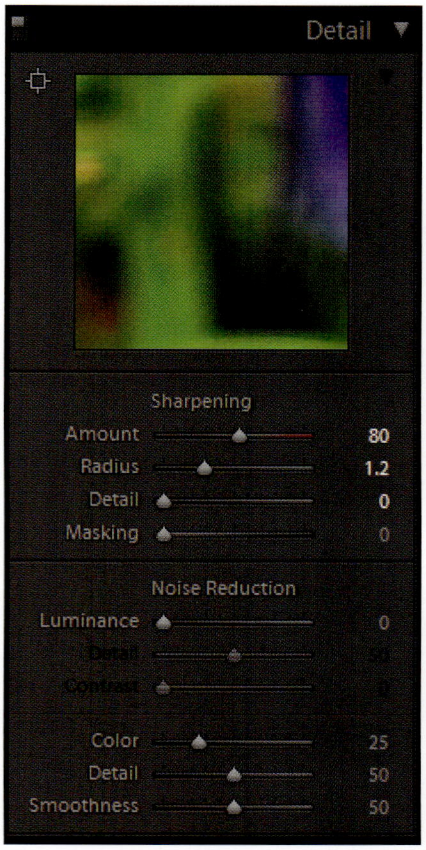

Then I sharpened the picture in the detail pallet. The first image doesn't look too bad. But every digital image needs to be sharpened in post-processing. So I put the sharpening to 80 and the radius to 1.2.

Before sharpening

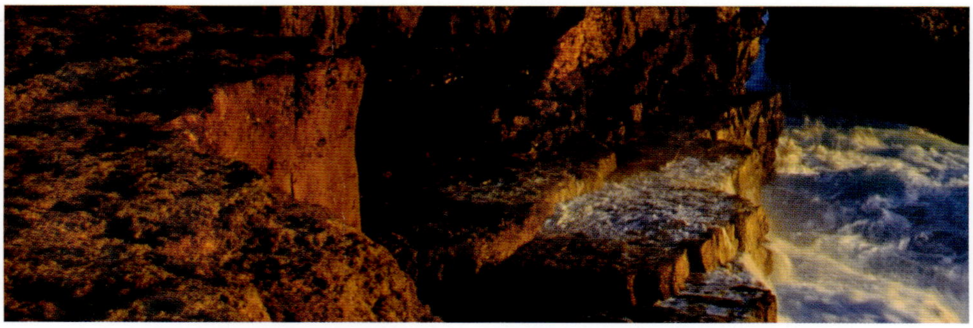

After sharpening

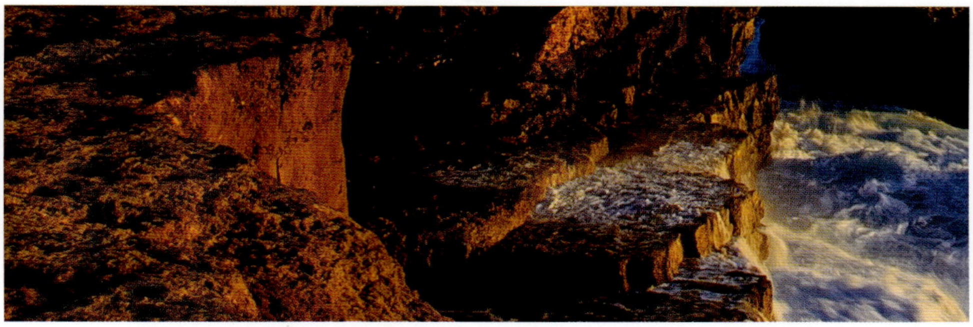

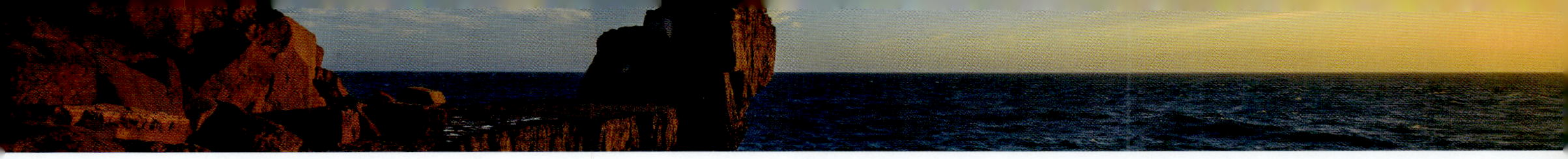

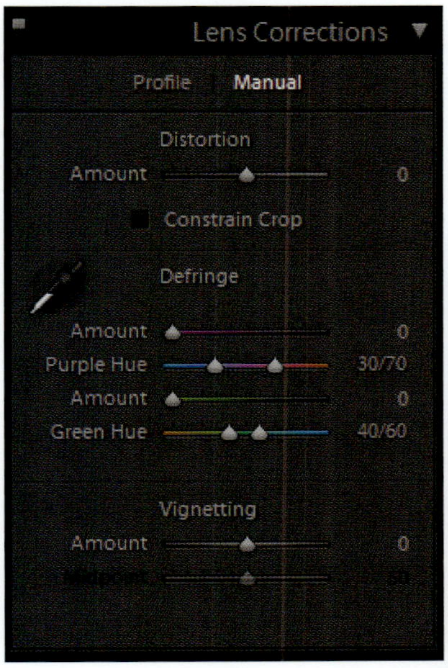

If you zoom in to the edges of objects in your image, in this case rocks, you can see there are two colour outlines; red and green. This is called 'chromatic aberration', and happens to some digital images (*below left*). In the lens correction panel, I ticked 'Remove Chromatic Aberration' and as you can, it has reduced these coloured outlines (*below right*).

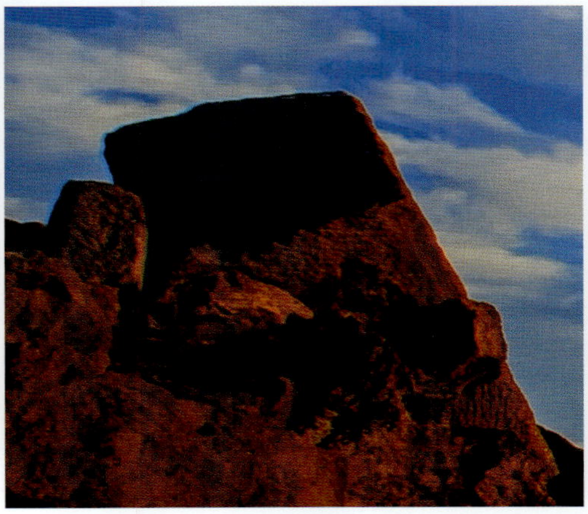

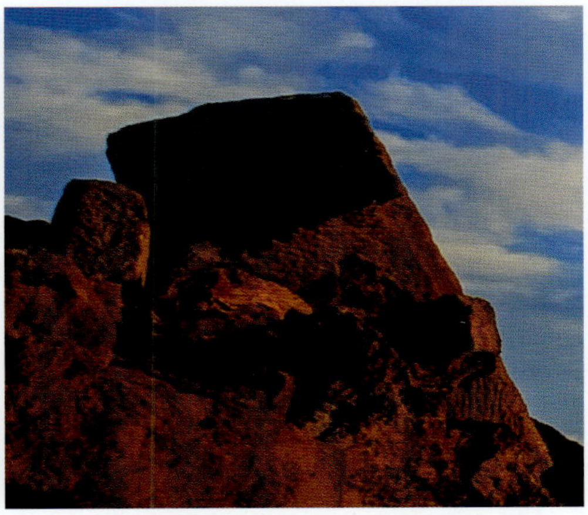

After that, I used the crop tool to improve the composition by having the clouds coming in from the top left of the frame.

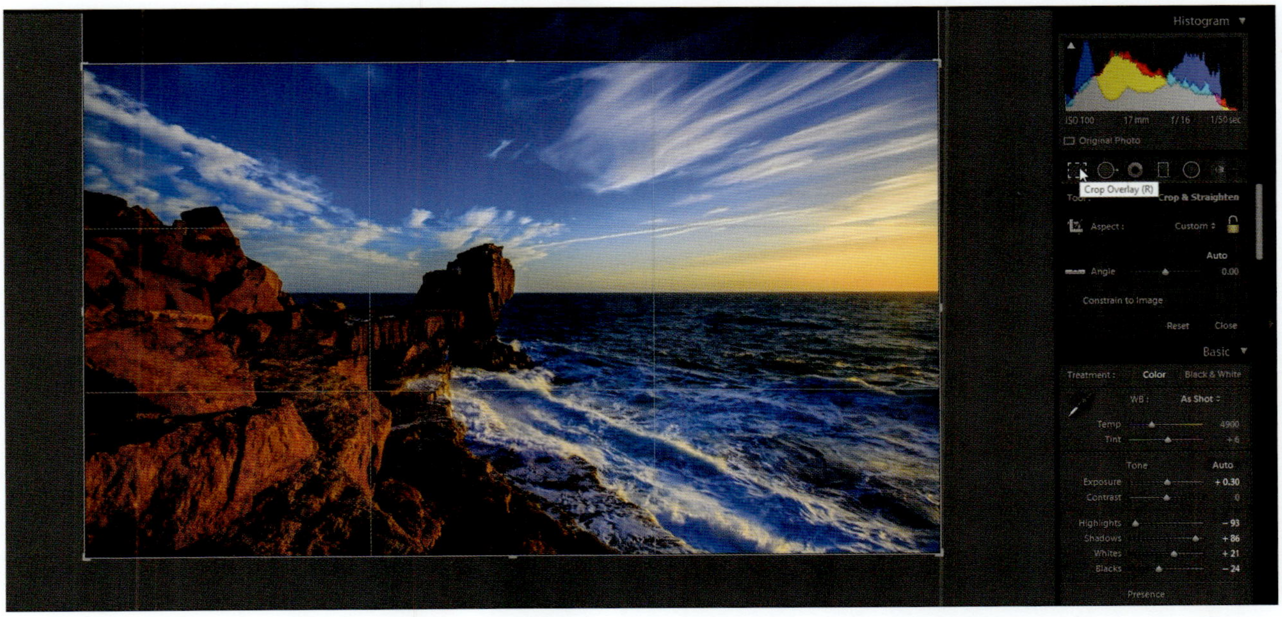

Finally, I added a slight vignette to the outside of the frame, in the effects panel.

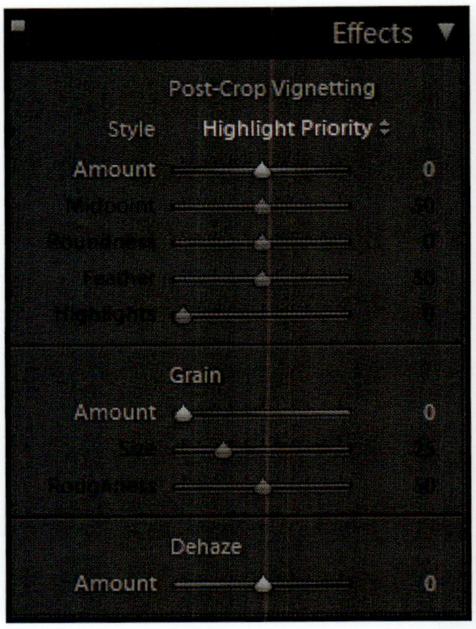

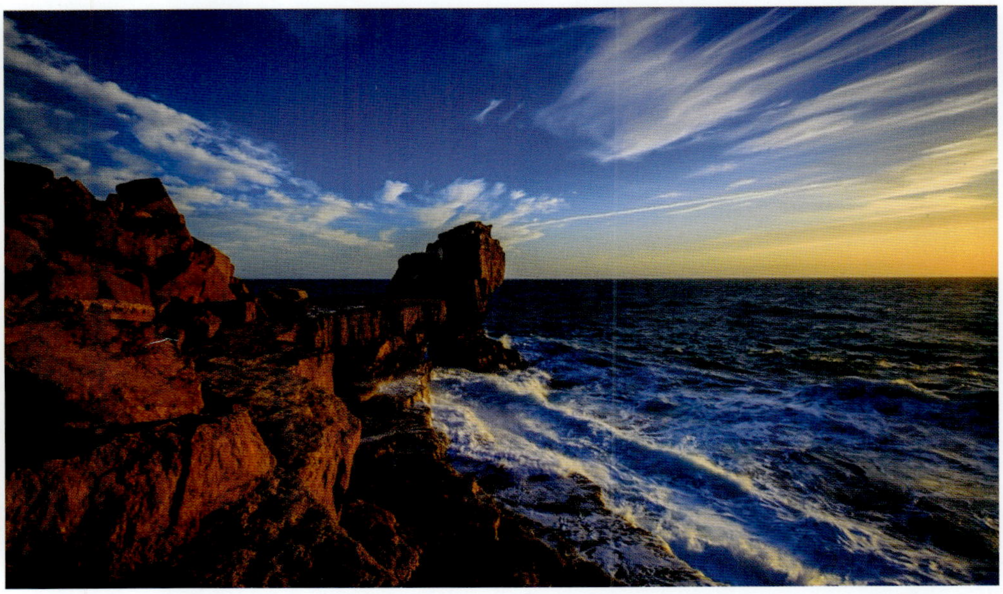

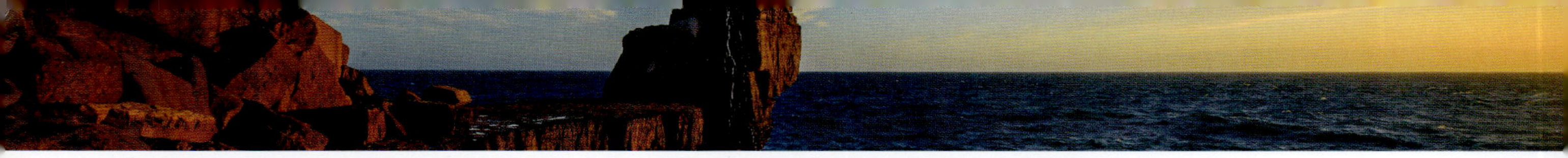

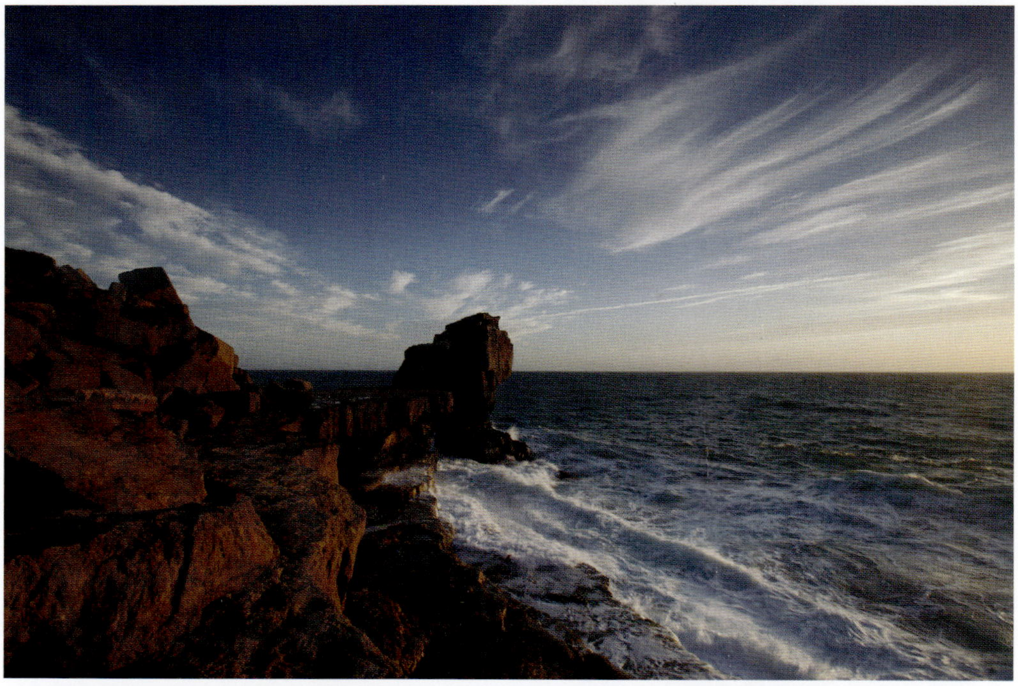

Original Raw File

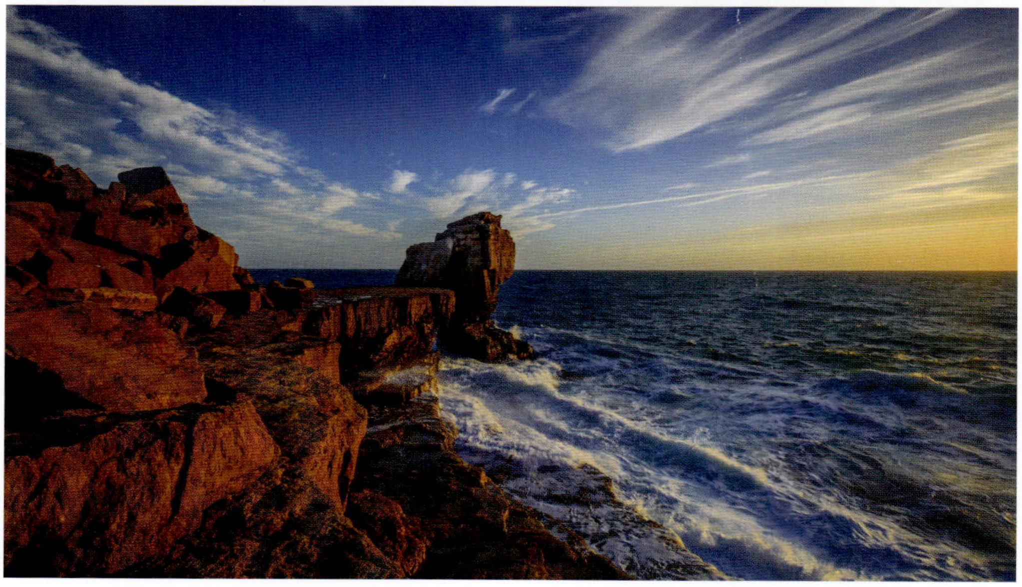

Processed Raw File

Processing a Jpeg in Photoshop

Although it's better to use Raw files when post processing, you can process Jpeg files as well.

I'm going to show you the same process but this time I will use a Jpeg and do it in Photoshop.

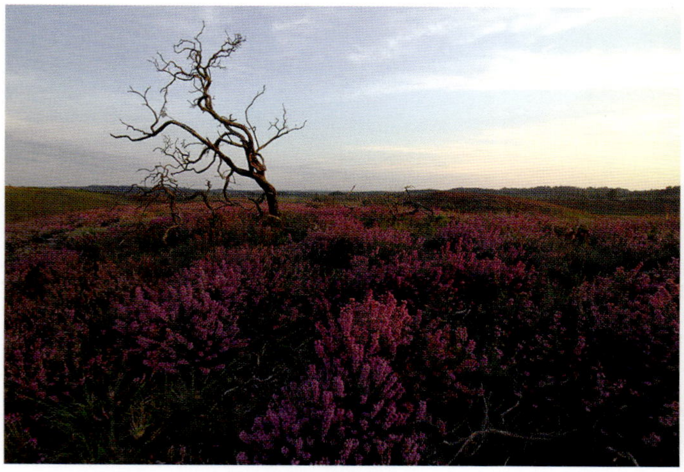

Original Jpeg file

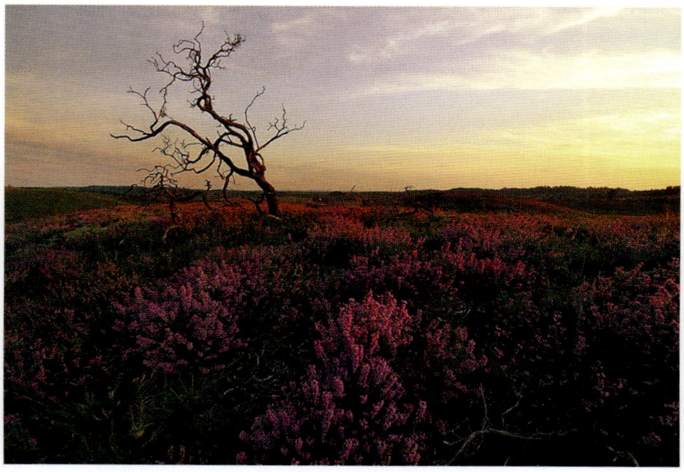

Processed Jpeg file

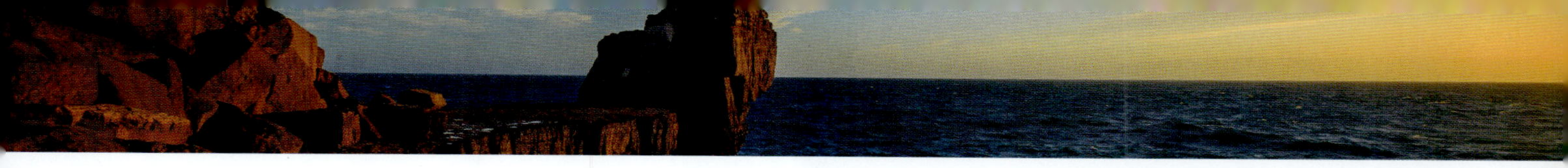

The first thing I did was sharpen the image by going to Filter > Sharpen > Unsharp Mask. Then I used the same sharpening settings that I used for Lightroom example – Amount 80, radius 1.2.

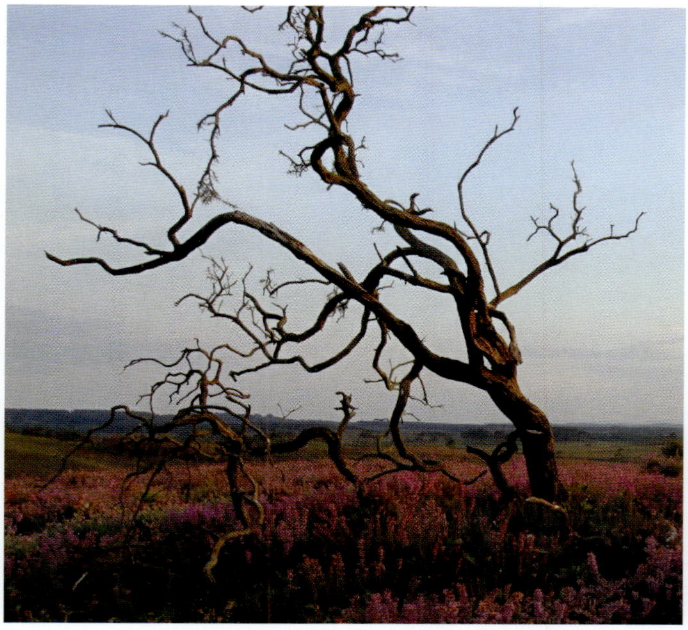

Before sharpening

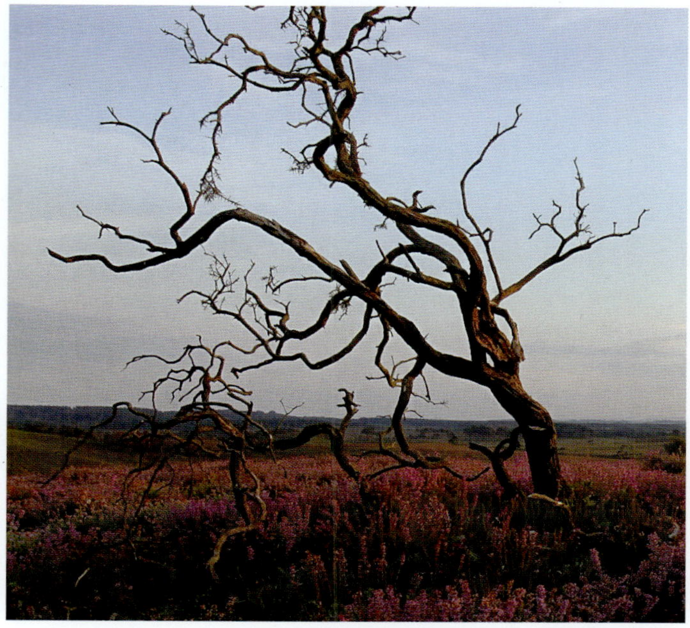

After sharpening

Next, I added a curves adjustment layer and gave it some contrast with a slight S curve.

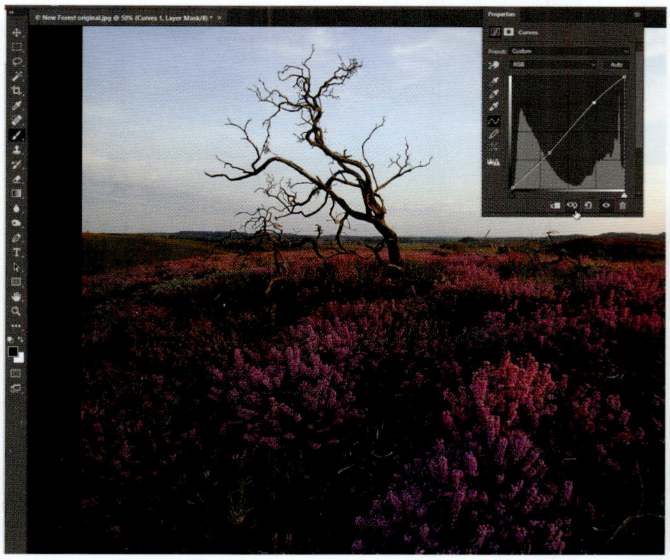

I then enhanced some colours using curves adjustment layers, this technique allows you to single out specific colours. For instance you choose a blue curve and enhance just the yellows and blues of the image.

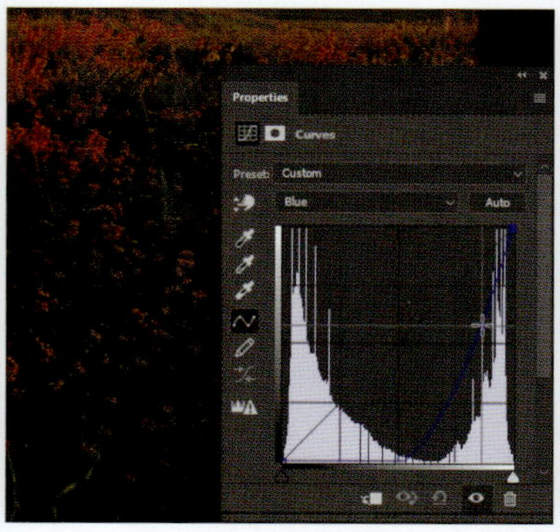

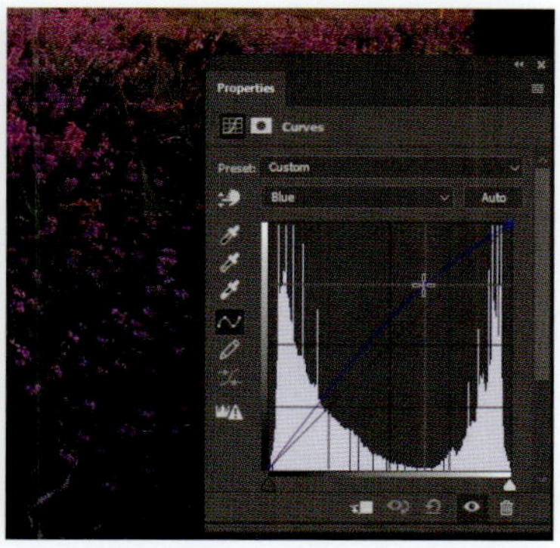

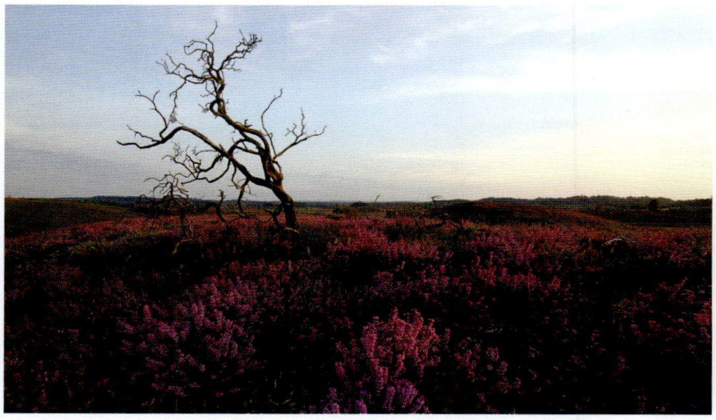

Before Curves Adjustments

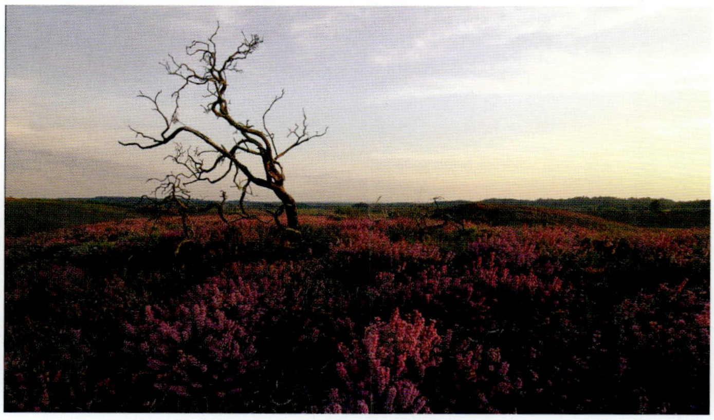

After Curves Adjustments

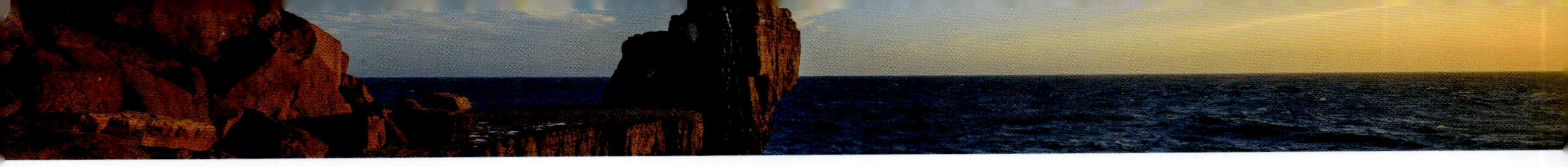

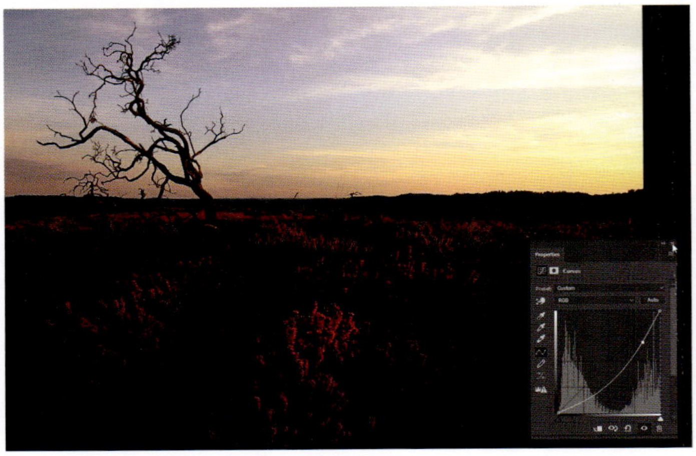

Next I added another curve adjustment layer but this time took the highlights down drastically, to darken the image.

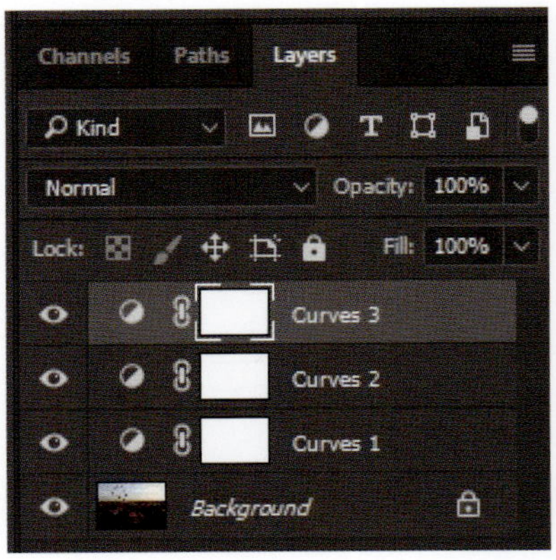

One of the benefits of Photoshop is you can work on individual layers and then work on masks within that layer.

On the mask of my darkened layer I removed the effect of the darkening from all parts of the image except the sky. Then adjusted the colour balance of the image. This gave me a rich warm tone to the sunset.

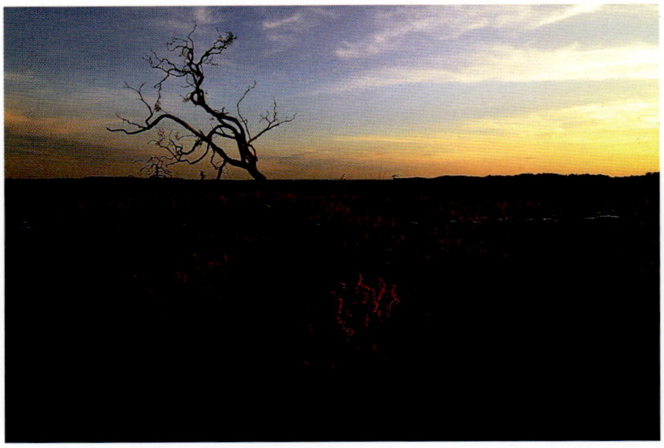

Darkened with curves adjustment layer

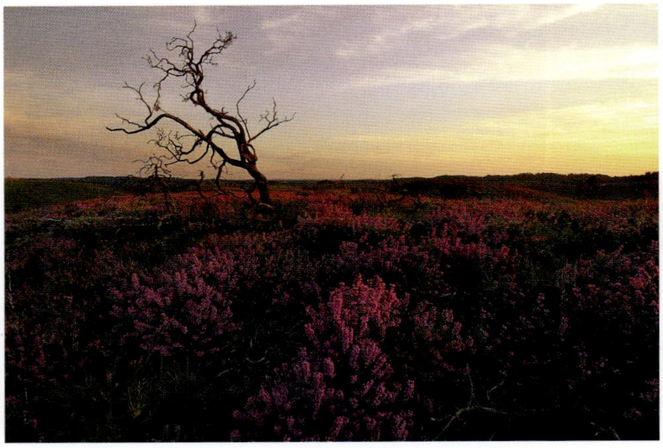

Darkened areas removed using layers and masking

To view video tutorials on post-processing go to www.theschoolofphotography.com and type curves or Lightroom or Photoshop in the search bar.

That's a brief introduction into what Photoshop and Lightroom can do in the post-processing of your images. Learning to use LR and PS are two totally new skills and this will be your next stage to becoming a great photographer. I recommend you learn Lightroom first then Photoshop.

And of course, we are a school of photography, so we have courses to get you starting in Lightroom and Photoshop; for more info on these courses, go to our website and click 'Online Courses'.

When you're comfortable with controlling photography, start shooting in RAW and learn about post-processing your images properly as it really does make a good image great.

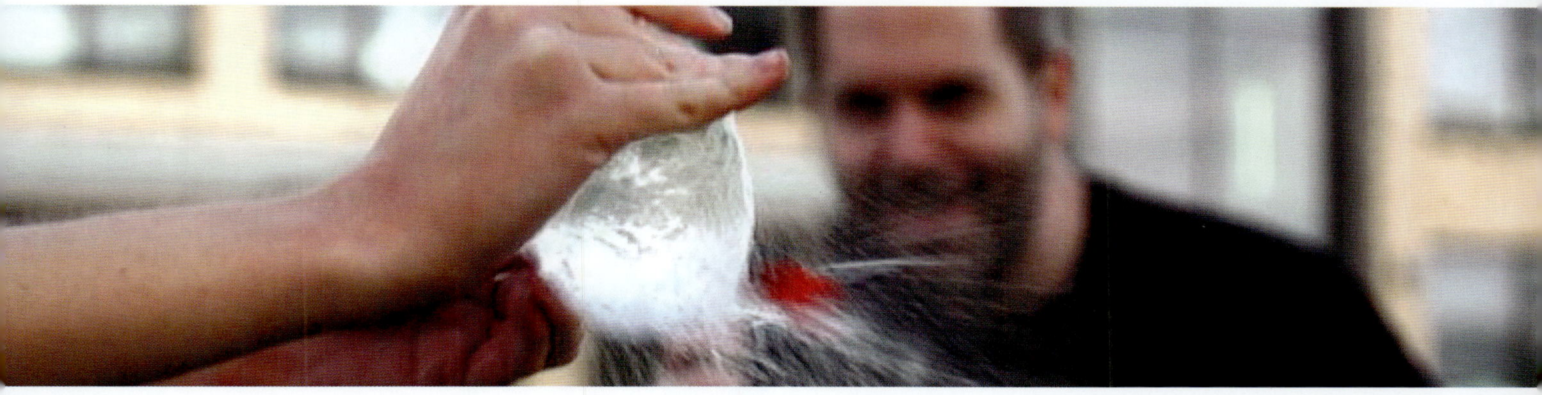

End of Book Recap

Chapter 17

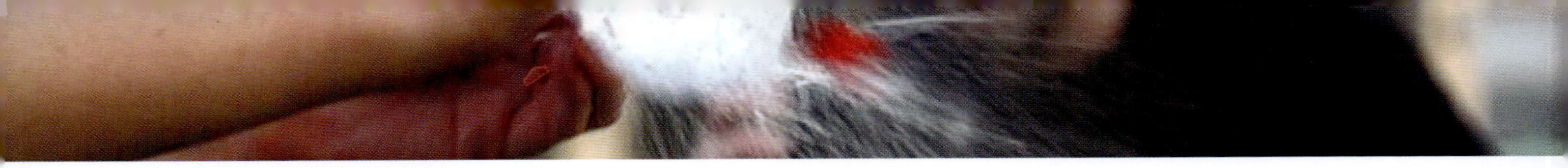

So that's the end of the *Complete Guide to Photography* Book. There's two things I hope you got from it. One is that I hope you learnt a lot and it has put you on a path to taking better photos. The other is that I hope you had fun doing it. It's very important to have fun whilst learning; it motivates you and pushes you to learn more.

Recap

First, we looked at camera kits and recommended equipment for when you're starting out in photography.

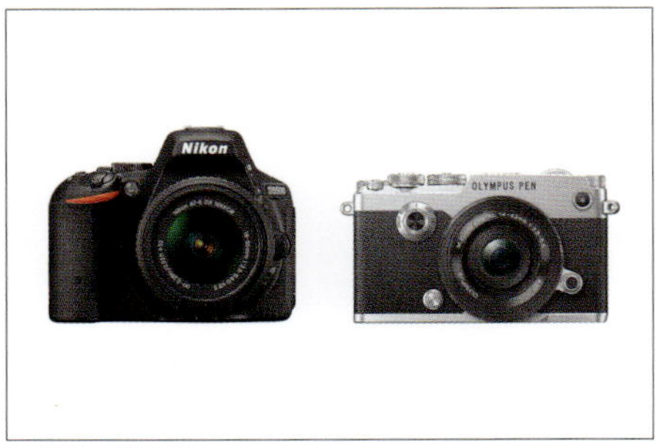

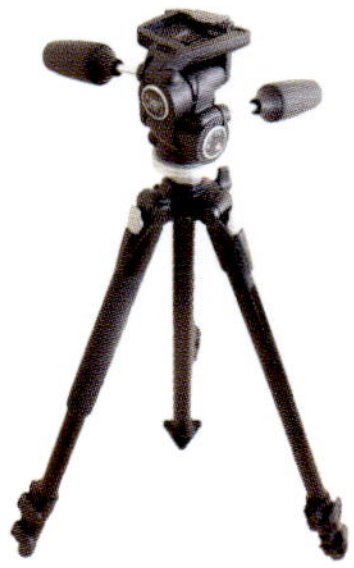

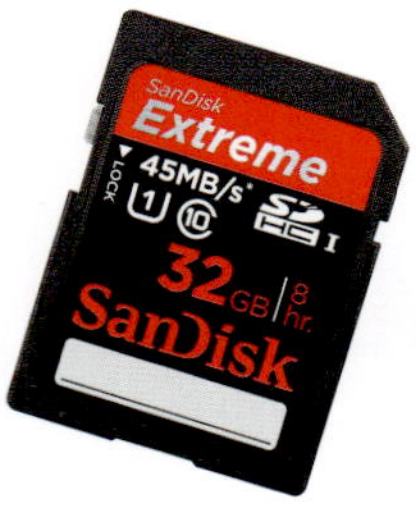

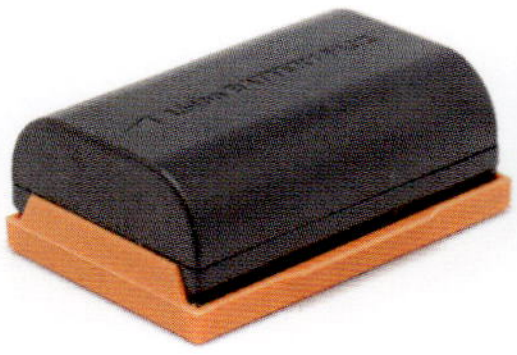

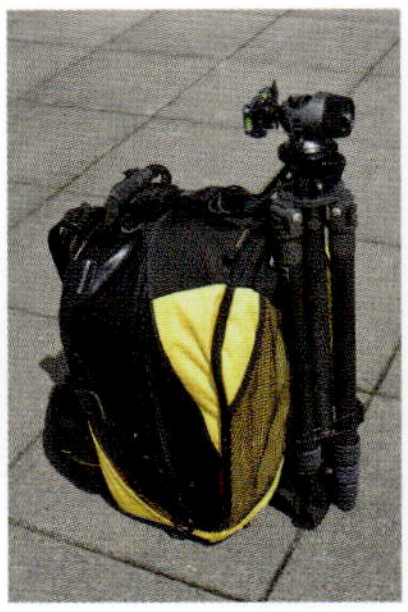

Then we looked at manual settings – you'll never use automatic modes again!

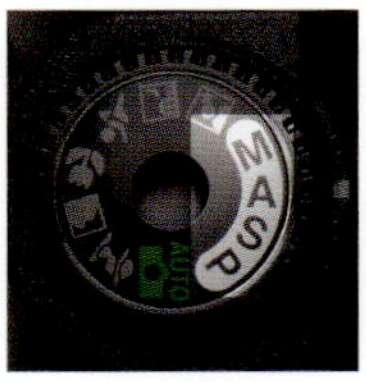

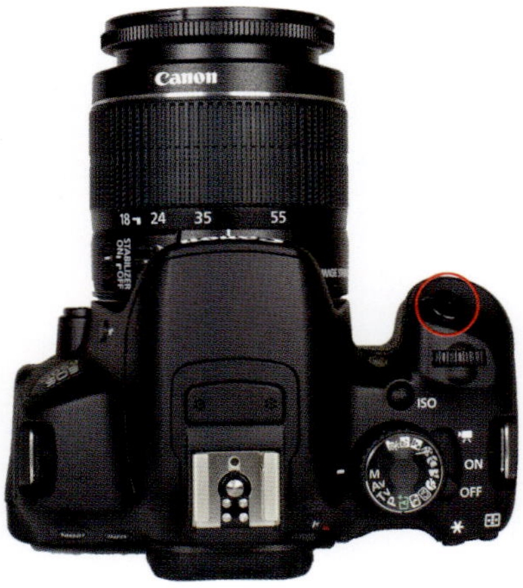

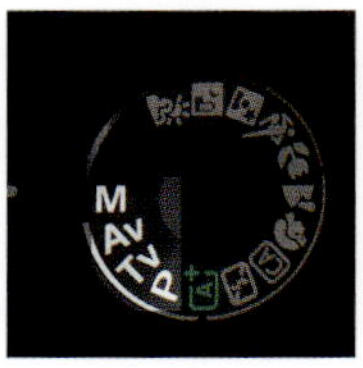

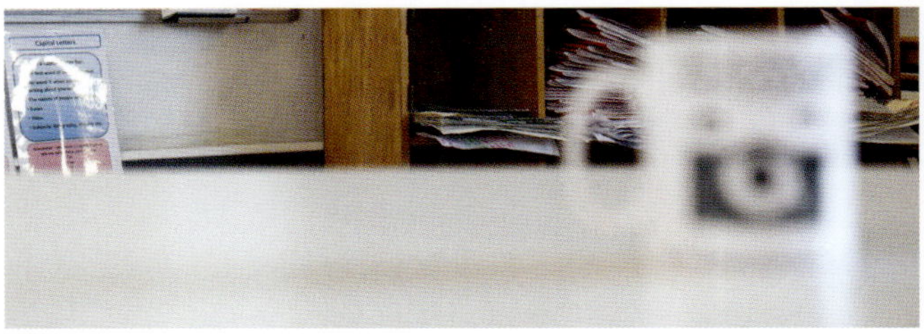

Next, we looked at focusing, and how to get your focus point exactly where you want it to be.

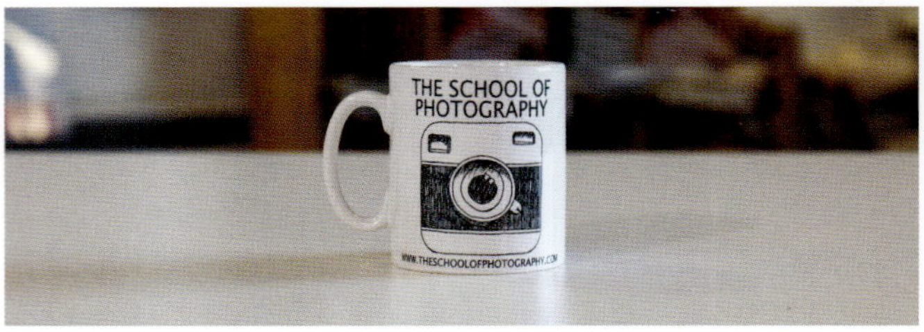

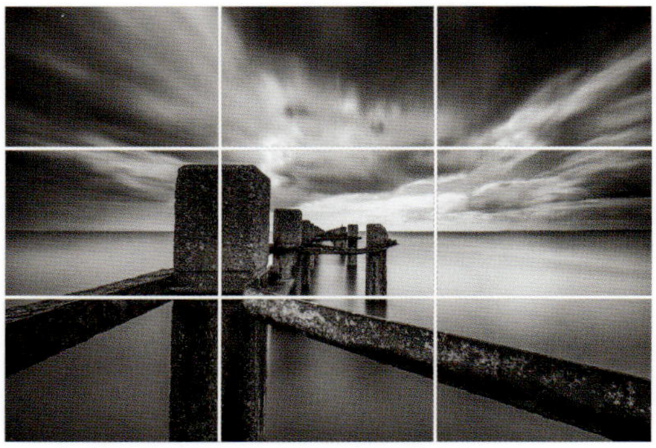

We then looked at composition; composition is the way you arrange the elements within your frame, and personally, I think it's one of the most important things to get right in any picture.

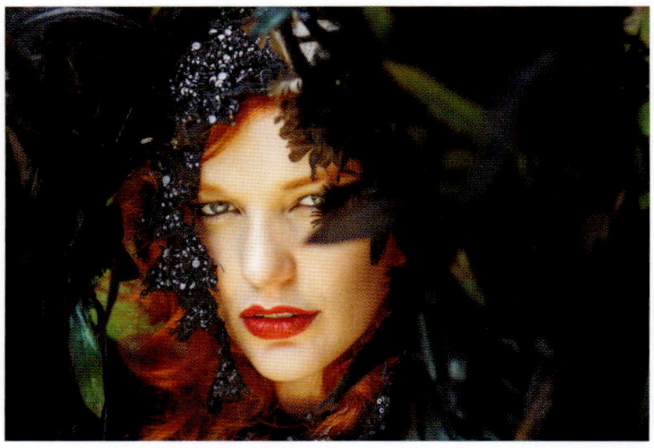

Then we looked at lenses and focal lengths. You use focal lengths to get a desired effect. Certain focal lengths will suit different situations. For example, a wide angle will suit landscapes, and zoomed in will suit portraits. Don't zoom in and out just because you can't be bothered to move forwards or backwards!

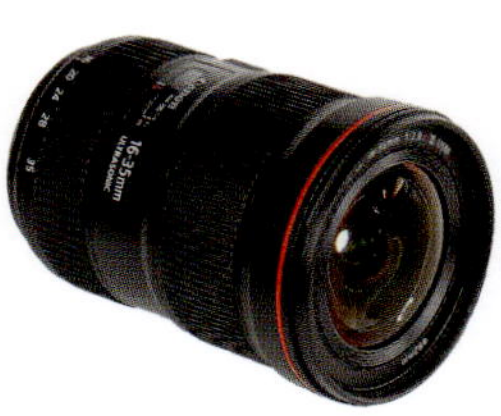

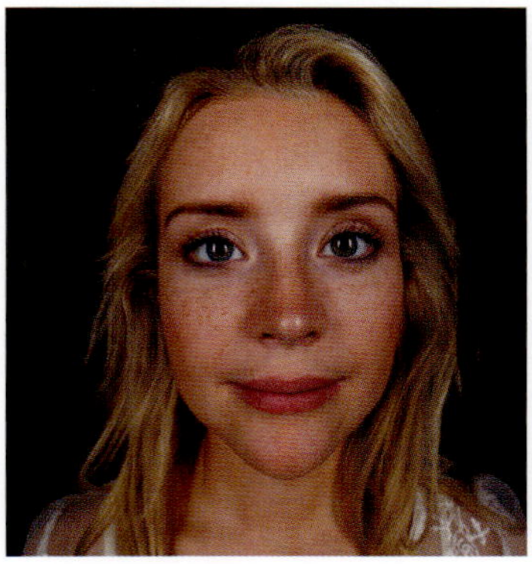

16mm

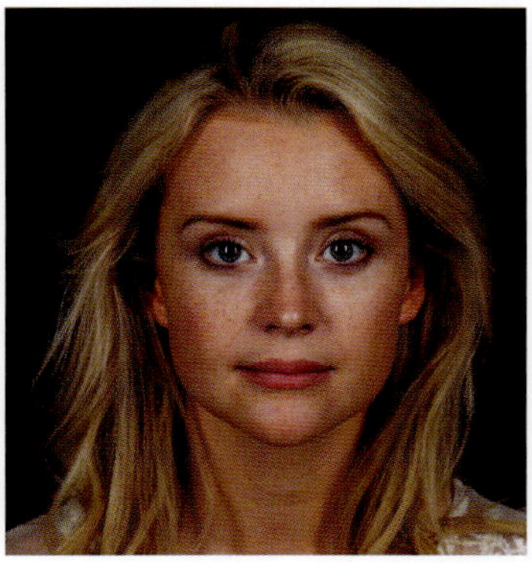

100mm

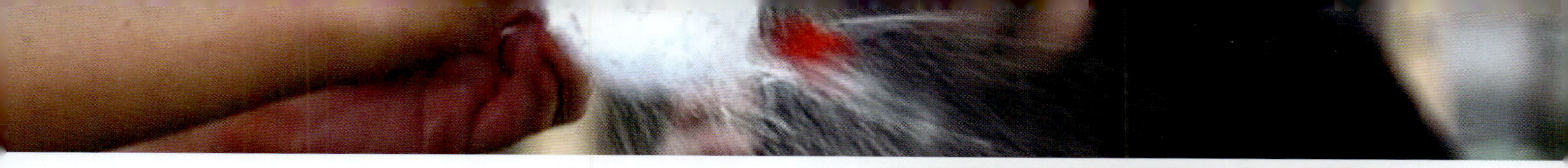

We looked at metering, how a camera measures light, and how to override this by increasing or decreasing the light, or by taking meter readings from specific parts of the frame

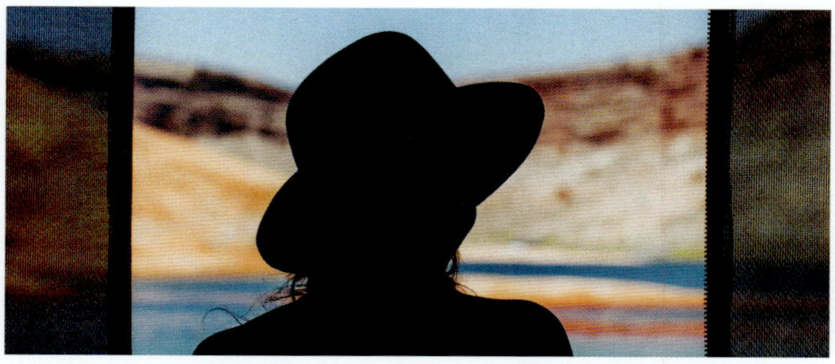

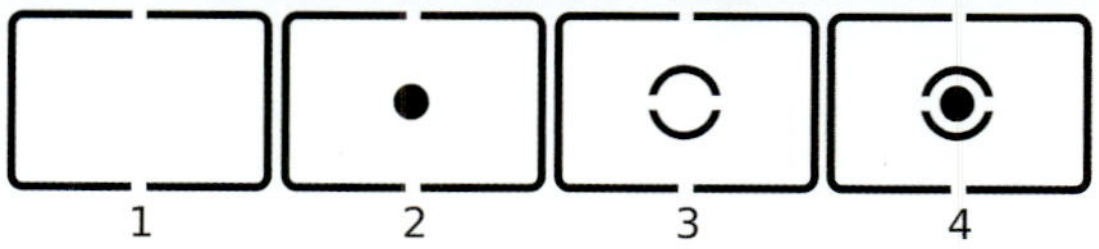

We looked at light and how you can create hard, soft, or diffused light, and how this effects an image.

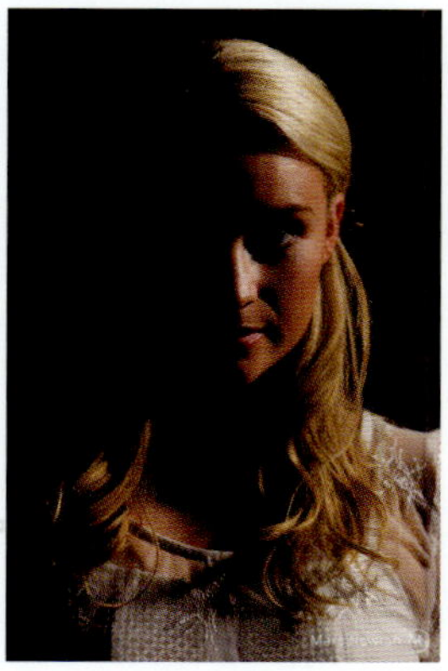

Hard light

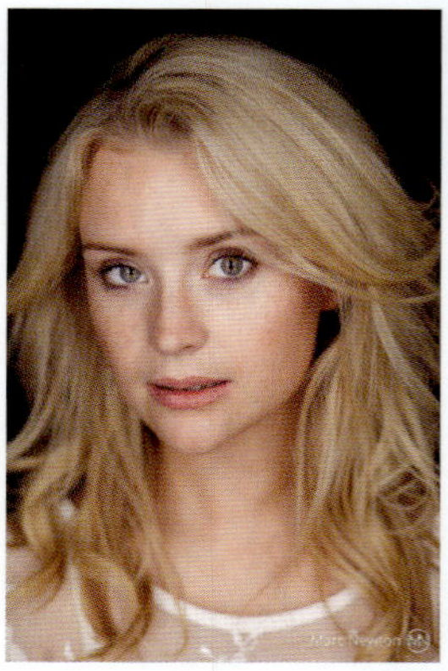

Soft light

We also looked at colour temperature and how you can use your camera's white balance to enhance or cancel out certain colours.

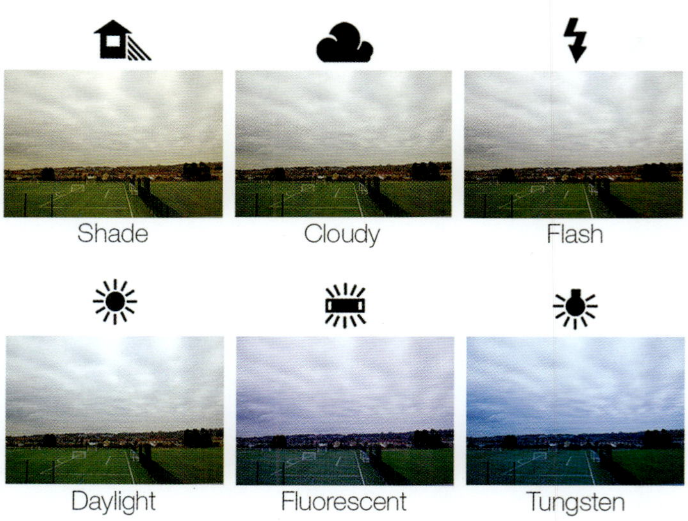

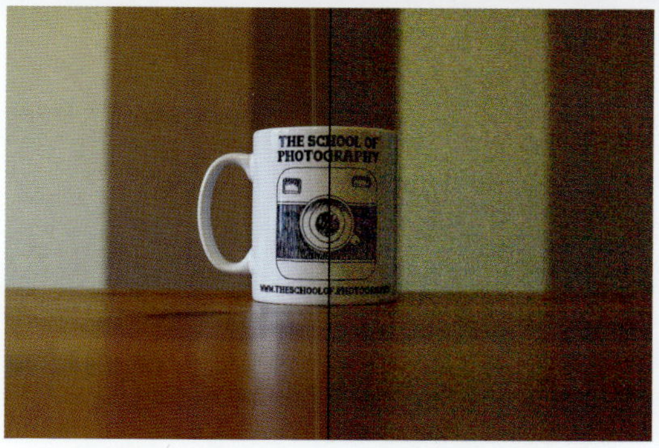

ISO 100 ISO 25600

Then we looked at ISO; what it is, how it affects your exposure, how you can reduce noise, and how you can make your camera more sensitive to light in low-light situations.

We looked at resolution and why you would use high and low res images.

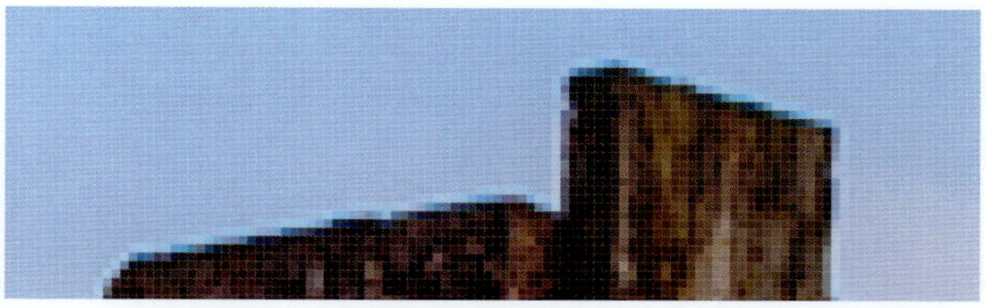

Name	Type	Size
High Res.jpg	JPG File	7,704 KB
Low Res.jpg	JPG File	1,131 KB

We looked at exposure in photography, which is how much light you let into your camera. We practiced our use of apertures and our control of depth of field. The three things that control depth of field are the aperture, focal length, and distance of your focus point from your lens.

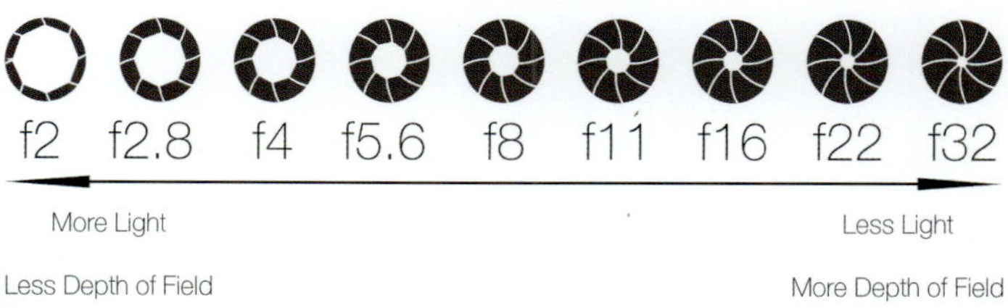

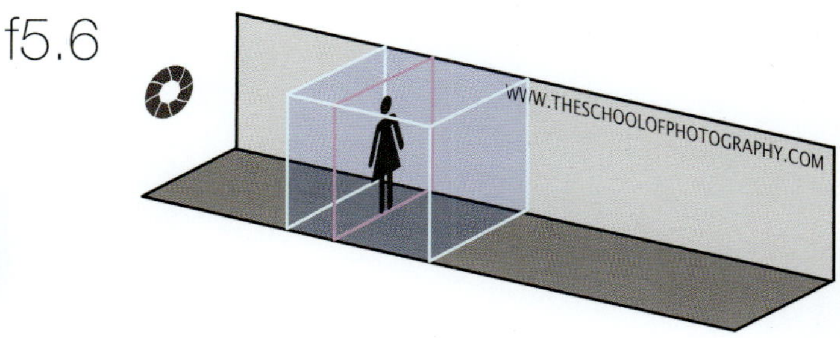

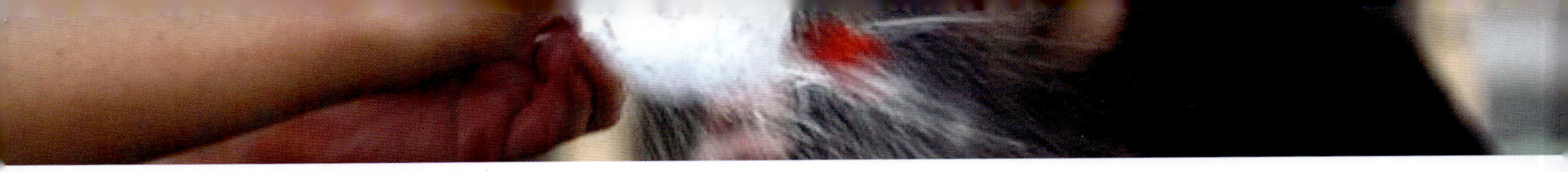

Next we looked at shutter speed and practiced many different techniques. The shutter speed lets in light over a period of time and can be used to freeze the action, or to show a sense a movement,

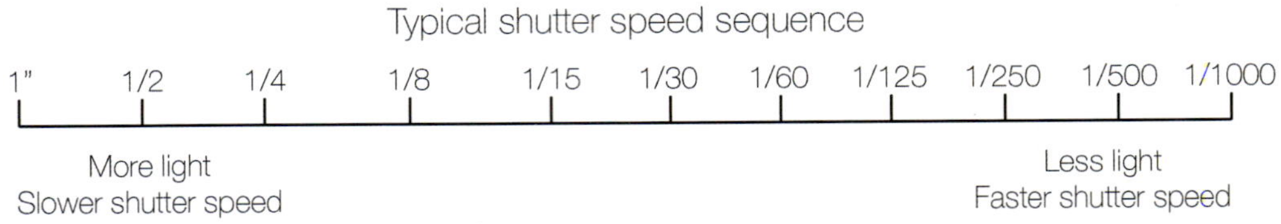

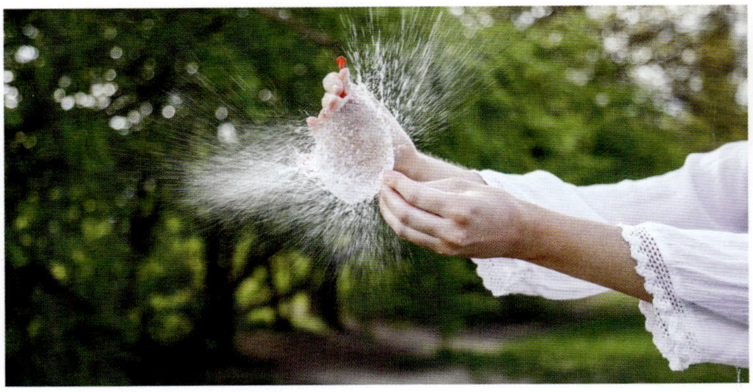

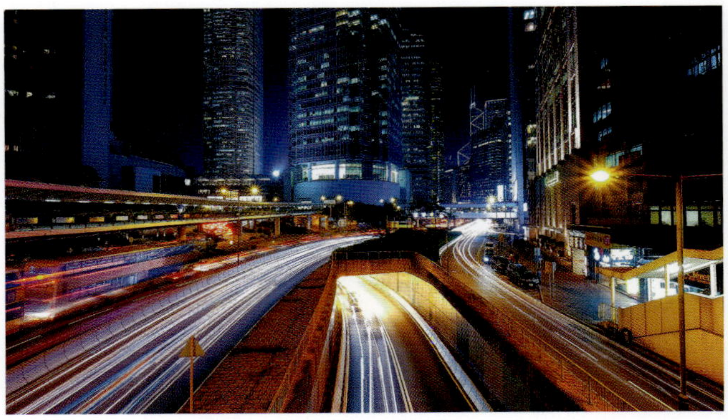

Then we moved on to learn about balancing exposures via your aperture and shutter speed. It's that balancing of light that makes you a photographer and not just someone who uses their camera on automatic. By balancing your exposure, you can let the same amount of light into your camera but create totally different visual effects.

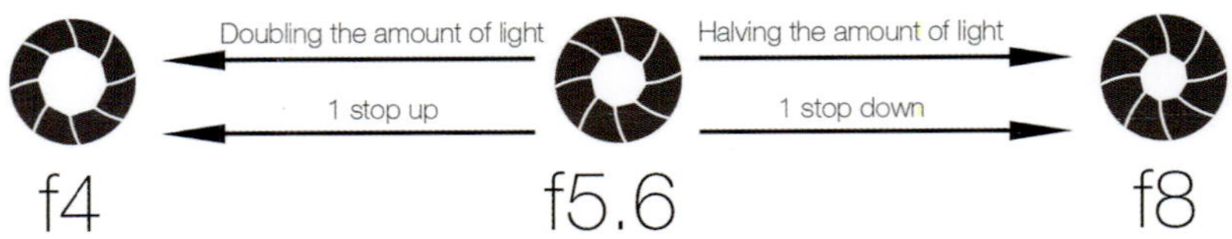

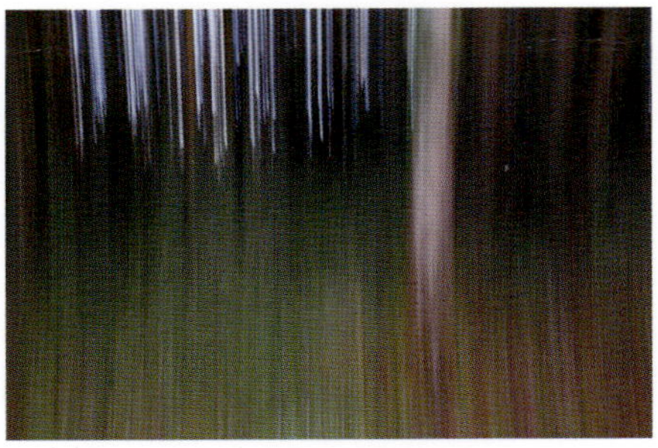

f8 - 1/2 sec - ISO 400

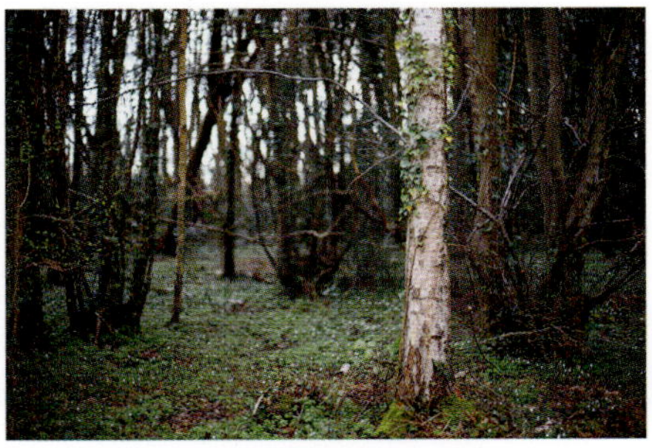

f1.4 - 1/60th - ISO 400

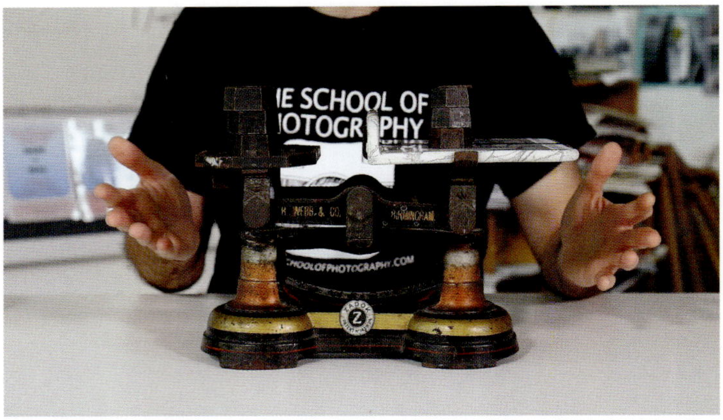

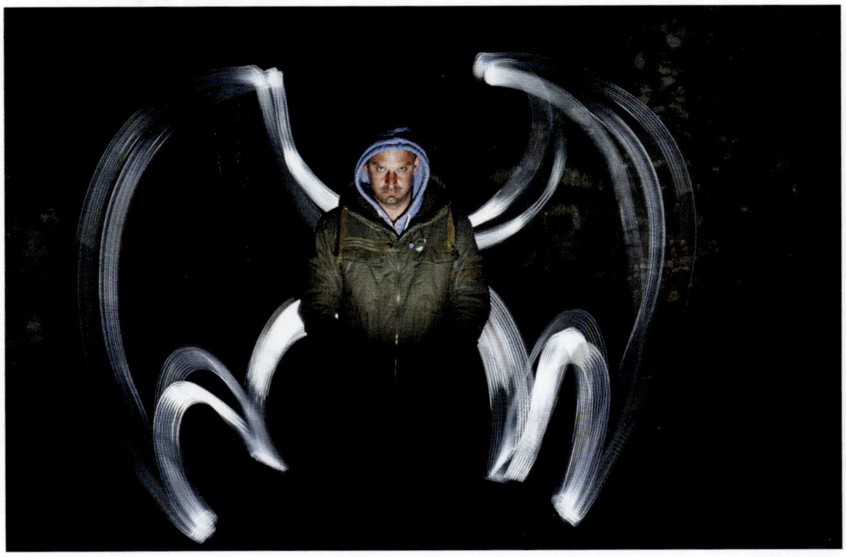

We practiced working in full manual mode by creating light paintings. A great way to mix all of what you have learnt and take control of photography.

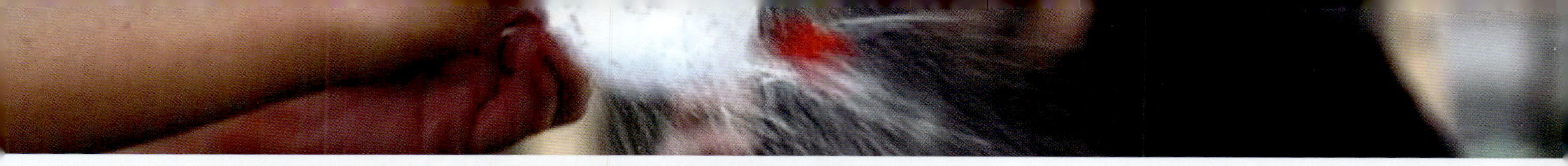

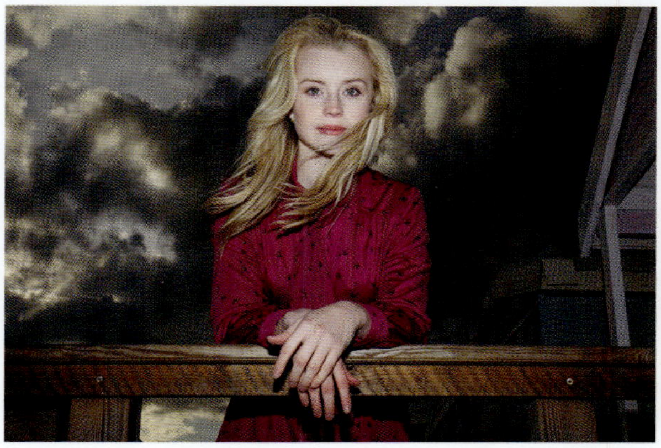

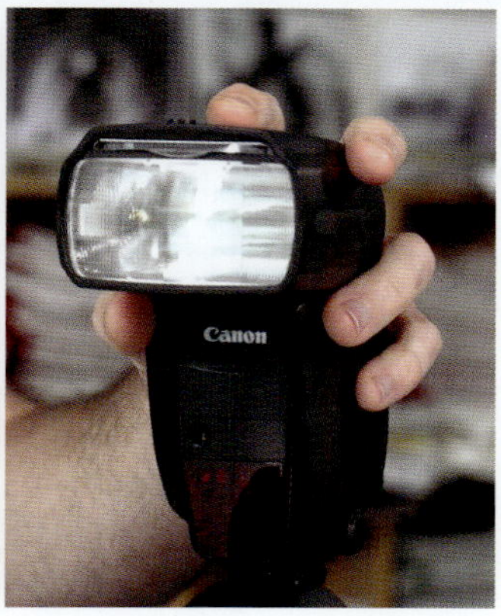

Then we got even more advanced by balancing exposures with flash, and in particular, how to use fill-in flash to create different visual effects.

Finally, we looked at the post-production of shots and examined using Raw or Jpeg files. I showed you some steps to enhance your photography, using Adobe Lightroom and Photoshop. Working in Raw and post-processing your shots are the next stages in your learning.

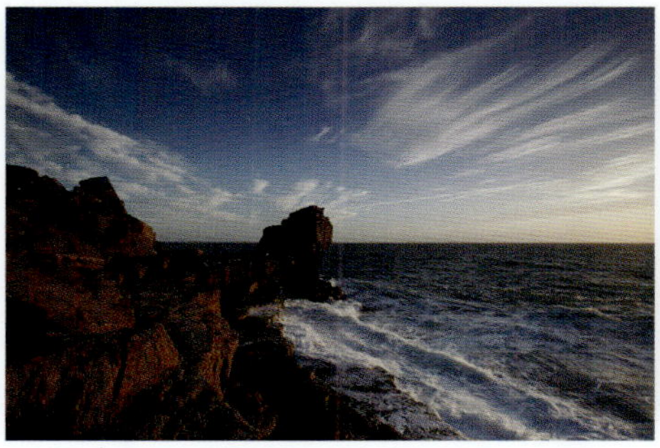

Original Raw file

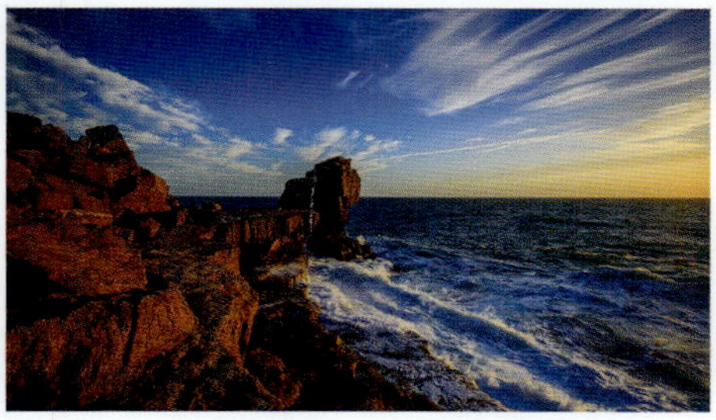

Processed Raw file

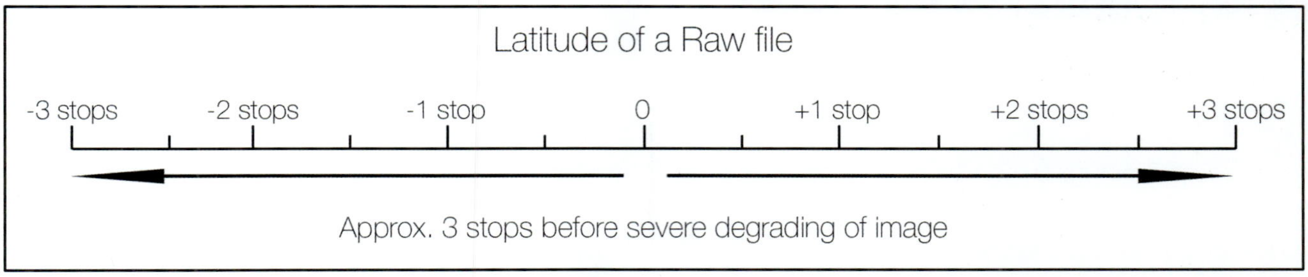

Get Social

I hope that this book has really helped you out, and I cannot wait to see some of your shots! Don't forget, you can show us your best shots on social media. Tag #theschoolofphotography

@theschoolofphotography1

@theschoolofphotography1

/c/theschoolofphotography

#theschoolofphotography

Follow us on social media too. We have a wonderful learning community of photographers, just like you.

It's been an absolute pleasure teaching you and I hope to see you on future courses at The School of Photography.

THE SCHOOL OF PHOTOGRAPHY

About The School of Photography

At TSoP we deliver high-quality photography courses online, in person, in books and are a leading provider of photography education to schools and colleges in the UK.

I'm Marc Newton and I run the team here. I'm a photographer, educational speaker, author and teacher of photography. Teaching Photography has been my passion for many years. I got my first paid photography job in 1997 whilst doing my photography degree, but in 2002 I decided to give teaching a go and I haven't looked back since. I loved seeing the stunning imagery my students produced. It filled me with a real sense of joy, and still does today.

My success in teaching led me to become an Advanced skills Teacher and I started to train UK school teachers to deliver the Photography GCSE and A Level curriculum. I wanted to take all of this experience and offer it up to a wider audience so in 2012 I started The School of Photography and now I teach people all over the world this beautiful craft.

My qualifications are as follows:

BA Honours degree in Photography.
Post Graduate Certificate in Education (PGCE).
Qualified Teacher Status (QTS).
Advanced Skills Teacher in Photography (AST).

Rest assured that you're in good hands!

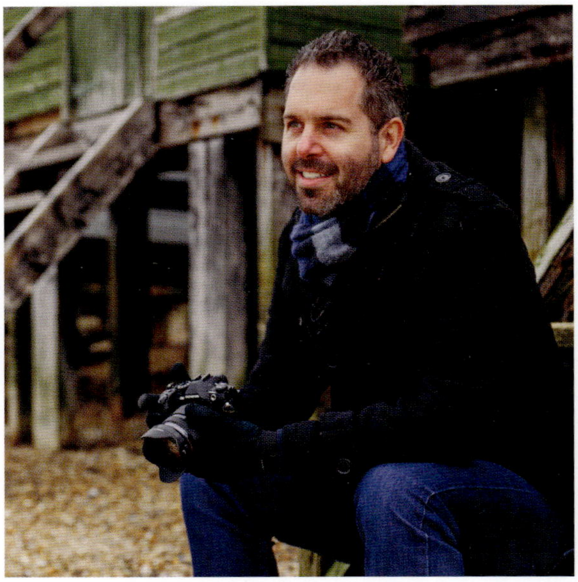

This is real learning delivered by Professional Teachers!

View my portfolio, exhibitions, awards and publications at www.marcnewton.com

---

Our Courses

Visit our website to see our full range of online video courses, books and eBooks

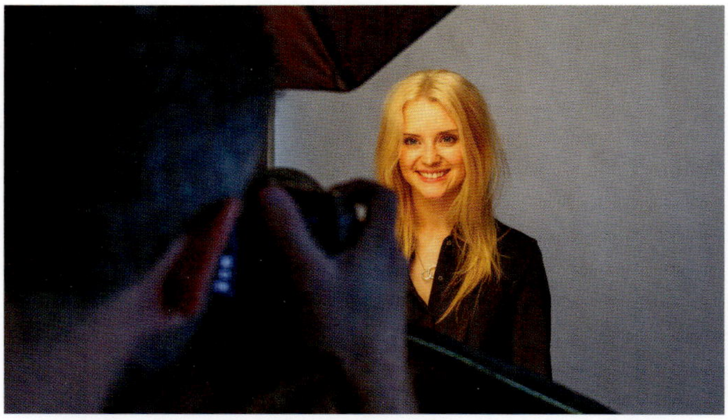

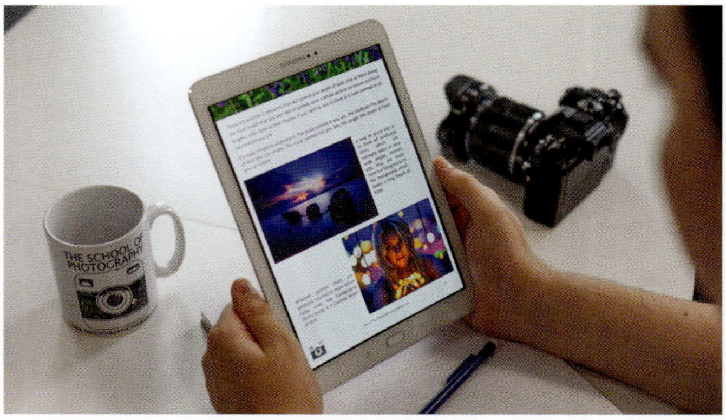

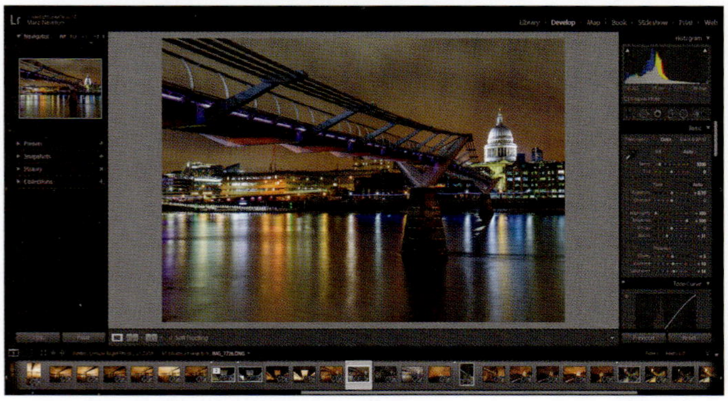

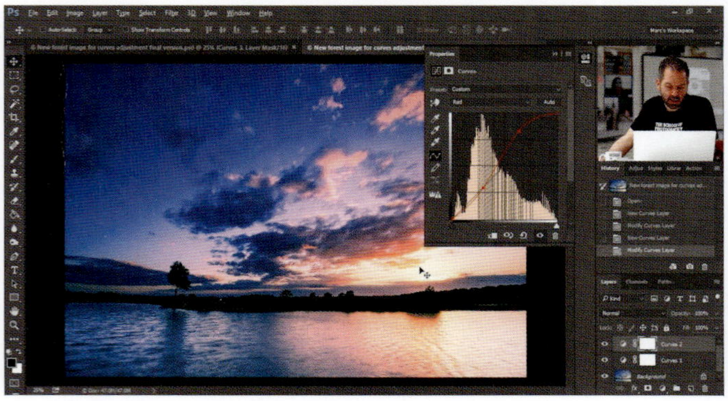

Go to www.theschoolofphotography.com